TURKEY AND THE EUROPEAN UNION

BOOKS OF RELATED INTEREST

TURKISH-AMERICAN RELATIONS:
200 YEARS OF DIVERGENCE AND CONVERGENCE
Edited by Mustafa Aydın and Çağrı Erhan

THE NEW GEOPOLITICS OF EURASIA
AND TURKEY'S POSITION
Edited by Bülent Aras

TURKISH-GREEK RELATIONS:
ESCAPING FROM THE SECURITY DILEMMA IN THE AEGEAN
Edited by Mustafa Aydın and Kostas Ifantis

POLITICAL PARTIES IN TURKEY
Edited by Barry Rubin and Metin Heper

TURKEY AND THE EUROPEAN UNION

Domestic Politics, Economic Integration and International Dynamics

Editors
ALİ ÇARKOĞLU
BARRY RUBIN

FRANK CASS
LONDON • PORTLAND, OR

First published in 2003 in Great Britain by
FRANK CASS AND COMPANY LIMITED
2 Park Square, Milton Park, Abingdon, Oxon, OX14 4RN

and in the United States of America by
FRANK CASS
270 Madison Ave,
New York NY 10016

Transferred to Digital Printing 2005

Copyright © 2003 Frank Cass & Co. Ltd

British Library Cataloguing in Publication Data

Turkey and the European Union: domestic politics, economic
integration and international dynamics
1. European Union – Turkey 2. Turkey – Foreign relations –
1980– 3. Turkey – Foreign relations – European Union
countries 4. European Union countries – Foreign relations –
Turkey 5. Turkey – Politics and government – 1980–
I. Carkoglu, Ali, 1963– II. Rubin, Barry
327.5'61'04

ISBN 0 7146 5402 7 (cloth)
ISBN 0 7146 8335 3 (paper)

Library of Congress Cataloging-in-Publication Data

Turkey and the European Union: domestic politics, economic integration,
and international dynamics / editors Ali Çarkoğlu, Barry Rubin.
  p.cm.
Includes bibliographical references and index.
  ISBN 0-7146-5402-7 – ISBN 0-7146-8335-3 (pbk.)
  1. Turkey–Foreign relations–European Union countries. 2. European
Union countries–Foreign relations–Turkey. 3. Turkey–Foreign economic
Relations–European Union countries. 4. European Union
countries–Foreign economic relations–Turkey. I. Çarkoğlu, Ali,
1963– II. Rubin, Barry M.
DR479.E85 T87 2003
327.56104–dc21   2002154406

This group of studies first appeared in a Special Issue of *Turkish Studies*
(ISSN 1468-3849), Vol.4, No.1 (Spring 2003) [Turkey and the European Union: Domestic
Politics, Economic Integration and International Dynamics].
Turkish Studies is a project of the Turkish Studies Institute (TSI) of the
Global Research in International Affairs (GLORIA) Center,
Interdisciplinary Center (IDC).

*All rights reserved. No part of this publication may be reproduced, stored in a retrieval
system, or transmitted in any form, or by any means, electronic, mechanical,
photocopying, recording or otherwise without the prior written permission of Frank Cass
and Company Limited.*

Contents

Introduction	*Barry Rubin*	1
Chronology: Turkey's Relations with the EU	*Özgül Erdemli*	4
Domestic Politics, International Norms and Challenges to the State: Turkey-EU Relations in the post-Helsinki Era	*Ziya Öniş*	9
Towards a European Security and Defense Policy: With or Without Turkey?	*Esra Çayhan*	35
The Cyprus Obstacle on Turkey's Road to Membership in the European Union	*Semin Suvarierol*	55
The Question of Asylum and Illegal Migration in European Union-Turkish Relations	*Kemal Kirişci*	79
Human Rights, the European Union and the Turkish Accession Process	*William Hale*	107
The Intellectual Roots of Anti-European Sentiments in Turkish Politics: The Case of Radical Turkish Nationalism	*Nergis Canefe and Tanıl Bora*	127
Turkey's Slow EU Candidacy: Insurmountable Hurdles to Membership or Simple Euro-skepticism?	*Gamze Avcı*	149
Who Wants Full Membership? Characteristics of Turkish Public Support for EU Membership	*Ali Çarkoğlu*	171
Turkish Parliamentarians' Perspectives on Turkey's Relations with the European Union	*Lauren M. McLaren and Meltem Müftüler-Baç*	195

Implementing the Economic Criteria of EU Membership:
How Difficult is it for Turkey? *Mine Eder* 219

Conclusion *Ali Çarkoğlu* 245

Abstracts 253

Notes on Contributors 257

Index 261

1
Introduction

BARRY RUBIN

The question of European Union (EU) membership is undoubtedly one of Turkey's most important foreign policy problems and also—as this series of studies makes clear—an extremely powerful domestic issue as well. This situation should not be taken for granted since, after all, it is an extraordinarily unusual one.

Dozens of countries in the last century have joined many international organizations without this issue becoming a focal point of their identity or the key political controversy of the day for them. In fact, it could be argued that the question of Turkish membership in the EU is proportionately the most important issue of this type for any state in history.

Why is this so? Clearly, while the country would receive certain benefits from EU membership of an economic nature—and less so regarding strategic and migration considerations—the EU question has understandably achieved mythic proportions for Turkey far beyond any material factors. It has become no less than the symbol for the successful completion of the long-term Ataturk revolution, involving the most basic and vital points of identity and orientation for Turkey.

To be a full "member" of Europe would mean Turkey's total, irrevocable acceptance as a Western state. It would mark the fulfillment of 80 years of labor and transformation for the Turkish people and state. While Moscow's former satellites crave EU membership as a symbol and promise of their permanent liberation from Russian control, no one else has such a stake in joining that organization as does Turkey.

By the same token, European opposition to Turkey's rapid and full incorporation in the EU also assumes tremendous importance for Turks. Clearly, there are a wide variety of factors slowing or blocking Turkey's admission to the EU. But in Turkey there is an understandable suspicion—which is often correct—that the basis for these hesitations go far beyond technical problems. For if Turks see membership as such a vital proof of Turkey's European and civilized nature, opposition to Turkey's entrance is construed as a rejection of those principles by those who hate, look down on, or discriminate against Turkey.

When asked about the reasons for the slow pace of Turkey's advance towards membership, one Turkish diplomat replied, "They think of new reasons every year." Actually, the full list of reasons is always present but the emphasis changes at different times.

Among those constraints and complaints which could be mentioned are Turkey's population size (and hence political weight and number of migrants in the EU), relative poverty (and thus the size of aid the EU would have to provide), Muslim population, anti-Turkish stereotypes, limits on democracy, human rights issues, the Armenian question, the Kurdish question, the Cyprus question, direct conflicts with Greece and the structure of the economy.

Consequently, while Turks tend to see the EU issue as a central element in their own identity, they also view it as the key indication of how others perceive them and will treat them now and in the future.

As if this were not enough, the EU question is of paramount importance to Turkey's domestic situation. At least five aspects should be mentioned here: the impact on identity, sovereignty, economy, society and polity. Each of these points is also involved with how high the price of admission will ultimately be and, indeed, if it will ever happen at all. If European demands on Turkey increase and the prize of membership is withheld for a long time, what might otherwise be a reasonable set of compromises would come to seem as a humiliating, futile series of concessions.

Regarding identity, if EU membership would be the completion of Turkey's westernization, those who oppose this outcome are reluctant to see that happen. Equally, strong nationalists worry that Turkey's sovereignty would be compromised by membership, especially the army whose political influence the EU wants diminished.

As for economic issues, every Turkish sector must calculate how it would benefit or be injured by membership. On this basis, domestic political forces take sides, not so much on their attitude towards membership but regarding the terms they are willing to accept.

Since the EU demands a range of social and political reforms as preconditions for admitting Turkey, these factors have sparked considerable debate as well. Some view the EU's conditions as a great opportunity to open Turkish society and politics while others regard them as unwarranted and dangerous interference. One camp thinks the changes might produce greater democracy and human rights; the other fears that the stability and even survival of the republic might be at stake.

Even this brief presentation shows that Turkey's quest for EU membership is no mere minor or technical issue but something which lies at the very core of that country's present and future. This comprehensive survey seeks to analyze all the above questions and many more besides.

Introduction

Given the complexity of the history of EU-Turkey relations, Özgül Erdemli has organized a chronology to pinpoint the key meetings and decisions along the way. Ziya Öniş examines the broader issues involved, especially in regard to the effect on Turkey's domestic scene.

Covering a range of specific issues are Esra Çayhan (strategic and defense issues), Semin Süvarierol (Cyprus), Kemal Kirişci (immigration issues) and William Hale (human rights questions).

The next stage of the analysis looks at Turkish attitudes towards the EU and membership process in the contributions of Nergis Canefe and Tanıl Bora along with that of Gamze Avcı. Ali Çarkoğlu examines Turkish public opinion while Lauren M. McLaren and Meltem Müftüler-Baç look at the views of Turkish parliamentarians. Mine Eder focuses on how Turkey can implement the EU's economic criteria for membership. Finally, Ali Çarkoğlu explains our main conclusions.

This work is based on cooperation between the Global Research in International Affairs (GLORIA) Center's Turkish Studies Institute and the Turkish Economic and Social Studies Foundation (TESEV). We wish to thank all those involved in both institutions and especially Ali Çarkoğlu of TESEV and Elisheva Rosman and Ozgul Erdemli of the GLORIA Center; Cameron Brown of the GLORIA Center also helped. We would also like to thank Vicky Johnson of Frank Cass for her assistance in publishing this project.

2
Chronology: Turkey's Relations with the EU*

ÖZGÜL ERDEMLI

September 11, 1959: The EEC (European Economic Community) Council of Ministers accepts Ankara's and Athens' applications for associate membership.

September 12, 1963: The Ankara Agreement (an Association Agreement) is signed, aimed at securing Turkey's full membership in the EEC through the establishment in three phases of a customs union. The first financial protocol is also signed.

December 1, 1964: The Ankara Agreement enters into force.

November 13, 1970: The Additional Protocol, signed and annexed to the Association Agreement between the EEC and Turkey, set out in detail how the Customs Union (CU) would be established between the two sides. Whilst the commitment to establish a Customs Union was provided in the Association Agreement, it was the Additional Protocol of 1970 that specified the program for bringing the CU into being.

October 26, 1970: First Customs Cooperation Committee meeting.

November 23, 1970: The Additional Protocol and the second financial protocol are signed in Brussels.

January 1, 1973: The Additional Protocol, approved in the Turkish Grand National Assembly (*Türkiye Büyük Millet Meclisi*—TBMM) in July 1971, enters into force.

January 1982: The European Community (EC) decides to suspend the Ankara Agreement officially and therefore freezes its political relations with Turkey as a result of the military *coup d'état* on September 12, 1980. The European Parliament also decides not to renew the European wing of the Joint Parliamentary Commission until a general election is held and a parliament established in Turkey.

September 1986: Turkey-EEC Association Council meets and relations between the EC and Turkey resume. During the September 1986 Association Council meeting Turkey signals its intention to go ahead with its long-expected application for full membership, opening a new chapter in relations.

April 14, 1987: Turkey applies for full EEC membership. The Foreign Ministers of the EC member states decide to refer the application to the Commission for an opinion in accordance with the routine procedure.

December 18, 1989: The European Commission's opinion on Turkey's Request for Accession stresses that enlargement for Turkey and other potential candidates could be contemplated only after the 1992 single market comes into operation. Moreover, a detailed analysis of Turkey's economic and social development states that—in spite of important progress since 1980 in restructuring and opening the economy to the outside world—a major gap still existed in comparison with EC levels of development. The Commission recommends the completion of a customs union stating that progressive completion of the customs union would give the Community the opportunity to associate Turkey more closely with the operation of the single market.

September 30, 1991: EEC-Turkey Association Council held in Brussels. The practical outcome of the meeting is the decision to relaunch regular sessions of the "association committee" in which Turkish and EC officials would carry out detailed work on trade and economic issues.

December 31, 1995: The EC and Turkey enter a formal customs union agreement. This was the EC's first substantial functioning customs union with a third state.

January 1, 1996: The Customs Union between the European Community and Turkey comes into effect, thereby creating the closest economic and political relationship between the EU and any non-member country. This Customs Union goes further than the abolition of tariff and quantitative barriers to trade between the parties and the application of a Common

External Tariff to imports from third countries, and envisages harmonization with EEC policies in virtually every field relating to the internal market.

July 13–14, 1996: The Dublin summit. The European Council urges Turkey to use its influence to contribute to a solution in Cyprus in accordance with UN Security Council resolutions. The European Council also emphasizes the need for the observance of the highest standards of human rights.

December 12–13, 1997: The Luxembourg summit. The European Council excludes Turkey from the list of formal candidates, effectively "rejecting" Ankara's request for accession.

December 1997: Turkey responds to the EU's Luxembourg declaration by partially suspending its dialogue with the EU. Furthermore, the Turkish government announces that it would go ahead with plans to integrate northern Cyprus should the EU launch accession talks with the island's Greek Cypriot government.

December 10–11, 1999: The Helsinki summit. The EU Council agrees to recognize Turkey as a candidate for membership. The European Council declares that building on the existing European strategy, Turkey, like other candidate states, would benefit from a pre-accession strategy to stimulate and support its reforms.

December 4, 2000: The General Affairs Council agrees on the framework regulation and on the Accession Partnership for Turkey.

December 7–9, 2000: The Nice summit. The European Council welcomes the progress made in implementing the pre-accession strategy for Turkey but requests Turkey submit its program for adoption of the *acquis*, basing it on the Accession Partnership.

March 8, 2001: The EU Council of Ministers adopts the EU-Turkey Accession Partnership, setting out the short- and medium-term measures necessary to ensure Turkey meets the criteria for membership.

March 19, 2001: The Turkish government adopts the National Program for the Adoption of the Acquis (NPAA). The NPAA sets out, for the first time, the large scale of reforms that Turkey is willing to address in all areas political and economic, and in relation to the alignment of Turkish legislation with the EU *acquis*.

October 3, 2001: The Turkish parliament adopts 34 amendments to the Constitution in order to meet the Copenhagen political criteria for EU membership. Among others, these include a partial abolition of the death penalty and authorize greater use of languages other than Turkish in public life.

December 14–15, 2001: The Laeken summit. The European Council states that Turkey made progress towards complying with the political criteria established for accession, in particular through the recent amendment of its constitution.

January–March 2002: The Turkish parliament passes amendments to the Penal Code and other legislation affecting the freedom of expression and the press, the activities of associations, the closure of political parties and the prevention of torture.

June 21–22, 2002: The Seville summit. The European Council reaffirms that the implementation of the required political and economic reforms would bring forward Turkey's prospects of accession in accordance with the same principles and criteria applied to the other candidate countries. The European Council states that new decisions could be taken in Copenhagen on the next stage of Turkey's candidature in the light of developments in the situation between the Seville and Copenhagen European Councils.

August 3, 2002: The Turkish parliament passes an EU Adaptation Law (*Avrupa Birliği Uyum Yasası*—APD) of 15 Articles to meet the remaining requirements of the APD in the human rights field. The reforms include the abolition of the death penalty, the allowance of broadcasting in different languages and dialects used traditionally by Turkish citizens in their daily lives, and the improved education possibilities for minority languages. These recent efforts were thought to lead to positive decisions being taken by the European Council at its Copenhagen summit (December 2002).

December 12–13, 2002: The Copenhagen summit. The 15 leaders of the EU embrace a plan for the enlargement of the EU eastward to include ten additional countries, but reject Turkey's demand to set a date to begin negotiations for its eventual admission. The leaders of the EU only agree to meet in December 2004 to review Turkey's candidacy.

NOTE

For a more detailed chronology, see the official website of the Republic of Turkey Prime Ministry Secretariat General for the EU Affairs, at <http://www.euturkey.org.tr/>.

Domestic Politics, International Norms and Challenges to the State: Turkey-EU Relations in the post-Helsinki Era

ZİYA ÖNİŞ

Potential European Union (EU) membership creates both conditions and incentives, constituting a powerful engine of democratization and economic transformation in candidate countries in the process. If the mix of conditions and incentives is inappropriate, however, and the emphasis is primarily on conditions or "negative incentives," this will tend to slow down the process of domestic political change in the candidate country. It will also help to strengthen those groups both within and outside the state who are likely to oppose democratic opening as well as the loss of sovereignty in certain key areas of policy that eventual EU membership naturally entails. Whilst an external anchor, such as potential EU membership, constitutes a powerful driving force for change, the primary impetus for change, nonetheless, needs to originate from domestic actors. Within this broad perspective, the present contribution attempts to provide a critical investigation of Turkey-EU relations in the post-Helsinki era.

The decision of the European Council to accept Turkey officially as a candidate country at its Helsinki summit of December 1999 represented a fundamental turning point in Turkey-EU relations. Previously, Turkey had become a member of the Customs Union by the beginning of 1996.[1] Without in any way underestimating the impact of the Customs Union, it is fair to argue in retrospect, that the Customs Union *per se* failed to provide an appropriate mix of conditions and incentives to induce a major transformation in Turkey's domestic politics and economy. Clearly, though, following the Helsinki decision, the incentives to undertake reform have increased considerably. The pressures to conform to EU norms, as well as to global norms specified by multilateral institutions such as the International Monetary Fund (IMF), have created major avenues for change in the recent Turkish context in both the economic and the political realms. This has been the case in spite of the historical legacy of a highly entrenched state tradition as well as the peculiarities of the Turkish modernization experience.[2]

Nevertheless, a powerful bloc that opposes the wider democratization agenda remains a persistent feature of the Turkish political system. This particular bloc played a key part in modifying the contents of the "National Report," a key document prepared to meet the accession criteria for full membership. It also played an important role in terms of delaying the passing of legislation on key elements of political reform in the more recent context. An attempt is made here to analyze the underlying reasons for widespread resistance to notions such as "liberal internationalism" and "cosmopolitan democracy" in the Turkish setting. This contribution also probes the question of whether the EU itself is doing enough to provide the kind of "signals" needed to create a virtuous cycle whereby domestic political and economic change and external inducements tend to reinforce one another. Special attention is given to economic considerations that constitute a vital component of Turkey-EU relations, particularly in view of the deep and recurrent economic crises experienced by Turkey in recent years.

TRANSNATIONALIZATION, CONDITIONALITY AND THE TRANSITION TO A "POST-MODERN STATE:" THE SIGNIFICANCE OF THE EU ANCHOR IN NEW DEMOCRACIES

The EU possesses an institutionalized regional framework which readily transmits the kind of influences and pressures that affect the course of democratization. Unlike other regional agreements such as NAFTA (North American Free Trade Agreement), meeting certain democratic credentials has been a prerequisite for EU (formerly the European Community—EC) membership ever since its very inception. More recently, in the course of the 1980s and the 1990s, "the New Europe" has placed even more emphasis on human rights and the quality of democratization as part of its emerging identity.[3] The positive role that the EC played in the process of democratic consolidation of the Southern European trio of Spain, Greece and Portugal during the course of the 1980s as part of the Mediterranean enlargement process has been widely documented. The EU has clearly helped consolidate nascent democracies in Southern Europe through a mix of political conditions and economic incentives over a relatively short period. Access to the Community's regional funds on a significant scale has helped to build the basic economic infrastructure in such states.

The positive signals provided by EU membership (initially potential, then actual) have enabled the countries concerned to attract considerable amounts of foreign direct investment. Rapid economic growth fuelled by expansion of foreign trade and investment has exerted a positive impact on the process of democratic consolidation in the domestic political sphere. The emergence of stable democracies, in turn, has contributed to economic stability and progress. Hence, favorable economic and political developments seem to have reinforced one another and have helped generate vibrant economies and mature democracies in recent decades. Similar processes have been at work, perhaps with a lower degree of intensity, in post-Communist Central and Eastern Europe as countries like Hungary, Poland and the Czech Republic line up for EU membership in the early years of the new century.[4]

It is also important to emphasize in this context that the European integration process involves a considerable "pooling of sovereignty," meaning a relocation of authority away from the individual nation-state to the supranational institutions of the EU. At the same time, there is a parallel process working in the direction of decentralization, involving a relocation of authority in a downward direction towards local and regional authorities. In addition, the domestic politics of individual nations are increasingly transnationalized as external actors—both states and increasingly non-state actors such as transnational civil society groups—become heavily involved in the domestic politics of individual states. Whilst the processes described are, in broad terms, a product of the globalization process itself, the impact of these forces is more evident in countries involved in the European integration process.[5]

The various processes described clearly present major challenges to the individual nation-state and create resentment among national elites—particularly in candidate countries—given the fact that their privileged positions are likely to be undermined by these processes. Stated somewhat differently, the economic benefits of integration for the society as a whole may be extremely high. However, at the same time, the costs of integration in political terms for particular groups might be considerable. Clearly, the groups concerned would be unwilling to relinquish their "sovereignty" over key areas of policy that would directly undermine their privileged positions or interests.

It is increasingly recognized that the European integration process is associated with a vision of a "post-modern state" with its emphasis on the pooling of sovereignty and decentralization at the same time.[6] A hallmark of this kind of post-modern state is recognition of multiple identities with a strong emphasis on the promotion of minority rights. This vision of a post-modern state and the associated notions of liberal internationalism come into direct conflict with the earlier vision of modernist or authoritarian visions of nationalism based on a single identity, creating significant tensions in the process. Nationalistic reactions to the European integration process are certainly not unique to Turkey. Indeed, such reactions are evident, though with varying degrees of intensity, in most states in both the Western European core and the Eastern European periphery. Nonetheless, it is fair to say that the tensions described are even more pronounced in the Turkish context given the country's historical legacies and the peculiarities of its nation-building experience.

THE HELSINKI SUMMIT AS A TURNING POINT: OFFICIAL REACTIONS AND THE IMPETUS TO REFORM

It is undoubtedly the case that the decision taken at the Helsinki summit has accelerated the momentum of political and economic reforms in the subsequent era. The process of change was actively initiated by the European Commission through the publication of its Accession Partnership (AP), which was made public in March 2000.[7] The AP highlighted the short- and medium-term priorities where radical steps had to be undertaken in order to satisfy the Copenhagen criteria in both the political and economic arenas. In the political arena the AP identified a rather comprehensive set of changes involving the extension of citizenship rights and the elimination of human rights violations. The targets set ranged from freedom of expression and freedom of association in the fullest sense of the term, elimination of torture practices to changing legal practices as a way of combating human rights violations. Reforms envisaged included improvements in the functioning and efficiency of the judiciary (including state security courts) as well as the removal of legal provisions forbidding the education of Turkish citizens in their mother tongue or the use of their native language in television and radio broadcasting. Finally, finding a comprehensive settlement to the Cyprus problem was delineated as a fundamental priority.

In the economic sphere, the requirements were very much in line with the expectations of the IMF program, involving disinflation and structural reforms initiated in December 1999. EU attention focused explicitly on control of public expenditure, financial sector reforms to establish transparency and surveillance, the reform of agricultural subsidies and further progress with privatization. The reforms aimed, essentially, at a dual transformation of the Turkish state. In the political sphere, the reforms proposed—involving a more liberal and pluralistic political order—presented a major challenge to the principles associated with "hard-core Republicanism" underlying the highly centralized Turkish state.[8] In the economic sphere, the objective was to transform the "soft state" characterized by populism, corruption and endemic fiscal instability to an effective regulatory state. This objective appeared to be crucial in terms of laying the foundations of sustained economic growth in a crisis-free environment.[9]

In response to the AP, the Turkish authorities prepared "The Turkish National Program for the Adoption of the Acquis," a document which was submitted to the EU Commission in March the following year (2001). The National Program (NPAA) represented an attempt on the part of the political authorities in Turkey to strike a balance between the need to meet the Copenhagen criteria and the unwillingness to implement reforms on the most sensitive issues in the short-term.[10] The reactions of the European Parliament and the Commission to the NPAA, outlined in their respective reports, were reasonably favorable.[11] Both institutions made it abundantly clear, however, that the actions proposed in the NPAA fell rather short of the expectations outlined in the Accession Partnership document. From the EU perspective, the NPAA represented significant progress, although the scale of transformation envisaged in the report failed to reach the threshold level set by the Community to open the critical accession negotiations for full membership. One should bear in mind that the EU is concerned not only with adoption of laws but also with their implementation. Hence, the adoption of the NPAA and the associated changes in the legal process do not necessarily mean that the EU is sufficiently satisfied with the implementation process to open negotiations.

Immediately following the official approval of the NPAA, the authorities initiated a process of implementation which involved the translation of the proposals embodied in the document into concrete action. Indeed, a record number of 34 Constitutional Amendments have been accomplished. These in turn were followed by "Harmonization Laws" designed to translate the Constitutional Amendments concerned into concrete action as part of the process of bringing Turkish law into line with the European *acquis*. Hence, the period from the beginning of 2000 onwards could be described as a period of profound and momentous change in Turkish history, a process that was ironically engineered by a relatively weak coalition government. Clearly, a change of this magnitude would have been impossible in the absence of a powerful and highly institutionalized EU anchor in the direction of full membership. During the summer of 2002, the process of change appeared to gather further momentum with the controversial harmonization laws having been approved by the parliament over an unexpectedly short period of time considering the depth of resistance involved. Particularly striking in this context was the August 2002 removal of the death penalty, including for those convicted of terrorist activity. This particular element of reform encountered major opposition from the military and nationalist parties, notably the ultra-nationalist Nationalist Action Party (*Miliyetçi Hareket Partisi*—MHP). Indeed, the MHP has been playing a major role as a key member of the coalition government in terms of explicitly blocking some of the major political reforms needed to meet the EU's democratic norms in the post-1999 era.[12] Another major element of progress involved allowing broadcasting and education in the mother tongues of minorities as well as the liberalization of laws restricting freedom of speech and association. This also constituted a remarkable development in the sense that the extension of the cultural rights of "minority groups" had presented particular difficulties in the Turkish context.

In spite of the significant progress recorded in terms of satisfying EU criteria over a relatively short period of time, four basic areas could be identified where—at the time when the present study was completed—considerable progress needed to be achieved in order to satisfy EU expectations. In broad terms, these included the Cyprus issue, the extension of the cultural rights of "minority groups" in practice, the role of the military and the performance of the economy. In retrospect, the failure to tackle the Cyprus issue constituted a major limitation of the NPAA: it appears to have largely ignored this issue. Clearly, unless an acceptable compromise is reached among the actors involved, the Cyprus issue will continue to present a major obstacle to Turkey's prospects for full membership.

In the sphere of minority rights, the fact that a major hurdle has been overcome by allowing minorities mother-tongue language education and broadcasting rights in principle should not be interpreted as a final state of affairs where all the difficulties have been resolved. In practice, in terms of the extension of cultural rights of "minority" groups, education in the mother tongue seems to be presenting particular difficulties. Indeed, this issue is likely to remain a considerable source of friction given the apparently irreconcilable differences between the official Turkey and EU positions on this issue. The EU has been rather insistent on the promotion of "minority rights," whereas a major component of the Turkish political system, notably the ultra-nationalist MHP, has traditionally been heavily opposed to any kind of change in this sphere.

Part of the problem lies with the definition of "minority rights." The official Turkish definition of "minority," which is in line with the Lausanne Treaty of 1923, recognizes non-Muslim groups as groups that should enjoy certain minority rights. According to this definition, non-Turkish minorities become part of the mainstream Muslim majority.

Hence, being part of the majority, ethnic Muslim minorities cannot benefit from the minority rights given to Greeks, Armenians and Jews, who enjoy the right to establish their own schools (within the parameters of the guidelines established by the Ministry of Education). The debate on this issue has generated considerable polarization in the political spectrum. Yet, even the more liberal wing of Turkish politics, represented—for example—by the right-of-center Motherland Party (*Anavatan Partisi*—ANAP), has been in favor of limited opening in this context in the form of providing extra language courses in the mother tongue. This in itself illustrates the weak foundations of liberal politics in the Turkish context. Moreover, nationalistic elements in Turkish society have interpreted even this kind of limited flexibility as an inherent threat to the unity of the Republic. Overall, it is fair to say that the vast majority of politicians in Turkey continue to support the idea that mother-tongue education can only be held in Turkish. Hence, the idea of instituting primary schools where only Kurdish or Arabic, for example, are taught will continue to generate widespread resentment. Even strictly limited proposals such as establishing individual courses to teach these languages as minor elements in the overall curriculum continue to elicit vigorous opposition from the nationalistic bloc, notably the MHP and the security establishment.[13] One should not be surprised, therefore, if more radical demands by the Kurds to establish their own secondary schools encounter intense opposition in the coming years.

The role of the military is an issue that the EU is particularly sensitive about and one on which major emphasis is placed in its attempts to monitor Turkey's progress towards a more open and democratic polity. The EU clearly visualizes a system whereby the military's role in Turkish politics is substantially reduced and placed under full civilian control.[14] A major institution that attracts EU attention and criticism in this context is the National Security Council (NSC), a military-dominated institution that has been a major organ of decisionmaking in the course of the past two decades. One concrete response to EU criticisms in this sphere in the context of the National Program has been to increase the number of civilians in the Council. Further civilianization of the institution alone, however, is unlikely to represent an acceptable alternative to EU demands.

Clearly, a number of rather subtle issues are involved in this context, but the underlying objective is to reduce the military's power. It is not obvious, however, that this could be achieved solely by institutionally limiting the presence of the military in executive circles. It is a far more complicated issue than is portrayed by the EU standards. A critical question in this context is how to reduce the weight of the military in the economic sphere. It is interesting that the EU itself has somewhat de-emphasized this issue in the past couple of years, perhaps coming to the conclusion that institutional arrangements are just the tip of the iceberg in Turkey. There also appears to be a realization on the part of the EU that an overemphasis on this issue in the short-run may achieve nothing more than simply alienating the military from the EU.

Last but not least, the performance of the economy is likely to pose a serious threat to Turkey's aspirations to become a full member of the EU. In spite of significant efforts aimed at reforming the Turkish economy in recent years, with pressures emanating from both the IMF and the EU, the Turkish economy has not been able to overcome its traditional problems of endemic instability and recurrent crises. The performance of the economy in recent years has been characterized by a low-growth, high-inflation equilibrium. Clearly, Turkey has not been able to generate the kind of performance in the economic sphere which would be synonymous with a steady convergence to EU norms in terms of per capita income and level of development over a reasonable period. All the work that goes towards satisfying the political components of the Copenhagen criteria will be severely undermined if the economic reform process is subject to further reversals and the economy fails to develop a certain momentum of rapid growth.

The four elements identified are likely to pose formidable challenges in the years ahead. In spite of the significant progress already made, major progress in all these areas must be accomplished before accession negotiations can even be initiated. It is obvious that softening the "hard state" in the political realm and hardening the "soft state" in the economic realm are unlikely to unfold themselves as inherently smooth processes.

REALIGNMENTS IN DOMESTIC POLITICS AND CHALLENGES FACING THE ESTABLISHMENT OF A GENUINELY LIBERAL AND PLURALISTIC POLITICAL ORDER IN THE POST-HELSINKI ERA

The process of institutionalized dialogue initiated by the Helsinki process and the resultant impetus to reform has exercised a profound impact on Turkey's domestic politics. What is also interesting in this context is that the kind of realignments that have taken place cannot be simply explained with reference to the traditional left/right axis. It would be interesting to examine the way that the positions of the principal political parties, interest associations and public opinion at large are transformed in Turkey following the critical turning point at the Helsinki summit.

Westernization has been a central objective of the Turkish political elite since the inception of the Turkish Republic in 1923. Indeed, the roots of the westernization drive can be traced back to Ottoman reforms of the late-eighteenth and nineteenth centuries. In the post-War period, and especially from the early 1960s onward, eventual membership in the EU has been interpreted as a necessary counterpart of the westernization and modernization drive, which itself has been proclaimed as official state ideology. Hence, it is fair to say that almost all of the major political parties in Turkey displayed a certain vague commitment towards the goal of EU membership. Even the Islamists in Turkey, who have traditionally looked towards the Middle East and the Islamic world as the natural point of Turkish foreign policy interests, appear to have shifted their position in favor of an active pro-EU stand in recent years.[15] Similarly, ultra-nationalist parties like the MHP have traditionally looked towards the former Soviet Union and the Turkic world as their primary point of reference. Nonetheless, even the MHP has not opposed EU membership in principle. Yet, the striking pattern in the pre-Helsinki era was that none of the major political parties on the right or left of the political spectrum actively pushed for the kind of reforms needed—notably in the political arena—to satisfy the conditions set by the EU. Indeed, none of the major political parties were able or willing to challenge the fundamental precepts of state ideology on key issues of concern such as "cultural rights" or "the Cyprus problem"—issues which appeared to lie beyond the parameters of the normal political debate.[16]

The intense process of interaction and pressure for reform initiated by the Helsinki summit, however, appear to have resulted in certain realignments in domestic politics, a process which has also forced individual political parties to develop sharper and more precise positions regarding their stand on the EU. What is quite striking in this context is that the center-right ANAP, under the leadership of former prime minister Mesut Yılmaz, has assumed a leadership role in pushing for EU membership and the associated reforms. ANAP, a representative of urban middle-class interests and a minor coalition partner since 1999, has been much more willing, relative to its competitors, to tackle the kind of sensitive issues related to EU conditionality. Hence, among the political parties, ANAP could be considered a key member of the emerging pro-EU coalition in Turkey, notably during the course of 2002. Indeed, the party leader's active stand on EU membership, not only in principle but also in terms of an underlying commitment to reforms, has generated widespread resistance from Turkey's military and security establishment as well as other components of the hardline Republican or nationalist bloc. Yet, it is fair to say that ANAP has started to play this role only very recently and its ability to play this particular role has been handicapped by its heavily nationalistic legacy. It is a striking fact that ANAP, as the principal party in opposition in 1994–95, had opposed the Customs Union as a tactic against its arch rival, the True Path Party (*Doğru Yol Partisi*—DYP).[17] This episode clearly added to its lack of credibility. Furthermore, the party has been associated with a number of alleged corruption episodes in recent years, which have contributed to the dramatic decline in its popularity towards the end of the 1990s. Finally, it was the party leader himself who took an active position on EU-related reforms. There is no firm indication that his pronouncements elicited the unified support of the party. Moreover, Yılmaz himself can be criticized for not being sufficiently consistent and vigorous in presenting and defending his case in favor of EU-related reforms, although admittedly he has played an instrumental role in the passing of the harmonization laws in August 2002.

At the opposite end of the political party spectrum, the ultra-nationalist MHP, a key member of the ruling coalition government, emerged as a leading element of the powerful "anti-EU coalition." This particular party, whilst not rejecting EU membership in principle, has vehemently opposed the type of reforms demanded by the EU, highlighting the threats posed by such reforms to national sovereignty and security. Indeed, one can immediately detect an exact correspondence between the basic perspectives of the MHP and the military-security establishment on EU-related issues. Other major political parties in Turkey could easily be located between the two extremes identified. None of them actively opposed the reform process as openly as the MHP, nor have they actively promoted EU-related reforms as vocally as ANAP did during the recent period. Even ANAP has been somewhat constrained in its actions on sensitive issues such as education in ethnic languages and the kinds of compromises needed to resolve the Cyprus dispute.

To an external observer, what is striking about the recent realignments in Turkish politics along a pro-EU versus anti-EU axis concerns the positions of the left-of-center social democratic parties. It is interesting to note that the Left has taken a highly nationalistic stand on many of the key issues involved. For a variety of historical reasons that require a separate treatment, parties of the center-left in Turkey do not appear to have been particularly influenced by debates on multiculturalism, liberal internationalism and third way politics, which seem to have occupied the European social democratic left during the recent era. Clearly, the reluctance of the Left in Turkey to transform itself and establish itself as a major component of the pro-EU coalition constitutes a factor that seems to be limiting the pace of progress on the path to EU membership. There are signs, however, that this pattern might change somewhat following the deep divisions that emerged within the left-wing, nationalist Democratic Left Party (*Demokratik Sol Parti*—DSP)—the premier member of the coalition government in office—during the summer of 2002. The substantial number of MPs who resigned from the party is characterized by their pro-EU outlook, whereas those who remained within the party can be distinguished by their strongly nationalistic outlook, which is perhaps not fundamentally distinct from the standpoint of the MHP on a number of the key issues involved.

An equally paradoxical feature of recent Turkish politics concerns the role of interest associations. Perhaps more than any political party, the principal pressure for EU-related democratic reforms originated from civil society organizations and, notably, from the representatives of the business community. Indeed, perhaps the single most vocal element in this context has been the voluntary association of big business in Turkey, namely TÜSİAD (*Türkiye Sanayici ve İşadamları Derneği*—Turkish Industrialists' and Businessmen's Association).[18] TÜSİAD's plea for the promotion of civil and human rights as well as for better governance in fact preceded the Helsinki summit. The organization published a highly controversial report in 1997 which outlined a series of needed major political reforms.[19] In addition to its activities in the domestic political sphere, TÜSİAD also played an active role of lobbying at Brussels and, in part, contributed to the favorable outcome of the Helsinki summit. The report on democratization published by the association, however, elicited widespread resentment and criticism from the military and other segments of the state. Consequently, TÜSİAD's push for democratic reforms has been somewhat subdued in the immediate aftermath of the Helsinki summit. On the other hand, the organization once again became extremely vocal during the course of 2002, stressing the urgency of the need to make progress on highly controversial issues such as the extension of cultural rights and a mutually acceptable resolution of the Cyprus dispute. In its widespread media campaigns to influence both the policymakers and the public opinion at large, the association has drawn increasing attention to the economic benefits of joining the EU for the population as a whole and has tried to justify political reforms as a necessary step in capitalizing on the economic benefits of the Union. The instrumental nature of TÜSİAD's commitment to the democratization agenda should not lead one to underestimate the fact that significant components of the business community embraced democratic reforms for their intrinsic benefit.

The pressures emanating from civil society have not been confined to TÜSİAD alone. Other organizations, primarily those with certain links to the private sector—notably the Economic Development Foundation

(*İktisadi ve Kalkınma Vakfı*—IKV) and the liberal think-tank organization, TESEV (Turkish Economic and Social Studies Foundation—*Türkiye Ekonomik ve Sosyal Etüdler Vakfı*)—have also been quite active in using the media to point towards the urgency of economic and political reforms.[20] Indeed, IKV has been trying to promote closer relations with the EU for three decades. Perhaps the major contribution of the IKV recently, with the principal impetus coming from the chairman of the organization, Meral Gezgin Eriş, has been its leadership role in creating an unprecedented broad-based civil movement in Turkey under the umbrella of *Avrupa Hareketi 2002* (Movement for Europe 2002). *Avrupa 2002* (Europe 2002) constituted a broad platform that mobilized 175 civil society organizations to take collective action in favor of Turkey's accession to the EU in June 2002. Clearly, the EU can play an instrumental role in this context by providing material support to broad-based civil initiatives, such as *Avrupa 2002*, and grass-roots initiatives, which are of critical importance of building mass support for EU membership in the Turkish context.

One should not be misled to believe that all the pressure for EU-related reforms originating from the NGOs stems from the business community.[21] Yet, it is interesting to draw attention to an anomaly of Turkish politics, which, to some extent, duplicates our observations regarding political parties of the center-left variety in Turkey. Major labor unions in Turkey, such as TÜRK-İŞ (*Türkiye İşçi Sendikaları Konfederasyonu*—Confederation of Turkish Labor Unions) have continued to be heavily nationalistic in outlook and, as a result, have excluded themselves rather decisively from the active pro-EU coalition. Their arguments appear to be heavily grounded in the loss of national autonomy/sovereignty discourse, arguments which look suspiciously similar to the kind of discourse presented by the ultra-nationalist MHP.[22]

From a broader analytical perspective, a striking aspect of the Helsinki decision to transform the possibility of EU membership from a vague promise to a concrete reality helped accentuate the divisions within the ruling power bloc, divisions that had already been evident in the late 1990s. There has been a close overlap between the economic interests of big business and the military-security arm of the state in Turkey, a relationship that has been steadily strengthened from the import-substitution era onwards.[23] Nonetheless, the concrete possibility of EU membership has resulted in a series of divisions within what could be described as the "ruling bloc" or the "power elite." What could be described as the "transnational business elites," including domestic business and the external investor community with an interest in the

Turkish economy, increasingly saw the EU anchor as a means of consolidating the kind of economic environment conducive to their long-term interests. In contrast, the privileged position of the military-security establishment, both in terms of its economic weight and social status, appeared to be particularly threatened by the kind of reforms proposed by the EU.

During the summer of 2002, the military, security and foreign policy wing of the traditional power bloc appeared to be somewhat on the defensive side as pressures from the EU and the transnational coalition of business interests mounted. It would be naive to suppose, however, that divisions within the ruling bloc have resulted in a complete rupture. A considerable overlap of economic interests remains intact between the two segments of the power bloc. It is a well-known fact that the military is an important economic actor in Turkish society and many private firms depend on contracts originating from the state or the military. This, in turn, limits the extent of the push for reforms originating from the large-scale business community and its constituent associations. The key inference that follows is that one should not underestimate the power of the anti-EU coalition in Turkey, of which the military-security arm of the state is one component, and its ability to resist the kind of reforms promoted by the EU.

Many observers commenting on the future of Turkey-EU relations in the immediate aftermath of the Helsinki summit, including this author, have focused their attention primarily on domestic political constraints and have placed much less emphasis on purely economic considerations in the process. The twin economic crises experienced by Turkey in November 2000 and February 2001, however, have brought economic considerations onto the center stage. This was something which was not anticipated by analysts of Turkey-EU relations in early 2000 given that the economic program supported by the IMF appeared to be intact during that period.[24]

Arguably, the deepest economic crisis that Turkey experienced during the post-War period, with the Helsinki decision in the background, had some rather unexpected consequences in terms of accelerating the kind of changes in Turkey's domestic politics that have already been highlighted. In immediate terms, the economic crisis seemed to have aggravated the prospects of becoming a full member of the EU over a reasonably short period. From a longer-term perspective, however, the economic crisis seems to have contributed quite dramatically to the emergence of a vocal pro-EU coalition. Increasingly, the transnational coalition of business interests conceived of the EU anchor as a necessary double anchor from the point of view of consolidating the kind of reforms pushed by the IMF in the Turkish context. Hence, the kind of explicitly political conditions proposed, on top of the economic conditions, were increasingly favored by the transnational business elites and representatives of the international financial community, primarily based on the positive economic impact of such reforms through ultimate EU membership. In other words, the implicit fear was that the economic reform process itself could easily be reversed in the absence of EU membership. Clearly, the actors concerned favored the presence of a permanent external anchor such as membership of the EU as a means of locking-in the reform process in Turkey. It is fascinating to observe the extent to which the EU-related political reforms are explicitly linked to the process whereby external investors and their representative agencies view and evaluate the prospects for the Turkish economy in the post-crisis period.[25] Apart from amplifying the support of business interests, the economic crisis was also instrumental in generating broader public support for the reform process. For the average citizen, the concrete material benefits associated with EU membership became even more appealing during a period of deep economic crisis.

It is becoming increasingly clear that overall public opinion is likely to play a progressively more important role in terms of influencing the outcome of the game played out by the different components of the power elite. The results of major public opinion surveys conducted in Turkey during the recent era convey interesting information in this respect. The most recent among these surveys is one undertaken by TESEV, the results of which are quite illuminating and deserve some comment in the present context. The TESEV survey is instructive in terms of showing broad support among the Turkish electorate for EU membership in rather general terms. Much more significant, however, is the result that shows the widespread demand for political reforms. Ninety percent of respondents appear to be extremely unhappy about the workings of Turkey's democracy and 74 percent indicate that the right to use ethnic languages should be allowed under all circumstances.

Yet, it is also quite interesting that the measures required for EU Copenhagen criteria receive mixed support: 52 percent do not support the removal of the death penalty in all cases and 58 percent would not support education and broadcasting in ethnic languages in the context of EU entry. There also appears to be deep suspicion about the EU itself, with 49 percent of the respondents viewing it as a "Christian club."[26]

Putting all these elements together, there has clearly been a pronounced shift in Turkey's domestic politics recently in terms of the emergence of a genuinely pro-active, pro-EU coalition. Moreover, a key component of this coalition is transnational business interests, drawing attention to the increasingly globalized nature of "domestic politics" in the present age. A genuinely pro-EU coalition means not only a commitment to EU membership in general terms but also a concrete commitment to undertake the kind of reforms specified as necessary conditions, even if these imply a certain loss of autonomy over critical policy areas. It is also the case, however, that a powerful anti-EU bloc continues to flourish in Turkey and presents a formidable obstacle to the reform process. Hence, there appears to be a stalemate, a pattern that seems to be consistent with the rather ambivalent results emerging from the recent public opinion surveys. Practical questions that need to be addressed, therefore, are how this stalemate could be resolved and what role the EU itself could play in this process.

THE RESOLUTION OF THE CYPRUS CONFLICT AS A KEY CHALLENGE FACING THE EMERGING PRO-EU COALITION IN TURKEY: IS THE EU DOING ENOUGH TO HELP?

Bilateral conflict with an EU member constitutes a natural barrier to full membership. Without overestimating its importance, it is fair to say that Greece's early membership in the EU has acted as an important constraint on the smooth development of Turkey-EU relations. The Greek veto, for example, meant that Turkey could not benefit from financial assistance, which became available in principle through membership in the Customs Union. Clearly, this represents a dilemma unique to Turkey, one that is not applicable to other candidate countries currently lined up for full membership. Indeed, there has been certain improvement in Greek-Turkish relations preceding the Helsinki summit. However, this recent rapprochement has not yet resulted in major progress with respect to the grand disputes involving the two countries, in which the Cyprus dispute occupies a very special role in this context. A detailed consideration of the Cyprus dispute lies beyond the scope of the present analysis. What is significant for our purposes is the impact of the Cyprus dispute on Turkey's domestic politics considering that it is probably the single overriding constraint on Turkey's progress to full membership and is also the issue area where the anti-EU coalition is perhaps least willing to compromise.

Taking into account the current stalemate in the relative powers of the emerging pro-EU coalition and the highly entrenched anti-EU coalition in Turkey, the EU, in principle, could play a decisive role in this context. In concrete terms, the EU could create the kind of incentives that would help to resolve the problem to the satisfaction of the various actors involved. This, in turn, would help tilt the balance of power within Turkey's domestic politics in favor of the pro-EU coalition. The current approach of the EU, however, has not been very helpful in this respect. The EU is in the process of completing accession negotiations with the Republic of Cyprus (RoC). The successful completion of the negotiations will mean the accession of "Southern Cyprus" as the sole representative of the island. As might be expected given the limited population and high per capita income of the RoC relative to other candidate countries, the accession negotiations have not presented any major problems. With the deadline for the end of negotiations set as December 2002, the membership of Southern Cyprus is likely to be realized over a short space of time.

Furthermore, it is interesting to note that the EU has not attached any conditions that would help pressure RoC to resolve its dispute with the Turkish Republic of Northern Cyprus (TRNC). The absence of explicit conditionality related to this issue with respect to the accession of Southern Cyprus has contributed to a certain asymmetry in power relations. This has increasingly rendered it more difficult for both parties to reach a workable compromise concerning the future of the island, a solution that is also of primary importance for the future of Turkey-EU relations. Clearly, this constitutes an area where the mix of conditions and incentives provided by the EU could have been more favorable to Turkey, in terms of facilitating Turkey's smooth transition to full membership. Given the crucial impact of the signals provided by the EU on Turkey's domestic politics, a more balanced approach on the part of the EU to the Cyprus issue would have made a major contribution towards the resolution of the dispute, which, in turn, would help jeopardize the position of the powerful anti-EU coalition in Turkey.[27] A more balanced approach on the part of the EU would mean setting explicit standards for Southern Cyprus to resolve its disputes with the North as a necessary step for accession to full membership.

Under the present rules governing the actions of the key actors involved and the incentive structure provided by the EU, the continued presence of the self-proclaimed Turkish Cypriot state on the northern part of the island does not appear to be a viable long-term option, at least in so far as Turkey's full membership remains a serious possibility. Moreover, the compromise solution proposed by the existing TRNC administration, involving essentially two largely independent Cypriot states entering the EU under a single umbrella, is not likely to elicit any kind of endorsement from Southern Cyprus. Southern Cyprus, under the present scenario, faces no such incentives to compromise. The key dilemma, however, is that members of the anti-EU coalition in Turkey, who strongly back the existing administration in the North, display no willingness whatsoever to consider any kind of serious compromise on this issue.

Perhaps on a slightly more optimistic note, the EU has indirectly contributed towards the resolution of the problem by triggering a process of change. The process initiated may not appear favorable from the Turkish perspective in the short-run, but it may nevertheless contribute towards some kind of compromise solution in the future. The EU signals are creating pressure for change in this context in two key respects. First, the increasingly unambiguous signals transmitted to the emerging pro-EU coalition in Turkey is that some kind of compromise, falling short of full-autonomy for the North, might ultimately be necessary in order to achieve a political settlement on the island, leading to the island's accession to the EU under a unified banner. This kind of signal has induced members of the pro-EU coalition in Turkey to exert increasing pressure on the government to revise the official policy stance. Indeed, key members of the pro-EU coalition such as TÜSİAD and, to a lesser extent, ANAP, have become increasingly vocal on this issue over the course of 2002. They have been making frequent public pronouncements, drawing attention to the urgency of finding a compromise solution, without actually being very precise about the nature of the compromise that needs to be made.[28] Such pronouncements have, in turn, generated intense reactions and criticisms from key components of the "anti-EU coalition," notably the military and the MHP. The debate seems to have acquired an additional urgency given the tight timetable facing the accession of Southern Cyprus to the EU and possible problems this poses to Turkey-EU relations in the future.

The second type of pressure brought about by EU action for change in the direction noted concerns the pressure upon Turkish Cypriots themselves. Clearly, there exists a major incentive on the part of Turkish Cypriots to be part of the EU as part of a unified Cypriot state, given the material and security benefits that such an arrangement would entail. The existing state of affairs—where the TRNC is not internationally recognized and its economy and security are dependent on mainland Turkey—surely does not constitute a durable and acceptable state of affairs from the perspective of the Turkish Cypriot Community. This EU pressure manifested itself in the resumption of negotiations between the representatives of the two communities on the island in November 2001, negotiations which had come to a complete standstill a few years beforehand. Although the series of negotiations conducted have so far failed to break the existing stalemate given the entrenched positions of the actors concerned, the opening of negotiations in itself might be interpreted as a sign of progress. The danger, however, is that if the Turkish Cypriot elites are unwilling to compromise, this will have significantly negative consequences in terms of strengthening the hand of the anti-EU factions in

Turkey. This negative possibility is unlikely to prevent Turkey's full membership in the end; however, it will undoubtedly frustrate Turkey's membership aspirations in the short-run.

The Cyprus dispute, therefore, is a clear case where the EU could have done much more to facilitate an equitable solution—taking into account the interests of all the actors involved—which would also pave the way for Turkey's relatively smooth accession to the EU. Nonetheless, one should also acknowledge the fact that the pressures presented by the EU and the incentives created by EU action have facilitated a process of change that may eventually lead towards a political settlement, paving the road to Turkey's full membership. From the Turkish perspective, however, one could anticipate a longer time frame and a less equitable outcome at the same time.

TOWARDS A CHANGE IN MUTUAL PERCEPTIONS AS A MEANS OF FOSTERING CLOSER TURKEY-EU RELATIONS

A typical argument frequently advanced by Turkey's military-security establishment concerns Turkey's unique importance for Europe from a geo-strategic perspective. The basic idea is that Turkey could make a significant contribution to European security through active participation in the emerging European Security and Defense architecture. The natural corollary of this argument is that there should be a major relaxation of the Copenhagen criteria in relation to sensitive areas such as cultural rights and the Cyprus dispute in return for the security advantages provided by Turkey's accession.[29]

Clearly, this is a rather naive argument for a variety of reasons. First, it represents a certain misunderstanding of the true meaning of EU integration and the role of the EU as a "security community."[30] The underlying logic of the EU as a security community is that a process of mutual democratization and economic integration, rather than using direct force and the threat of military action, provides peace.

Second, the argument fails to take into account that, as Turkey is a NATO member, few security "carrots" exist on the part of the EU that could function as true incentives. Thirdly, it is a paradoxical argument for the nationalists to make in the sense that it implicitly conveys an underlying inferiority complex by suggesting that the only serious contribution Turkey could make to the EU is through improved security based on the size of its army and security forces.

This is not to suggest, however, that security conditions are not important and should be automatically minimized. The central point to emphasize is that security considerations *per se* cannot act as a substitute for democratic reforms and, hence, such considerations cannot be used as a means for bypassing the Copenhagen criteria in the first place. Indeed, once Turkey experiences major democratic reforms and resolves its central internal and external dilemmas it will be in a much better position to contribute to European security as a full member of the Union. Resolution of the Cyprus dispute would be a proof that Turkish membership would be a concrete security asset. Otherwise, in the European mind, Turkey in its present mold would still be regarded as security consumer rather than a security provider. This perception, in turn, will naturally reduce the incentives on the part of the EU to admit Turkey as a full member.

The emerging pro-EU coalition in Turkey could make an important contribution by challenging the orthodox, security-conscious mindset in Turkey and conveying what EU integration is all about in the first place. It is also crucial that the reform process is "internalized" in the sense that the kind of reforms needed to satisfy Copenhagen criteria ought to be portrayed as reforms which are intrinsically valuable and not simply accomplished to meet EU criteria in purely instrumental fashion. The proponents of Turkey's membership in the EU should also try to contemplate in a more positive fashion the possible contributions that Turkey could make to the broader integration process.

In terms of trade the Turkish economy is already heavily integrated into the European Union. Following the Helsinki summit, a number of new opportunities have emerged involving possibilities for active participation in Community-wide projects in education, technology and other areas.[31] Clearly, the ability to benefit from such cooperative schemes depends heavily on Turkey's own initiatives and internal capabilities. In a sense, substantial informal integration will have to precede formal association through full membership. Increased interaction through civil society networks and the participation of non-state actors are likely to play a central role in this kind of bottom-up integration process. Ultimately, Turkey's attraction to the EU will rest heavily on her concrete achievements in such diverse areas as science, technology, education, culture, sports, communications and entrepreneurship, achievements which are likely to be far more important than its contribution in the narrowly defined security realm.

Turkey could also make a significant contribution towards the evolution of a genuinely multicultural Europe, a kind of Europe which is not only interested in what is happening within her own borders but extends her horizons to develop relations with the neighboring Islamic world. Europe has a greater incentive to develop such a close relationship than the United States given that Europe is geographically closer to the Islamic world and contains a significant Islamic minority within its borders. Indeed, Turkey's contribution to a multicultural Europe would transcend the realm of Islam and include the significant non-Islamic elements in her rich cultural heritage. For this vision to be meaningful, however, especially after September 11, two basic preconditions have to be satisfied. First, Turkey needs to transform itself into a genuinely democratic state if it wishes to present itself as a model of multiculturalism, both to Europe and to the Islamic world. Second, Europe needs to undergo a major transformation itself from being an inward-oriented entity towards a genuinely global actor, interested not only in its own internal dynamics but also in broader regional and global processes. The origins of the current problems in Turkey-EU relations are, to a certain extent, due to the inward-oriented nature of the EU. In such a scenario, a reformed Turkey—based on a role extending well beyond that of security provider—could claim to have importance for the EU in terms of having a stronghold in the strategically important Middle East and the former Soviet Union. Clearly, these are long-term visions and some drastic changes need to take place on both sides if such ideas are to have any concrete meaning. It is clear, for example, that Europe itself does not constitute a monolithic entity. Deep divisions exist between different elements of the political spectrum concerning the meaning and limits of multiculturalism in the European context. The idea of a genuinely multicultural Europe is close to the visions of the European Left but tends to generate considerable resentment from the European Right, which is very much on the ascendancy at present. Similarly, the vision of Europe as a unified global actor appears to be somewhat distant. The kinds of obstacles that Turkey itself, moreover, needs to overcome to conform to this long-term vision are quite formidable.

In the meantime, the EU in the present setting could contribute further to Turkey's accession by improving the mix of conditions and incentives. Ambiguous signals provided by the EU and the vision of full membership as a long-term possibility tends to strengthen the position of the powerful anti-EU coalition in Turkey. Through improved financial assistance and diplomatic signaling, as well as greater support for broad-based civil initiatives in Turkey, the EU could significantly alter the balance of power in favor of the emerging pro-EU coalition, as has been the case in other candidate countries, both in the context of southern and eastern enlargement. Furthermore, greater sensitivity on the part of the EU to Turkey's security concerns and a more balanced approach to its disputes with its neighbors are also likely to be particularly helpful in this context.

CONCLUDING OBSERVATIONS

The Helsinki decision created a powerful set of incentives for change and reform in Turkey's domestic politics. Previously, change had been under way, but was less pronounced given that membership in the Customs Union in and of itself failed to provide an appropriate mix of conditions and incentives. The end of the armed conflict in the southeast during the early part of 1999 also paved the way for significant change in the direction of political reforms. Observing the Turkish scene two-and-a-half years after the Helsinki summit, one can clearly detect the beginnings of an influential pro-EU coalition in Turkey committed to undertaking the kind of economic and political reforms necessary to facilitate full membership. It is fair to say that, hitherto, civil society associations, rather than political parties, have been the principal actors of this newly emerging pro-EU coalition. Key political parties are yet to establish themselves as active members of this coalition.[32]

At the same time, one needs to take into account the formidable obstacles on the way to full membership in the presence of a highly entrenched anti-EU coalition. The term "anti-EU coalition" contains a precise meaning in the present context. It certainly does not mean that key constituencies making up this broad coalition are against EU membership at all cost. What it does mean is that members of this coalition do not like the conditions associated with full membership and are unwilling to delegate authority on what they consider to be key national decisions to a supranational authority like the EU. But by arguing that domestic politics should be totally independent from transnational influences, they clearly fail to diagnose the increasingly "post-modern" character of the EU in recent times. Ideally, they would like Turkey to become a member of the EU on their own terms, meaning the absence of any major change in the *status quo* in the domestic sphere. Members of the anti-EU coalition tend to exaggerate the internal and external security threats confronting Turkey and regard major political reform, such as the extension of cultural rights, as a major threat to the unity of the nation. Clearly, the EU itself can help break the existing deadlock and shift the balance in favor of the emerging pro-EU coalition as it has effectively done in the past in other national contexts. Incomplete commitment on the part of both Turkey and the EU at present seems to be slowing down the process of change in the direction of full membership, a process which would have been far smoother if both sides could display a greater degree of commitment to the key Helsinki decision.

POSTSCRIPT

Important developments have occurred in Turkey-EU relations in the aftermath of September 2002 when the present study was completed. The general elections of November 2002, the UN Plan for Cyprus, which became public during the same month, and the outcome of the European Council's Copenhagen summit of December 2002 all represent critical turning points in the long-trajectory of Turkey-EU relations.

The Justice and Development Party (*Adalet ve Kalkınma Partisi*—AKP), emerged as the winner of the November elections and managed to form a majority government in Turkey for the first time since 1991. Although the party had strong Islamist roots, it presented itself as a center-right conservative party with moderate leanings and an underlying commitment to secularism. What is even more striking is that the AKP, much more than any political party of the previous era, demonstrated a high degree of commitment to the goal of full EU membership. Hence, the party constituted a key component of Turkey's pro-EU coalition by the end of 2002. This not only showed its readiness to accelerate the reform process that had already gathered momentum during the course of the year, but also expressed its willingness to diverge from the official state line in resolving the Cyprus dispute, even before the UN Plan on Cyprus became public. The party was clearly willing to challenge the military-security establishment on a critical issue of Cyprus; something that political parties of the previous era, including ANAP, were not able to do. The AKP clearly faces a number of challenges. A major test of success will be in the economic sphere. Similarly, the party is confronted with major challenges in terms of staying within the boundaries of the secular constitutional order. Nonetheless, the fact that after November 2002 Turkey obtained a strong government with a deep commitment to EU membership clearly constituted a favorable development.

The second major turning point involved the comprehensive plan prepared by UN Secretary General Kofi Annan to settle the Cyprus conflict. Most commentators would agree that the "Annan Plan" represents a critical step towards resolving the Cyprus dispute. The plan clearly satisfies the basic demands of the Turkish and Greek communities on the island, as well as the major states involved. The plan offers the Turkish community political equality with the Greek Cypriots and envisages the formation of a common state composed of politically equal component states enjoying legal equality with the central level and exercising sovereign powers in their respective spheres of jurisdiction. It also allows for the continuation of a Turkish military presence on the island, although on a reduced scale. The Greek community will also gain from the reunification of the island and will obtain control over a larger proportion of the island's territory.[33]

It is interesting that the main impetus for an equitable solution to the Cyprus dispute originated not from the EU, but from the UN under the explicit pressure of the United States. Nonetheless, one could argue that the EU triggered this process by offering Southern Cyprus the possibility of full membership and encouraging the process of reunification and the entry of a united Cyprus into the EU. Yet there remains considerable resistance to the Annan Plan both from the leadership of TRNC as well as the military-security establishment in Turkey. Although the anti-EU coalition was on the defensive towards the end of 2002, the Cyprus issue will undoubtedly emerge as the real test of the respective strengths of the pro- and anti-EU coalitions in Turkey during the next phase of Turkey-EU relations.

Finally, the EU's Copenhagen summit held in December 2002 was of critical importance. The key outcome of the meeting involved the offer of a firm date (December 2004) for opening up accession negotiations with Turkey, provided that Turkey could satisfy all aspects of EU conditionality by then. The agreement on this date means that the mix of conditions and incentives has improved for Turkey although, admittedly, the EU could have improved the mix further by offering an earlier target date of December 2003. Arguably, an early target date could play an instrumental role in shifting the balance of power in Turkish society even more rapidly in favor of the pro-EU coalition. This, in turn, would help to accelerate the process whereby the reforms are successfully accomplished and the Cyprus conflict is resolved.

NOTES

The author would like to thank Ali Çarkoğlu, Dietrich Jung, Wolfango Piccoli and Kamil Yılmaz for their valuable comments on an early version of the essay and Hatice Burcu Şahin for her able assistance. An earlier version of this essay was presented at the Annual Meeting of the Middle East Studies Association held in Washington DC, November 23–26, 2002.

1. On the evolution of Turkey-EU relations—both from a historical perspective and the recent context—see, among others, Ziya Öniş, "Luxembourg, Helsinki and Beyond: Towards an Interpretation of Recent Turkey-EU Relations," *Government and Opposition*, Vol.35, No.4 (Fall 2000), pp.463–83; Meltem Müftüler-Baç, "Through the Looking Glass: Turkey in Europe," *Turkish Studies*, Vol.1, No.1 (Spring 2000), pp.21–35; Ziya Öniş, "An Awkward Partnership: Turkey's Relations with the European Union in Comparative-Historical Perspective," *Journal of European Integration History*, Vol.7, No.1 (2001), pp.105–19; William Park, "Turkey's European Union Candidacy: From Luxembourg to Helsinki to Ankara?," *Mediterranean Politics*, Vol.5, No.3 (Autumn 2000), pp.31–53; Chris Rumford,

"From Luxembourg to Helsinki: Turkey, the Politics of EU Enlargement and the Prospects for Accession," *Contemporary Politics*, Vol.6, No.4 (Dec. 2000), pp.331–43; Canan Balkır, "The Customs Union and Beyond," in Libby Rittenberg (ed.), *The Political Economy of Turkey in the Post-Soviet Era: Going West and Looking East?* (Wesport, CT: Praeger, 1998), pp.51–77; Ersel Aydinli and Dov Waxman, "A Dream to become a Nightmare? Turkey's Entry into the European Union," *Current History*, Vol.100, No.649 (Nov. 2001), pp.381–93; Mehmet Uğur, "Europeanization and Convergence via Incomplete Contracts? The Case of Turkey," *South European Society and Politics*, Vol.5, No.2 (Autumn 2000), pp.217–42.

2. On Turkey's state tradition and peculiarities of her modernization experience, see Sibel Bozdoğan and Reşat Kasaba (eds.), *Rethinking Modernity and National Identity in Turkey* (Washington DC: University of Washington Press, 1997).
3. On the New Europe, see Karl Cordell (ed.), *Ethnicity and Democratisation in the New Europe* (London: Routledge, 1999).
4. On the role of international influences, and especially the role of the EU, in the democratization process, see Jean Grugel, *Democracy Without Borders, Transnationalization and Conditionality in New Democracies* (London: Routledge, 1999) and Phillippe C. Schmitter, "The Influence of the International Context upon the Choice of National Institutions and Policies in Neo-Democracies," in Laurence Whitehead (ed.), *The International Dimensions of Democratization: Europe and the Americas* (New York: Oxford University Press, 1996), pp.26–58.
5. On the transnationalization of domestic politics in response to pressures from globalization in general—and for specific countries from the EU *per se*—see Grugel (1999).
6. On the post-modern state in Europe, see Thomas Diez (ed.), *The European Union and the Cyprus Conflict: Modern Conflict, Postmodern Integration* (Manchester: Manchester University Press, 2002).
7. Accession Partnership (Turkey: 2000 Accession Partnership) at <http://www.deltur.cec.eu.int/english/apwithturkey.pdf>.
8. Concerning the need to adapt Kemalist ideology to the environment of the twenty-first century, thereby shedding some of its hardline Republican features in the process, see Nathalie Tocci, "21st Century Kemalism: Redefining Turkey-EU Relations in the Post-Helsinki Era," *CEPS Working Documents*, No.170 (July 2001), <http://www.ceps.be/Pubs.php#WD>. On the dual characterization of the Turkish state, "hard" in political terms and "soft" in economic terms, see Metin Heper and Fuat Keyman, "Double-Faced State: Political Patronage and the Consolidation of Democracy in Turkey," *Middle Eastern Studies*, Vol.34, No.4 (1998), pp.259–77.
9. On the political economy of the Turkish state in the neo-liberal era and its relationship to recurrent financial crises following the opening up of the capital account, see Emre Alper and Ziya Öniş, "Financial Globalization, the Democratic Deficit and Recurrent Crises in Emerging Markets: The Turkish Experience in the Aftermath of Capital Account Liberalization," *Russian and East European Finance and Trade* (forthcoming), <http://www.ku.edu.tr/ir/>.
10. For the details of the National Report, see the Turkish National Program for the Adoption of the Acquis at <http://www.deltur.cec.eu.int/english/nationalprogtr.html>.
11. The respective reports are available at 2001 Regular Report on Turkey's Progress towards Accession, <http://www.deltur.cec.eu.int/english/e-g-regular-01.htm>.
12. On the MHP see Hakan Yavuz, "The Politics of Fear: The Rise of the Nationalist Action Party (MHP) in Turkey," *Middle East Journal*, Vol.56, No.2 (Spring 2002) and Ziya Öniş, "Globalization, Democratization and the Far Right: Turkey's Nationalist Action Party in Critical Perspective," *Democratization* (forthcoming), available at <http://www.ku.edu.tr/ir/>.
13. For clear evidence on this issue see Sedat Ergin, "312'nin Bu Şekliyle Geçmesinde Karalıyız" [We are Determined that the Relevant Constitutional Amendment Should be Approved by Parliament Without Further Revisions], NTV <http://www.ntvmsnbc.com> (Jan. 26, 2002).
14. On the role of military in Turkish politics, see Ümit Cizre, "Politics and Military in Turkey into the 21st Century," *EUI Working Papers*, RSC No.2000/24 Mediterranean Programme Series, Robert Schuman Centre for Advanced Studies (2000). On EU criticisms in this

context, see *2001 Regular Report on Turkey's Progress towards Accession*, p.19 at <http://www.deltur.cec.eu.int/english/e-g-regular-01.html>.
15. On the link between the EU and the evolution of Islamist politics in Turkey, see Ziya Öniş, "Political Islam at Crossroads: From Hegemony to Co-existence," *Contemporary Politics*, Vol.7, No.4 (Dec. 2001), pp.281–98.
16. The left-of-center Social Democratic Populist Party (SHP) was perhaps the forerunner of change in this sphere in the sense that it developed a wide democratization agenda. This included advocating the extension of cultural rights leading up to the general elections of 1991. However, the party has subsequently abandoned this agenda. Indeed, its successor, the Republican People's Party (*Cumhuriyet Halk Partisi*—CHP) recently became rather indistinguishable from its nationalistic counterparts.
17. A major qualification is called for in the sense that one may question the desirability of a customs union agreement on purely economic grounds. Indeed, many candidate countries have chosen a less restrictive free trade agreement with the EU, as opposed to a customs union agreement. Turkey preferred the Customs Union in order to demonstrate her strong economic commitment to the EU as a substitute for her lack of political commitment. The Turkish political elites at the time were clearly reluctant to abide by these conditions after a major economic crisis in 2001 and towards the end of the deadline.
18. On the role of TÜSİAD, see Ziya Öniş and Umut Türem, "Business, Globalization and Democracy: A Comparative Analysis of Turkish Business Associations," *Turkish Studies*, Vol.2, No.2 (2001), pp.94–120 and Ziya Öniş and Umut Türem, "Entrepreneurs, Democracy and Citizenship in Turkey," *Comparative Politics*, Vol.34, No.4 (2002), pp.439–56.
19. TÜSİAD's democratization report of 1997 is available at <http://www.tusiad.org.tr>. Subsequent reports on democratic reforms, both in general and in relation to EU membership, have also been published. See TÜSİAD, *Türkiye'de Demokratik Standartların Yükseltilmesi: Tartışmalarve Son Gelişmeler* [Raising Democratic Standards in Turkey: Debates and Recent Developments] (Istanbul: Turkish Industrialists' and Businessmen's Association, 1999); TÜSİAD, *Avrupa Birliğine Uyum Sürecine Doğru Siyasal Kıstaslar ve Uyum Süreci* [Political Conditions Attached to EU Membership and the Process of Adjustment to EU Norms] (Istanbul: Turkish Industrialists' and Businessmen's Association, 1999); and TÜSİAD, *Türkiye'de Demokratikleşme Perspektivi AB Kopenhag Siyasal Kriterleri* [A Perspective on Democratization in Turkey and the Political Components of the EU's Copenhagen Criteria, Vols.1 and 2] (Istanbul: Turkish Industrialists' and Businessmen's Association, 2001), also available at <http://www.tusiad.org.tr>.
20. For a comparative analysis of the role of business associations in relation to democratization and EU membership, see Öniş and Türem (2001), pp.94–120.
21. In fact, not all business associations are equally enthusiastic about this project. The semi-official "Union of Turkish Chambers and Stock Exchanges" (TOBB) and "Turkish Employers' Federation" (TISK) are examples of two associations which displayed a somewhat lukewarm attitude towards EU-related reforms, if not directly towards EU membership.
22. The TÜRK-İŞ (*Türkiye İşçi Sendikaları Federasyonu*—Confederation of Turkish Labor Unions) report entitled *AB Türkiye'den Ne İstiyor?* [What Does the EU Demand from Turkey?] is available at <http://www.turkis.org.tr/AB%20RAPORU.doc>.
23. On the military-industrial complex in Turkey, see Taha Parla, "Mercantile Militarism in Turkey, 1960–1998," *New Perspectives on Turkey*, No.19 (Fall 1998), pp.29–52.
24. On the crises of 2000–1 and the role of the IMF in the process, see Emre Alper and Ziya Öniş, "Emerging Market Crises and the IMF: Rethinking the Role of the IMF In the Light of Turkey's 2000–2001 Financial Crises," *Boğaziçi University Department of Economics Working Papers*, Feb.–March 2002. Available at <http://www.ku.edu.tr/ir>.
25. See the Lehman Brothers' report as a typical example. Lehman Brothers, "Cliff-hanger," *Focus Turkey*, Nov. 30, 2001.
26. The TESEV survey is available at <http://www.tesev.org.tr/etkinlik/TESEVyolsuzluk Sunumu.pdf>.
27. For an elaboration of this perspective see Ziya Öniş, "Greek-Turkish Relations and the European Union: A Critical Perspective," *Mediterranean Politics*, Vol.6, No.3 (Autumn

2001), pp.31–45. For a series of diverse perspectives on Greek-Turkish relations and the Cyprus Conflict, see Dimitris Keridis and Dimitrios Triantaphyllou (eds.), *Greek-Turkey Relations in the Era of Globalization* (Herndon, VA: Brassey's, 2001).

28. For an innovative proposal involving the integration of a bi-communal Cyprus to the EU along the lines of the Belgian model, see Michael Emerson and Nathalie Tocci, *Cyprus as a Lighthouse of the Eastern Mediterranean* (Belgium: Centre for European Policy Studies, 2002), also available at <http://www.ceps.be>.
29. For an articulate exposition of this frequently advanced, but highly problematic, thesis see Onur Öymen, *Türkiye'nin Gücü* [Turkey's Power] (Istanbul: AD Kitapçılık A.Ş, 1998).
30. For a powerful argument along these lines, see Dietrich Jung, "Turkey and Europe: Ongoing Hypocrisy?" (Copenhagen: Copenhagen Peace Research Institute Working Papers), No.35 (2001), also available at <http://www.copri.dk>.
31. Examples of programs which became available to Turkey after the Helsinki summit are: PHARE, ISPA and SAPARD, LIFE (2000–4) and 5th EC Framework Programme on R&D (1998–2002), 6th EC Framework Programme on R&D (2002–6), Leonardo da Vinci II, Socrates II, Youth (2000–6), ETAP, Carnot and SURE.
32. At least this was the case until the general elections of November 3, 2002 that marked another crucial turning point in the trajectory of Turkey-EU relations.
33. Details of the UN Plan on Cyprus are available at <http://www.mfa.gov.tr/grupa/ad/annan.doc>.

4
Towards a European Security and Defense Policy: With or Without Turkey?

ESRA ÇAYHAN

The European Economic Community (EEC), which was established by six Western European countries in 1957, aimed at creating a common market. However, during a life span of 44 years, it has successfully turned into a monetary union with a single currency. With this unique process of economic integration Europe indeed deserves to be thought of as an economic "giant." On the other hand, in the political realm, there has been no equivalent success over the years. This difference has often been reflected in the opposite characterization of the Community as a political "dwarf." In the last few years, significant steps have been taken to change this image. The European Union (EU), with 15 members, seems to be determined to become an influential actor in international relations.

In order to go beyond economic integration, the Union has undertaken the task of forming a common foreign and security policy by the implementation of the Maastricht Treaty. Previously, foreign policy issues were tackled intergovernmentally. Since 1970, member states had been involved in the mechanism of "European Political Cooperation" (EPC) while dealing with international political problems. The Single European Act legalized the EPC in 1986, without changing its intergovernmental nature. Together with the Maastricht Treaty, which came into force in 1993, the creation of a Common Foreign and Security Policy (CFSP) has become one of the objectives of the EU. Indeed CFSP found its place in the framework of the Union as the second pillar.[1] Later, the Treaty of Amsterdam, which was put into effect in 1999, and the Treaty of Nice, signed in 2001 (will enter into force on February 1, 2003), revised the provisions for CFSP.

While enhancing the security of the Union in all ways, CFSP also aims at preserving peace and strengthening international security. Such goals signal a Union that wishes to assert its identity on the international scene. In order to do this, the Union has decided to develop its own military capabilities in recent years. In other words, the security dimension of CFSP has been on the agenda with the aim of progressively building a common defense policy, which might lead to a common defense.

Will this new process of framing a security and defense policy in Europe include Turkey? How is it going to effect Turkey's future accession to the Union? This contribution serves as an introduction to this important issue. In the following sections, the evolution of European Security and Defense Identity/Policy (ESDI/ESDP) will be explained, largely by using official documents. This will be followed by an evaluation of the policy's main challenges. Finally, Turkey's position will be assessed, before making a conclusion.

FROM ESDI TO ESDP: A UNION WITH MILITARY "TEETH"?

The first half of 1990s witnessed attempts to develop a European Security and Defense Identity (ESDI) within NATO. It was claimed that ESDI would improve the European contribution to NATO-led operations and give Europe a capability to act where NATO as an organization would not be engaged. In other words, ESDI was designed to improve the flexibility of Euro-Atlantic crisis management. This type of strengthening of the European pillar of NATO required a new framework of cooperation between NATO and the EU. This was provided by the Maastricht Treaty, which designated the Western European Union (WEU) as the defense component of the EU. The WEU was expected to be able to use NATO assets.

NATO members supported such cooperation between NATO and the WEU. In fact, the development of ESDI within NATO was encouraged in light of the socio-economic and political transformations in Europe. However, ESDI would not compete with NATO and jeopardize its leading role. For example, the declaration of the heads of state and government, following the ministerial meeting of the North Atlantic Council/North Atlantic Cooperation Council on January 10–11, 1994,[2] underlined the fact that the Alliance was the essential forum for consultation among its members and the venue for agreement on policies bearing on the security and defense commitments of allies. Reaffirmation of the strong commitment to the transatlantic link, and the wish to continue the direct involvement of the United States and Canada in the security of Europe, showed that NATO would continue to be the leading organization for European security.

The sensitivity regarding the key role of NATO in European security was once more reflected when the Treaty of Amsterdam was signed in 1997. It was carefully stated that CFSP was going to be compatible with the common security and defense policy established within the framework of NATO.[3] In this context the WEU (with the possibility of being integrated into the Union, should the European Council so decide) would elaborate and implement the decisions and actions of the EU with defense implications.

Such decisions and actions would include the so-called "Petersberg tasks,"[4] namely humanitarian and rescue tasks, peacekeeping tasks and tasks of combat forces in crisis management, including peacemaking.

Until 1998, discussions on ESDI revolved around the main theme of declaring NATO as the centerpiece of European security. Any steps that the EU would take within the realm of security would only strengthen the European pillar of the Atlantic Alliance, taken from this point of view. In 1998, however, there were certain developments which marked a new turn in the Union's quest for a greater role in international relations.

The joint declaration on European defense issued at the British-French summit in St Malo on December 3–4, 1998 marked a new approach regarding the search for a common defense policy in the EU.[5] The declaration stated that the EU needs to have the capacity for autonomous action, backed up by credible military forces, in order to be in a position to play its full role on the international stage. This signaled a turning point in the discussions on ESDI. Stressing that Europeans would operate within the institutional framework of the EU and use European capabilities—pre-designated within NATO's European pillar or national or multinational European means outside the NATO framework—the British and French leaders were proposing, for the first time, autonomous European action by using autonomous European forces.

The importance of NATO was not denied. In fact, respective obligations in NATO were underlined as usual. In order to contribute to the vitality of a modernized Atlantic Alliance, however, Europe had to make its voice heard in world affairs. This depended, to a large extent, on strengthening European armed forces that could rapidly react to new risks and be supported by a strong and competitive European defense industry and technology. In short, the St Malo declaration revealed the first signs that the EU would try to develop its own military capabilities outside NATO in its search for a greater role on the international scene.

The significance of this new dimension in ESDI discussions was enhanced by the Kosovo crisis. Once more it became obvious that European security was too dependent on the United States. The technological gap between the American and European military capabilities was enormous and Europeans had to do something in order to exert more influence on issues related to their own security. Thus, it was not difficult to gain support for the St Malo spirit, and security and defense aspects of CFSP were thoroughly tackled in the Cologne and Helsinki European Council Presidency Conclusions, in June and December 1999, respectively.

The Franco-British initiative to develop the EU's own military capabilities was accepted by other member states of the Union and started to take its place in EU discourse together with the Cologne European Council Presidency Conclusions. The determination of the EU to assume its tasks in conflict prevention and crisis management was put forward by stressing the commitment to "further develop more effective European military capabilities from the basis of existing national, bi-national and multinational capabilities" and the need to strengthen the EU's own capabilities.[6]

Following the Cologne and Helsinki summits, the term ESDI was replaced by "ESDP" in discussions about European security. The switch in terms, from "identity" to "policy," indicated that security and defense issues would no longer be mere topics for theoretical debates in Europe. The change in language corresponded to the transformation from conceptual analysis to the application of policies with security and defense implications.

This transition from conceptual to concrete language was evident in Helsinki. Here, the European Council underlined the EU's "determination to develop an autonomous capacity to take decisions and, where NATO as a whole is not engaged, to launch and conduct EU-led military operations in response to international crises."[7] According to the Helsinki European Council Presidency Conclusions on common security and defense policy, "cooperating voluntarily in EU led operations, member states must be able, by 2003, to deploy within 60 days and sustain for at least one year military forces of up to 50,000–60,000 persons capable of the full range of Petersberg tasks."[8] To reach this headline goal, "new political and military bodies and structures will be established within the Council to enable the Union to ensure the necessary political guidance and strategic direction to such operations, while respecting the single institutional framework."[9]

A few months after the Helsinki summit, in March 2000, temporary structures that would prepare the future Political and Security Committee of ambassadors, European Military Committee of senior officers and European Military Major Staff, started to operate in Brussels. In November 2000, the member states participated in the Capabilities Commitment Conference, at which specific national commitments corresponding to the military capability goals set by the Helsinki European Council were drawn together.

Also, as it was decided in Helsinki, there were attempts to establish a non-military crisis management mechanism in order "to coordinate and make more effective the various civilian means and resources, in parallel with the military ones, at the disposal of the Union and the member states."[10] The experience and resources of the member states and the EU "in a number of areas such as civilian police, humanitarian assistance, administrative and legal rehabilitation, search and rescue, electoral and human rights monitoring" would be of great value as civilian instruments of crisis management.[11] It was agreed to develop the civilian aspects of crisis management in four priority areas, namely police, strengthening of the rule of law, strengthening civilian administration and civil protection. Member states should be able to provide 5,000 officers by 2003 for international missions.

All these developments suggested that, at the beginning of the twenty-first century, the EU would no longer stand as a "civilian power." For the first time in its history the Union was openly declaring major aspects of its future military forces and establishing new institutional structures that would direct future military operations. However, these new institutional structures raised serious concern among non-EU members in Europe because they would not be a part of the EU's own decisionmaking mechanisms. The merger of the WEU into the EU deprived them of the access they had gained via several types of membership in the WEU.

When the WEU was designated as the defense component of the EU by the Maastricht Treaty it was expected to act as a bridge between the EU and NATO. Since membership in the WEU was only open to EU member states, in an effort to make the WEU an inclusive pivotal organization "associate membership" and "associate partnership" were introduced in order to involve non-EU members in this framework. The non-EU European NATO members Turkey, Iceland and Norway became associate members of WEU in 1992 (when they became NATO members in 1999, Hungary, Poland and the Czech Republic were also accepted as associate members). EU members Denmark and Ireland preferred to have observer status in the WEU in 1992 (as did Austria, Finland and Sweden in 1995, when they were admitted to the Union). Finally, Estonia, Latvia, Lithuania, Bulgaria, Slovenia, Slovakia and Romania acquired associate partnership in 1994.

The differentiated membership system of the WEU turned it into a large forum for dialogue in which all participants could have an impact on the decisionmaking process, regardless of having full membership status. This all-encompassing approach presented an opportunity for non-EU members to have a say in the EU's security and defense issues. Similarly, for the EU it became a healthy way of incorporating non-EU European NATO members—namely Turkey, Norway and Iceland—whose approval would be necessary in future EU operations that would require the using of NATO assets.

At the Cologne European Council, when it was agreed to include into the EU framework "those functions of the WEU which will be necessary for the EU to fulfil its new responsibilities in the area of Petersberg tasks,"[12] it was expected that this development would not be welcomed by those non-EU members with associate membership in the WEU. Later, in the Feira European Council Presidency Conclusions, in June 2000, principles and modalities for arrangements were put forward "to allow non-EU European NATO members and other EU accession candidates to contribute to EU military crisis management."[13] The European Council also welcomed the offers made by Turkey, Norway, Poland and the Czech Republic that would contribute to the expansion European capabilities for EU-led operations.

While building consultation and cooperation mechanisms with non-EU European NATO members and other countries that are candidates for accession to the EU, it was carefully stressed that the decisionmaking autonomy and the single institutional framework of the EU would be fully respected. Bearing this in mind, "there will be a single, inclusive structure in which all of the 15 countries concerned (the non-EU European NATO members and the candidates for accession to the EU) can enjoy the necessary dialogue, consultation and cooperation with the EU."[14] Within this framework, there will be "exchanges with the non-EU European NATO members where the subject matter requires it, such as on questions concerning the nature and functioning of EU-led operations using NATO assets and capabilities."[15]

In the event of a crisis, then, the EU will address participation of non-EU NATO members and other countries that are candidates for EU accession before deciding on the military option.[16] When the Council decides to launch an operation requiring recourse to NATO assets and capabilities, the non-EU European NATO members will participate, if they wish to do so. Where NATO assets are not used, their participation will depend on the invitation of the Council. The Council may invite candidates for accession to the Union to join EU-led operations. The countries that participate in an EU-led operation by deploying significant military forces will have "the same rights and obligations as the EU participating member states in the day-to-day conduct of that operation."[17]

The initiatives taken by the EU in order to become an influential actor in international relations in the last decade reached a climax when ESDP was activated in Laeken in December 2001. The process that started with attempts to develop ESDI within NATO changed course, enabling the EU to gain its own military capabilities.

ESDP: STRENGTHENING OR WEAKENING EUROPEAN SECURITY?

To the optimistic federalist, the long-standing dream of a united Europe is becoming a reality. Europe seems to have developed a common security and defense policy and established an independent military of its own. Such attempts failed previously in the 1950s, but at the turn of the twenty-first century Europe stood very close to political and military integration. To the pessimistic Euro-skeptic, who distrusts further integration, another step has been taken to "Brussels-ize" the highly critical issues of security and defense without the consent of the citizens of Europe. Therefore, the democratic deficit in the EU is becoming greater.

Regardless of the type of value judgments that can be made, one has to point out that major steps have been taken in the direction of creating a Europe with military "teeth" in the last few years. Until recently, the Union has exerted influence on international relations through its trade policies and development aid. Thus, economically speaking, it has always been a significant "civilian" actor in the international arena. When it came to security and defense, NATO was always the main organization in Europe. However, as of the Laeken European Council in December 2001, where ESDP was declared operational,[18] the EU has started to turn into a "military power" in order to exert regional and global influence.

It should be noted that all official documents related to this process have always carefully stated that the Union does not intend to create a European army. This has been supported by explanations that a standing army is not being established. However, NATO does not have a standing army either. Member states assign some of their forces to NATO, and this is also the case regarding the military forces of the EU. Despite denial in the official EU documents, in day-to-day discussions everyone speaks of the "European army."

However, these attempts to create an army should not be exaggerated. We have witnessed only the beginnings of a long and painful process of framing a common security and defense policy in the EU. There is still a lack of political doctrine in the sphere of ESDP.[19] It is not going to be easy to develop a European strategic concept. How the transatlantic relationship will be influenced by ESDP will in turn have an important impact on determining the future of ESDP. While it is highly difficult to develop ESDP in a Union of 15 member states, enlargement will worsen the problem of reaching common grounds in security and defense issues. Furthermore, if the non-EU NATO members in Europe are not satisfied with the degree of their connection to the ESDP mechanisms, it will be very difficult not to alienate them.

If ESDP is developed in such a way that does not compete with—but contributes to—NATO's ability to effectively manage crises within and beyond the borders of Europe, then it will turn into a success story. In fact, to achieve a healthier transatlantic relationship in the future, the Europeans must increase their military capabilities. In the post-cold war period, the transatlantic Alliance has witnessed mutual criticisms. Americans believe that Europeans are not sufficiently committed to their own security. Thus, the United States often encouraged Europe to spend more on security and defense. On the other hand, Europeans have been critical of American dominance of NATO. The only way to have an equal say was to increase the European contribution to the Alliance.

Europe's capacity to contribute to transatlantic security has been limited in various aspects, especially regarding mobility of forces and capability to sustain them in the field. Also, in comparison to the United States, there have been deficiencies in high-tech communications and weapons. The capability gap between the two sides of the Alliance has been obvious, since the United States spends more than double what the European allies spend on equipment and about six times what they spend on research and development.[20] Such investments mean more capabilities, which were clearly demonstrated in the Kosovo air campaign.

In this respect, Kosovo proved to be something of a turning point for the EU:

> Until the Kosovo war began, the European Union remained obsessed with the creation of a common currency, the euro. Efforts to develop shared defense and security policies were largely stalled. But NATO bombardment of Kosovo, dominated by the United States, appears to have changed that. Europe's need for new military technologies such as laser-guided bombs, its dependence on Washington strategic reconnaissance and its lack of aircraft were clear. As a result, a debate that had been confined to a few foreign policy and military experts about Europe's growing dependence on the United States and its failure to keep up with new technologies has become a subject of wide public discussion.[21]

The United States may possess dominating bombing capabilities, but deploying ground troops is a different story. Due to the Vietnam syndrome, the American administration is extremely hesitant to put US troops on the ground as the American public does not want to see American soldiers killed abroad. This meant that it was up to the Europeans to deploy troops in the Balkans, which is considered to be their "backyard."

In fact, Britain, France, Germany and Italy took the lead, committing troops in Kosovo. In this context, Germany's first involvement in a major military role since 1945 and Britain's attempts to assume a leading role in the development of European defense have been two extraordinary developments, while France kept stressing the old-time theme of countering American hegemony. The fact that an international presence in the Balkans would be necessary to guarantee peace in the coming decades had an important impact on the EU's attitude. Efforts to speed up the development of a common security and defense policy have had much to do with that outlook on the future. In other words, the EU seemed to be willing to take the initiative in its "backyard," and this determination launched discussions on ESDP.

There are certain challenges that are to be met in order to develop an effective ESDP. The Clinton administration summarized them as the famous three Ds that are to be avoided: "de-coupling" the United States from Europe; "duplication" of NATO structures and capabilities; and "discrimination" against non-EU member allies. In other words, the role of NATO and the American presence in Europe should not be undermined; real capabilities should be developed by increasing defense budgets; and non-EU European NATO members should not be alienated.

American presence in Europe and NATO's position as the leading defense organization in Europe are critical matters. If ESDP evolves in such a way that competes with NATO and excludes the United States from European security issues, Americans are likely to review their commitments regarding Europe. From the very beginning of the discussions on ESDI, Washington stressed that isolationist trends in America may become dominant if there are any signs of the de-coupling of Europe from NATO and the United States:

> A European contribution to fairly share burdens within the alliance is indispensable to the health and future of the alliance. Having said this, though, Americans should not refrain from asking questions both about the process itself and the ultimate objectives of the EU's defense project. And here, our European friends should understand the constructive spirit in which these questions are raised. They should remember that it is the Atlanticists in the US who ask hard questions, precisely because they do take Europe and our partnership seriously. If misunderstandings and misperceptions grow, however, it will be the isolationists and the global unilateralists who benefit as a result and to the profound detriment of us all.[22]

In a nutshell, the Atlanticists have been trying to convey the message that ESDP should be developed in the right direction in order to prevent the United States from saying, "if Europeans want to defend themselves, let them." Warnings about a possible US withdrawal from Europe have been constantly repeated, directly or indirectly, especially following the St Malo declaration. It is a very serious threat, when we consider the fact that none of the twentieth-century wars in Europe could have come to an end without American involvement.

In fact, Europeans have been very careful not to make any statements or engage in actions that would amount to distancing Europe from America. That is why all official EU documents have underlined the significance of NATO and ESDP has been put forward as an attempt to strengthen the European pillar of the Atlantic Alliance.

It should be kept in mind that the EU intends to take on a range of missions, which include humanitarian and rescue tasks, peacekeeping and crisis management operations, including peacemaking. These Petersberg tasks have nothing to do with collective defense. ESDP does not have a dimension that is related to the collective defense of Europe. NATO continues to be the cornerstone of European security, since it has the mandate and capacity to take on the full spectrum of missions, ranging from conflict prevention and crisis management to collective defense, including times of war.

However, this should not be evaluated as a division of labor between NATO and the EU. A two-tier Alliance, in which the EU-member allies focus on Petersberg-type, low-intensity situations, and non-EU allies are responsible for collective defense, is not welcome. "This would not be healthy for the transatlantic relationship. It also would not be good for the Europeans, since all crises are unpredictable and could, in the end, require more than modest capabilities."[23] If a crisis handled by the EU escalates into a major problem that has direct implications for the security and defense of some of the allies, then Article 5 commitment may come into play.[24]

These considerations make it obvious that the EU should work in close contact with NATO. There is an attempt to develop the EU's own capabilities, but NATO's support in terms of assets, capabilities and force planning are indispensable. This means that NATO and the EU, which have never had any cooperation and collaboration in the past, are bound to establish a partnership. It is essential that the two different organizations can work together efficiently under the pressure of time, when there is a crisis to be handled as soon as possible. The bureaucracies in either of them should not slow down the process of crisis management.

In short, it may be said that whenever the strategic interests of both Europe and North America make it necessary to handle a security crisis, NATO will take the lead. If NATO refrains from intervening, then the EU may carry out the Petersberg tasks. In other words, the EU is trying to develop a rather modest capacity allowing it to engage in military operations. However, the crucial factor is that these capabilities should really be built. The United States has been rather skeptical about European seriousness on defense: "There is a danger that the European allies will concentrate on institutions rather than actually building the military capabilities needed to help manage crises."[25]

The headline ESDP goal calls for being able to deploy, by 2003, 50,000–60,000 persons capable of the full range of Petersberg tasks within

60 days, for at least one year. "In reality, this means raising a force of some 200,000 men because of rotation. At a time of declining defense budgets in Europe, there is some reason to doubt whether the Europeans will be willing to provide the funds needed to pay for the manpower and logistics support needed to sustain such a force."[26] It is not easy to rationalize the need to increase defense spending to public opinion in Europe. Europeans tend to choose "butter" instead of "guns." However, the EU governments have to spend more on defense issues if they wish to increase their military capabilities.

While developing ESDP, coherent defense planning between NATO and the EU is vital in order to prevent costly and inefficient duplication. In this process the position of non-EU member European allies, namely Turkey, Norway, Iceland, Hungary, the Czech Republic and Poland, is of crucial importance (the last three of these will become EU members as of May 1, 2004). If ESDP discriminates against these countries, new problems may be created while trying to prepare for potential conflicts in Europe. As explained above, the integration of the WEU into the EU meant that advantages of the differentiated membership structure of the WEU were lost. This was a major problem for the non-EU members who had associate membership status in the WEU. They became highly apprehensive, thinking they were to lose their channels of communication with the EU regarding security matters. Thus, the EU has tried to bring them into the new decisionmaking process. Turkey's approach to ESDP presented a major obstacle for some time. The following section describes Turkey's position *vis-à-vis* European security.

ESDP AND TURKEY:
MUTUALLY EXCLUSIVE OR INDISPENSABLE?

For more than 40 years now, Turkey and the EEC/EC/EU have had restless relations, mostly built upon mutual misunderstandings and disappointments. In a context of divergent perceptions, there have been several periods of crises, during which conflict and dissatisfaction, rather than cooperation and positive attitudes, prevailed. Despite problems, a unique position has been achieved in that Turkey is the only associate member to establish a customs union with the EU without having full membership status.

The uneasy patterns of interaction between the two sides should not prevent anybody from observing that Turkey and the EU are indispensable partners. For Turkey, membership in the EU is the long-overdue step that is to be taken towards westernization. Ankara has never perceived the

Customs Union as a target in itself. Rather, it has been evaluated as one of the stages in its long-time endeavor towards accession to the EU. As a regional power, situated between the Balkans, the Middle East, the Caucasus and Central Asia, Turkey may be too difficult to digest, but is also much too important to be neglected and left alone by Europe.

This is especially true when it comes to European security and defense: "As far as Turkey is concerned, it is in close proximity to existing and potential crisis areas. Therefore, arrangements to be formulated for the security of Europe are of the utmost importance to her, given the fact that Turkey's vital interests would be at stake."[27] From the standpoint of the EU, it makes sense to include Turkey in the framework of ESDP considering the fact that Turkey has played a pivotal role in the defense of Europe during the cold war. Turkey also has the second largest standing army in NATO after the United States, in other words, the largest European NATO army. Another asset is that Turkish armed forces have had considerable experience in peacekeeping in several countries, ranging from Somalia to Bosnia. It should also be taken into consideration that, unlike most European armies, the Turkish army has actively been engaged in war fighting for extended periods. For these reasons, technically and politically, it would be useful to integrate Turkey into the mechanisms of ESDP.

For half a century, NATO membership has been the cornerstone of Turkey's defense and security policy. With the understanding that European security and defense is indivisible and Turkey is an inseparable part of this system, efforts have been made for the inclusion of Turkey in every security organization unique to Europe.[28] In the first half of the 1990s, through associate membership to the WEU, Turkey gained a foothold in the decisionmaking mechanism of the EU on security issues, albeit not an impressive one. Later on, the decision to integrate the WEU into the EU annoyed Turkey very much. Since the EU had already declared that it was going to establish its autonomous military capabilities, Turkey began to perceive these developments as aimed at turning the EU into a security fortress. A widespread feeling of exclusion dominated the Turkish civilian and military structures.

This psychology of "being left out of the game" still prevails in Turkey, but the EU has partially understood the problem and tried to adopt some reassuring measures in Feira (June 2000). Arrangements were made to allow non-EU European NATO members to take part in EU military crisis management. This was done largely thanks to the American warnings against discrimination:

> it is essential that non-EU European allies, such as Turkey, enjoy a special status in their security relations with the EU because of their

NATO Treaty Article V commitment to the 11 EU allies. If a crisis being handled by the EU were to escalate, that Article V commitment could come into play—a fact often forgotten by some of our EU partners.[29]

The Turkish side has not been satisfied with the Feira arrangements:

> proposed EU arrangements limit the participation of non-EU European allies only to the day to day conduct of operations through a so-called Ad Hoc Committee of Contributors. This is an arrangement that does not make sense politically or militarily since only a military commander can undertake the day to day conduct of an operation. What the non-EU European allies should be involved in is the political control and strategic direction of an EU-led operation.[30]

The dialogue mechanism between the 15 EU member states and the six non-EU NATO members has not been appreciated by Ankara either: "Most importantly, the suggested EU format for dialogue, consultation and cooperation is a restrictive one that cannot be the basic structure for a true dialogue, cooperation and consultation on European security issues. A single and permanent structure of 21 should be the regular basis for such an exchange."[31]

Another point of concern for Turkey is that non-EU European allies do not participate in the interim and permanent phase EU military bodies. In addition, the fact that non-military aspects of crisis management do not allow the non-EU European allies a substantial role has been criticized by Turkey.[32]

Under these circumstances, Turkey's warnings to the EU can be summarized as follows:

- A non-Article 5, Petersberg-type operation may eventually transform into an Article 5 contingency, having direct implications on the security and defense of all allies;
- Any possible EU operation will make use of the same set of forces and capabilities assigned for the full range of Alliance missions;
- Any EU operation, regardless of the capabilities used, might affect the legitimate security interests of allies, like Turkey.[33]

Although there have been some gestures of good will—such as the welcoming by the EU of Turkey's proposal to participate in the headline goal with a brigade-level unit supported by a sufficient number of air force and navy units[34]—relations between the EU and Turkey regarding ESDP had been very tense until the end of 2001. Basically, "the problem of Turkey"[35] can be described as the Turkish veto on letting the EU use NATO assets and capabilities, unless its demand for inclusion in the ESDP decisionmaking mechanisms is fulfilled, even without being an EU member. The EU has responded by claiming that Turkey cannot veto autonomous EU actions that do not involve Turkish military forces.

Turkey's blockage has prevented the EU from having guaranteed access to NATO's planning facilities at SHAPE (Supreme Headquarters Allied Powers Europe), and this has been perceived as a Turkish attempt to hamper EU efforts to build up its military organization.[36] In December 2001, this deadlock was solved by a deal between the United States, Britain and Turkey. Two important concessions were made in order to remove the Turkish veto. First, Turkey's disadvantage stemming from being left outside of the EU decisionmaking mechanisms was tackled. It was accepted that an intensive consultation procedure would be applied whenever Turkey's security interests are at stake due to an EU operation, or when an operation in Turkey's "near abroad" is under discussion. Second, Turkey's concern about a likely EU interference in case of a conflict with Greece had to be addressed. It was agreed that the EU military forces would not intervene in conflicts between NATO and EU members.[37]

These principles disturbed Greece very much. As an EU member state, Greece expected the EU to side with it in event of a conflict with Turkey over the Aegean or Cyprus. Thus, the attempt by the United States and Britain to lift the Turkish veto immediately prompted a Greek veto in the EU. This problem was expected to be solved during the Spanish Presidency, during the first half of 2002. However, no consensus could be reached. It seems that "the problem of Turkey" regarding ESDP has turned into an internal matter of the EU. However, Greece has a chance to be assertive in the second half of 2002, during the Danish Presidency. Since Denmark is not going to handle issues related to security and defense as it is a neutral country, Greece will be responsible for policy in that sphere. It is therefore highly likely that ESDP will be a prominent issue.

It is important to note that, due to "the problem of Turkey" and "the problem of Greece," the EU has not yet finalized security arrangements with NATO. European military forces have been declared operational as of 2003, but the EU does not have guaranteed access to NATO's assets, capabilities and operational planning. For this reason it is essential to conclude the necessary agreements with NATO as soon as possible. The end of 2002 should be characterized by intensive diplomatic bargaining in order to please both Turkey and Greece or else the problems between both will present a real impediment to the EU's attempt to become a military power.

CONCLUSIONS

Contemporary security risks emanate from quite different sources and are mostly impossible for an individual state to deal with alone. Problems such as terrorism, ethnic conflicts, organized crime, the mass movement of people, environmental disasters, religious fundamentalism and biochemical warfare are transnational issues that require international action. The September 11 terrorist attacks in the United States have proved the seriousness of such issues. Today, when we talk about European security, there is no clear-cut threat in the form of a group of enemy states against which collective security should be maintained. Rather, there are many risks to be taken into consideration.

In such an international context, the EU has been trying to develop a security and defense policy in order to become a major power in world affairs. Formerly, it had been one of the most important economic actors in international relations, but had no political weight. Recently, the Union has been working to increase its military capabilities so that it will be involved in crisis management activities. Ethnic conflicts in the Balkans have enhanced this attitude of the EU. The Union intends to deal with future crises in its backyard and contain them before they reach the point of threatening the security of Europe as a whole.

This attempt has been described as an initiative that will strengthen the European pillar of NATO. The US position, from the very beginning of the Clinton administration in 1993 and into the present Bush administration, has been supportive of a stronger European pillar within NATO. The European allies were encouraged to take greater responsibility to manage security problems in Europe:

> The Administration position reflected broad sentiment within the US Congress and American public opinion that, fifty years after the end of World War II, it was high time for the Europeans to shoulder a greater share of the burden. At the same time, President Clinton was convinced that maintaining domestic support for US engagement in Europe after the end of the Cold War would be easier if there were a more equitable share of responsibility within the Alliance.[38]

The American perspective on ESDI/ESDP has been positive, in principle. But there are certain conditions to be met, as the "three Ds" described above illustrate. American concerns have been very clearly explained at every possible occasion:

> As a practical matter, the United States may have little to worry about. The Europeans are shrinking their defense budgets with such

abandon that it will be a long time before they have an autonomous capacity to act militarily without US backing. So the odds are that this EU concept will be empty without the constant involvement of NATO. If managed wisely, it could all work out for the better. However, the more that either EMU or CFSP has an anti-American undercurrent, and the more that EU efforts seem to take a form that tears at the integrity of NATO procedures, then concerns could only mount in this country that damage is being done to the Alliance. If NATO is thought by Europeans to be dispensable, the same idea might catch on here.[39]

If the position of the United States is the major external dynamic that will have an impact on how ESDP evolves, the main internal dynamic is the harmonization of priorities among the member states regarding common security and defense. Today, the key element that is missing in ESDP is a strategic concept, which should link the Union's military capabilities to its political objectives. Such a concept has to state the political and strategic rationale for ESDP and address questions such as "*where* and *when* Europe will make use of its military capabilities, *what kind* of operations will be conducted under the auspices of the European Union and *how* such operations will be conducted ... Any attempt to define clear cut strategic guidelines is likely to reveal disagreements and different priorities among EU countries" (original emphasis).[40]

Yet the general consensus achieved so far regarding ESDP objectives should not be misunderstood. The more specific aspects are put on the table the less the chances of further consensus. This presents a real dilemma to the Union. On the one hand, there is the need to develop a strategic concept in detail in order to have a sense of direction for ESDP. On the other hand, such efforts may lead to disintegration. It is an extremely difficult task to reach a consensus on such delicate matters as security and defense when there are 15 member states sitting around the table, each with its own interests and priorities. Not surprisingly, the future enlargement of the EU will make this problem even worse. For the time being, it may be wise not to push this new common policy too far too soon. Only small steps can be taken without causing irritation among the member states, some of which have a neutral status. A low-profile ESDP seems to be the best choice for the EU, at least for the next few years.

As for secondary external dynamics, namely the position of the non-EU member NATO allies, Turkey's standpoint deserves special attention. In fact, Turkey's attitude has presented a real problem for ESDP for some time. Turkey's chief concern has been that the EU might intervene in areas such as Cyprus, the Aegean and the Balkans, which are of strategic interest to Turkey. When such operations are to be conducted by using NATO assets Turkey would have the power of veto in NATO. However, if autonomous EU military forces are to be used, then Turkey would have no say in the decisions. Turkey is also "concerned that Greece could use its membership of NATO to block a NATO military mission in these sensitive areas, with the result that the EU—soon to contain two Greek speaking countries—would have to run the operation."[41]

From the point of view of the EU, Turkey's stubborn policy has been perceived as an impediment against the establishment of a "European army." It was annoyed that a non-member state was demanding access to the EU's own decisionmaking mechanisms, which involves only the 15 member states. However, one should not miss the point that European security policy cannot be compared to common agricultural policy or monetary union. It is highly understandable that such areas are strictly matters for the Union itself. However, when the Union claims to develop a new security and defense policy in Europe, it should be remembered that this will have a direct impact on Europe as a whole, of which Turkey is a part. With its critical geopolitical position Turkey is bound to be taken into account whenever Europe becomes involved with new security and defense arrangements.

As stressed at the beginning of this contribution, the EU is a unique example of successful economic integration that aspires to become a major actor in international relations. Turkey has always paid close attention to the integration process in Europe. The movement that began with the aim of establishing a common market has evolved into a highly developed system of economic and monetary union. Furthermore, the political dimension has been brought to the forefront by the recent efforts to create a European army. With or without Turkey, the EU will continue taking steps in the sphere of security in order to become a global power. It is not likely that the EU will completely exclude Turkey from ESDP. It remains to be seen to what extent Turkey will participate in this framework.

So far, Turkey's future participation in ESDP is as unclear as future membership in the EU. If Turkey is going to be treated as an "outsider" by the EU while it frames a security and defense policy in Europe, the accession process will be negatively influenced. On the other hand, if Turkey is allowed to take part in ESDP to a considerable extent, this will have a positive impact on efforts to integrate this long-time associate member into the EU.

POSTSCRIPT

The Copenhagen European Council (December 12–13, 2002) proved to be a turning point for ESDP in terms of resolution of conflicts between

Turkey and Greece. According to the Presidency Conclusions,[42] when the EU conducts military operations using NATO assets, only "EU Member States which are also either NATO members or parties to the 'Partnership for Peace',[43] and which have consequently concluded bilateral security agreements with NATO" will participate. This means Cyprus and Malta will not take part in such military operations.

> This concession had been demanded before the summit by Turkey, which was disappointed by the Copenhagen meeting's decision to schedule its EU candidacy in 2005, after Cyprus gains membership in 2004. Pessimism about a defense accord deepened on the summit's eve when EU foreign ministers were told by Greece's George Papandreou that his country would reject the compromise unless Cyprus agreed. Cyprus then came under intense pressure from European leaders to accept the concession and get the NATO deal that has proved an essential precondition, both technically and politically, for the EU to develop an autonomous defense force.[44]

Receiving the concession from Cyprus, and thus guaranteeing the lifting of the Turkish blockage, meant a breakthrough in NATO-EU relations.[45] With the NATO-EU arrangements finally rid of all barriers:

> the European Council confirmed the Union's readiness to take over the military operation in fYROM [Former Yugoslav Republic of Macedonia] as soon as possible in consultation with NATO, and invited the relevant bodies of the EU to finalize work on the overall approach to the operation, including development of military options and relevant plans. The European Council also indicated the Union's willingness to lead a military operation in Bosnia following SFOR.[46]

Thus, the first ESDP mission may start early in 2003, with the handing over of NATO's small peacekeeping program in Macedonia to the EU. Also, the EU may develop a bigger role in peacekeeping in Bosnia. If these missions are put into effect, it will be possible to free the American forces there for possible use in US military operations in other parts of the world. Such a prospect will no doubt please the US while intervention in Iraq remains a possibility.

NOTES

1. The first pillar being the European Community (EC), and the third Justice and Home Affairs.
2. Ministerial Meeting of the North Atlantic Council/North Atlantic Cooperation Council, *Declaration of the Heads of State and Government*, NATO Headquarters, Brussels, Jan. 10–11, 1994, <http://www.nato.int/docu/comm/49-95/c940111a.htm>, July 3, 2002.

3. See Treaty on European Union, Article 17, as amended by the Treaty of Amsterdam, <http://www.europa.eu.int/eur-lex/en/treaties/dat/eu_cons_treaty_en.pdf>, July 3, 2002.
4. See *Western European Union Council of Ministers Petersberg Declaration*, Bonn, June 1992, <http://www.cip.fuhem.es/ueh/documentos/ueo/92-petersberg.htm>, July 3, 2002.
5. *Joint Declaration issued at the British-French Summit*, Saint-Malo, France, Dec. 3–4, 1998, <http://www.fco.gov.uk/news/newstext.asp?1795>, July 3, 2002.
6. "Annex III: European Council declaration on strengthening the common European policy on security and defense," Cologne European Council, *Presidency Conclusions*, <http://ue.eu.int/en/Info/eurocouncil/index.htm>, July 3, 2002.
7. Helsinki European Council, *Presidency Conclusions*, <http://ue.eu.int/en/Info/eurocouncil/index.htm>, July 3, 2002.
8. Ibid.
9. Ibid.
10. Ibid.
11. "Annex II: Presidency Report on Nonmilitary Crisis Management of the European Union," to "Annex IV: Presidency reports to the Helsinki European Council on strengthening the common European policy on security and defense and on nonmilitary crisis management of the European Union," Helsinki European Council, *Presidency Conclusions*, <http://ue.eu.int/en/Info/eurocouncil/index.htm>, July 3, 2002.
12. "Annex III: European Council declaration on strengthening the common European policy on security and defense," Cologne European Council, *Presidency Conclusions*, <http://ue.eu.int/en/Info/eurocouncil/index.htm>, July 3, 2002.
13. Santa Maria da Feira European Council, *Presidency Conclusions*, June 19–20, 2000, <http://ue.eu.int/en/Info/eurocouncil/index.htm>, July 3, 2002.
14. "Appendix 1: Arrangements to be concluded by the Council on modalities of consultation and/or participation that will allow the non-EU European NATO members and other countries which are candidates for accession to the EU to contribute to EU military crisis management," to "Annex 1: Presidency Report on strengthening the common European security and defense policy," Santa Maria da Feira European Council, *Presidency Conclusions*, June 19–20, 2000, <http://ue.eu.int/en/Info/eurocouncil/index.htm>, July 3, 2002.
15. Ibid.
16. Regarding the situation of non-EU European NATO members, Turkey's objections to ESDP turned out to be the principle problem. The US attitude towards ESDI/ESDP and Turkey's considerations will be analyzed in detail below. December 2001 saw an attempt to solve this problem through an agreement between the United States, Britain and Turkey. The Greek rejection of this attempt prevented the EU from reaching an agreement with NATO before the Laeken European Council in December 2001.
17. "Appendix 1: Arrangements to be concluded by the Council on modalities of consultation and/or participation that will allow the non-EU European NATO members and other countries which are candidates for accession to the EU to contribute to EU military crisis management," to "Annex 1: Presidency Report on strengthening the common European security and defense policy," Santa Maria da Feira European Council, *Presidency Conclusions*, June, 19–20, 2000, <http://ue.eu.int/en/Info/eurocouncil/index.htm>, July 3, 2002.
18. See *Presidency Conclusions*, European Council Meeting in Laeken, Dec. 14–15, 2001, <http://ue.eu.int/pressData/en/ec/68827.pdf>, July 3, 2002.
19. See Giovanna Bono, "European Security and Defense Policy: Theoretical Approaches, the Nice Summit and Hot Issues," *Research and Training Network: Bridging the Accountability Gap in European Security and Defense Policy (ESDP)/ESDP and Democracy*, Feb. 2002, <http://www.europeansecurity.net/Documents/documents/ESDP&Democracy.pdf>, July 4, 2002.
20. For defense expenditures of NATO countries (1980–2000), see *NATO Handbook*, <http://www.nato.int/docu/handbook/2001/hb090803.htm>, July 31, 2002.
21. Roger Cohen, "A bigger Military Role for Germany," *International Herald Tribune*, June 15, 1999, web edition, <http://www.iht.com>.
22. Jeffrey Gedmin, "NATO and the EU's European Security and Defense Policy," *Prepared Statement for a Hearing before the Committee on Foreign Relations, Subcommittee on European Affairs, United States Senate*, March 9, 2000, p.4.

23. Alexander Vershbow, "The American Perspective on ESDI/ESDP," *Perceptions*, Vol.5, No.3 (Sept.–Nov. 2000), pp.100–1.
24. Article 5 of The North Atlantic Treaty (NATO's founding treaty) states that: "The Parties agree that an armed attack against one or more of them in Europe or North America shall be considered an attack against them all and consequently they agree that, if such an armed attack occurs, each of them, in exercise of the right of individual or collective self-defense recognized by Article 51 of the Charter of the United Nations, will assist the Party or Parties so attacked by taking forthwith, individually and in concert with the other Parties, such action as it deems necessary, including the use of armed force, to restore and maintain the security of the North Atlantic area.
    Any such armed attack and all measures taken as a result thereof shall immediately be reported to the Security Council. Such measures shall be terminated when the Security Council has taken the measures necessary to restore and maintain international peace and security." See *The North Atlantic Treaty, Washington D.C., 4 April 1949*, <http://www.nato. int/docu/basictxt/treaty.htm>, July 30, 2002.
25. Stephen Larrabee, "ESDI and US Interests: The European Security and Defense Identity (ESDI) and American Interests," Prepared Statement for a Hearing before the Committee on Foreign Relations, Subcommittee on European Affairs, United States Senate, March 9, 2000, p.1. At <http://www.rand.org/publications/CT/CT168.pdf>, July 4, 2002.
26. Ibid., p.2.
27. Ömür Orhun, "European Security and Defense Identity-Common European Security and Defense Policy: A Turkish Perspective," *Perceptions*, Vol.5, No.3 (Sept.–Nov. 2000), p.119.
28. Turkish Ministry of Defense, *White Paper 2000*, <http://www.msb.gov.tr/Birimler/GnPPD/GnPPDBeyazKitap.htm>, July 4, 2002.
29. Vershbow (2000), p.103.
30. Orhun (2000), p.121.
31. Ibid.
32. Ibid., p.122.
33. Ibid.
34. Turkish Ministry of Defense (2000).
35. Charles Grant, "A European view of ESDP," *IISS/CEPS European Security Forum*, Sept. 10, 2001, <http://www.eusec.org/grant.htm>, July 4, 2002.
36. Ibid.
37. Zeynel Lüle, "Atina Direniyor" [Athens resists], *Hürriyet*, Dec. 11, 2001, p.14.
38. Vershbow (2000), pp.96–7.
39. Peter W. Rodman, "NATO and the European Union's Common Foreign and Security Policy," *Remarks prepared for the Subcommittee on European Affairs, Committee on Foreign Relations, United States Senate*, March 24, 1999, <http://www.nixoncenter.org/publications/testimony/3_24NATO.htm>, July 4, 2002.
40. Alfred van Staden, Kees Homan, Bert Kreemers, Alfred Pijpers and Rob de Wijk, "Towards a European Strategic Concept," *Netherlands Institute of International Relations 'Clingendael'*, Nov. 2000, p.5, <http://www.europeansecurity.net/Documents/documents/ m1.pdf>, July 4, 2002.
41. Grant (2001).
42. Copenhagen European Council, *Presidency Conclusions*, <http://ue.eu.int/newsroom/council HomePage.asp?LANG=1>, Dec. 20, 2002.
43. Members of the NATO Partnership for Peace (PfP) are as follows: Albania, Armenia, Austria, Azerbaijan, Belarus, Bulgaria, Croatia, Estonia, Finland, Georgia, Ireland, Kazakhstan, Kyrghyz Republic, Latvia, Lithuania, Moldova, Romania, Russia, Slovakia, Slovenia, Sweden, Switzerland, Tajikistan, the Former Yugoslav Republic of Macedonia, Turkmenistan, Ukraine and Uzbekistan. For details, see <http://www.nato.int/pfp/sig-cntr.htm> and <http://www.nato.int/docu/facts/2001/part-coop.htm>, Dec. 22, 2002.
44. Joseph Fitchett, "NATO agrees to help new EU force," *International Herald Tribune*, Dec. 16, 2002, web edition, <www.iht.com>.
45. NATO and the EU adopted a framework for cooperation on December 16, 2002 after the Copenhagen summit. See <http://www.nato.int/docu/update/2002/12-december/e1216 a.htm>, Dec. 22, 2002.
46. Copenhagen European Council, *Presidency Conclusions*, <http://ue.eu.int/newsroom/councilHomePage.asp?LANG=1>, Dec. 20, 2002.

5

The Cyprus Obstacle on Turkey's Road to Membership in the European Union

SEMIN SUVARIEROL

Turkish-Greek relations and the Cyprus problem following the Turkish intervention of 1974 have occupied an important place throughout the evolution of the relations between Turkey and the European Union (EU).[1] These two issues, often linked, figured among the most difficult to handle. The fact that Greece became a member of the EU in 1981 has complicated matters further, especially for the EU. From that point on, the EU could no longer keep its benevolent neutrality towards its two allies. Consequently, the road towards the amelioration of Turkish–EU relations passed via Athens and Nicosia,[2] despite Turkey's desire to keep the resolution of these issues separate from the question of its accession to the EU.

The divided island of Cyprus constitutes one of the "thousands of problems" the current EU enlargement process entails as a whole.[3] Each candidate obviously has its own particular problems; yet, even a brief look at the list of candidate countries may indicate that the case of Cyprus is the most exceptional case at present. The paradox is that, at the economic and administrative level, Cyprus is the best candidate. It is the most prosperous among the candidate countries and has all the administrative structures necessary for membership. But which Cyprus? Due to the Cyprus conflict, which has remained unresolved for 39 years, this preoccupying question has framed the Cypriot case as a politically problematic candidacy.

The link between the Cyprus issue and the accession of Turkey to the EU has become especially pronounced since Cyprus and Turkey both became candidates for EU membership. As a result of the European Council's 1999 Helsinki summit decisions, the resolution of the Cyprus problem is not a precondition to the accession of the Republic of Cyprus (RoC) or Turkey to the EU. Nevertheless, Ankara is expected to play an active role in bringing about a settlement in Cyprus as all parties concerned perceive it as having a key part in achieving the resolution of this imbroglio. Given this expectation and the noting of this issue as a short-term priority of Turkey's Accession Partnership, Cyprus is a *sine qua non* for Turkey's membership. Turkey thus finds itself obliged to modify its stance on this issue if it truly wants to become a part of the EU and to contribute to the stability of the region and the wellbeing of Cypriots.

This contribution does not aim to analyze the details of the Cyprus problem. In order to assist the reader and provide context, a chronology of the key events in the history of Cyprus, including the major turning points of Cyprus' and Turkey's relations with the EU, appears at the end of this piece. This contribution aspires to show how and why it is in Turkey's best interest to see Cyprus join the EU once a settlement is reached. As the Greek Cypriots will be accepted to the Union even without a settlement, an eventuality that may potentially trouble Turkey's own European course, Ankara will benefit from an early, rather than late, settlement. First, the Cyprus policies of Turkey and the EU will be examined in detail. Next, the Greek influence on the shaping of the European attitude will be emphasized, followed by a depiction of the links between the Turkish and Cypriot accessions to the EU and an anticipation of what lies ahead in the near future.[4]

TURKISH POLICY ON CYPRUS

Turkish policy on Cyprus is quite paradoxical. On one hand, Cyprus remains a national cause (*milli dava*) and a bastion of strategic interests for Turkey. On the other hand, Turkey argues that the resolution of the Cyprus problem is the sole responsibility of Greek and Turkish Cypriots. As a result of this double-edged policy, Turkey finds itself simultaneously demanding that its interests be taken into account with regard to any decision regarding Cyprus and denying it has any role in bringing about a solution in Cyprus, apart from declaring that it encourages all efforts to reach a settlement.

Why is Cyprus a national cause for Turkey? As an ancient Ottoman territory, Cyprus has historical significance for Turkey. There is thus a sense of national solidarity towards the Turkish Cypriots, similar to that felt towards other Turkish populations previously under Ottoman rule. Turkish presence on the island symbolizes and guarantees the upholding of Turkish interests, which are predominantly of strategic value. Only 40 nautical miles away from Anatolian coasts, the extension of the Karpaz peninsula offers Cyprus the possibility of blocking the exit from the gulf of Iskenderun and thus threatens Turkey's naval maneuverability.[5] For this reason, Cyprus is perceived as a dagger aiming at the stomach of Turkey. This rather outdated military vision (outdated when one considers the current technological circumstances) dominates the handling of the Cyprus issue by Ankara. Beyond this rhetoric, the strategic significance of Cyprus seems to currently lie in the fact that it is basically a "stationary aircraft carrier" (*sabit uçak gemisi*).[6] There is also the argument that the loss of Cyprus to Turkey's historical enemy, Greece, signifies a threat against vital Turkish interests. If Cyprus became "Greek," the Anatolian coasts would be encircled by a string of Greek islands. Consequently, the balance of forces between Greece and Turkey would be destroyed, the safeguarding of which is always of great psychological importance for Turkey.[7]

It was these considerations which brought about the Turkish intervention of 1974, rather than the humanistic pretext of the protection of the Turkish Cypriot minority. This strategic bastion has to be preserved in one way or another at all costs. Prime Minister Bülent Ecevit, a staunch hardliner on the Cyprus issue, is said to have claimed in 1998 that Cyprus is so indispensable for the strategic interests of Turkey that Ankara would not withdraw its troops even if there were not a single Turkish Cypriot living on the island.[8] Therefore, compromises on the rights of Turkey over Cyprus are out of the question. In addition, it is the first territory won against the enemy, the first contemporary victory of the Turkish army and the first expression of the determination of Turkey to protect its interests and to display publicly its strategic priorities.[9] Consequently, none of the political parties dare to make far-reaching concessions on Cyprus—an issue with high nationalistic connotations—for whatever objective it may be. Decisions like the compromise of March 6, 1995, which guaranteed Cyprus that its accession negotiations will begin six months after the conclusion of the 1996 IGC (Intergovernmental Conference) in return for the lifting of the Greek veto on the customs union agreement with Turkey, provoked comments such as "Cyprus has been sold" from the public and media. Turkish nationalists especially emphasize that compromising on Cyprus would trigger losses of other vital interests of the country.

Turkish Reaction to the Republic of Cyprus' Application for EU Membership

When the Republic of Cyprus applied for membership to the EU in 1990, Turkish leaders were alarmed. The Greek presence in the EU already prevented the amelioration of relations between Turkey and Europe, and now the Greeks would obtain a second veto against Turkey, in addition to their own. The balance established by the treaties founding Cyprus was being threatened.

Turkey insisted that the Cypriot application, as such, should be unacceptable to the EU. Consequently, Turkey requested the advice of experts on international law, namely Maurice H. Mendelson[10] and Christian Heinze,[11] to convince Europe and the rest of the international community that the Greek Cypriot application was against principles of international law, which the EU claims to always respect. Mendelson pointed to Article 185 of the Constitution of the Republic of Cyprus—an "unamendable" disposition—which stipulates, "The integral or partial union of Cyprus with any other State is excluded." He argued that the intention of the treaties establishing the Republic of Cyprus was to prevent the possibility of giving Greece or Turkey a more favorable economic position on the island which would amount to an economic *enosis* (unification of Cyprus with Greece). For this reason Article 8 of the Constitution underlined that "The President and the Vice President separately or conjointly, shall have the right of final veto on any law or decision concerning foreign affairs, except the participation of the Republic of Cyprus in international organizations and pacts of alliance in which Greece and Turkey both participate." This was interpreted as the president and the vice president having a veto right on the accession of Cyprus to organizations of which only one of these two states was a member, which of course would include the EU. Mendelson concluded that the Greek Cypriot administration had no right to apply for membership to the EU nor could it become a member as long as Turkey remained outside the EU.

These arguments, however, have not succeeded in persuading the European Union, since it interpreted the Cyprus question differently. Furthermore, for EU officials, the issue of Cyprus' accession is an eminently political debate, and law can adapt itself to any political solution.[12] On the other hand, Turkey's staunch emphasis on international law with regard to Cyprus has become rather hypocritical following the rulings of the European Court of Human Rights on Cyprus that Turkey still refuses to abide by.

Turkey had hoped that accession negotiations with Cyprus would not be launched before the resolution of the Cyprus conflict. Ankara has stated repeatedly that it neither wants the Union to become involved in the Cyprus question, nor does it approve of the EU having an active role in the negotiations for settlement in Cyprus. As Greece is a member of the EU, Turkey is convinced the Union cannot be impartial. Accordingly, Turkey even resented the appointment of an EU observer to these settlement talks.[13]

When the decision to open accession negotiations with Cyprus was taken simultaneously with the decision to put into force the customs union with Turkey, the prime minister at the time, Tansu Çiller, was fiercely criticized. The opposition parties blamed her government for having agreed to this historical compromise which "sold Cyprus," even though the minister of foreign affairs, Murat Karayalçın, declared during the March 6, 1995 Association Council meeting—where these decisions had been finalized—that Turkey's Cyprus policy had not changed at all.

This historical compromise by Turkey naturally had repercussions in the Turkish Republic of Northern Cyprus (TRNC). Many Turkish Cypriots had the impression that Turkey could abandon them for the sake of its own interests, seeing the TRNC as but a bargaining card.[14] To counter this perception, Turkey and the TRNC signed a common declaration on December 28, 1995, which asserted that they only approve the accession of Cyprus to the EU within the framework of a definite solution of the Cyprus problem. The same declaration maintained that the ties between the two countries would be reinforced at the economic and political levels.

Meanwhile, Greece and the Republic of Cyprus launched the "Joint Defense Dogma" in December 1993 with the aim of improving the coordination of the defense of Hellenic space against Turkish expansionism. The Dogma has been put into action through joint military exercises (called *Nikiphoros*) and the construction of a new air base in Paphos. Alarmed by this attempt to change the balance of power in the region, the Turkish government protested vigorously when the Republic of Cyprus announced its decision to purchase Russian S-300 missiles with a range of 150km in January 1997.[15] These missiles have been perceived as a direct threat to the security of Turkey, and the Turkish army has indicated that the move will be perceived as a *casus belli* and threatened preventive bombing should the missiles be deployed in Cyprus.[16]

The common declaration of January 20, 1997, signed between Turkey and the TRNC, was orchestrated within this context. The two parties were convinced that the Greek Cypriots aimed for indirect *enosis* through membership in the EU. To restore balance, they announced their intention of creating a concept of common defense: any attack against the TRNC would be considered an attack on Turkey. Furthermore, the declaration warned, "All steps taken by the Greek Cypriot Administration towards accession to the EU will accelerate the integration of the TRNC with Turkey."[17]

Similar declarations followed, finally resulting in an agreement on August 6, 1997, establishing the Association Council between Turkey and the TRNC, engineering partial integration at the economic, military and foreign policy levels. When the European Council Luxembourg summit declared that the EU would start accession negotiations with Cyprus and excluded Turkey from the list of candidates for the next wave of EU enlargement, the TRNC President Rauf Denktaş and Mesut Yılmaz, the Turkish prime minister of the time, firmly indicated that this decision left them a single option: integration. The TRNC followed Turkey's path of breaking off all contacts with the EU. Symbolically, the first meeting of the Association Council between Turkey and the TRNC took place on March

31, 1998, the day the EU began accession negotiations with the Republic of Cyprus.

Gradually, the Turkish stand moved further away from the idea that the solution of the Cyprus problem should be through the formation of a federation. The Turkish and Turkish-Cypriot governments started stating openly that the two sovereign states on the island should be recognized. This position, relatively softened with the proposition of Rauf Denktaş in favor of establishing a Cypriot federation, was made public on August 31, 1998. Turkey gave this proposition full support with a common declaration on July 20, 1999.[18] All these acts were a manifestation of Turkish foreign policy that proclaims itself as reactive, in the sense that it is formed as a response to positions taken by Greece, the Republic of Cyprus, and the EU. Turkey argued that since these three had modified all the parameters of the Cyprus question, Turkey and the TRNC could do the same.[19]

When the Agenda 2000 and the European Council Luxembourg summit Declaration excluded Turkey even from the list of candidates for the second round of enlargement, this provoked an outcry in Turkey. The EU, aware of the risk of alienating Turkey by excluding it from the list of candidates, had invited it to the European Conference to show that Turkey would one day become a candidate for membership. However, Turkish leaders were offended by the text of the Presidency Conclusions of the Luxembourg summit referring to the European Conference which underlined the following:

> The members of the Conference must share a common commitment to peace, security and good neighborliness, respect for other countries' sovereignty, the principles upon which the European Union is founded, the integrity and inviolability of external borders and the principles of international law and a commitment to the settlement of territorial disputes by peaceful means, in particular through the jurisdiction of the International Court of Justice in the Hague. Countries which endorse these principles and respect the right of any European country fulfilling the required criteria to accede to the European Union and sharing the Union's commitment to building a Europe free of divisions and difficulties of the past will be invited to take part in the Conference.[20]

This diplomatic formulation, which conditioned the participation in the Conference to a commitment to these principles, troubled Turkish national pride. Basically, the EU was imposing what it considered as the viable solution to Greek-Turkish problems and the Cyprus issue. It was also pressing forward the idea that Cyprus could accede to the Union once it fulfilled the accession criteria. Yet, the Turkish government was convinced that the decisions on these issues concerned Turkey alone. The EU should not encroach upon the sovereignty of the country. Above all, it should not interfere with issues considered of critical national importance. As a result, Turkey categorically refused all the above conditions and did not participate in the European Conference.

The strategies developed by the EU exclusively for Turkey, namely the French idea of assembling all the candidate countries at the European Conference, proved insufficient for overcoming the resentment of Turkish leaders. Ankara cut off all political dialogue with the EU until the Union abandoned what the Turkish officials saw as its discriminatory attitude towards Turkey, and waited for the EU to correct its "historical error." This long-awaited day came with the Helsinki summit, when Turkey finally became the thirteenth candidate for accession.

Prior to the Helsinki summit, the EU strategy had been to pressure Turkey by highlighting that Turkish-EU relations could be improved if, among other conditions, Turkey contributed to a resolution of the Cyprus question that would reunite the island and lead to the accession of Cyprus to the EU. This strategy would surely help to resolve the Cyprus question, as well as the problems related to the accession of Cyprus to the EU, *if* Turkey acknowledged that the revision of its policy on Cyprus constituted virtually a precondition for its own accession. Turkey, however, has refused viewing the revision of its policy on Cyprus as a precondition and, to the contrary, has taken measures towards closer integration with the TRNC. The fact that it felt alienated by the EU has therefore complicated matters further in Cyprus.

The 1999 Helsinki Summit and its Aftermath

As the strategy of excluding Turkey from the list of candidates only caused the hardening of the Turkish position, the EU changed its policy towards Turkey by announcing Turkey's official candidacy for membership at the European Council Helsinki summit. It was hoped that Turkey's accession process would also contribute to the resolution of the Cyprus problem. The expectation was that Turkey, as one of the major actors in Cyprus, would modify its position to break the deadlock on the island. Yet, Turkish politicians still tend to separate the Cyprus problem from the issue of Turkey's EU membership, mainly due to domestic political concerns.

The ambiguous language of the Helsinki conclusions initially led Turkish leaders to mistakenly believe that the EU would not undermine Turkey's interests, so that when the time came the EU would not let the Greek Cypriots join without the resolution of the Cyprus question. When the President of the European Commission, Romano Prodi, made it clear during his visit to the Republic of Cyprus in October 2001 that Cyprus would be among the first wave of EU members, irrespective of a political settlement, there was finally a realization that "the Cyprus issue was not going well for Turkey."[21] This acknowledgment was accompanied by a recourse to threats: the Turkish Minister of Foreign Affairs at the time, İsmail Cem, declared that "Turkey might be forced to take drastic measures" in the event of a Greek Cypriot accession prior to an agreement on the Cyprus question.[22] This was followed by statements by Prime Minister Ecevit that Turkey could annex the TRNC if the EU admitted Cyprus before a settlement.[23]

These unexpected threats led an EU Commission spokesman to express regret over the hardening tone and warned that annexation of Northern Cyprus would probably jeopardize Ankara's own hopes of joining the EU.[24] The European Parliament had already made it clear in its report published in July 2001 that "if Turkey were to carry out its threat of annexing the north of Cyprus in response to Cypriot accession to the EU and to proclaim the northern part as its 82nd province in clear breach of international law, it would put an end to its own ambitions of European Union membership."[25] This tension has relatively declined with the opening of direct talks between the two community leaders in Cyprus.

THE CYPRUS POLICY OF THE EU AND THE GREEK FACTOR

Whereas Turkish politicians have concerns (mentioned above) which shape Turkish policy on Cyprus, the EU has had its own internal considerations and precedents that generated its Cyprus policy. First, EU members in general seek to use the enlargement process for promoting their own interests or for exteriorizing their interior problems.[26] That said, Cyprus presents a fundamental political interest for an EU member: Greece. Greece has utilized all possible instruments within the EU to support the membership application of Cyprus. Even though Greece is a small country in the Union it has managed to make its voice heard concerning issues of importance for Greek foreign policy.[27] Wielding the veto stick in the Council of Ministers, Athens has influenced EU policy *vis-à-vis* Cyprus. The Greek influence can be described as a negative influence as this influence has led the EU, at times, to take certain unwanted decisions.[28] However, this claim is rejected by Greek diplomats, who point out that Greece has not been confronted with any pressure to refrain from using its right to veto.[29]

Nevertheless, as the EU machinery functions on compromise, the EU has managed to balance this negative influence by linking every compromise made to Greece to a compromise by Greece on other issues that the EU wanted to press forward. Thus, each substantial success that Greece has obtained towards the progress of the Cypriot candidature was a result of a compromise it made regarding the progress of the Turkish candidature. Even though the EU had hoped that Greece's accession would not affect Turkey-EU relations,[30] the functioning of EU organs constrains the EU sphere of action. No one can say that Greece has no right to insist on issues concerning its national interests because this is the right of each EU member state.

In principle, though, the EU has always sought to maintain a balanced approach towards its two allies, Greece and Turkey, by avoiding involvement in Greek-Turkish conflicts. This benevolent neutrality is notably observable in the fact that the Association Agreement with Greece was followed by the Association Agreement with Turkey. Allegedly, once Greece applied for membership to the EU, Turkey was encouraged to follow suit in order to safeguard the equal treatment of these two NATO allies—although this recommendation was not undertaken by the Turkish government at the time. Consequently, when Athens joined the EU in 1981, the Community found itself inevitably drawn into the relations between these two countries.[31] From that point on, the Community was obliged to be careful in order not to push Turkey away from Europe, or the West in general, which would have had undesirable consequences (especially during the cold war). This cautious policy prevented it from taking a firmer stance towards Turkey, even if it continued to deplore the Turkish military presence in Cyprus. The cost of sanctions, for example, would be too high. As long as Turkey remained outside, the EU could afford to be more flexible in order to preserve its ally.

Once Turkey and Cyprus materialized their European vocations through their applications for membership, the Community developed its Cyprus policy.[32] The European Parliament had notably adopted several resolutions conveying that the solution of the Cyprus problem would lead to the amelioration of the relations between the EU and Turkey.[33] The December 1989 opinion of the European Commission on the Turkish application also stated resolutely that the evaluation of the political aspects of the application would be incomplete if it did not take into consideration the negative effects of the disagreements between Turkey and a member state (Greece), but also the situation in Cyprus. Thus, the Cyprus problem had to be resolved if Turkey genuinely wanted to join the EU.

Once it became evident that the Cyprus policy of Turkey was incompatible with its vocation to join the Community, the fact that Turkey did not alter this policy not only allowed Greece to gain the support of its

European partners but also reflected the non-credibility of the European orientation of Turkey.[34] Meanwhile, three developments during the 1980s forced the Community to take a more activist position regarding Cyprus:[35]

- The accession of Greece to the EU;
- The denunciation by the Greek Cypriot political elite of *enosis* as a political objective (November 1981);
- The progressive consolidation of the Turkish Cypriot administration as a separate state.

The accession of Greece has rendered the option of *enosis* obsolete as the annexation of Cyprus by Greece would clearly violate the sovereignty of an associated state by a member state.[36] The viability of the Cypriot state was hence reinforced. As a result, the pro-*enosists* in Greece and Cyprus were weakened, which allowed the removal of *enosis* from the agenda of the Greek Cypriot government. The EU has therefore willingly let Greece Europeanize the Cyprus question. After all, while the *enosis* option ceased to exist, the occupation of the Turkish army remained.[37]

Turkey, however, has chosen to blame the influence of Greek pressure and has accused the EU of submission to Greek blackmail. Particularly because of the three developments aforementioned, there were many other voices within the Union favoring a more activist position, as advanced by Greece.[38] Yet, on each relevant occasion, Ankara severely criticized the European stance on Cyprus, repeating that it had not occupied Cyprus. In Turkey's eyes, the EU persisted in its erroneous assessment of the Cyprus question and thus adopted a Cyprus policy based on the Greek view.[39]

The Greek Presidency of the EU had already established during the Corfu summit in 1994 that the next enlargement would include Cyprus. However, the "historical compromise" of 1995 marked the beginning of the give-and-take process on Cyprus.[40] During the 1997 Luxembourg summit, it has been claimed that Greece again asserted that it would only approve the list of the first-wave candidates if Cyprus was included and negotiations with it would begin.[41] One eurocrat claims that this Greek influence was the only reason the EU started accession negotiations with Cyprus, denying analyses which argue that the Union wanted to increase its political role by contributing to the resolution of the Cyprus conflict.[42]

While the accession negotiations with the RoC moved forward successfully, there was no progress on the resolution of the Cyprus problem. To the contrary, the inter-communal talks which broke down in 1997—under the Turkish Cypriot party's pretext of the European Council's decision to open accession negotiations with Cyprus—were interrupted until December 1999. It is in this context that the new Helsinki package was orchestrated in order to obtain Greek agreement to

Turkey's candidacy.⁴³ The European Council of Helsinki, while welcoming the launch of the talks aiming at a comprehensive solution of the Cyprus problem and underlining that a political settlement will facilitate the accession of Cyprus to the European Union, concluded: "If no settlement has been reached by the completion of accession negotiations, the Council's decision on accession will be made without the above being a precondition. In this the Council will take account of all relevant factors."⁴⁴

While the European Union still bases its position with regard to Cyprus' accession on the Helsinki decisions, the conclusions of the June 21–22, 2002 Seville European Council confirmed that the EU's preference continues to be for the accession of a reunited island.⁴⁵ Yet, if the current negotiations in Cyprus fail, the undesirable eventuality of the accession of a divided Cyprus appears predictable. Any other option would endanger the entire enlargement project: Greece repeats its threat of vetoing the accession of Central and East European states in the event that Cyprus is excluded from the first wave of enlargement.⁴⁶ Greece's argument refers to the accession criteria, emphasizing that a candidate who fulfills these cannot be prevented from joining the Union. Thus, if the EU is a community of values, the exclusion of Cyprus will not be morally justifiable. Clearly, this argument is highly valid for the EU, which aspires to function according to well-established principles. Yet again, it can be recalled that the EU had asked the Central and Eastern European countries to settle their minority and border disputes through the Balladur Stability Pact before accession. Still, settling the Cyprus problem is not a condition that the RoC has to fulfill, as stated in the Helsinki decisions. This means that the EU will be accepting a state that claims to be occupied and therefore unable to apply accession criteria to those occupied territories. The EU, then, can obviously be selective on what set of principles or criteria to apply for a given case, according to its interests, which makes the moral argument advanced in European circles questionable.

The truth is, since the Eastern enlargement constitutes a major interest for all EU members, they do not want to see the entire process blocked because of a small Mediterranean island. Moreover, at the moment of the first round of enlargement, there will be a package of candidate states. The EU may continue to say that since the Helsinki summit it has adopted the principle of evaluating each candidate on its own merit. However, at the end of the day, this appears to be more rhetorical than what will happen in practice. As in the past, the EU prefers the accession of a group of countries to single accessions. Therefore, when the moment comes, even the member states that are reticent regarding the accession of a divided

Cyprus will not be able to vote against the accession of Cyprus when they wish to see other candidates accede.

THE LINKS BETWEEN THE TURKISH AND CYPRIOT ACCESSIONS

The compromise packages made so far concerning Turkey and Cyprus confirm the linkage between the Turkish and Cypriot candidatures for membership to the EU. Although Turkey cannot block the accession of Cyprus to the EU by refusing to contribute to the resolution of the Cyprus conflict, this strategy would jeopardize the accession of Turkey, as well as the accession of Turkish Cypriots. Therefore, the *status quo* is only to the benefit of the Greek Cypriots, who will be able to join the EU even if the Cyprus problem is not settled. Consequently, instead of having mixed Cypriot delegations within EU organs and the voice of Turkish Cypriots in favor of Turkey, there will be Greek Cypriot officials insisting on more EU pressure on Turkey, especially regarding Cyprus issues. It is likely that the Greek Cypriot government will not be favourable towards Turkey's membership of the EU.

Greek and Turkish Cypriots, as well as EU officials, list such key arguments demonstrating that it is in the interest of Turkey to see the settlement of the Cyprus problem. After all, Cyprus—as an EU member—would not threaten the strategic interests of Turkey in any way. Accordingly, they are convinced that Turkey would not sacrifice the prospect of its membership because of the Cyprus problem.

On the other hand, the fact that the progress of the Cypriot and Turkish applications was made through compromising should not give the impression that Cyprus is a valuable bargaining card in Turkey's hands. Although Turkey's contribution to the reunification of the island will definitely improve its relations with Europe, as well as with Greece, unification alone will not guarantee Turkish membership in the EU. Cyprus is only one of the short-term priorities included in the Accession Partnership with Turkey. As a matter of fact, the withdrawal of Turkish troops from Northern Cyprus is the minimum price Turkey will be required to pay,[47] as "it is inconceivable in a community based on the rule of law that one Member State should station troops in part of the territory of another Member State without the explicit agreement of the latter."[48] No one denies that Turkey is an important partner whose degree of satisfaction matters to the EU, but it should not abuse the Cypriot card.[49] The decision at Helsinki stipulating that the resolution of the Cyprus problem would not constitute a precondition to the accession of Cyprus signaled precisely that to Turkey. Some predict that an encouraging move towards Turkey will take place if Ankara works toward improving the situation in Cyprus, but this move will not be accession to the Union,[50] contrary to Turkish hopes.

However, many Turkish politicians do not agree with these arguments. There is a tendency in general to overestimate the influence of Turkey. There is also a belief that realpolitik requires that the EU take Turkey's opinions into consideration; otherwise, Europe will have to face the consequences.[51] Furthermore, strategists continue to claim that Cyprus is of primary strategic importance, especially since the construction project of the Baku-Ceyhan pipeline makes the security of this part of the Mediterranean even more vital than before.

If Turkey has managed to maintain its Cyprus policy since 1974, at the risk of alienating its allies,[52] it should not compromise now. If Turkey is to renounce its rights on Cyprus, that should only be done in exchange for an important gain, that is, membership to the EU. Yet Euro-skeptics in Turkey claim that the EU will never admit Turkey to its ranks; therefore, there is no need to concede regarding Cyprus, hoping that this would bring Turkey closer to Europe. Jean-François Drevet argues that Turks have an interest in keeping their "booty," selling it for the best price when the time comes.[53] If the Europeans do not want Turkey's accession, the island could indefinitely remain hostage, according to Drevet, who points out that—paradoxically—its candidature could lead Turkey to stick more vehemently to its conquest. As for the official Turkish foreign policy line on Cyprus, it constantly insists that Turkey does not consider the Cyprus issue a precondition to stronger relations with the EU. Therefore, in Turkey there is either an overestimation or an underestimation of the role of the Cyprus question on Turkish-EU relations.

It is clear that Turkey's attitude towards a potential settlement in Cyprus counts considerably. It is unclear to outside observers to what extent the TRNC authorities are dependent on, or independent from, Turkish authorities when it comes to decisionmaking regarding the fate of Turkish Cypriots. Nevertheless, given that the Turkish army and Turkish economic support constitute the most important bases of power for the TRNC, Turkish Cypriots would obviously have even more incentive for arriving at a settlement should Turkey pressure the TRNC. At the very least, if Turkey gave a clear and unambiguous signal that it wants to see the Cyprus problem solved—instead of merely declaring support for the negotiations—it would give a strong impetus to the talks on Cyprus. Such a clear message would also refute the Greek Cypriot argument that Turkey and the TRNC are intransigent and do not genuinely want a solution in Cyprus.

CONCLUSION

The dialogue of the deaf between the Union and Turkey with regard to Cyprus has continued despite overtures made to Turkey, which began at Helsinki.[54] The EU insists that the pre-accession strategy for Turkey is closely linked to the improvement of Greek-Turkish relations and the resolution of the Cyprus problem. Turkey is adamant that its Cyprus policy remains the same: the Cyprus problem belongs to the two communities on the island and is theirs to solve. As Turkish leaders insist on Turkey's sensitivities, so the EU insists on its own interests. The EU does not accept a third party blocking the accession of Cyprus, which means it will not accord a voice to Turkey on this issue. Europe is wary not to create precedents which could possibly open the way for other third countries to claim a similar right concerning their national interests.

If the EU is convinced that Turkey is capable of contributing to the solution of the Cyprus problem it is because of the well-founded conviction that Turkey has decisive leverage on the TRNC. Given its close political ties and dialogue with the Turkish Cypriot community, Turkey has more capacity to make itself heard in Northern Cyprus than any other actor.[55] The Turkish Cypriots are also aware of this strong Turkish influence, and they judge that the prospect of the EU membership will eventually oblige Turkey to work for a solution in Cyprus. Turkish Cypriots have thus welcomed the Helsinki decisions, as many of them believe that Turkey will preserve Cyprus as a bargaining card until its own accession.[56] It is therefore essential that Turkey dedicates itself to preparing for its own membership so that it could start its accession negotiations as soon as possible.

Certainly, symbolic declarations of support for the talks in Cyprus are important, but it is time that Turkey effectuate a fundamental change of attitude and policy regarding Cyprus. Furthermore, Turkey's threats of annexing the TRNC are not regarded as credible by the Greek Cypriots or in Europe, as Turkey has used this diplomatic arm before to push for its national interests. This recourse to threats is rather a self-defeating policy for Turkey as enforcing them will demand a high price, which brings into question the actual credibility of these threats and, therefore, largely renders them ineffective.

Turkey's membership process retains its uncertainty, as it is still unclear when Turkey will be able to begin actual accession negotiations, despite the Turkish parliament's crucial decisions to amend the Constitution in line with the EU accession criteria in the hope of obtaining a date during the Copenhagen European Council. Before the adoption of these reforms, the Commissioner for Enlargement, Günter Verheugen, signaled that the European Commission was against politically motivated bargaining with respect to Turkey, underlining that Turkey was still lagging behind in fulfilling the political criteria of membership.[57] Hence, Verheugen has played down the raised expectation of a date for accession negotiations at the upcoming Copenhagen European Council even if Turkey would adopt a positive attitude on the issues of Cyprus and NATO-ESDP (European Security and Defense Policy) cooperation.[58] On the other hand, the June 2002 Seville European Council noted, "New decisions could be taken in Copenhagen on the next stage of Turkey's candidature in the light of the developments in the situation between the Seville and Copenhagen European Councils."[59] This could well be interpreted as encouragement and support of Turkey's EU membership efforts.

As for Cyprus, the question seems to be more whether it will join the EU as a unified island or not rather than whether Cyprus will be included in the first wave of enlargement. The answer to that question will depend on whether the direct talks, started between the Greek and Turkish Cypriot leaders in January 2001, will finally lead to the surpassing of the antagonisms between the two communities in Cyprus. Even though the pressure on the parties to arrive at a resolution is stronger than ever, it is uncertain whether the two sides will be able to agree on a settlement. If one thing is clear, though, it is that any eventual settlement will be far from the ideal solution each side envisages for Cyprus. The challenge, as always, is to accept compromises, however painful they might be, as they are essential for arriving at a solution.

The prospect of accession of Cyprus to the EU has not served as a catalyst for the settlement of the Cyprus problem, as was hoped by many. Nevertheless, one cannot ignore the fact that "the approaching EU deadline for the accession of the Republic of Cyprus was one of the critical factors inducing the Turkish Cypriot and Turkish sides to re-embark upon a peace process."[60]

Many in Europe hoped that the significance of the relations between Turkey and the EU and the aspirations of Turkey of becoming a member of the EU would lead Turkey to change its Cyprus policy so as to bring about a solution in Cyprus. Accordingly, the Greek Cypriots believed that the EU could force Turkey to contribute to the solution of the Cyprus problem through the membership process to the EU. The resolutions by EU organs linking Turkey's accession to the settlement of the Cyprus issue have thus encouraged the Greek Cypriots who already firmly believed that "the key to a solution in Cyprus is Ankara."[61] Greek Cypriots, as well as others, anticipated that Turkey would finally be obliged to change its intransigent stance and abandon the Turkish Cypriots in order to ameliorate its international image and be accepted to the European club.[62]

Turkey has had difficulty meeting the political requirements since its accession partnership agreement was signed in March 2001. Even though there have been significant amendments of legislation, the problem lies at the level of implementation. Moreover, due to the economic crisis the country has experienced as of the end of 2000, the economic criteria have also become a problematic area. Turkey is thus in urgent need of working seriously on its membership track. As nobody is forcing Turkey to become a member of the EU, it is up to Turkey now to prove the seriousness of its European vocation. It is time to take concrete measures, and the Cyprus question could be the easiest to tackle if Turkish leaders realize (or perhaps decide) where their real interest lies.

Furthermore, it is up to Turkey to transcend its national pride,[63] which is incompatible with its vocation to join the EU. It is Turkey that aspires to become a member of the European club; it is thus Turkey that has to adapt itself to the values of this club. Clearly, this adaptation requires also a reorientation of its political attitudes.[64]

After all, the prospect of EU accession necessitates a fundamental change of vision, especially concerning policies based on a traditional perception of national sovereignty. Today, sovereignty depends very much on the inter-subjective relations between states: states are sovereign only through their counterparts; it is the "other," through its behavior or acts, which determines sovereignty or the "degree" of sovereignty.[65] This applies to Turkey as well as for the both parties in Cyprus. All three parties need to embrace the principles of the EU if they see their future in the Union, where even the smallest countries prosper without regretting the loss of sovereignty membership entails.[66]

POSTSCRIPT

Following the November 2002 parliamentary elections in Turkey, the new Justice and Development Party (*Adalet ve Kalkınma Partisi*—AKP) government has been advocating policy change with respect to Cyprus. The AKP leader Erdoğan's public statements mark a departure from the previous Turkish policy of passive support for the negotiations towards a settlement in Cyprus. Acknowledging that "no-solution is not a solution,"[67] the government wants the Cyprus issue resolved. Erdoğan has also recognized the link between the Cyprus issue and Turkey's EU membership and tried to convince EU officials and member states that giving a date for Turkey's accession negotiations would pave the way to settlement in Cyprus.

After Kofi Annan presented the *Basis for Agreement on a Comprehensive Settlement of the Cyprus Problem* on November 11, 2002 the Turkish government has actively encouraged the TRNC President Denktaş to accept the plan as a basis for further negotiations.[68] In view of the concerns expressed by the two sides, Annan presented a revised proposal on December 10, 2002. If both sides had signed this, then the Copenhagen Council Conclusions would have referred to the "United Cyprus."

The agreement was not signed, the Copenhagen Council announced, as expected, that Cyprus would become a member of the EU on May 1, 2004. February 28, 2003 has been set as the final date for arriving at a comprehensive settlement of the Cyprus problem. In case of a settlement, the Council, acting by unanimity on the basis of proposals by the Commission, shall decide upon adaptations of the terms concerning the accession of Cyprus to the EU with regard to the Turkish Cypriot community. In the absence of a settlement, the application of the *acquis* to the northern part of the island shall be suspended, until the Council decides unanimously otherwise, on the basis of a proposal by the Commission.[69]

Despite the legislative reforms passed and the declared commitment of the new government to EU membership, Copenhagen failed to give any definite perspective on Turkey's membership track. It only asserted that the EU will open accession negotiations if the European Council in December 2004 decides, on the basis of a recommendation by the Commission, that Turkey fulfills the Copenhagen criteria.[70]

It remains to be seen whether a settlement will be reached by the February 28, 2003 deadline. So far, the Greek Cypriot side has appeared willing to sign the agreement despite the fact that recent public opinion surveys in the RoC have shown that 59 percent of the Greek Cypriot population would vote against the "Annan Plan" if a referendum were to take place now.[71] The forthcoming February 7, 2003 presidential elections in the RoC also constitute a pressing reason to agree on a settlement sooner rather than later, as it cannot be guaranteed that the successive president will be equally prepared to sign the agreement, given public opinion.

Even though the Turkish Cypriot side has expressed its willingness to negotiate a final settlement on the basis of the revised Annan Plan, it still has some major reservations about the proposal. However, opinion polls indicate that 51.5 percent of Turkish Cypriots approve of the plan.[72] The legitimacy of Denktaş is thus increasingly questioned, while civil society groups in the TRNC demonstrate *en masse* in support of the Annan Plan.[73]

The current Turkish government is evidently committed to reform in view of EU membership and Cyprus constitutes one of the first obstacles to overcome. It is still uncertain whether the Turkish government's moderate stance will prevail over the traditional Cyprus policy favored by the Turkish Foreign Ministry and the current Turkish Cypriot leadership. The press statement by the Turkish Foreign Ministry on December 18, 2002 was very much in line with the longstanding Turkish position.[74] Remarkably, the statement also declared that Turkey does not accept the Copenhagen Conclusions with regard to Cyprus on legal and political grounds. Obviously, the extensive public debate on Cyprus will continue; only time will tell if the outcome will bring the winds of change or keep the *status quo*.

CHRONOLOGY

February 11, 1959: Zurich Agreements signed between the United Kingdom (UK), Greece, and Turkey about the founding principles of the Republic of Cyprus (RoC).

February 19, 1959: London Agreements signed between the UK, Greece, and Turkey about the founding principles of the RoC.

August 16, 1960: Proclamation of the independence of the RoC.

September 12, 1963: Association Agreement (the Ankara Agreement) signed between Turkey and the EU.

November 30, 1963: Archbishop Makarios proposed to his vice president, Fazıl Küçük, 13 amendments that would facilitate the functioning of the state apparatus, as the inapplicability of several dispositions of the Constitution had been proven in the eyes of Greek Cypriots.

December 21, 1963: "Bloody Christmas" is claimed to have caused the death of two Turkish Cypriots, murdered by Greek Cypriot policemen, aimed to force Turkish Cypriots to accept the 13 constitutional amendments. Following these events, the Turkish Cypriots abandoned their places in the parliament and the administration.

March 4, 1964: The United Nations (UN) Security Council passed Resolution 186 (1964), which stationed a force—the UNFICYP (United Nations Peacekeeping Force in Cyprus)—for maintaining peace and putting an end to violence in Cyprus. The reference in this resolution to the "Government of the Republic of Cyprus" marked the first instance of the recognition of the Greek Cypriot administration as the legal government of Cyprus.

December 1, 1964: Association Agreement between Turkey and the EU came into force.

December 19, 1972: Association Agreement between the Republic of Cyprus and the EU signed.

June 1, 1973: Association Agreement between the Republic of Cyprus and the EU came into force.

July 15, 1974: *Coup d'état* organized by the Greek military junta in power and executed by EOKA-B (the Greek acronym for "the national organization of Cypriot fighters") against President Makarios.

July 20, 1974: Turkish intervention in Cyprus to prevent *enosis*, to put an end to inter-communal fighting and to save the Turkish Cypriots.

August 16, 1974: Second offensive move by the Turkish army, which led to the occupation of 37 percent of the northern part of the island by the Turkish army and subsequently to the territorial regrouping of the populations of the two communities.

February 13, 1975: Proclamation of the establishment of the Turkish Cypriot Federal State (*Kıbrıs Türk Federe Devleti*).

February 12, 1977: High-level Agreement between President Rauf Denktaş and Archbishop Makarios setting the basis for the inter-communal talks.

May 19, 1979: Ten-point Agreement between Presidents Rauf Denktaş and Spyros Kyprianou setting the basis for the inter-communal talks.

November 15, 1983: Proclamation of independence of the Turkish Republic of Northern Cyprus (*Kuzey Kıbrıs Türk Cumhuriyeti*—TRNC). Only Turkey recognizes the TRNC, whereas the RoC, which only controls the Southern zone and includes only the Greek Cypriots, Maronites, Armenians, and other minorities, is recognized as the sole legitimate state by all other states.

November 18, 1983: The UN Security Council adopts Resolution 541 (1983), which deplores this declaration of secession, considers the proclamation invalid, and demands its annulment and calls for all the states to recognize no other state than the Republic of Cyprus.

April 14, 1987: Application for full membership to the EU by Turkey.

January 1, 1988: Customs union protocol between the Republic of Cyprus and the EU came into force.

December 18, 1989: Opinion of the European Commission rejected the Turkish application but confirmed the eligibility of Turkey for membership.

July 4, 1990: Application for full membership to the EU by the government of the Republic of Cyprus in the name of the whole island.

June 30, 1993: European Commission's opinion in favor of the opening of accession negotiations with Cyprus.

October 4, 1993: European Council approves the Commission's opinion during its summit in Luxembourg.

June 24–25, 1994: European Council of Corfu declared that the next enlargement of the Union would encompass Cyprus and Malta.

March 6, 1995: The "historical compromise" that guaranteed Cyprus its accession negotiations would begin six months after the conclusion of the 1996 IGC. In return, Greece lifted its veto on the customs union agreement with Turkey.

January 1, 1996: Entry into force of the Customs Union between the EU and Turkey.

December 12–13, 1997: The decision to start negotiations with the RoC taken by the European Council of Luxembourg.

March 12, 1998: The Greek Cypriot President, Glafcos Clerides, invited the Turkish Cypriot community to join the Cypriot negotiation team. The British Presidency of the EU transmitted the invitation extended to Turkish Cypriot leaders during the European Conference in London. The invitation was refused by the TRNC.

March 31, 1998: Accession negotiations started with the RoC.

November 10, 1998: Beginning of substantial negotiations for accession with the RoC.

December 10–11, 1999: European Council Helsinki summit asserted that the political settlement in Cyprus would not constitute a precondition for the accession of Cyprus to the European Union; the candidacy of Turkey made official after Greece lifted its veto.

December 4, 2001: Decision to start face-to-face talks between Presidents Denktaş and Clerides.

December 14–15, 2001: European Council meeting in Laeken expressed its determination to bring the accession negotiations to a successful conclusion—by the end of 2002—with those countries that will be ready, and listed Cyprus as one of the countries which could be ready if the present rate of negotiations and reforms is maintained.

January 21, 2002: Beginning of intensive and open-ended rounds of negotiations between the Greek and Turkish Cypriot leaders.

November 11, 2002: UN Secretary General Kofi Annan presented the *Basis for Agreement on a Comprehensive Settlement of the Cyprus Problem.*

December 12–13, 2002: European Council of Copenhagen welcomed Cyprus as a member of the EU from May 1, 2004 regardless of the resolution of the Cyprus issue.

NOTES

1. The European Community became the European Union on November 1, 1993, with the Maastricht Treaty. The term European Union (EU) will be used throughout the essay for the sake of simplicity.
2. Interview with Kostas I. Hatzidakis, Alternate Member of the Committee of Foreign Affairs, Human Rights, Common Security and Defense Policy, European Parliament, Strasbourg, June 14, 2000.
3. Words of a Spanish diplomat (who spoke on the basis of confidentiality) during an interview at the Permanent Representation of Spain to the European Union, Brussels, May 18, 2000.
4. The analysis here is based on the literature on the issues in question, the coverage of these issues in the Turkish, Cypriot, Greek, and European press, as well as interviews conducted in 2000 in Cyprus, Brussels, Strasbourg, and Paris with politicians, European bureaucrats, diplomats, and academics, within the framework of the master's thesis project of the author. Since 2001, the author's involvement within the TESEV (Turkish Economic and Social Studies Foundation) project on Cyprus has confirmed the findings of these interviews via encounters in Turkey, Cyprus and Europe during related conferences and meetings.
5. Marie-Pierre Richarte, "La question chypriote dans la politique étrangère de la Turquie," *Trimestre du monde*, Vol.4, No.36 (Oct.–Dec. 1996), p.105.
6. Words of Kürşat Eser, Nationalist Action Party member of the Turkish Grand National Assembly at the "Conference on Cyprus' Accession to the European Union" on May 4, 2002

at Boğaziçi University, Istanbul.
7. Confidential interview with an official at the Embassy of Turkey, Paris, July 17, 2000.
8. Hansjörg Brey, "Turkey and the Cyprus Question," *International Spectator*, Vol.14, No.1 (Jan.–March 1999), p.111.
9. Richarte (1996), p.107.
10. Maurice H. Mendelson, *EU and Cyprus: An Expert View – Opinion on the Application of Republic of Cyprus to Join the European Union* (Lefkoşa, 1997).
11. Christian Heinze, *On the Question of the Compatibility of the Admission of Cyprus into the European Union with International Law, the Law of the EU and the Cyprus Treaties of 1959/60*, Appraisal study presented to the Republic of Turkey (Munich, March 1997).
12. Interview with Georges Vandersanden (Lawyer, Professor at the Université Libre de Bruxelles, Brussels), May 16, 2000. One should note that the treaty establishing Austria, which assigned it a status of neutrality in order to prevent its union with Germany, did not constitute an obstacle to Austria's accession to the EU in 1995.
13. *Le Monde*, Dec. 25, 1993.
14. Interview with Ferdi Sabit Soyer, Secretary General of CTP (*Cumhuriyetçi Türk Partisi*— Republican Turkish Party), Lefkoşa, April 6, 2000.
15. It is worth noting that Cyprus is the most militarized island in the world. For further information on this and the crisis over the S-300 missiles, see Madeleine Demetriou, "On the Long Road to Europe and the Short Path to War: Issue-Linkage Politics and the Arms Build-up on Cyprus," *Mediterranean Politics*, Vol.3, No.3 (Winter 1998), pp.38–51.
16. Christophe Chiclet, "Chypre aux portes de l'Union européenne," *Politique Internationale*, No.77 (Autumn 1997), p.116.
17. Sabahattin İsmail, *150 Soruda Kıbrıs Sorunu* [The Cyprus Problem in 150 Questions] (Istanbul: Kastaş Yayınevi, 1998), pp.362–3.
18. Korkmaz Haktanır, *A Time to Remember* (Gazimağusa: Eastern Mediterranean University Center for Cyprus Studies Publications, 1999), pp.28–34.
19. Erol Manisalı, *Dünden Bugüne KIBRIS* [CYPRUS from Past to Present] (Istanbul: Çağdaş Matbaacılık ve Yayıncılık, 2000), p.120.
20. European Council of Luxembourg, *Presidency Conclusions*, Dec. 12–13, 1997.
21. Briefing of the Turkish Minister of Foreign Affairs in *Kathimerini* (English Edition), Nov. 3–4, 2001.
22 Ibid.
23. *Cyprus Mail*, Nov. 6, 2001.
24. Ibid.
25. Jacques F. Poos (Rapporteur), *Report on Cyprus's Application for Membership to the European Union and the State of Negotiations* (European Parliament, Committee on Foreign Affairs, Human Rights, Common Security and Defense Policy, July 17, 2001).
26. Christopher Preston, *Enlargement and Integration in the European Union* (London: Routledge, 1997), p.22.
27. Confidential interview with an official at the French Ministry of Foreign Affairs, Paris, June 7, 2000.
28. Ibid.
29. Interview with Dimitrios Triantaphyllou, Research Fellow at the Institute for Security Studies of the European Union, Paris, July 21, 2000. The opinions expressed are the personal views of the interviewee and do not represent the views of the Institute.
30. See the Report of the Commission of the European Communities, Jan. 27, 1976, quoted in Semih Vaner, "Chypre et l'Union européenne," *Politique Étrangère*, 61e année, No.3 (Autumn 1996), p.660.
31. Panos Tsakaloyannis, "The European Community and the Greek-Turkish Dispute," *Journal of Common Market Studies*, Vol.19, No.1 (1980), p.52.
32. Mehmet Uğur, *The European Union and Turkey: An Anchor Credibility Dilemma* (Aldershot: Ashgate, 1999), p.20.
33. See the resolutions of the European Parliament of July 8, 1982, July 10, 1986, July 9, 1987, and Dec. 15, 1988 in *La Position européenne sur Chypre* (Nicosia: Republic of Cyprus Press and Information Bureau, 1998), pp.68, 82, 84, 89.
34. Uğur (1999), p.21.

35. Ibid., p.163.
36. The prosperity of the Republic of Cyprus is another factor that obstructs the idea of *enosis* with Greece. Greek Cypriots are currently richer and better administered compared to their counterparts in Greece.
37. Confidential interview with a diplomat at the Embassy of the Netherlands, Paris, June 19, 2000.
38. Confidential interview with an official at the Permanent Representation of Greece to the EU, Brussels, May 18, 2000.
39. See the *Bulletin Quotidien Europe* of Nov. 9–10, 1998 (No.7339) for the declaration of the Turkish Minister of Foreign Affairs following the first regular progress report of the European Commission on Turkey's accession process, released on Nov. 4, 1998.
40. According to Andrew Apostolou, this affair was the work of two politicians outside the EU: Tansu Çiller, the Turkish prime minister at the time, and Glafcos Clerides, the President of the Republic of Cyprus. The two supposedly concluded a deal through indirect channels. During a visit to London just before the elections in Turkey, Çiller spoke to Tony Blair, who was the leader of the opposition Labour Party at the time, and said that the Socialist Group in the European Parliament (EP) should vote in favor of the customs union with Turkey. Otherwise, she warned, the Islamists would come to power. At the same time, Clerides is said to have contacted the Labour Party and told them that the Socialist Group of the EP, with whom the Greek Cypriot community in the UK has close links, should vote in favor of the customs union with Turkey because he had made a deal with Çiller. See Andrew Apostolou, "Turkey, the European Union, and Cyprus," *Mediterranean Quarterly*, Vol.10, No.4 (Fall 1999), pp.120–21.
41. Ibid.
42. Confidential interview with an official of the European Commission, DG Enlargement, Cyprus Team, Brussels, May 15, 2000.
43. Confidential interview with an official at the Permanent Representation of Italy to the EU, Brussels, May 15, 2000.
44. Helsinki European Council, *Presidency Conclusions*, Dec. 10–11, 1999.
45. Seville European Council, *Presidency Conclusions*, June 21–22, 2002.
46. Confidential interview with an official at the Permanent Representation of Greece to the EU, May 18, 2000.
47. John Redmond, *The Next Mediterranean Enlargement of the European Community: Turkey, Cyprus and Malta?* (Aldershot: Dartmouth, 1993), p.54.
48. Jacques F. Poos (Rapporteur), *Report on Cyprus's Application for Membership to the European Union and the State of Negotiations* (European Parliament, Committee on Foreign Affairs, Human Rights, Common Security and Defense Policy, Sept. 19, 2000). Nevertheless, the EU is ready to accept any settlement of the Cyprus problem reached by both parties in Cyprus. Verheugen declared in March 2000 during a visit to Cyprus that the existence of foreign troops did not constitute an obstacle to the accession of Cyprus.
49. Confidential interview with an official of the European Commission, DG Enlargement, Turkey Team, Brussels, May 16, 2000.
50. Interview with Kostas I. Hatzidakis.
51. Interview with a diplomat at the Permanent Delegation of Turkey to the European Union, Brussels, May 16, 2000.
52. The United States imposed an arms embargo on Turkey following the Turkish intervention of 1974 due to the pressure of the Greek lobby of the American Congress and despite the cold war; the embargo lasted for three years. This decision led Turkey to realize its isolation: it could not even count on its allies. At this point Turkish foreign policy was revised and Turkey began to search for other partners, such as the USSR and Middle Eastern countries. From that point on, the construction of military might that would allow Turkey to defend itself alone was emphasized.
53. Jean-François Drevet, *Chypre île extrême: Chronique d'une Europe oubliée* (Paris: Syros/Alternatives, 1991), p.305.
54. For example, the decision of the European Council (Laeken, Dec. 2001) to include Turkey in the European Convention on the Future of Europe alongside the other candidate countries, even though Turkey was not accounted for in the modifications brought about by the Treaty of

Nice in 2000.
55. Confidential interview with an official of the European Commission, DG Enlargement, Turkey Team.
56. Interview with Fatma Azgın (Pharmacist, Participant of bi-communal activities), Lefkoşa, April 6, 2000.
57. See the briefing of Günter Verheugen, "Öncelik Kıbrıs değil siyasi kriterler" [Priority political criteria, not Cyprus], *Frankfurter Allgemeine Zeitung*, July 1, 2002, <http://www.ntvmsnbc.com/news/161330.asp>.
58. The EU would like to use NATO assets for the planned European rapid reaction force. Turkey has blocked this because of differences with Greece. Some argue that the whole concept of the ESDP will be under threat unless the row is resolved. See <http://news.bbc.co.uk/1/hi/uk_politics/2162493.stm>.
59. Seville European Council, *Presidency Conclusions*.
60. Nathalie Tocci, "Cyprus and the EU: Catalyst for Negotiations or Settlement?," *Turkish Policy Quarterly* (Spring 2002), p.48.
61. Interview with Georges Zodiates, Counselor at the Permanent Delegation of the Republic of Cyprus to the European Union, Brussels, May 17, 2000. The Greek Cypriot argument is that if Ankara decides to solve the problem the Turkish Cypriot leaders will follow the Turkish line without question. The Commissioner for Enlargement, Günter Verheugen, has also commented that the key to a solution in Cyprus was in Ankara's hands, adding that the standpoint of the Turkish army was not clear either. See Verheugen's briefing to *Frankfurter Allgemeine Zeitung*.
62. Tozun Bahcheli and Nicholas X. Rizopoulos, "The Cyprus Impasse: What Next?," *World Policy Journal*, Vol.13, No.4 (Winter 1996/97), p.32.
63. Confidential interview with an official at the Permanent Representation of Spain to the EU.
64. Preston (1997), p.29.
65. Bertrand Badie, "La Souveraineté sur la scène mondiale: concept reconsidéré ou fiction renouvelée?," *La Revue Tocqueville/Tocqueville Review*, Vol.19, No.2 (1998), p.7.
66. Interview with Jacques F. Poos (Questeur), Member of the Committee of Foreign Affairs, Human Rights, Common Security and Defense Policy, Strasbourg, June 14, 2000. Poos gave the example of his own country, Luxembourg, stating that it felt itself at ease within the EU. In other words, it lost nothing by transferring a part of its sovereignty to the EU.
67. Fikret Bila, "Erdoğan'ın Kıbrıs'a bakışı," *Milliyet*, Dec. 18, 2002.
68. Details of the Annan Plan, including revisions, are available at <http://www.pio.gov.cy/other/revised_un_Plan.pdf>.
69. European Council of Copenhagen, *Presidency Conclusions*, Dec. 12–13, 2002, Articles 11–12.
70. One wonders why the EU has opted for this December 2004 date, as the Commission publishes its regular report on candidate countries each autumn. Perhaps the dates rest on the presumption that Turkey will not fulfill the political criteria by the end of 2003? Even though the Turkish government interpreted this date optimistically as a clear commitment on the part of the EU, as the conclusions promise to open accession negotiations without delay, the Commission and the Council will eventually decide whether Turkey has addressed its shortcomings, not only with regard to legislation but also implementation.
71. "Opinion poll by 'Politis' and 'Ortam' Newspapers on Annan's Plan: Turkish Cypriots approve by 51%, Greek Cypriots still opposed by 59%", at <http://www.european-cyprus.net/cgibin/hweb?-A=760&-V=from_the_press&w=>.
72. Ibid.
73. Some have also suggested that a referendum be held right away in order to act according to the demands of the Turkish Cypriot population. For articles on civil movements and views, see *Kıbrıs*, Dec. 25, 2002.
74. The contents of this statement are available at <http://www.mfa.gov.tr/turkce/gruopc/ca/2002/12/default.htm>.

6

The Question of Asylum and Illegal Migration in European Union-Turkish Relations

KEMAL KİRİŞCİ

One of the important issues on the agenda of the European Union (EU) is the issue of asylum and illegal migration. Over the last few years there has been an increase in xenophobia in the EU member countries. This, for example, was reflected in a very conspicuous manner during the presidential elections in France in 2002: the leader of the right-wing and ultra-nationalist National Front, Jean-Marie Le Pen, made it to the second round of elections on an anti-immigrant platform. In Britain, the increase in the number of illegal migrants apprehended and a surge in the number of asylum applications led the Prime Minister, Tony Blair, to also advocate a tough stand against immigration. In cooperation with his Spanish counterpart Jose Anzar at the European Council summit in Seville in June 2002, Blair called for a common asylum policy and also a common effort to stem illegal migration. There were even calls for the introduction of sanctions against countries failing to cooperate against illegal migration. A similar mood exists in Denmark, too, where the government has been introducing restrictive new legislation on asylum and immigration.

These immigration and asylum issues are increasingly seen from a security perspective rather than from a human rights perspective. Governments are not only concerned about basic law and order matters but also feel increasing domestic political pressure to address the public's perception of what is a threat to the national identity of their countries. Hence there is a growing tendency to frame these issues in terms of "soft security" and introduce policies that emphasize "control" and "prevention." The nature of these policies is leading many to argue that the EU is becoming "Fortress Europe."[1]

These developments put Turkey at the center of attention for a number of reasons. Turkey has long been a country of emigration: there are currently close to 3.5 million Turkish citizens living in the EU. During the 1990s, large numbers of Turks—particularly Kurds—sought asylum in

European countries. Although the movement of asylum seekers is slowing down, Turkey is still among the top countries of origin for asylum seekers in Europe. Turkey has also become a major country of destination—as well as transit—for illegal migration. Many third country nationals from the Middle East and Asia try to travel through Turkey in an attempt to reach Europe. There are frequent reports of illegal migrants being apprehended in Turkey or news of boats full of illegal migrants trying to make it across to Greece, Italy or France. An important number of Turkish citizens immigrate to Europe as a part of family reunification arrangements. Clearly, therefore, Turkey is a very central country in terms of EU concerns about immigration and asylum issues.[2] Turkey is also important for the member governments of the EU in terms of combating illegal migration. Similarly, in respect to asylum, the EU wants to see Turkey increasingly fulfill the tasks of a first country of asylum and develop a capacity to process asylum applications as well as permit those who are granted refugee status to stay on in the country.

Turkish-EU relations entered a new era with the decision to declare Turkey a candidate country for membership at the Helsinki summit of December 1999. Since then, the adoption of the Accession Partnership Document (APD), issued by the EU in December 2000,[3] and the National Program for the Adoption of the Acquis (NPAA), issued in April 2001 by the Turkish government,[4] have set an agenda of issues to be addressed in preparing Turkey's accession. Although considerable public attention has been given to the reforms that Turkey must introduce to meet the Copenhagen criteria and to foreign policy issues, such as the question of Cyprus, asylum and immigration issues are also extensively dealt with in both documents under the heading of Justice and Home Affair (JHA) issues. JHA is an area of the European integration process that has not yet become supranational. Instead, member countries have preferred to address issues to do with JHA through intergovernmental cooperation. Nevertheless, an impressive level of EU *acquis* has been developed and candidate countries are expected to harmonize their legislation and abide by it. The 1997 Treaty of Amsterdam includes a commitment by member states to move JHA issues into the realm of common policy subject to qualified majority voting by 2004. Asylum—and illegal migration in particular—is central to JHA issues. At Tampere, Finland in 1999 the EU governments agreed to enhance efforts to develop a common asylum and immigration policy.

Against this background Turkish authorities are finding themselves obligated to respond to the demands included in the APD, which range from the need to harmonize Turkish visa policy with the Schengen visa regime to signing readmission treaties and upgrading the control of Turkey's eastern borders. The latter issue gains particular importance considering that, if Turkey were to become a member of the EU, these borders would become the borders of the EU. These are borders adjacent to regions where an important proportion of irregular migration and refugee movements to the EU originate from. Furthermore, if Turkey were to be admitted to the EU, in accordance with the existing EU *acquis* Turkey would become a country of first asylum and hence have to process these demands itself. Yet, as the JHA Expert Mission report also recognizes, Turkey is far from implementing its own refugee status determination and currently the quality of the protection granted to asylum seekers and refugees in Turkey falls short of EU *acquis* standards.[5]

Turkish authorities recognize that cooperation with the EU is a *sine qua non* of the smooth progress of the accession process. Yet, Turkish officials face a major dilemma. They fear a situation where they may actually choose to cooperate with the EU in harmonizing their asylum policies—as well as broader issues regarding immigration—without this revision leading to actual membership. In other words, they do recognize that these issues are very important for the EU and that EU membership is dependent on Turkey's cooperation. On the other hand, in light of the controversial nature of the Turkish candidacy, Turkish officials fear a situation where cooperation with the EU will not be accompanied by membership, leaving Turkey exposed and forced to deal alone with difficult problems associated with asylum and irregular migration. This dilemma captures both the extent as well as the manner in which the EU's immigration and asylum policies deeply impact Turkey and also Turkey's relations with a host of countries neighboring Turkey. This dilemma frames these issues in a "security" context in the minds of Turkish officials. Many officials believe that Turkey's security would be fundamentally undermined if Turkey were to adopt the *acquis* without membership. In respect of these issues the purpose of this contribution is twofold: to survey Turkish policy and practice in respect to asylum and irregular migration and to explore the consequences of harmonizing Turkish policy with the EU.[6]

ASYLUM

In Europe, Turkey is not well known as a country of immigration, let alone asylum. The image of Turkey is one that tends to emphasize labor migration from Turkey to Europe as well as refugee movements from Turkey.[7] The bulk of labor migration occurred in the 1960s and 1970s; this was later accompanied by migration resulting from family reunification. The 1980s and 1990s were, in turn, characterized by a conspicuous growth in the number of asylum seekers, many of whom were Kurds. According to UNHCR (United Nations High Commission for Refugees) statistics, during the course of the 1990s alone there were almost 340,000 Turkish citizens who applied for asylum in various European countries.[8] Although over the last few years a significant drop has occurred, an unidentified number of Turkish citizens continue to migrate to Europe, often in an irregular manner. The financial and economic crisis which rocked Turkey in February 2001 has actually increased the pressures of emigration out of Turkey in the direction of Europe. Today, it is estimated that approximately 3.4 million Turks, including Kurds from Turkey, live in the European Union.[9]

Yet, at the same time, Turkey has always been a country of immigration, especially for Muslim ethnic groups, ranging from Bosnians to Pomaks and Tatars, as well as Turks from the Balkans and, to a lesser extent, from the Caucasus and Central Asia.[10] From the establishment of Turkey in 1923 to 1995 more than 1,686,163 immigrants settled in Turkey.[11] Since the collapse of the Soviet Union, Turkey has also become a country receiving an increasing number of illegal workers and immigrants from Balkan countries and former Soviet republics, as well as Iran, northern Iraq and Africa. These often include people who overstay their visas and work in the black market. There are no reliable figures, but there have been claims that put their numbers at more than 1 million.[12] These are probably exaggerated figures, but nevertheless the phenomenon has been on the rise throughout the 1990s and can be observed easily in the streets of Istanbul.[13]

At the same time, Turkey has also been a country of asylum. The onset of the Nazi regime in Germany in 1933, for example, made Turkey a popular country of asylum, particularly during the second half of the 1930s. These refugees also included Jews from various parts of occupied Europe.[14] There are no definite figures for the number of Jews that benefited from temporary asylum in Turkey until their resettlement, for the most part, in Palestine and subsequently in Israel. However, it is estimated that around 100,000 Jews may have used Turkey as their first country of asylum. During the course of the Second World War many people from the German-occupied Balkans, including Bulgarians, Greeks from the Aegean and Italians from the Dodecanese islands, also sought refuge in Turkey. There are no public records available for their number but, according to one source, there were approximately 67,000 internees and refugees in Turkey at the end of the Second World War.[15] Most of these people returned to their countries at the end of the war, although there were some Bulgarians who stayed on because of the change of regime in their country.

Similarly, the civil war in Greece led some Greeks to stay on for an additional period of time.

The origins of the current asylum policies of Turkey can be traced to the early years of the cold war when Turkey signed the 1951 Convention relating to the status of refugees. Subsequently, the Convention became the major source of codified international law on the rights of asylum seekers and refugees.[16] Turkey was among a group of countries who took an active role in the production of a definition of "refugee" and is likely to have been among those countries who pushed for the introduction of a geographical and time limitation to the Convention as expressed in Article 1.B(1)(a).[17] Accordingly, Turkey accepted to be bound by the terms of the Convention for refugees fleeing persecution in Europe as a result of events prior to 1951. In 1967, when signing the 1967 Protocol relating to the Status of Refugees, Turkey agreed to lift the time limitation but chose to maintain the geographical limitation. This geographical limitation has been a central characteristic of Turkey's asylum policies and has traditionally drawn criticism from western governments as well as refugee advocacy and human rights groups. In spite of these criticisms, in the past the Turkish government resisted lifting the limitation citing national security reasons and fears of a mass influx of refugees. The influx of more than half a million Kurdish refugees from Iraq in 1988 and 1991 reinforced these security concerns.

This geographical limitation led to the evolution of a two-tiered asylum policy.[18] The first tier applied to asylum seekers to whom Turkey has upheld the Convention. By and large, these have been asylum seekers fleeing communism in Eastern Europe and the Soviet Union during the course of the cold war. In general, Turkey, in close cooperation with the UNHCR, granted refuge to such asylum seekers with the understanding that recognized refugees would, eventually, be resettled in third countries. Such refugees, during their stay in Turkey, enjoyed all the rights provided for in the Geneva Convention. Only a very small number were allowed to stay on in Turkey, often as a result of marriages that took place with Turkish nationals. Consequently, there were never any of the economic, political and social problems often associated with integrating refugees. Furthermore, the fact that the costs of sheltering and resettling these refugees were often met by international agencies, such as the International Catholic Migration Commission and the UNHCR, helped sustain the policy. Although it is very difficult to obtain accurate statistics on their numbers, the Ministry of Interior (MOI) has indicated that some 13,500 asylum seekers benefited from the protection of the 1951 Convention between 1970 and 1996.[19] Statistics for previous years were not available.

The flow of asylum seekers from Eastern Europe came to a virtual halt with the collapse of Communism. However, the eruption of violence and ethnic strife in the former Soviet Union territories and the Balkans has led to the displacement of Muslim and Turkic groups. There have, therefore, been a number of asylum demands from nationals of the republics of the former Soviet Union. Even though these countries appear to be considered part of Europe and within the 1951 Convention's applicability, Turkish authorities in general have refrained from granting refugee status to Azeris, Ahıska Turks, Chechens and Uzbeks. Instead, they have been allowed to stay in the country on an unofficial basis or have been allowed to benefit from the laws that allow people considered to be of Turkish descent to settle, work and eventually obtain Turkish citizenship. Political considerations and the fear of offending the governments of Azerbaijan, Russia and Uzbekistan have been an important factor in this practice.

An additional factor has been the fear that a liberal and open refugee policy would attract greater numbers of asylum seekers to Turkey. This was clearly kept in the minds of Turkish officials when a large group of Chechen refugees turned up at the Turkish border with Georgia in February 2000.[20] In spite of strong public opinion in support of their admission into Turkey, the government insisted that these refugees were safe in Georgia and that Turkey was providing humanitarian assistance.[21] Yet, Turkey has followed quite a liberal visa policy towards nationals of the former Soviet Union republics. Chechens with proper travel documents, for example, enter Turkey easily, many overstaying their visa. There is also the case of Meshketian Turks, also known as Ahıska Turks. These are people who have tried to return to their ancestral homes in Georgia, from where Stalin had displaced them to Central Asia in 1944. Some have been trying to seek asylum in Turkey claiming mistreatment and persecution, especially in the Krasnodar region of Russia.[22] In their case, too, Turkey has been reluctant to grant asylum. Instead, there are an estimated 15,000 Ahıska Turks who have settled with their relatives in various parts of Turkey, having entered the country mostly on old Soviet passports.[23]

An estimated 20,000 Bosnians Muslims from the former Yugoslavia also sought asylum in Turkey during the war in former Yugoslavia. In their case, too, Turkish officials refrained from applying the provisions of the 1951 Convention. Instead, and in line with practice elsewhere in Europe, the government granted them temporary protection. The overwhelming majority of the Bosnian refugees who were housed in camps returned to their country subsequent to the Dayton Peace Treaty in 1995. A similar situation occurred in late 1998 and 1999 when a growing number of Albanians and Turks from Kosovo began to enter the country as tourists.

There were also a large group of Albanian refugees who were brought over to Turkey from Macedonia as part of the Humanitarian Evacuation Programme during the spring of 1999. They were housed in the very same refugee camp where Bosnians had stayed. At its peak, 8,700 refugees were housed there.[24] It is also estimated that in total there were roughly 18,000 Kosovars who entered Turkey for protection.[25] The ones in the refugee camps have mostly returned to Kosovo. Some of the others outside the camp have also returned or, often, are actually moving back and forth between Kosovo and Turkey.

The second tier of Turkey's asylum policy concerns what might be referred to as "non-Convention" refugees. Basically, these are refugees who have come from geographical regions outside of Europe. For a long time, Turkey did not have any provisions governing the status of such asylum seekers and refugees. Instead, a policy based on pragmatism and flexibility was permitted to evolve during the 1980s as a growing number of Iranians fleeing Ayatollah Khomeini's regime began to arrive. According to this practice a large number of Iranians, including former Shah Supporters, regime opponents, Kurds and members of the Jewish and Bahai communities fled to Turkey. The absence of visa requirements for Iranian nationals made their entry into the country relatively easy. There are no accurate statistics on their numbers, although a member of the Turkish Parliament put the total number of Iranians that came through Turkey between 1980 and 1991 at 1.5 million.[26] By and large, these people found their way to third countries on their own while only a small proportion actually approached the UNHCR. Turkish officials granted residence permits for those Iranians whose cases were being examined by the UNHCR or those who were waiting to be resettled. From the late 1980s onwards, asylum seekers from countries other than Iran also began to benefit from this arrangement, including many Iraqis, but also nationals of Afghanistan, Somalia, Sri Lanka, Sudan and Tunisia, as well as Palestinians. The largest group among them came from Iraq.

This arrangement worked until the aftermath of the mass refugee crisis of April 1991, when Turkey began to change its policy. As a result of a military onslaught launched by the Iraqi government against a Kurdish rebellion in the north of the country, close to half a million refugees fled to Turkey. Turkey's diplomatic efforts culminated in the adoption of the United Nations Security Council Resolution 688 that enabled the declaration of a "safe haven" for refugees north of the 36th parallel. This was accompanied by Operation Provide Comfort, which assisted the repatriation of the overwhelming majority of the refugees to northern Iraq.[27] The remaining refugees were resettled over the years in third countries. Subsequently, Turkey began to refuse Iraqis coming from northern Iraq the right to seek asylum, arguing that northern Iraq is safe from the persecution of the central government, and Turkish authorities reserved the right to deport such persons. However, some of them did approach the UNHCR in Ankara and had their refugee status recognized. On many occasions, Turkish officials refused to allow them to leave the country when they did not have passports with valid entry stamps into Turkey.[28] Furthermore, officials were also concerned that among these asylum seekers were PKK militants trying to enter Turkey from northern Iraq and make their way to Europe.

Turkish authorities, then, became increasingly reluctant to apply the working relationship to asylum seekers from this area. They considered northern Iraq to be safe from Iraqi governmental persecution, viewed asylum seekers from that region as illegal immigrants looking for a better economic life and tended to deport them.[29] This led to disputes between UNHCR and the Turkish authorities. Amnesty International bitterly criticized this practice.[30] On the other hand, Turkish officials also became uneasy about the growing number of asylum seekers from distant countries and began to argue that they had no obligation to recognize asylum seekers reaching Turkey via third countries, and likewise increasingly considered such people to be illegal migrants.

These developments also coincided with a period when Turkey came under increasing criticism over deportations of persons that the international community considered to be genuine asylum seekers or refugees. This was accompanied by growing pressure from western governments and refugee advocate organizations to respect the principle of *non-refoulement* for "non-Convention" refugees.[31] They argued that the forced return of asylum seekers and refugees constitutes a breach of Turkey's international legal obligations. There were also arguments that Turkey, as a party to the European Human Rights Convention, had additional obligations given that this Convention is meant to apply to the citizens of Council of Europe members as well as to aliens in these countries. These pressures and the intensification of the conflict with the UNHCR over who is an asylum seeker and who is not saw the end of the fragile working relationship in due course. Instead, the government introduced the Asylum Regulation in November 1994.[32]

The Asylum Regulation aimed to bring status determination under the control of the Turkish government and also introduce strict regulation governing access to the asylum procedures.[33] The practice that evolved from the first few years of the application of the Regulation attracted serious and concerted criticism from western governments as well as major international human rights advocacy groups.[34] Critics argued that Turkey was violating the rights of asylum seekers and refugees by denying them access to asylum procedures or failing to provide them adequate protection. These criticisms appear to have had some impact and, as a result of this, a climate of cooperation evolved between the Turkish authorities and the UNHCR.

The government, as a result of this cooperation, increased the time limit for filing an asylum application from five to ten days in 1999. The 1994 Asylum Regulation had introduced a five-day limit, which gave the officials the possibility to reject those who filed their application late without addressing the actual substance of the application. However, the new policy in 1999 significantly improved access to asylum procedures. More importantly, in terms of human rights and rule of law standards, with the initiative of the UNHCR negative decisions of the Turkish government on asylum application were appealed to administrative courts. On a number of cases, the courts ruled in support of applicants, and the Council of State, the highest court of appeal, ruled against the Ministry of Interior, which had appealed against the ruling of a lower court. Accompanied by a critical ruling of the European Human Rights Court, these rulings have made the government much more sensitive towards the enforcement of the time limit rule and respecting the principle of *non-refoulement*.[35] Most importantly, Turkish authorities have unofficially adopted a practice of cooperating very closely with the UNHCR in respect to status determination. It is possible to argue that, in effect, it is the UNHCR that determines status and the Turkish government grants UNHCR-recognized refugees temporary asylum by issuing residence permits. In return, the expectation from the Turkish side is that the UNHCR helps to make sure that asylum seekers also register with the Turkish police and that recognized refugees are resettled out of Turkey. These are clearly positive developments and the credit goes both to the Turkish authorities and to the UNHCR, and, to some degree, to a number of western governments as well as the EU and several non-governmental organizations.

The December 1999 decision to include Turkey among the official candidate countries for membership to the EU opened the possibility for the EU to influence Turkish asylum policy in an unprecedented manner. The section of the APD dealing with Justice and Home Affairs issues make it clear that adopting the EU *acquis* on asylum will be an integral part of Turkey's accession process. The APD also boldly states that the lifting of the geographical limitation to the 1951 Convention will be needed. The JHA Expert Mission report underlines the importance of this as well. The Turkish NP, issued in response to the APD in April 2000, has responded quite favorably to these demands. Most striking is the apparent willingness to consider the lifting of the geographical limitation. Even if an eventual decision to lift is made conditional on the introduction of "legislative and infra-structural measures" and "the attitudes of the EU Member States on the issue of burden-sharing,"[36] it must be viewed as nothing short of a revolutionary departure from previous practice.

Nevertheless, it must also be noted that the decision to actually lift the geographical limitation will not be an easy one. The inclusion of the existing formulation into the NP was the product of considerable negotiation and careful wording to appease the concerns of the advocates of the traditional policy. Military and security circles still remain very reluctant and especially fear the possibility of a mass influx from neighboring Middle Eastern countries. Additionally, they continue to be apprehensive of Turkey becoming a buffer zone where asylum seekers and refugees congregate as they fail to enter the EU. Furthermore, public opinion in the country seems to be divided. There are those who see the lifting of the geographical limitation as opening the floodgates of asylum and argue that Turkey would become a haven for refugees who cannot make it to Europe.[37] The opposing argument sees it as part of the process of living up to the legal and political standards of becoming an eventual member of the EU.[38] In any event, the lifting of the geographical limitation will be a function of a long bargaining process between the EU and Turkish authorities, who will try to extract from their counterparts commitments to burden sharing. For the Turkish authorities the continuation of the present resettlement commitments would be regarded as an important element of burden-sharing expectations. Furthermore, the issue will also be intricately linked to legal and political reforms in Turkey and the way the EU responds to these reforms. A critical factor in the lifting of the limitation will be whether the EU can engender confidence among officials that the EU is serious about Turkish membership. An important measure of this will be whether the EU will be able to offer a date for the beginning of accession negotiations with Turkey. Lastly, the lifting of the geographical limitation will also need a transformation in the mindset of those who have governed policies towards immigration.

The mindset issue is particularly important. Currently, the Turkish practice regarding immigration and asylum is one that restricts the possibility of settlement and integration to people of "Turkish descent and culture."[39] This is reflected in the wording of the Law on Settlement dating from 1934.[40] According to this law—and the practice accompanying it—only people with an ethnic and religious affinity to Turkey are able to immigrate and settle in Turkey. These have primarily included different ethnic groups from the Balkan countries, who were not necessarily always Turkish speakers but are Sunni Muslims. Similarly, this law only allows asylum seekers of "Turkish descent and culture" to become refugees in Turkey. This partly explains the cultural and ideological background the geographical limitation as well as the practice of emphasizing resettlement or repatriation rather than integration for refugees in Turkey. Therefore, one of the important changes that would have to accompany the lifting of the geographical limitation will be allowing the possibility of recognized refugees staying on in Turkey and integrating. This will require either a substantive amending of the Law on Settlement or the introduction of a new law solely addressing asylum and immigration issues.

Another problem awaiting Turkey, concerning both the lifting the geographical limitation and the adoption of the EU *acquis*, is the question of whether Turkey has the capacity to carry out the tasks associated with such changes. Currently, Turkey is not ready to carry out these tasks bureaucratically, organizationally or socio-economically. This will not only require a major training program for the relevant personnel but also a whole restructuring of the existing asylum process. At a minimum, Turkey would have to become capable of performing status determination tasks in a manner that meets the 1951 Convention as well as EU standards. Furthermore, Turkey is far from having the economic base and resources to sustain a support system for asylum seekers and refugees that would meet the requirements of the Convention. It is no surprise that in 1961, when the 1951 Convention was ratified, this was done with the reservation that refugees would not be granted rights that go beyond those Turkish citizens enjoy.[41] In theory, asylum seekers and refugees are entitled to work and receive social assistance in Turkey. In practice, however, acquiring a work permit is virtually impossible. This often forces people into illegality, which in turn makes them vulnerable to deportation for violation of Turkish law. The government, then, has no social assistance programs for asylum seekers and refugees. Moreover, the network of non-governmental organizations addressing refugee needs is still extremely limited, although the UNHCR does provide some assistance of a very limited nature.

Even if Turkey may have come a long way in terms of economic development since the 1950s, it is not evident that it has reached a level where it can manage status determination and integration of refugees easily. Hence, assistance from the EU will be critical, as are further economic and political changes in Turkey. Inevitably, the transformation will be a long-term one. Nevertheless, it should be recognized that Turkey is on the verge of overhauling its asylum policy. This, in turn, is largely a function of the relations developing between Turkey and the EU, as well as the EU policy to increasingly transfer the task of addressing asylum issues to the borderlands of the EU—to members or candidates for membership.[42] If this task is to be performed successfully by Turkey there will have to be very close cooperation between Turkey and the EU. In this regard, Turkey will need to become much more transparent in its asylum policy and practice. This will include developing a habit of working much more closely with EU officials and experts. On the other hand, EU officials will need to be sensitive to the relatively unique geographical location of Turkey in terms of refugee movements as well as to Turkish officials' expectations that there will be a close, convincing and generous commitment to burden sharing. This will be critical to nurturing the mutual goodwill and trust that will be crucial to a successful cooperation between the two sides.

The question of where all of this would leave the asylum seekers and refugees is open to debate. The accession process, if it works, will put considerable pressure on Turkey to develop and regularize its asylum admission and processing structures in line with the EU.[43] It will also compel Turkey to meet the higher EU standards for legal and human rights, especially with respect to appeal procedures and *non-refoulement*. Yet, as will be studied in the following section, achieving such an improvement may well be complicated by increasing pressure on Turkey to cooperate with the EU in preventing illegal transit migration through Turkey. Under these circumstances the line between an asylum seeker and an illegal migrant may become blurred. This situation may become particularly aggravated if the EU becomes inclined to give more importance to the prevention of illegal migration then promoting asylum law.[44] Clearly, this would not benefit the asylum seekers in Turkey.

On the other hand, it can also be argued that the current system is a more flexible, pragmatic and possibly liberal one. Recognition rates in the current system are dramatically higher in Turkey than many other European countries. According to the UNHCR, during the 1990s EU member countries granted refugee status—or some form of stay for asylum seekers—to between 15 and 23 percent of the asylum applications filed during this time.[45] Calculating the recognition rate in Turkey is complicated; however, if one excludes cases that are still pending, the recognition rate in Turkey between 1995 and 2001 was more than 60 percent. In the existing system asylum seekers and refugees enjoy also some degree of freedom from close government supervision and control. The introduction of reception centers advocated by the EU may well take away some of the freedom and flexibility in the existing Turkish system. In addition, the current system—again often because of a lack of funds—

does not pursue asylum seekers who have had their cases rejected for the purpose of deportation. Such persons often remain in Turkey illegally, attempt to go on to Europe, or pursue alternative ways of seeking asylum in or immigration to a third country. The danger here is that it exposes such persons to the abuse of smugglers as well as unscrupulous employers who use them as cheap labor. Yet, as Turkey adopts EU standards, such people once deported would most likely try to return and be exposed to similar risks. Also, Ankara may institute the kind of border control that might make it much more difficult for asylum seekers to access the system. In turn, they may resort to illegal entry using the services of smugglers, with all the risks that this method entails.

According to the UNHCR statistics covering the period since 1995, there are roughly 5,550–6,000 asylum applicants in Turkey per year. Turkish authorities do not provide statistics on a yearly basis, but a total was given for the period covering 1995 to November 2000. Turkish statistics suggest a lower level of applicants of just over 20,000 for this period. There is, then, a discrepancy of more than 11,000 applications between the Turkish and UNHCR statistics. This stems from the problem of irregular asylum seekers[46]—asylum seekers who have failed to register with the Turkish authorities and have their status determination carried out only by the UNHCR. Frequently, these are persons who have either entered the country illegally or have let the time limit pass and hence have been reluctant to approach the Turkish authorities. An important consequence of this is that—if and when the UNHCR recognizes them as refugees—these persons encounter serious difficulties in exiting Turkey for resettlement.[47]

The question of such irregular asylum seekers would obviously be resolved when Turkey takes over status determination completely. Currently, a draft law addressing unresolved issues in Turkey's asylum policy is in the process of being finalized. However, it was not included in the package of reforms adopted in August 2002. This is primarily because of the controversy over the lifting of the geographical limitation. The new legislation would have to address this question as part and parcel of status determination. There are two sensitive issues involved here. First, with the lifting of geographical limitation, Ankara would—in a major break from past practice—have to consider integration of recognized refugees in Turkey itself. Previously, the emphasis was on resettlement into third countries. However, there are indications that traditional countries of resettlement would at least in the near future continue to maintain a resettlement policy in cooperation with Turkey as part of a burden-sharing responsibility. Nevertheless, in return Turkey would have to show in practice a willingness to allow for integration.

The second issue is a more problematic one and not immediately resolvable. Turkish authorities consider the geographical limitation as a tool that allows them to serve Turkish national security, especially in the face of mass influxes. The fact that Turkey in the recent past experienced major mass influxes of Kurdish refugees from northern Iraq at a time when Turkish security forces were waging an armed struggle against the Kurdistan Workers Party (PKK) makes them acutely aware of the national security dimension of this issue. Hence, they will be most reluctant to lift this limitation unless they become sure that the EU is serious about Turkey's membership. It clearly is a question of trust and, most likely, nothing short of receiving an unambiguous date for the beginning of accession negotiations would be considered as the necessary minimum condition for actually lifting the geographical limitation.

The question of asylum is also closely linked to the issue of illegal migration. The movements of asylum seekers and illegal migrants are intertwined. EU member governments, as well as the Turkish one, have international obligations to respect the rights of asylum seekers and refugees. Hence, distinguishing between asylum seekers and illegal migrants becomes very important. Often, soft security considerations make governments overlook their obligations under international law. A country like Turkey is particularly prone to overlooking the need to distinguish between illegal migrants and the potential asylum seekers who might be mixed among them. This is especially due to growing EU pressure on Ankara to cooperate more rigorously against illegal migration. The next section will examine the place of illegal migration in Turkish-EU relations.

ILLEGAL MIGRATION

Over the last few years Turkey has emerged as a central news item in connection with illegal migration. There are frequent media reports of ships originating from Turkey crowded with illegal immigrants landing on the coast of Greece, Italy or France. Occasionally, human tragedies are also reported when these ships run aground or sink. Illegal migrants usually pay fees well into thousands of US dollars and fall into the hands of unscrupulous smugglers who force them to travel under inhumane conditions. Furthermore, there are also frequent media reports in Turkey of irregular immigrants being apprehended in Turkey. It is not possible to estimate the number of people that actually transit through Turkey. However, as observed in Figure 1, since 1995 there has been a steady increase in the number of illegal immigrants apprehended by Turkish authorities, reaching a peak of 94,514 in 2000 and slightly dipping in 2001.

FIGURE 1
NUMBER OF ILLEGAL IMMIGRANTS ARRESTED BY TURKISH SECURITY FORCES BETWEEN 1995 AND 2001

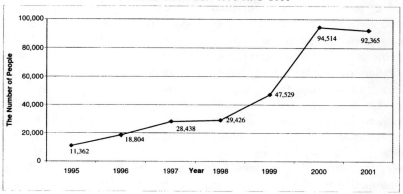

Source: Data obtained from the Foreigners Department of MOI.

Closely associated with the problem of irregular migration is the problem of trafficking of human beings. Unlike the previous group, these are people who are being forced across frontiers against their will. Often these are young women who have been lured to accept work abroad and instead find themselves forced into prostitution and trapped in the hands of organized crime. There is no reliable information on trafficked persons in Turkey, but there is considerable prostitution taking place in Turkey by women from, in particular, former Soviet republics or Balkan countries. However, it is very difficult to tell what proportion of such persons are actually victims of trafficking and what proportion come to Turkey on their own for purely economic reasons. Currently, Turkish legislation to combat trafficking was non-existent until the introduction of a new article into the Turkish penal code during the adoption of the EU reforms in August 2002. This should allow the Turkish police to confront the phenomenon more effectively and activate measures that may help alleviate widespread international criticism for not doing enough against the trafficking of human beings.

A breakdown of the numbers of illegal migrants by nationality is given in Table 1. However, it should be noted that the statistics cover two types of illegal migrants. The first group includes people who overstay their visas in Turkey or are caught working in Turkey illegally; these are mostly Romanian and former Soviet citizens. The second group is composed of illegal transit migrants, although there may be a few Iranians and Iraqis apprehended in Turkey for overstay or illegal work. Otherwise, the majority of illegal transit migrants stopped in Turkey are from Iraq, Afghanistan and Pakistan. Those from Iraq are mostly Kurds but also include small numbers of Turkmen and Arabs. The political instability in northern Iraq along with deep economic difficulties and the negative consequences of sanctions on the country are the principle factors driving people to seek their fortunes in Europe.[48] Furthermore, the near lawless situation of northern Iraq makes the possibility of obtaining forged documents and contacting networks of human smugglers much easier. Turkish authorities complain that illegal migrants who are deported to northern Iraq often try again. This suggests that—as long as there is no fundamental change in the political and economic situation in northern Iraq—the flow of illegal migrants will continue, independent of Ankara's countermeasures. The concern that EU governments have here is that an important proportion of illegal migrants apprehended in Europe come from northern Iraq. On the other hand, a major security concern for Turkey is that PKK elements can infiltrate Turkey or attempt to reach Europe through Turkey. Although the leader of the PKK, Abdullah Öcalan, was apprehended in 1999 and called on PKK militants to end their armed struggle, there continue to be armed elements of the PKK in northern Iraq.

It is difficult to tell whether the steady increase in the number of people apprehended in Turkey is a sign that illegal transit migration is increasing or that Turkish authorities are becoming stricter. Turkey has been under growing pressure from the EU, as well as the United States, to cooperate in the prevention of irregular migration.[49] In Europe, there have also been

TABLE 1
BREAKDOWN OF ILLEGAL IMMIGRANTS ARRESTED BY TURKISH SECURITY FORCES BETWEEN 1995 AND 2001 BY NATIONALITY

Nationality	Number of People
Afghanistan	22,017
Bangladesh	9,062
Pakistan	15,754
Iran	17,714
Iraq	73,045
Syria	3,741
Former Soviet Republics (Russia, Ukraine, Moldovia, Georgia, Azerbaijan, Armenia)	58,072
Bulgaria	4,812
Romania	13,001
Turkey	10,678
Other	94,543
Total	322,439

Source: Data obtained from the Foreigners Department of Turkish Ministry of Interior.

occasions when Turkey has been accused of using irregular transit migration as a political weapon. In February 2000, when a freighter called the *East Sea* ran aground the Mediterranean coast of France with more than 900 illegal migrants, there were many media reports in France blaming the Turkish government.[50] There were even reports that the Turkish government used this as a punishment for the French parliament's recognition of the Armenian genocide in March 2000.[51] These were accompanied by allegations that Turkish coastguard vessels actually escorted boats carrying the illegal migrants.[52] Turkish officials, on the other hand, argue that not only is this not true but that they actually informed authorities in Europe that they had been shadowing this particular ship and had called on the European authorities to take measures against it.

Similar accusations were also directed towards Turkey from 1997 to 2000, when a series of boats, and sometimes ships, carrying Kurds, many from Southeast Turkey, landed on the Adriatic coast of Italy.[53] Many of these ships carrying illegal immigrants landed in Italy just before, during and immediately after a bitter conflict erupted between Italy and Turkey in October 1998 over the extradition of the PKK leader, Abdullah Öcalan, who had been arrested in Italy. The aggravation engendered by the crisis, as well as the illegal immigrants, led the Italian Prime Minister, Massimo D'Alema, who was visiting the United States in March 1999, to argue that there were similarities between the situation in Southeast Turkey and Kosovo. He appealed to his host Bill Clinton that "If we defend the rights of the Albanians in Kosovo, and rightly so, then I think we have to defend the rights of the Kurdish minority."[54] These two cases are indicative of the degree of importance, as well as frustration, that the issue of irregular migration through Turkey can cause.

The allegation that Turkish authorities abuse irregular migration or support it for political goals is probably exaggerated for a number of reasons. First, for a long time Turkey was concerned that the PKK was actually involved in the business of smuggling people to Europe. Officials believed this was the case because smuggling constituted an important source of income, as well as constituting part of a concerted effort to create a base of support, for the PKK in Europe.[55] Hence, during the 1990s this was a major security concern for the Turkish authorities, which they tried to prevent. Another reason was that the smugglers were also often part of larger organized crime networks involved in drug trafficking and illegal arms trade. A third reason had to do with the growing trend for some of these immigrants to stay on in Turkey and become involved in criminal activities. Hence, government officials have always had an interest in at least trying to stop illegal migration because of the connection between illegal migration and other forms of activity threatening Turkish security and law and order in a more direct manner.

However, this interest often failed to translate itself into actual concerted action against preventing irregular migration. One important reason for this has to do with insufficient police funds. The police also complain about the difficulties in getting the cooperation of the countries illegal immigrants originate from and add that they themselves often lack the resources to arrange for the deportation of illegal immigrants, particularly those who are not nationals of neighboring countries. They have also complained that existing laws in Turkey are inadequate to deter criminals from organizing smuggling and trafficking in human beings.[56] Many observers also argue that these illegal migrants could not cross the whole length of the country if somewhere along the line there were not corrupt officials.[57] Turkish authorities have also complained that officials in Western Europe often accuse Turkey of not doing enough while making statements and adopting policies that encourage irregular migrants to try their fortunes.[58] However, recently adopted legislation, which is part of the EU reforms, should help to alleviate the problems associated with combating illegal migration. This legislation defines assisting human smuggling and trafficking as a very serious crime with severe penalties.

Turkey itself has also been a source of illegal immigrant flow towards Europe. As Table 1 indicates, Turkish nationals were among those apprehended in 2001. Most of them were Turkish citizens of Kurdish origin. During the 1980s and 1990s Kurds constituted a large proportion of the asylum seekers entering Europe from Turkey; many claiming the persecution of the Turkish state against them. This was a period when the struggle between the PKK and the Turkish security authorities in the southeastern provinces of Turkey was particularly violent, culminating in widespread human rights violations as well as massive internal displacement. This violence has subsided since Abdullah Öcalan was apprehended in February 1999. Although the Kurdish problem in Turkey is far from resolved, the decision of the PKK to give up armed struggle has created a much more positive climate for reforms.[59]

In a manner unprecedented in recent Turkish history, the Turkish parliament adopted a series of liberal amendments to the Constitution in October 2001. These amendments subsequently led to the adoption of a series of reforms. Most important of them all, in terms of Kurds seeking asylum in Europe, is the adoption in August 2002 reforms that opens the way for broadcasting in Kurdish as well as the learning of the Kurdish language. This is considered to be an important step in the direction of addressing the grievances associated with the Kurdish question in Turkey. Yet, the same cannot be said in terms of the economy of the areas inhabited by most Kurds. The region is economically depressed and still bears the scars of years of violent conflict. The situation is also aggravated because of the economic embargo on neighboring Iraq. Hence, many Kurds who are economically disenchanted are trying to migrate to Europe. Given the current economic crisis in Turkey, it is highly likely that this trend will continue. However, there may be a significant drop in the number of Kurdish asylum seekers from Turkey filing applications in Europe.

Currently, there are few forums where irregular migration issues can be discussed by Turkey and the EU. Most of the interactions are more of a bilateral nature. For example, Italian and Turkish officials have been meeting regularly in an effort to cooperate against illegal transit migration to Italy via Turkey.[60] Furthermore, the governmental dialogue between Turkey and Greece has included the issue of illegal transit migration and agreements signed in this regard have been heralded as a sign of improving Turkish-Greek relations. Currently, the only official forum where these issues—as well as the broader ones dealing with immigration—can be raised is the subcommittee under the Association Council (AC) between the EU and Turkey. The AC is the formal body where issues to do with the accession process are handled, in which there are eight subcommittees dealing with various issues. One such committee deals with JHA issues.

So far, it is the Budapest process that has constituted the major multilateral forum where most of the cooperation in Europe on irregular migration takes place. However, this process operates outside the EU framework and is a consultative forum of more than 40 governments and ten international organizations aiming to prevent irregular migration. One of the critical issues that have come up at the Budapest process is the question of readmission agreements. Members of the EU have been keen to get Central and Eastern European countries to reach such agreements in order to accept their own returning nationals, as well as the ones of third countries. Candidate countries from Eastern and Central Europe have been eager to comply as such agreements constitute part of the criteria they are expected to meet for membership in the EU. The APD for Turkey also notes the expectation from Turkey to sign similar readmission treaties.

Turkey long resisted this and shied away from negotiating such agreements with third countries. Instead, Ankara's official position was that Turkey would be prepared to accept the return of persons present in Europe of Turkish nationality or a legal resident of Turkey. This also applied to persons who may have legally transited to Europe via Turkey and were arrested for illegal entry into Europe, as long as the demand for readmission is made within 48 hours of transiting Turkey. During the presidency of Britain in 1998, there were even offers to Turkey to mediate readmission agreements between Turkey, Pakistan and Bangladesh. However, since the adoption of the NP Turkey's position has changed. The NP clearly refers to the objective of adopting the EU *acquis* and reaching the required readmission agreements by 2004. In this regard, Turkey is negotiating such agreements with Bulgaria, Iran and Syria and considerable progress has been reported. In November 2001 such a readmission agreement was signed with Greece. In the case of Pakistan and Bangladesh, efforts to negotiate such agreements have met with little progress. Turkey has also proposed to negotiate similar agreements with China and Romania.[61]

However, these agreements are also grounds for concern as Ankara fears that Turkey will become a dumping ground for irregular migrants apprehended in the EU. It also argues that readmission agreements are not always effective, as people who are returned to their country of origin soon reattempt to reach Europe. This is particularly the case with irregular migrants from northern Iraq and explains why Turkey has had a longstanding reluctance to accept the return of Iraqis via Turkey.

Turkish officials also argue that the liberal visa policy Turkey has followed during the course of the 1990s enabled many citizens of countries of the former Soviet Union to travel to Turkey quite freely.[62] This encouraged an informal trade—often referred to as suitcase trade—between Turkey and these countries, making it possible for many individuals and families to survive the worst of the economic crisis that followed the dissolution of the Soviet Union. Hence, they argue that their visa policy became a factor contributing to the reasons why a massive migration from the former Soviet Union and Eastern Europe towards Western Europe did not happen (at the end of the cold war many European officials were worried about a mass influx of immigrants). This visa policy is in the process of revision as Turkey prepares to adopt the Schengen visa system. This will mean that the entry of nationals of a large number of countries from Ukraine to Mongolia will become more strictly controlled and, consequently, more difficult. This may actually become an additional factor forcing an increase in illegal migration and possibly asylum application. A case in point may be Iran. Nationals of Iran have enjoyed visa-free entry to Turkey since the 1970s. This has enabled some Iranian nationals to use Turkey as an informal asylum country or a country where they can take temporary refuge. The introduction of a visa arrangement would change that and increase the prospects of some of these people formally seeking asylum or joining the caravan of illegal migrants.

In general, Turkish officials have often argued that the problem of irregular migration stems from large economic gaps between Europe and other countries of the region. Hence, they argue that police measures in and of themselves are not adequate. MOI officials have also complained of western government officials pressuring them to prevent transit migration through Turkey on the one hand, and on the other making statements which, they argue, encourage people to become illegal migrants in an effort to get to Europe. Furthermore, they add that the tight visa regime prevailing in Europe aggravates the situation by forcing people to try illegal means to reach Europe. It is interesting to note that in Germany in July 2001 and in Britain in October 2001 interior ministry reports have been adopted recommending a loosening of the tight immigration policies in favor of allowing more immigrants into the country. The idea of adopting an EU immigration policy that would give economic migrants a chance to enter the Union was taken up by the EU Commissioner responsible for JHA matters, Antonio Vitorino, in London in July 2001. Similarly, the European Parliament in October 2001 adopted a report recommending similar measures as part of efforts to develop a Community immigration policy.[63] However, it is difficult to say whether the implementation of the ideas advocated by these reports would actually stem the flow of irregular migration. Commissioner Vitorino did add that each year 500,000 illegal immigrants penetrate the territory of the Union and that encouragement of legal immigration would have to be accompanied by a fight against illegal immigration.[64]

Therefore, it is likely that irrespective of the police measures taken in Turkey to control and prevent illegal transit migration the phenomenon will continue and will remain an important item on the agenda of Turkish-EU relations. At the same time, Turkey is slowly but surely harmonizing its legislation with that of the EU. The adoption—as part of the EU reforms introduced by the European Parliament in August 2002—of two amendments concerning illegal migration and trafficking in human beings to the Turkish Penal Code is a concrete sign of this.

CONCLUSION

Asylum and illegal migration are two issues that are increasingly being handled in a soft security context in many EU countries as xenophobic fears and reaction against foreigners and immigrants emerge. These two issues are having a growing impact on Turkish-EU relations. This is an inevitable function of Turkey's interest in becoming a member of the EU but also of Turkey's geographic location at the crossroads of countries of origin in Asia and asylum in Western Europe. Turkey is coming under growing pressure to cooperate with the EU and control the flow of transit illegal migrants and introduce an asylum system that can allow recognized refugees to stay in Turkey. Turkey's asylum policy used to be criticized from a human rights perspective. Ironically, since Turkey's performance improved significantly it is now being asked to take a security-driven approach, especially towards illegal migration if not also asylum.[65]

The extension of candidate status to Turkey has significantly increased EU leverage over Turkey. The reforms that Turkey is expected to adopt in these areas are stated in quite an unequivocal manner in the APD. Turkey has responded to the APD with the NP, which demonstrates a will to adopt these reforms. This is most conspicuous in respect to the lifting of the geographical limitation, which is expected to transpire by 2004. This will require Turkey to introduce major changes to its asylum policy, above and beyond what other candidates have had to do. In particular, this will mean making it possible for refugees to be integrated in Turkey and not rely solely on resettlement and repatriation. A most significant implication of this will be a reconsideration of the Turkish definition of national identity and even national security. Individuals and groups that were not seen as organically tied to the notion of "Turkish descent and culture" and that were often seen as potential sources of threat to Turkish national security will need to be viewed from a very different perspective. Furthermore, due to the geographic location of Turkey and given the nature of the EU *acquis*, Turkey is likely to become a country of first asylum. This will bring a considerable administrative as well as economic burden to Turkey. However, the harmonization policy also brings the possibility of benefiting from financial as well as technical assistance. During the negotiation process Turkey should be able to insist on a commitment from the EU to burden sharing, particularly in the form of some resettlement of refugees.

In the case of illegal transit migration, Turkey is under particular pressure to stem it. An important objective is to prevent irregular migration from becoming a path for accessing asylum procedures in the EU. In this respect Turkey faces an important challenge. It is expected to stem illegal migration but also at the same time be able to weed out potential asylum seekers from outright economically motivated illegal migrants and process their applications. The need for Turkey to leave behind a relatively liberal visa policy and replace it with the much tighter Schengen visa regime is meant to serve a similar end of stemming illegal migration into the EU. Turkish legislators showed their commitment to controlling illegal migration by including in the most recent set of EU reforms provision to facilitate efforts to combat this phenomenon.

Traditionally, the question of who can enter a country and who can become integrated as a citizen of a country has been at the very heart of national sovereignty. Is Turkey ready to take that step? If so, then the Turkish government will need to cooperate with EU officials and experts much more closely and professionally. The issue of protecting the Union geographically from unregulated movements of people is a very central aspect of the enlargement process. Hence, the EU will give utmost care to assessing the candidate countries' capacity to fulfil the standards of the Union. Turkey's geographic location will make these issues all the more sensitive for the EU.

This leaves Turkey facing several tough dilemmas and consequences. The cost of meeting the EU requirements in the area of asylum and illegal migration is quite significant in the economic as well as the bureaucratic, social and political sense of the term. Undoubtedly, making the necessary adjustments may be seen as a worthwhile price to pay as part and parcel of the grander exercise of transforming Turkey into a more democratic and pluralistic country driven by rule of law. It is quite possible that some of the more administrative and economic aspects of the costs may be cushioned by EU financial and technical support. Yet, Turkish decisionmakers do face a major dilemma: What if after the adjustment process Turkey is not admitted to the European Union as a member? This could leave Turkey facing major difficulties all on its own without the benefits of EU membership and, more importantly, the sense of security that comes with that membership.

Another dilemma that faces Turkey is the immediate future. EU governments, especially in the area of controlling or stemming irregular migration, seem to be asking Turkey to perform tasks that would be questioned by many liberal circles in Europe. At times, EU governments seem to demand a tough performance—bordering on authoritarianism— from Turkey in order to appease conservative anti-immigration circles in Europe while taking a more liberal approach towards those irregular migrants who arrive in Europe. In this manner, EU governments are not only able to satisfy liberal circles but also meet the growing needs of cheap labor in Europe at a time when demographic trends in Europe suggest that Europe's population is decreasing. This pattern of behavior appears to be translating itself into a situation where Europe may increasingly introduce controlled and closely supervised immigration to meet labor needs while keeping the economically, socially or politically disadvantaged out of the EU.[66]

Having served as the bastion of Western Europe's defense during the cold war against the Soviet Union thanks to its geo-strategically important location, Turkey, at present, would serve yet another security objective by becoming a buffer zone for checking the unwanted and/or uncontrolled movement of people into the EU. This is a risk worth taking. The absence of cooperation on asylum and illegal migration would further complicate Turkey's membership potential. Adopting the EU *acquis* in this area and shouldering the costs associated with it can also be seen as a price worth paying for the larger advantages that membership to the EU would bring to Turkey. Furthermore, once Turkey is genuinely engaged in the accession process, it will have ample opportunity to bargain and make its voice heard. This would give Turkey a much better opportunity to make a case for the particular difficulties and problems it faces compared to a situation where Turkey fails in its membership bid. In turn, the EU ought to take an approach towards Turkey on these issues that gives preference to engaging Turkey constructively rather than dictating to Turkey the measures to be taken. The advantage of a policy of engagement and empathy is that it can help overcome the deep mistrust that both Turkish public opinion and officials have of the EU and, in particular, its seriousness to assist Turkey's accession to membership. Turkish officials, once more confident about the EU's intentions, would be in a better position to adopt what they consider to be high-risk decision, such as the lifting of the "geographical limitation" to the 1951 Convention relating to the status of refugees.

NOTES

This essay is a substantially revised and updated version of the paper that appeared as *Justice and Home Affairs Issues in Turkish-EU Relations* (Istanbul: Turkish Economic and Social Studies Foundation, 2001). This monograph is available at <http://www.tesev.org.tr>.

1. For an analysis of the "Fortress Europe" phenomenon, see Andrew Geddes, *Immigration and European Integration: Towards Fortress Europe?* (Manchester: Manchester University Press, 2000).
2. For coverage of immigration, illegal and transit migration in Turkey, see Kemal Kirişci, "'Coerced Immigrants:' Refugees of Turkish Origins since 1945," *International Migration*, Vol.34, No.3 (1996), pp.385–412; Sema Erder, "Uluslararası Göçte Yeni Eğilimler: Türkiye 'Göç Alan' Ülke mi?" [New Trends in International Migration: Is Turkey an Immigration Country?], in F. Atacan *et al.* (eds.), *Mübeccel Kıray için Yazılar* (Istanbul: Bağlam Yayınları, 2000), pp.235–59; Ahmet İçduygu, "Transit Migration and Turkey," *Boğaziçi Journal*, Vol.10, Nos.1–2 (1996), pp.127–42; *Transit Migration in Turkey* (Budapest: IOM Migration Programme, 1996); Alimet İçduygu, "SOPEMI Report for Turkey," Meeting of the SOPEMI Correspondents, Paris, Dec. 5–7, 2001; Ahmet İçduygu and Fuat Keyman, "Globalization, Security, and Migration: The Case of Turkey," *Global Governance*, Vol.1, No.6 (2000), pp.383–98.
3. General Affairs Council of the European Union, *Accession Partnership Document: 2000* (December 2000); <http://www.deltur.cec.eu.int>.
4. The Turkish and English versions of these documents are available at the Secretariat General for European Affairs website: <http://www.abgs.gov.tr/> (July 19, 2001). Furthermore, the entire schedule and plan for adopting the *acquis* is outlined in a massive worksheet known as *Follow-Up Instrument on the Turkish National Programme for the*

The Question of Asylum and Illegal Migration 103

Adoption of the Acquis (NPAA) (Secretariat General for EU Affairs, Ankara). This document is also available on the website of the Secretariat. The English version is currently being prepared for posting.
5. In September 2000, the EU sent its first JHA Expert Mission to Turkey to examine Turkish policy and practice in JHA-related issues. The results of this extensive and detailed study was published as *General JHA Expert Mission to Turkey 18–29 September 2000: Mission Report on the Situation in the Field of Justice and Home Affairs in Turkey* (Internal Document).
6. For a detailed study of these issues and other JHA issues, such as visa policy, see Kemal Kirişci, *Justice and Home Affairs Issues in Turkish-EU Relations* (Istanbul: TESEV, 2001).
7. For a concise analysis of labor migration to Europe from Turkey, see Nermin Abadan-Unat, "Turkish Migration to Europe," in Robin Cohen (ed.), *The Cambridge Survey of World Migration* (Cambridge: Cambridge University Press, 1995), pp.279–84. For asylum movements to Europe, see Anita Böcker, "Refugee and Asylum-Seeking Migration from Turkey to Europe," *Boğaziçi Journal*, Vol.10, Nos.1–2 (1996), pp.55–75.
8. United Nations High Commissioner for Refugees, *The State of the World's Refugees: Fifty Years of Humanitarian Action* (New York: Oxford University Press, 2000), Annex 10, p.325.
9. Information obtained from Office of the Prime Minister, Directorate General of Press and Information <http://www.byegm.gov.tr/yayinlarimiz/AnadolununSesi/165/T8.htm> (July 12, 2001).
10. For details see Kirişci (1996) and Kemal Kirişci, "Disaggregating Turkish Citizenship and Immigration Practices," *Middle Eastern Studies*, Vol.36, No.3 (July 2000), pp.1–22.
11. See Table 1 in Kirişci (2000), p.8.
12. The Turkish Minister for Labor Affairs and Social Welfare, Yaşar Okuyan, announced that there were approximately 1 million illegal immigrant workers in Turkey. See *Radikal*, Dec. 30, 2000. The Ministry of Foreign Affairs put their numbers at 1.2 million. See *Radikal*, Jan. 4, 2001.
13. For coverage of this phenomenon, see Erder (2000).
14. Stanford Shaw, *The Jews of the Ottoman Empire and the Turkish Republic* (New York: New York University Press, 1991), p.256.
15. Jacques Vernant, *The Refugee in the Post-War World* (New Haven, CT: Yale University Press, 1953), p.244.
16. For an assessment of the Convention and refugee law in general, see G.S. Goodwin-Gill, *The Refugee in International Law* (Oxford: Claredon Press, 2nd Edn. 1996).
17. Ivor C. Jackson, *The Refugee Concept in Group Situations* (The Hague: Martinus Nijhoff, 1999), p.68. The time limitation gave the possibility for states to accept the Convention only for individuals who became refugees before 1951. The geographical limitation, on the other hand, gave states the possibility to accept the applicability of the Convention only to individuals who became refugees as a result of events in Europe. In 1967 the United Nations adopted an additional protocol to the Convention which gave states the possibility to lift both limitations.
18. For an analysis of the origins and early years of this policy, see Kemal Kirişci, "The Legal Status of Asylum Seekers in Turkey: Problems and Prospects," *International Journal of Refugee Law*, Vol.3, No.3 (1991), pp.510–28.
19. Statistics and information obtained from the Foreigners Department in Ankara.
20. *Milliyet*, Feb. 22, 2000, reported that there was a group of 104 Chechen refugees waiting at the border in temperatures of minus 30°C.
21. *Radikal*, Feb. 25, 2000.
22. See *Russian Experience of Ethnic Discrimination: Meskhetians in Krasnodar Region* (Moscow: Memorial Human Rights Center, 2000).
23. Opening speech given by Abdulhaluk Çay, State Minister responsible for immigrants and refugees, at the *Workshop on Ahıska (Meshketian) Turks: Identity, Migration and Integration*, Dec. 14–15, 2000.
24. NA, *Annual Activity Report for 1999* (Ankara: Anatolian Development Foundation).

25. Estimates provided by officials from the Foreigners Department in Ankara.
26. *Cumhuriyet*, Feb. 15, 1991.
27. For a detailed analysis of the crisis and the subsequent effort to assist the refugees, see Kemal Kirişci, "'Provide Comfort' and Turkey: Decision Making for Refugee Assistance," *Low Intensity Conflict and Law Enforcement*, Vol.2, No.2 (Autumn 1993), pp.227–53.
28. For a report on such a case, see *Turkish Daily News*, Jan. 7, 1994.
29. *Cumhuriyet*, Jan. 13, 1994; *Sabah*, Dec. 5, 1995.
30. Amnesty International, *Turkey: Selective Protection – Discriminatory Treatment of Non-European Refugees and Asylum Seekers* (London: International Secretariat, March 1994).
31. *Non-refoulement* is considered not only as a pillar of the 1951 Convention but also as a rule with the status of customary international law, binding even on countries not party to the Convention. The principle basically prohibits asylum seekers from being returned to their country of origin against their will and without their application being properly examined. Refugees enjoy the same right too. Goodwin-Gill (1996), p.167.
32. For an unofficial translation of the text of the Regulation and an early evaluation of it, see Kemal Kirişci, "Is Turkey Lifting the 'Geographical Limitation?:' The November 1994 Regulation on Asylum in Turkey," *International Journal of Refugee Law*, Vol.8, No.3 (1996), pp.293–318. For a more critical analysis of the Regulation, see Bill Frelick, "Barriers to Protection: Turkey's Asylum Regulations," *International Journal of Refugee Law*, Vol.9, No.1 (1997), pp.8–34.
33. For a more detailed study of the background and problems arising from the implementation of the Regulation, see Kirişci (2001), pp.19–22.
34. See, for example, the following reports: *US Department of State: Turkey Country Report on Human Rights for 1996* (Released Jan. 1997) obtained from <http://www.state.gov> (Dec. 28, 2000); Bill Frelick, *Barriers to Protection: Turkey's Asylum Regulations* (Washington DC: Report issued by the US Committee for Refugees); *Turkey: Refoulment of non-European Refugees – A Protection Crisis* (London: Amnesty International Secretariat, Document EUR 44/031/1997).
35. For a brief analysis of these court rulings, see Kemal Kirişci, "UHNCR and Turkey: Cooperating Toward and Improved Implementation of the 1951 Convention," *International Journal of Refugee Law*, Vol.13, Nos.1–2 (2001), pp.71–97. The Turkish court rulings can be found in United Nations High Commissioner for Refugees Ankara Branch Office, *Sığınmacı, Mülteci ve Göç Konularına İlişkin Türkiye'deki Yargı Kararları* (Ankara: Birleşmiş Milletler Mülteciler Yüksek Komiserliği, Ankara, 2000).
36. Secretariat General for the EU Affairs, *Turkey: National Programme for the Adoption of the Acquis* (Ankara, 2001), Section "4.25.2 Asylum."
37. Başak Kale, "'Mülteci Cenneti' Oluruz" [We Will Become a Haven for Refugees], *Radikal*, Dec. 5, 2000.
38. Adem Arkadaş, "Sığınma ve Kaçak Göç" [Asylum and Illegal Migration], *Radikal*, Jan. 23, 2001; Cengiz Aktar, "Çağdaş Bir İltica Politikası İçin: Hoşgörü Değil Hukuk" [For a Modern Asylum Policy: Law In Place of Tolerance], *Radikal*, 28 June, 2001.
39. Kirişci (2000). See also Soner Çağaptay, "Kemalist dönemde göç ve iskan politikaları: Türk kimliği üzerine bir çalışma" [Migration and settlement policies during the Kemalist era: A study of Turkish identity], *Toplum ve Bilim*, No.93 (Summer 2002), pp.218–41.
40. *Official Gazette* (Resmi Gazete), June 14, 1934, No.2733. This law has since been heavily amended but the basic articles that define who can be an immigrant and refugee remain unchanged.
41. For the ratification text, see *Official Gazette*, Sept. 5, 1961, No.10898.
42. For the argument, see Geddes (2000), pp.104–6.
43. There are reports that the Turkish government is currently drafting a completely new asylum law. However, as of December 2002, the draft law has not been made available to the public. Therefore, it is not possible to comment as to whether the new law that is being considered will actually live up to the EU *acquis* as well as international refugee law.
44. See Geddes (2000), pp.104–5.
45. See Figure 7.11, *The State of the World Refugees* (2000), p.175.

46. For these statistics, see Kirişci (2001), Tables 2 and 3, pp.32–3.
47. For a detailed study of this problem and efforts to resolve it, see Kirişci (2001), pp.33–4.
48. For first-hand coverage of this situation, see article by Rizgar Khoshnaw, "Why are the Kurds Leaving their Homeland?," *KurdishMedia.com*, June 14, 2001.
49. For an American perspective, see *Victims of Trafficking and Violence Protection Act of 2000: Trafficking in Persons Report* (US Department of State, July 2001), <http://www.state.gov/g/ inl/rls/tiprpt/2001/>, July 18, 2001.
50. See French dailies such as *Le Monde* and *Liberation*, Feb. 19, 2001.
51. *Radikal*, March 1, 2001, noted that a substantial part of these reports was based on a report carried by *Armeniannews*.
52. For critical coverage of these allegations by a Turkish journalist based in Paris, see M. Kırıkkanat, "Figaro' nun Kürt Düğünü," *Milliyet*, Feb. 25, 2001 (<http://www.milliyet. com. tr>).
53. *CNN.Com*, Jan. 1, 1998, reported that during the course of 1997 boats and ships carrying 5,000 illegal immigrants had been intercepted and that 3,000 were either from Turkey or had transited Turkey. In an earlier report (Dec. 21, 1997), *CNN.Com* reported that Italian officials alleged there were 18–20,000 Kurds waiting to set sail toward Italy from Turkey.
54. *New York Times*, March 4, 1999, A12.
55. For an analysis of the activities of the PKK, see Michael Radu, "The Rise and Fall of the PKK," *Orbis*, Vol.45, No.1 (Winter 2001), pp.47–64.
56. See story by Ayşe Karabat, "Kâr Tatlı, Ceza Komik" [High Returns for Comical Penalties], *Radikal*, Jan. 4, 2001.
57. There have been news reports of police officers arrested in smuggler rings. Corruption is a chronic problem in Turkey. The former Minister of the Interior, Saadettin Tantan, openly admitted that the problem existed in the Turkish bureaucracy, vowed to combat this problem and actually supported a research project on corruption in Turkey. For the results of this research project, see Fikret Adaman, Ali Çarkoğlu and Burhan Şenatalar, *Hanehalkı Gözünden Türkiye'de Yolsuzluğun Nedenleri ve Önlenmesine İlişkin Öneriler* (Istanbul: TESEV, 2001). In addition, a prominent politician from the right-wing nationalist National Action Party highlighted the role of security forces in drug trafficking during an interview in *Radikal*, June 12, 2000.
58. Confidential interview with a high-level MOI official on *NTV*, Yakın Plan, May 14, 2001. This official also said that the *East Sea* had been closely monitored and the police had been alerted in Europe but that their counterparts had not expressed any interest in following up the matter before the ship ended up running aground in France in February 2001.
59. For a detailed analysis of the origins of the Kurdish problem in Turkey, see Kemal Kirişci and Gareth Winrow, *The Kurdish Question and Turkey* (London and Portland, OR: Frank Cass, 1997). For an evaluation of developments since the capture of Abdullah Öcalan, see Svante Cornell, "The Kurdish Question in Turkish Politics," *Orbis*, Vol.45, No.1 (Winter 2001), pp.31–46.
60. In spite of the bitter recriminations that both sides directed towards each other, Italian and Turkish officials have also been cooperating in an effort to stem illegal migration. It is in this context that the Minister of the Interior, Saadetin Tantan, met his Italian counterpart to discuss closer cooperation in this area. See *Radikal*, Jan. 24, 2001.
61. For work in progress concerning readmission agreements, see *Follow-Up Instrument on the Turkish National Programme for the Adoption of the Acquis*, Section 4.25.4, Migration subsection 6.
62. For details of this visa policy, see Kirişci (2001), pp.47–53.
63. The report is also known as the Pirker Report of the European Parliament (published on Sept. 14, 2001).
64. For the speech by the Commissioner given in London on 9 July, 2001, see <http://europa.eu.int/comm/commissioners/vitorino/index_en.htm>.
65. For an analysis of the improvements in Turkey's asylum policy and the background to it, see Kemal Kirişci, "UNHCR and Turkey: Cooperating Towards An Improved Implementation of the 1951 Convention on the Status of Refugees," *International Journal*

of Refugee Law, Vol.13, Nos.1–2 (2001), pp.71–97. Ironically, the improvement can be said to have taken place as a function of Turkish asylum policy being to some degree moved out of a security perspective into a human rights perspective.
66. See feature entitled "Europe's Immigrants: A Continent on the Move," *Economist*, May 6, 2000, which, under the subsection "Don't give me your tired, your poor," raises the preference of the EU to allow in only skilled immigrants and keep the unskilled out of the EU.

Human Rights, the European Union and the Turkish Accession Process

WILLIAM HALE

In the midsummer of 2002, Turkey was in the throes of yet another of its periodic political crises, which was ended only by the general elections of November 3, 2002. With the prolonged illness of the 77-year-old Prime Minister, Bülent Ecevit, and with the resignation of a deputy premier and five other ministers, there were widespread predictions that his three-party coalition government could not last for long and that Turkey would soon be engaged in early general elections. The cabinet was gravely weakened and divided, not only by Ecevit's illness but also by disagreements over the completion of political reforms which were required by the European Union (EU) as a prerequisite for the start of accession negotiations. Two of the ruling parties—Ecevit's Democratic Left Party (*Demokratik Sol Parti*—DSP) and the Motherland Party (*Anavatan Partisi*—ANAP), led by Mesut Yılmaz—claimed that they were fully prepared to enact the required human rights improvements. Nonetheless, the way was effectively blocked by the third coalition partner, the Nationalist Action Party (*Milliyetçi Hareket Partisi*—MHP), led by Devlet Bahçeli. Since Ecevit refused to dismantle his government by excluding the MHP, the process of preparing Turkey for eventual accession seemed to have reached an impasse. The widening of human rights thus became Turkey's most pressing political question alongside the survival of the government.

Given constraints of space, this contribution gives only a brief summary of the background conditions that led to the evolution of this situation, which is, in any case, covered by a number of previous studies.[1] Instead, it concentrates on analyzing current developments in four crucial areas of reform: first, freedom of expression and association and of political parties; second, the treatment of ethnic minorities (particularly as regards cultural rights); third, the abolition of the death penalty; and, fourth, the reduction of the political role of the military. This is very far from exhausting the list of conditions stipulated by the EU, which included—among other things—the elimination of torture by the police and security forces, the improvement of prison conditions and the rights of civil associations, and enhancement of the functioning and efficiency of the judiciary. However, the four issues considered here were clearly at the top of the agenda and likely to arouse most controversy in Turkey, besides raising some important questions about the definition and extent of human rights in general.[2]

EUROPEAN PROJECTS AND TURKISH REACTIONS

The political reforms which have been pressed on Turkey since the EU's Helsinki summit of December 1999 recognized Turkey as an official candidate for eventual accession were not specially invented to meet the Turkish case but have been an established part of the EU's agenda for several years and are equally applied to all the candidate countries.[3] Until the 1990s, the main instrument for advancing these reforms was the Council of Europe, which in 1953 established the European Court of Human Rights (ECHR)—set up as the main instrument for enforcing the European Convention on Human Rights. Where states accepted the right of individual application to the Court by their citizens (which Turkey has done since 1991) the Convention became internationally justiciable. However, as the European Union's program for enlargement into Eastern Europe got off the ground, respect for human rights was made a *sine qua non* for candidate countries. At its meeting in Copenhagen in June 1993 the European Council made it clear that "membership requires that the candidate country has achieved stability of institutions guaranteeing democracy, the rule of law, human rights and respect for and protection of minorities."[4] Meeting in Luxembourg in December 1997, the Council decided that "compliance with the Copenhagen political criteria is a prerequisite for the opening of any accession negotiations."[5] Hence, when the European Council meeting in Helsinki in December 1999 declared that "Turkey is a candidate State destined to join the Union on the basis of the same criteria as applied to the other candidate States,"[6] it was emphasized that it would have to meet the political criteria before accession negotiations could start.

In November 2000 the EU Commission put flesh on the bare bones of the Copenhagen criteria by issuing its Accession Partnership Document (APD) for Turkey.[7] This was accepted by the EU leaders at the Nice meeting of the European Council in December 2000. So far as the political criteria were concerned, the APD outlined the measures which Turkey was required to implement in the "short term" (that is, apparently, by the end of 2001) and in the "medium term" (of indefinite duration). The government's official reaction to this came in March 2001 when the cabinet approved a "National Program" for the implementation of the EU *acquis*, the first part of which dealt with the political criteria.[8] In October 2001 the Turkish parliament began to give effect to these commitments by passing a package of 34 amendments to the Constitution affecting, in particular, freedoms of expression, organization and assembly, the use of minority languages, the partial abolition of the death penalty, and the role of the military in politics. Parliament followed this up in January–March 2002 by passing amendments to the Penal Code and other legislation affecting the freedom of expression and the press, the activities of associations, the closure of political parties and the prevention of torture. However, these still left crucial parts of the APD unimplemented, notably as they affected the application of capital punishment and cultural rights for the Kurds. These issues were not addressed until August 2002, shortly before the end of the Ecevit government (see below).

Within Ecevit's government, as already noted, opposition to reform of the human rights regime came almost exclusively from the MHP, which regarded any constitutional liberalization—especially on the Kurdish issue—as an insult to those who had died during the long struggle against the militants of the Kurdistan Workers' Party (*Partiya Karkaren Kurdistan*—PKK). Even allowing cultural rights to the Kurds was regarded as a serious threat to Turkey's territorial integrity by the ultra-nationalists. Officially, the MHP supported Turkey's application for eventual accession, but party spokesmen maintained that, since the EU was unlikely to admit Turkey anyway, there was no point in making these "concessions." Among the opposition parties the True Path Party (*Doğru Yol Partisi*—DYP), led by Tansu Çiller, supported EU accession, but could not be expected to help the government unless a pledge for early general elections was part of the deal. In June 2001 the pro-Islamist Virtue Party (*Fazilet Partisi*—FP) was closed down by the Constitutional Court for engaging in "activities contrary to the principle of the secular republic."[9] It was succeeded by two parties, in the shape of the Felicity Party (*Saadet Partisi*—SP), nominally led by Recai Kutan but actually controlled by the veteran Islamist leader Necmettin Erbakan from behind the scenes, and the Justice and Development Party (*Adalet ve Kalkınma Partisi*—AKP), led by Recep Tayip Erdoğan, the formerly pro-Islamist mayor of Istanbul. According to their published party programs, both parties were committed to achieving Turkish accession to the EU, and the leaders of both claimed that they supported the human rights reforms which would be necessary to achieve this. In effect, there seemed to be a rapprochement between Islamists and secularist liberals on this point, since both wished to widen civil liberties, albeit with different motives.[10] More broadly, within an emerging civil society there was general support for the EU project and for the improvement of civil rights, especially in the business community.[11] As a crucial force in Turkish politics, the military broadly supported the goal of eventual EU accession as a natural extension of Turkey's NATO membership, which would further cement its relationship with the western powers. Apparently, the commanders of the armed forces accepted political liberalization—even on the Kurdish issue—as an inevitable corollary, even though there may have been severe misgivings on this point on the part of many military officers.[12] Public opinion polls also suggested that the big majority of ordinary citizens supported Turkey's bid for EU membership even though many opposed the complete abolition of capital punishment or allowing minority cultural rights.[13]

FREEDOM OF EXPRESSION AND ASSOCIATION, AND OF POLITICAL PARTIES

Articles 22–26 of the Turkish Constitution state that everyone has the right to "freedom of communication," "freedom of residence and movement," "freedom of conscience, religious belief and conviction," "freedom of thought and opinion" and "the right to disseminate his thoughts and opinions." Article 28 states that "the press is free and shall not be censored."[14] Article 33 decrees that "everyone has the right to form associations without prior permission," while Article 34 confirms the "right to hold peaceful meetings and demonstration marches without prior permission." However, the original text of the Constitution, enacted under the military regime of 1980–83, stipulated quite severe restrictions on the actual exercise of these rights. Although it is not clear whether its provisions have the same legal force as those contained in particular articles of the Constitution, the original Preamble to the Constitution provided that "no protection shall be accorded to thoughts and opinions contrary to Turkish national interests, the principle of the indivisibility of the existence of Turkey with its state and territory, Turkish historical and moral values or the nationalism, principles and reforms of Atatürk." More specifically, the original texts of Articles 13 and 14 placed severe restrictions on the freedom of expression. In its original text, Article 13 stated:

> Fundamental rights and freedoms may be restricted by law, in conformity with the letter and spirit of the Constitution, with the aim of safeguarding the indivisible integrity of the State with its territory and nation, national sovereignty, the Republic, national security,

public order, general peace, the public interest, public morals and public health, and also for specific reasons set forth in the relevant Articles of the Constitution.

In its original version, Article 14 extended the same principle by stipulating that:

> None of the rights and freedoms embodied in the Constitution shall be exercised with the aim of violating the indivisible integrity of the State with its territory and nation, of endangering the existence of the Turkish State and Republic, of destroying fundamental rights and freedoms, of placing the government of the State under the control of an individual or a group, or establishing the hegemony of one social class over the others, or creating discrimination on the basis of language, race, religion or sect, or of establishing by any other means a system of government based on these concepts and ideas.

Article 68, which outlines the rights and duties of political parties, and remained unchanged by the amendments of 2001, requires that the "statutes and programmes, as well as the activities of political parties, shall not be in conflict with the independence of the State, its indivisible integrity with its territory and nation ... [or] the principles of the democratic and secular republic" (paragraph 4). Article 69 allows for the closure of political parties by the Constitutional Court "owing to activities violating the fourth paragraph of Article 68," if the Court determines that "the party in question has become a centre for the execution of such activities."

Infraction of these provisions does not by itself constitute a criminal offence unless there is a provision of the Penal Code or other statutes giving effect to them. The statutes most frequently used by the courts to restrict freedom of expression were Articles 159 and 312 of the Penal Code,[15] and Article 8 of the Law for the Struggle against Terrorism (Law No.3713) of 1991.[16] The original wording of Penal Code Article 159 provided that "those who publicly insult or deride the moral character of Turkishness, the Republic, the Grand National Assembly [the Turkish parliament] or the Government, or the Ministries, the military or security forces of the State or the moral character of the judiciary, shall be punished by between one and six years of severe imprisonment." According to the original text of Penal Code Article 312, "anyone who openly incites the public to hatred and enmity with regard to class, race, religion, religious sect or regional differences shall be punished by between one and three years of imprisonment." Article 8 of Law No.3713 is directed more specifically at statements alleged to support Kurdish separatism: in its original text it declared that *"Regardless of with whatever method, aim or purpose, written or oral propaganda, together with meetings, demonstrations and marches which have the objective of destroying the indivisible integrity of the State of the Republic of Turkey, with its territory and nation, shall not be carried out"* (emphasis added). As part of amendments to this law enacted in 1995, the words reproduced here in italics were removed.[17] Nonetheless, even in its revised wording, the statute still made statements deemed to be in support of "separatism" illegal. Besides restricting the freedom of expression of individuals, legal statutes also limit the freedom of print and electronic media as well as political parties.[18]

These statutes were used in Turkey for many years to restrict freedom of expression and association, particularly for those supporting dissident views on the Kurdish or Islamist issues. Penal Code Article 312, in particular, was used to prosecute such people on the grounds that calling for greater political or cultural rights for the Kurds, or adherence to Islamic principles in politics, constitute an incitement to racial or religious hatred. Many other journalists were prosecuted and imprisoned under Article 8 of the Law for the Struggle against Terrorism or Penal Code Article 159.[19] Similarly, the Political Parties Law was used to close down parties deemed to have supported separatism or advanced illegal Islamist ideas. Notable examples are two previous pro-Kurdish parties, the People's Labour Party (*Halkın Emek Partisi*—HEP), which was dissolved in 1993, and the Democracy Party (*Demokrasi Partisi*—DEP), closed down in the following year. Its successor, the People's Democracy Party (*Halkın Demokrasi Partisi*—HADEP), was allowed to compete in the general elections of 1995 and 1999 (though it failed to win any seats on either occasion) and is itself currently faced with a closure suit. In the pro-Islamist camp, Necmettin Erbakan's Welfare Party (*Refah Partisi*—RP) achieved far more electoral success, but was in turn closed down by the Constitutional Court, as of February 1998.[20] As already noted, its successor, the Virtue Party, suffered the same fate in 2001.

The fact that these and other legal provisions have been judged quite contrary to human rights norms was made clear by the EU and the Council of Europe. Hence, in the Accession Partnership Document—and as a "short-term" measure—the EU called on Turkey to "strengthen legal and constitutional guarantees for the right to freedom of expression in line with article 10 of the European Convention on Human Rights [and to] address in that context the situation of those persons in prison sentenced for expressing non-violent opinions."[21] The government would also be required to "strengthen legal and constitutional guarantees of the right to freedom of association and peaceful assembly and encourage development of civil society." Steps to be taken in the medium term included legal changes so as to "guarantee full enjoyment by all individuals without any discrimination and irrespective of their language, race, colour, sex, political opinion, philosophical belief or religion of all human rights and fundamental freedoms [and to] further develop conditions for the enjoyment of freedom of thought, conscience and religion."[22]

Article 10 of the European Convention on Human Rights, to which both the EU and the Turkish government refer, is not entirely unambiguous as to how far complete freedom of expression should be allowed. In its words, "everyone has the right to freedom of expression. This right shall include freedom to hold opinions and to receive and impart information and ideas without interference by public authority and regardless of frontiers."[23] However, the second paragraph of the same Article states that:

> The exercise of these freedoms, since it carries with it duties and responsibilities, may be subject to such formalities, conditions, restrictions or penalties as are prescribed by law and are necessary in a democratic society, in the interests of national security, territorial integrity or public safety, for the prevention of disorder or crime, for the protection of health or morals, [or] for the protection of the reputation or rights of others ...[24]

The right to "peaceful assembly and to freedom of association with others" is defined in Article 11 of the Convention. The list of objectives for which this right can be restricted are the same as those given in Article 10, except that the aim of protecting territorial integrity is omitted.

As part of the package of constitutional amendments enacted in October 2001, important changes to the Preamble and to Articles 13 and 14 of the Constitution were enacted. In the case of the Preamble, the words "thoughts or opinions" in the passage quoted above were replaced with "actions."[25] The previous texts of Articles 13 and 14 were deleted, with the new wording of Article 13 stating that:

> Fundamental rights and freedoms may be restricted only by law and in conformity with the reasons mentioned in the relevant articles of the Constitution without infringing upon their essence. These restrictions shall not be in conflict with the letter and spirit of the Constitution and the requirements of the democratic order of the society and the secular Republic and the principle of proportionality.

The new version of Article 14 reads as follows:

None of the rights and freedoms embodied in the Constitution shall be exercised with the aim of violating the indivisible integrity of the State with its territory and nation, and endangering the existence of the democratic and secular order of the Turkish Republic based upon human rights. No provision of this Constitution shall be interpreted in a manner that enables the State or individuals to destroy the fundamental rights and freedoms embodied in the Constitution or to stage an activity with the aim of restricting them more extensively than stated in the Constitution. The sanctions to be applied against those who perpetrate these activities in conflict with these provisions shall be determined by law.

The package of constitutional amendments passed in October 2001 also included an addition to Article 69 giving a closer definition of the phrase "centre for the execution" of activities contrary to the provisions of Article 68 that could be the basis for the closure of a political party by the Constitutional Court. Under the new wording, such actions would have to be "carried out intensively by the members of that party" or "shared implicitly or explicitly" by the General Congress (in effect, the national convention of the party) or its leader or parliamentary group. As an alternative to closure, the Constitutional Court could also deprive the party of the state subsidy normally payable to parties.

In January 2002, Bülent Ecevit's government began the job of bringing the Penal Code and other statutes into line with these constitutional amendments. On February 6 parliament passed changes to Articles 159 and 312 of the Penal Code and Article 8 of the Law for the Struggle against Terrorism (No.3713), together with some other legislation.[26] Under the successful amendment to Article 312, statements inciting the public "to hatred and enmity with regard to class, race, religion, religious sect or regional differences" would only be counted as a crime if they were delivered "in a manner which could be dangerous for public order." However, Penal Code Article 159 remained unaltered, except that the maximum punishment which could be applied was reduced from six to three years. Similarly, Article 8 of Law No.3713 remained essentially unchanged.[27] A second package of statute reforms was passed by parliament on March 26, 2002. Among other changes—and repeating the wording of the previous amendment to Article 69 of the constitution—Article 101 of the Political Parties Law was altered so that parties could be closed down by the Constitutional Court only if allegedly pro-Islamist or pro-"separatist" actions had been adopted as clear party policy by its governing bodies.[28]

While these changes can at least be judged to have been a step in the right direction, critics could reasonably argue that they did not go far enough. On the positive side, the alterations to Articles 13 and 14 of the constitution appeared to bring them into rough correspondence with Articles 10 and 11 of the European Convention on Human Rights, notably by shortening the list of unconstitutional aims mentioned in the previous version of Article 14. The amendment to the Preamble also removed the provision that merely having "thoughts or opinions" deemed contrary to Turkey's national interests could be deemed illegal, but the substitution of "actions" did not remove the objection that the restriction as a whole was dangerously vague and catch-all. There were similar shortcomings in the two packages of legislative amendments—in particular the fact that Article 159 of the Penal Code and Article 8 of Law No.3713 were left virtually unchanged, except for some reduction of the punishments applied. It was not until August 2002 that Article 159 was further ammended to bring it into line with the EU's requirements (see below). The addition of a perceived threat to public order was a useful amendment to the restrictions contained in Penal Code Article 312, but it would still be open to courts to decide whether such a "danger" was present in contested cases. More generally (and before deciding whether the amendments marked a real advance), it remained to be seen how courts would interpret the new legislation and constitutional clauses in practice.

Similar considerations applied to an assessment of the changes to the rules affecting political parties. By specifying how a party was to be judged a "centre for the execution" of unacceptable policies the new versions of Article 69 of the constitution and Article 101 of the Political Parties Law appeared to remove the possibility that a party could be closed down purely on the basis of individual remarks by its leader or other members which could not be proved to be part of established party policy—as happened in the case of the Welfare Party in 1998. On the other hand, most of the restrictions contained in the Political Parties Law remained in place, so Turkish parties remained far more restrained in what they could do or say than those of most European states. The argument for far more liberal laws on political parties was not entirely clear cut, however, since it is not universally accepted that, within a democracy, parties cannot legally be closed down, especially if they advance principles which are seen as quite contrary to democratic values.[29] Probably for this reason the APD did not call specifically for reform of the laws regarding political parties. In fact, the main initiative for this was internal—primarily, though not exclusively, from the political Islamists.

THE TREATMENT OF ETHNIC MINORITIES

Although the rights of individuals are fairly well established in international human rights instruments, those of collectivities—in particular, what are known as "national minorities"—are not. As an example, the European Convention of Human Rights nowhere mentions minority rights as such. In particular, it is not generally accepted that national minorities (however defined) are necessarily entitled to independent statehood—or even to territorial autonomy within an existing state as an alternative.[30] In the absence of a clear entitlement to independence or autonomy, the question of cultural rights (in particular the use of minority languages in education and for other official purposes) appears to be the most critical issue.

Apart from the difficulty of establishing what rights a minority is entitled to, it is not even clear what a "national minority" is. How big does a minority need to be—and does it have to inhabit a definable territory within the state—if it is to be counted as such? Does it have to have a separate language or religion? There is no generally accepted answer to these questions. As the introduction to the Framework Convention for the Protection of National Minorities drawn up by the Council of Europe in 1994 admits, it was decided "not to include a definition of the notion of a 'national minority' in the Framework Convention as, at this stage, it was impossible to arrive at a definition capable of mustering general support of all Council of Europe member states."[31] The Turkish case, moreover, is particularly problematic, since the Turkish state accepts as "minorities" only those groups who were defined as such in the Treaty of Lausanne of 1923, that is the non-Muslim citizens of Turkey—primarily Jewish, Armenian and Greek—to whom some special rights were granted. Members of ethnic minorities who are Muslims—notably the Kurds—are not accepted as "minorities" but as full and normal citizens of Turkey, hence are entitled to no special privileges. Kemalist principles, on which Turkish approaches to this problem firmly rest, assert the homogeneity of the Turkish nation and the principle of equal citizenship. However, as Will Kymlicka puts it, "the problem is not that Turkey refuses to accept Kurds as Turkish citizens. The problem is precisely its attempt to force Kurds to see themselves as Turks."[32]

Since the early 1990s attitudes have generally changed: it is no longer officially claimed that the Kurds in Turkey do not exist or are really ethnic Turks. However, this change is not fully reflected in the laws and constitution. Until their revision as part of the package of amendments passed in October 2001, Article 26 of the constitution forbade the use of "any language prohibited by law" (in effect, Kurdish) for "the expression and dissemination of thought," while Article 28, affecting the press, decreed that "publication shall not be made in any language forbidden by law." The amendments of October 2001 withdrew these clauses from both the affected Articles. The effect of this was not substantial, however, since in practice these clauses had been virtually void since April 1991 when Law No.2932 (1983) was repealed, a law which had effectively defined Kurdish as a "language prohibited by law." As there was no language which was now so defined, books, newspapers and magazines in Kurdish and other languages now appear. On the other hand, until a further package of reforms was passed in August 2002 (see below), the ban still affected broadcasting, education and some other activities, which are covered by separate legislation. Article 3 of the constitution also confirms Turkish as the sole language of the state, while Article 42 stipulates that "no language other than Turkish shall be taught as a mother-tongue to Turkish citizens in institutions of training and education." The phrase "as a mother tongue" was apparently inserted to allow the teaching of foreign languages such as English, French and Arabic. Other restrictions on the use of the Kurdish language are contained in the legislation affecting political parties, elections and broadcasting. In particular, political parties may not use any language other than Turkish in their internal proceedings or election propaganda,[33] and all terrestrial broadcasting in Kurdish was banned.[34]

In trying to elaborate on the commitment to the "protection of minorities" contained in the Copenhagen criteria, the EU's Accession Partnership Document was circumspect as it did not specifically use the word "Kurdish" and restricted its requirements to cultural rights. As a short-term measure, it called on the Turkish government to "remove any legal provisions forbidding the use by Turkish citizens of their mother tongue in TV/radio broadcasting." In the medium term, Turkey would be required to "ensure cultural diversity and guarantee cultural rights for all citizens irrespective of their origin. Any legal provisions preventing the enjoyment of these rights should be abolished, including in the field of education."[35]

On the first point, as the foregoing discussion makes clear, Turkey clearly fell short of the EU's requirements but could overcome the problem by a fairly simple amendment to the broadcasting law. The question of allowing "cultural rights ... in the field of education" was far more complex, however, since it was not at all clear what the EU was demanding. In fact, as in the case of the regional devolution of power, the practice in existing EU member states varies quite widely.[36] In practice, it is likely that the EU would probably be satisfied with the introduction of some Kurdish language lessons as an option in state schools or maybe merely official permission to private institutions to provide such lessons. From the Turkish point of view, it is arguable that such permission would not by itself endanger Turkey's territorial integrity. What is important in this context is what is taught, rather than what language is used, and on this score the numerous constitutional and other rules protecting the territorial integrity of the country would still apply. It might even be possible to achieve this change without altering Article 42 of the Constitution—if, for example, it was decided that Kurdish could not be counted as the "mother tongue" of Turkish citizens, however illogical this might appear from the outside.

ABOLITION OF THE DEATH PENALTY

Although abolition of the death penalty is now widely advocated by liberal opinion throughout the world, capital punishment is not universally recognized as being incompatible with democratic government. It is, for example, retained for murder in several states in the United States and in US federal law. The main text of the European Convention of Human Rights, moreover, does not outlaw capital punishment. In fact, it was not until the promulgation of the Sixth Protocol to the Convention in 1983—in which signatory states agree to abolish it except "in respect of acts committed in time of war or imminent threat of war"—that this could be said to have become part of the European political agenda.[37] In practice, all the current EU member states have abolished the death penalty, except in the circumstances mentioned in the Sixth Protocol, as have all the current candidate states. Until August 2002, the Turkish Penal Code, which dates from 1926 and is based on that of Italy at the time, still allowed for the death penalty to be applied in certain cases of homicide (Article 450), besides some "felonies against the state," notably in time of war and in cases of those attempting to "separate a part of its territory from the Administration of the State" (Article 125), or attempting "by force" to alter or overthrow the Constitution or the government or encourage others to do so (Articles 146–7).[38] However, under Article 87 of the Constitution, death sentences could only be carried out if parliament passed a positive vote to that effect. Since 1984 no such motions have been tabled—and a number of prisoners were effectively left on "death row."

In the Accession Partnership Document, the EU clearly required Turkey to maintain the *de facto* moratorium on the application of capital punishment, then to abolish the death penalty and to sign and ratify the Sixth Protocol.[39] The problem thus became a black-and-white issue without any of the areas of doubt left in other parts of the EU's list of requirements: either Turkey abolished the death penalty—with the reservations contained in the Sixth Protocol—or it did not. Nearly all the parties represented in parliament supported abolition in principle, the only significant exception being the MHP, which wished to retain parliament's right to order the execution of Abdullah Öcalan, the leader of the PKK, who had been sentenced to death in June 1999 under Penal Code Article 125. As the MHP was the second partner in Ecevit's coalition it was able to insist on this reservation. Hence, as part of the package of constitutional amendments passed in October 2001, a sentence was added to Article 38 stating that "the death penalty shall not be imposed except in cases in time of war, imminent threat of war *and terrorist crimes*" (emphasis added). The MHP's motivation was that Öcalan, like some other PKK prisoners, was a terrorist who—in the party's view—deserved to be executed. If it were to meet the EU's demands, parliament still had to eliminate the death penalty entirely (except possibly in times of war or imminent threat of war). This could be done by changing the wording of those Articles of the Penal Code which prescribed the death penalty by substituting sentences of life imprisonment, and would not necessarily require a further amendment of the Constitution.[40] There was also some public debate of the idea that, if the death penalty were abolished in the case of "terrorist crimes," then a clause should be added to the Constitution to the effect that anyone serving a life sentence for such crimes could not subsequently benefit from a general amnesty—the objective being to prevent a future government from releasing Öcalan.[41] Disagreements on this and related points prevented an agreement between those parties in the government which favored full abolition (that is, the Democratic Left and Motherland Parties) and the opposition parties until a deal was struck in August 2002 (see Postscript).

THE POLITICAL ROLE OF THE MILITARY

The fact that the armed forces have played a crucial role in Turkish politics for many years hardly needs repeating here. In a tradition going back to the Ottoman era, military officers regard themselves as the bedrock of the state and, in the republican era, the guardians of Kemalist modernism. Apart from those times of crisis in which the military have themselves ruled the republic (that is, during 1960–61, 1980–83 and, indirectly, during 1971–73), they have carried out their professional functions virtually independently of the government and have played a crucial political role—notably in protecting Atatürk's secularist legacy and upholding the principle of the unitary republic. This goes a good deal further than that of their counterparts in most other democracies, who in peacetime merely advise the government on questions of defense and national security.

During the PKK's campaign of violence of 1984–99, and under legislation passed in July 1987, the armed forces were also given special and much criticized powers in the southeastern provinces, which were classified as a "Special Situation Region" (*Olağanüstü Hal Bölgesi*) under a "Special Regional Governor."

Under the Turkish Constitution, the chief of the general staff—as the commander of the armed forces—is appointed by the president on the proposal of the government and is responsible to the prime minister rather than to the minister of defense, as in most democratic systems (Article 117). Article 118 of the Constitution outlines the composition and powers of the National Security Council (NSC)—a body bringing together the commanders of the armed forces, the president, prime minister and other ministers. According to the original text of 1982, the NSC membership was to consist of the prime minister, the ministers of defense, the interior and foreign affairs, the chief of the general staff and the commanders of the army, navy, air force and gendarmerie, meeting under the chairmanship of the president. Counting the president as neutral, this gave the military members of the NSC a 5:4 majority over the representatives of the government. More crucially, the original version of this Article gave the Council the power to make decisions on a wide range of issues—some of them outside the normal military orbit—and implied that these should be taken as orders to the government, not recommendations. In the original wording of Article 118:

> The National Security Council shall submit to the Council of Ministers its views on taking decisions and ensuring necessary coordination with regard to the formulation, establishment, and implementation of the national security policy of the State. The Council of Ministers shall give priority consideration to the decisions of the National Security Council concerning the measures that it deems necessary for the preservation of the existence and independence of the State, the integrity and indivisibility of the country and the peace and security of society.

In the Accession Partnership Document the EU required the government to "align the constitutional role of the National Security Council as an advisory body to the government in accordance with the practice of EU member states" (without specifying exactly what this was) and to "lift the state of emergency in the South-East."[42] On the first requirement, and as part of the package of constitutional amendments of October 2001, Article 118 was altered in two ways: first, the minister of justice was added to the list of ministers included in the NSC; second, the passage quoted above was amended as follows:

The National Security Council shall submit to the Council of the Ministers its views on the advisory decisions that are taken and ensuring the necessary coordination with regard to the formulation, establishment, and implementation of the national security policy of the state. The Council of Ministers shall evaluate decisions of the National Security Council concerning the measures that it deems necessary for the preservation of the existence and independence of the state, the integrity and indivisibility of the country and the peace and security of society.

As a further step towards meeting the EU's criteria, a meeting of the NSC held on May 30, 2002, decided—as of June 30—to end the "Exceptional Situation" regime in the provinces of Hakkâri and Tunceli, and to extend it for the last time for four months in the two remaining provinces (Diyarbakır and Şırnak) in which it was still applied.[43] As a result, the role of the armed forces as the virtual rulers in much of the southeast would be ended by the beginning of November 2002, meeting an important part of the EU's political agenda. The effects of the amendments to Article 118 of the Constitution were harder to predict, however. In principle, the change in the composition of the NSC gave the military chiefs and the members of the government equal representation (again, counting the president as neutral. With Ahmet Necdet Sezer, a former chief justice of the Constitutional Court, as chairman, the NSC could be said to have a civilian majority). By replacing "decisions" with "advisory decisions" and the phrase "give priority consideration" with "evaluate," the new wording also implied that decisions of the NSC could not be considered mandatory for the government. It nevertheless remained doubtful how much effect this would have in practice. Essentially, the political power of the military members of the NSC appeared to depend, not on their numbers, but the high regard in which they were still held by most of the public, which meant that the politicians had to take them seriously whatever their numerical strength in the Council. As the Chief of the General Staff, General Hüseyin Kıvrıkoğlu, had been quoted as saying some time earlier, "if they want 100 civilians as members of the National Security Council, so be it," implying that this would not make much difference.[44] While the new wording of the Constitution appeared to reduce the powers of the NSC over the government, it remained to be seen how far this would go in practice. Even the position of the EU on this point was ambiguous. As the Foreign Affairs Committee of the British House of Commons put it in April 2002: "there is an awkward tension between the EU's emphasis on democratic standards and civilian control of the military, and the concern of Turkey's NATO allies (many of which are of course also EU member states) that Turkey should remain a western-oriented secular society at all costs."[45] Hence, even if there was no dramatic reduction in the military's actual role in Turkish politics in the near future, it seemed unlikely that the EU would use this as an explicit reason for not starting accession negotiations.

POSTSCRIPT

Following Bülent Ecevit's illness and continued disagreements within his coalition over human rights reforms, his Democratic Left Party (DSP) fell apart in July 2002 as İsmail Cem led a group of over 60 ex-DSP deputies out of the party to form a new party, christened the New Turkey Party (*Yeni Türkiye Partisi*—YTP). Parliament was reconvened and, on July 31, passed a bill providing for early general elections to be held on November 3, 2002. Although it had technically lost its majority, the Ecevit government would apparently remain in office pending the elections. On August 3, with the support of most of the opposition deputies, the Assembly passed a European Union Adaptation Law (*Avrupa Birliği Uyum Yasası*) of 15 Articles which, at least on paper, appeared to meet the remaining requirements of the APD in the human rights field. In particular, in changes to the Penal Code the death penalty was removed in the case of charges involving the use of "terrorism" by changing such sentences to read "life imprisonment." However, capital punishment could be retained in times of war or imminent danger of war, and the new wording provided that those sentenced to life imprisonment for terrorist crimes could not benefit from any subsequent amnesty or reduction of sentences. In an alteration to Penal Code Article 159, statements made with the aim of "criticizing" (rather than "insulting") the government, parliament, ministries or the security forces, would not be counted as a crime. The broadcasting law was also altered to permit broadcasts in "different languages and dialects which are traditionally used by Turkish citizens in their daily lives"[46] (in effect, regional languages like that of the Laz of the Black Sea region, as well as Kurdish) with the proviso that these should not be contrary to the basic principles of the Constitution or the territorial integrity of the state. On the vexed question of the teaching of languages "traditionally used by Turkish citizens in their daily lives," the new law would allow this to be carried out by non-governmental organizations, subject to control by the ministry of education and the permission of the cabinet. Other reforms allowed associations to establish links and branches abroad, allowed the non-Muslim minorities free disposal of their real estate in Turkey and introduced harsh punishments for those found guilty of smuggling illegal immigrants in or out of the country.[47] Welcoming these proposals, Bülent Ecevit claimed that "except for a few details, Turkey will have all the freedoms and rights of a member-country of the EU," and that there were now no obstacles to the start of accession negotiations.[48] The EU appeared to be more cautious, however. In a statement issued on August 5, a spokesman for the Commission also welcomed the reforms as "positive steps," but cautioned that the EU would monitor the situation to see that they were applied, and that deciding on a starting date for accession negotiations would depend on this.[49] Subsequently, however, it appeared that the EU's political leaders were prepared to be more positive. Accordingly, at its meeting in Copenhagen on December 12–13, 2002 the European Council agreed that if the reforms detailed above were actually put into practice, accession negotiations could start "without delay" after December 2004.

NOTES

1. See, in particular, Bertil Dunér and Edward Deverell, "Country Cousin: Turkey, the European Union and Human Rights," *Turkish Studies*, Vol.2, No.1 (2001), pp.1–24.
2. For a discussion of the issues not covered here see, in particular, Human Rights Watch, *Turkey: Human Rights and the European Union Accession Partnership* (London: Human Rights Watch, September 2000), text from the Human Rights Watch website, <http://www.hrw.org/reports/2000/turkey2>, hereinafter abbreviated as "HRW Report 2000," and Bertil Dunér and Liv Hammergren, "Turkey: Politization of Torture Care?," *Turkish Studies*, Vol.2, No.2 (2001), pp.41–62.
3. For the background to this process see, for example, William Park, "Turkey's European Candidacy: From Luxembourg to Helsinki—to Ankara?," *Mediterranean Politics*, Vol.5, No.3 (2000), pp.31–53; Ziya Öniş, "Luxembourg, Helsinki and Beyond: Towards an Interpretation of Recent Turkey-EU Relations," *Government and Opposition*, Vol.35, No.4 (2000), pp.463–83; William Hale, *Turkish Foreign Policy, 1774–2000* (London and Portland, OR: Frank Cass, 2000), pp.233–43.
4. *Conclusions of the [EU] Presidency, Copenhagen, June 21–22, 1993*; copy kindly supplied by Foreign and Commonwealth Office, London.
5. Luxembourg European Council, *Presidency Conclusions*, Dec. 12–13, 1997, para.25; available at <http://www.europa.eu.int/council/off>.
6. Helsinki European Council, *Presidency Conclusions*, Dec. 12–13, 1999; available at <http://www.ue.eu.int/newsroom>.
7. *Turkey: 2000 Accession Partnership* (Annex to *Proposal for a Council Decision*, Commission of the European Communities, Brussels, Nov. 8, 2000), from website of Representation of EU Commission in Turkey (<http://www.deltur.cec.eu.int>), hereinafter abbreviated as "APD."
8. *National Programme, Introduction and Political Criteria* (Unofficial Translation), from website of Turkish Prime Ministry, General Secretariat of EU Affairs, <http://www.abgs.gov.tr>.
9. In the words of the Constitutional Court's judgment. Reported on website of NTV television, <http://www.ntvmsnbc.com>, June 22, 2001.
10. For the party programs, see the websites of the Felicity Party (<http://www.saadetpartisi.org.tr>) and the Justice and Development Party (<http://www.akparti.org.tr>).

11. For details, see Dunér and Deverell (2001), pp.6–8.
12. In March 2002 a temporary flurry was caused when General Tuncer Kılınç, the Secretary of the National Security Council, expressed the view that Turkey should abandon its bid for eventual EU membership. However, General Hüseyin Kıvrıkoğlu, the Chief of the General Staff, quickly overruled General Kılınç by declaring that he had been speaking purely for himself and that membership of the EU was a "geostrategic" necessity for Turkey. Quoted in *Briefing* (Ankara, weekly) March 18, 2002, p.8. Meeting on May 30, 2002, the National Security Council also declared that "it was deemed appropriate that efforts with regard to our other obligations foreseen in the National Program [for the application of the *acquis communautaire*] should be speeded up," although this was linked to the condition that the EU should give a definite date for the start of accession negotiations. Obtained from the NTV website, May 30, 2002.
13. See, for instance, the survey by the widely respected Turkish Economic and Social Studies Foundation (TESEV) issued in June 2002 and summarized in *Briefing*, July 1, 2002, pp.7–9.
14. The English translation of the original text of the 1982 Constitution which is used here is that previously published on the website of the Ministry of Foreign Affairs in Ankara, <http://www.mfa.gov.tr>. All quotations given here are from this text.
15. *Türk Ceza Kanunu*. Besides being published in the Official Gazette, the texts of legal statutes are issued by private publishers in Turkey. The text quoted here is that edited by Sedat Bakıcı (Istanbul: Adalet Yayınları, 2000).
16. *Terörle Mücadele Kanunu*, text in İbrahim Pinar (ed.), *Terörle Mücadele Kanunu ve İnsan Hakları Sözleşmeleri* [Law for the Struggle against Terrorism and Human Rights Agreements] (Ankara: Seçkin Yayınları, 1998).
17. Other changes were to reduce the prison sentences of those previously convicted under this Article, resulting in a number of releases. See ibid., pp.32–3.
18. Notably, the Press Law and the Political Parties Law. For details, see Human Rights Watch, *Turkey: Violations of Free Expression in Turkey* (New York: Human Rights Watch, Feb. 1999), Section V, hereinafter abbreviated as "HRW Report 1999," text taken from Human Rights Watch website, <www.hrw.org/reports/1999/turkey>, and *Siyasi Partıller Kanunu* (No.2820), text taken from Mustafa Everdi (ed.), *Seçim Mevzuatı* [Election Regulations] (Ankara: 21 Yüzyıl Yayınları, n.d.), pp.96–159.
19. For details on many such cases see, for example, HRW Report 2000, section on "Safeguarding Freedom of Expression" and HRW Report 1999.
20. See, for example, Michael M. Gunter, "The Silent Coup: The Secularist-Islamist Struggle in Turkey," *Journal of South Asian and Middle Eastern Studies*, Vol.21, No.3 (1998), pp.1–12, and Mehran Kamrava, "Pseudo-Democratic Politics and Populist Possibilities: The Rise and Demise of Turkey's Refah Party," *British Journal of Middle East Studies*, Vol.25, No.2 (1998), pp.275–301.
21. APD, Annex.
22. Ibid.
23. For the full text of the Convention and its Protocols see, for example, Ian Brownlie (ed.), *Basic Documents on Human Rights* (Oxford: Clarendon Press, 3rd Edn. 1992), pp.326–62.
24. Ibid., Article 10.
25. The present English language text of the constitution, including these amendments, is published on the website of the Grand National Assembly of Turkey, <http://www.tbmm.gov.tr/anayasa/constitution.htm>. The quotations given here are drawn from this text. They cover only a fraction of the total package of amendments; for some others, see below.
26. *Bazi Kanunlarda Değişiklik Yapılmasına Dair Kanun* (No.4744), available on website of Grand National Assembly of Turkey, <http://www.tbmm.gov.tr/kanunlar/k4744.html>.
27. Ibid., Articles 1–4.
28. *Çeşitli Kanunlarda Değişiklik Yapılmasına Dair Kanun* (No.4748), Articles 2–5, available on website of Grand National Assembly of Turkey, <http://www.tbmm.gov.tr/kanunlar/k4748.html>. For explanatory summaries see, for example, reports on NTV website, March 27, 2002, and in *Milliyet* newspaper, internet edition (<http://www.milliyet.com.tr>), March 27, 2002.

29. An example is that of the former West Germany, where the Constitutional Court banned the Communist Party in 1956 on account of its undemocratic principles. A more crucial case affecting Turkey arose in 2001, when the former leaders of the Welfare Party appealed to the European Court of Human Rights in Strasbourg for annulment of the closure of the party by the Turkish Constitutional Court two years earlier. In a majority verdict of 4:3 the judges in Strasbourg decided that the closure had been justified on the grounds that it answered a "pressing social need" and, hence, did not violate the provisions of Article 11 of the Convention. See European Court of Human Rights, Section 3, *Case of Refah Partisi (The Welfare Party) and Others vs. Turkey: Judgement: Strasbourg, 31 July 2001*, paragraphs 83–4; text taken from website of Council of Europe, <http://hudoc.echr.coe.in t/hudoc>. However, in December 2001 the plaintiffs were given leave to appeal against this verdict, so there was a chance that it might be overturned. See NTV website, December 13, 2001.
30. For discussion of these points see, for example, Conor Cruise O'Brien, "What Rights Should Minorities Have?," in Georgina Ashworth (ed.), *World Minorities* (Sunbury: Quatermaine House and Minority Rights Group, 1977), p.xiv, and R.J. Vincent, *Human Rights and International Relations*, Vol.1 (Cambridge: Cambridge University Press, in association with the Royal Institute of International Affairs, 1986), p.80.
31. Council of Europe, *Framework Convention for the Protection of National Minorities* (Strasbourg, Council of Europe, European Treaty Series No.157, 1995). Text taken from Council of Europe website, <http://www.coe.int/eng/legaltxt>.
32. Will Kymlicka, "Misunderstanding Nationalism," *Dissent* (Winter 1995), p.132, quoted in Ümit Cizre Sakallıoğlu, "Historicizing the Present and Problematizing the Future of the Kurdish Problem: A Critique of the TOBB Report on the Eastern Question," *New Perspectives on Turkey*, No.14 (1996), p.6.
33. *Siyasi Partiler Kanunu* (see footnote 18), Article 81; *Seçimlerin Temel Hükümleri ve Seçmen Kütükleri Hakkında Kanun* (No.298), Article 58. Text quoted in Everdi (ed.), *Seçim Mevzuatı* (n.d.), pp.134–5, 217.
34. This ban was originally contained in Article 4 of the broadcasting law of 1994 (Law No.3984). The wording of the law carefully avoided the use of the word "Kurdish," stating that "radio and television broadcasts will be made in Turkish: however, for the purpose of teaching or imparting news those foreign languages which have made a contribution to the development of universal culture and scientific works can be used." This allowed the state broadcasting corporation (TRT) to broadcast programs in English and other languages, whereas Kurdish was apparently classed as a language which has not "made a contribution to universal culture." Text taken from HRW Report 1999, Section V, footnote 60. In July 2001 this law was amended by Law No.4746, Article 2 of which states that "The basis of broadcasts is that they should be in Turkish. However, broadcasts may be made for the purpose of teaching languages which have made a contribution to universal culture and scientific works or for broadcasting music or news in these languages." Text taken from website of Grand National Assembly of Turkey, <www.tbmm.gov.tr/kanunlar/k4746.html>. This provision was then further amended in August 2002 (see below).
35. APD, Annex.
36. The Council of Europe's European Charter for Regional or Minority Languages of 1992 provides that signatory states may take a number of measures ranging from the provision of primary and/or secondary education "in the relevant regional or minority languages" to "the teaching of the relevant regional or minority languages as an integral part of the curriculum ... at least to those pupils whose families so request and whose number is considered sufficient." However, only eight of the EU's existing member states have both signed and ratified the Charter and the APD gave no indication that Turkey would be required to do so. Council of Europe, *European Charter for Regional or Minority Languages*, Strasbourg, 5.XI.1992, European Treaty Series No.148, Article 8. Text taken from Council of Europe website, <http://www.coe.inst>.
37. For text, see Brownlie (1992), p.362.
38. *Türk Ceza Kanunu* (see note 15), Articles 125, 146–7, 450.
39. APD, Annex.

40. After a good deal of public discussion on this point, the first division of the Administrative Court (*Danıştay*) issued a decision to this effect on March 27, 2002. See NTV website, March 27, 2002.
41. The precedent cited was that of the ex-Nazi war criminal Rudolf Hess. See NTV website, May 28, 2002.
42. APD, Annex.
43. NTV website, May 30, 2002.
44. Quoted in Dunér and Deverell (2001), p.3.
45. House of Commons, Foreign Affairs Committee, *Turkey: Sixth Report of Session 2001–02*, HC 606 (London: Stationery Office, April 2002), p.22.
46. Quoted on NTV website, Aug. 3, 2002.
47. Ibid., July 31, Aug. 3, 2002.
48. Ibid., Aug. 5, 2002.
49. *Hürriyetim*, Aug. 5, 2002.

8
Intellectual Roots of Anti-European Sentiments in Turkish Politics: The Case of Radical Turkish Nationalism

NERGIS CANEFE and TANIL BORA

The aim of this contribution is to examine the intellectual roots of current anti-European sentiments actively embraced in select sectors of modern Turkish society and politics. Issues of Europe and Europeanness have long been contentious subjects among Turkish intellectuals, ideologues, revolutionaries, academics, bureaucrats and, of course, politicians. However, the current political climate, pre- or post-November 2002 elections, almost unilaterally points to radical Turkish nationalism and its parliamentary representative *Milliyetçi Hareket Partisi* (Nationalist Action Party—MHP) as the prime protagonist of anti-European attitudes and discourse. This is particularly true in the aftermath of the recent legislative reforms in Parliament. The MHP and its leaders indeed appear to be the only group that oppose Turkish efforts to fulfil the legal criteria regarding full membership in the European Union (EU).

Meanwhile, concerns raised by the party's leaders and the cynicism that has become a characteristic trait of radical nationalist politics and hints at the "hidden agenda" of the Europeans have a long history in Turkish political thought. It is, therefore, of crucial importance to examine contemporary anti-European debates in the context of existing intellectual traditions if one is to reach an assessment about the representativeness and rootedness of these current political gestures of a nativist nature. The most appropriate context for discussing such negative conceptions of European identity, European values and Europe's expectations and impositions on Turkey is the Republican tradition of nationalism/conservatism (*milliyetçi muhafazakarlık*). This intellectual and political tradition dates back to the early days of the National Assembly and the "Second Group" within it, which was later discarded from politics until the exercise of multi-party politics in the 1950s. In this work we present some of the key debates internal to this particular tradition of thought that had, and continues to have, wide-ranging repercussions in the fields of both party politics and grass-roots political movements alike. Our aim in doing so is to point out the parallels between the offerings of this well-embedded intellectual heritage and current arguments presented by the leaders of the MHP regarding Turkey's relations with Europe.

It is our belief that one of the weakest points of the discipline of political science is its lack of engagement with cultural and intellectual history, particularly the history of ideas. We strive to refurbish such a lack in the case of anti-European politics of the radical nationalist camp in Turkey. The benefits of this approach are threefold. First and foremost, this study reveals that the MHP in particular, and the radical nationalist movement in general, do not constitute a singular example of anti-European sentiments and criticism bordering on chronic cynicism in Turkish politics. Instead, the select intellectual history presented here confirms that they have been, and still are, part and parcel of a relatively long tradition of thought and political engagement in Republican Turkey—namely, the nationalist-conservative one. Therefore, the anti-European attitude presented by the Party is not to be regarded as unique or novel. It seems that with the rise of the MHP to political power in the 1999 elections anti-European ideas and sentiments found a new venue for circulation. Consequently, until 2002 they constituted a staple item in parliamentary discussions and ministerial speeches when the issue at hand was presumed to concern Turkey's national sovereignty. The remaining question concerns the segments of the population that the MHP represents and whether the party was elected primarily on the basis of its anti-European bias or other items in its agenda. Although this line of inquiry falls beyond the scope of the present study, it is of enough importance to keep in mind for the full assessment of the role played by radical nationalists in Turkish politics.

Second, undertaking an informed analysis of the intellectual history of the current political stand of radical Turkish nationalists confirms that ideological approaches and normative values articulated among these circles are not necessarily idiosyncratic truisms. On the contrary, they reflect the intertwined traditions of Turkism, Islamism, cultural purism, defensive nationalism and reverse Orientalism in Turkish political culture. Finally, as this study emphasizes, anti-European attitudes of radical nationalist pedigree are an integral part of grander political transformations, rather than an end in and of themselves. In the end, these three outcomes give us a better sense of the occurrences within Turkish society in terms of perceptions of Europe and Europeanness as well as modern Turkish identity. Furthermore, they provide an insight into the workings of the most xenophobic branch of Turkish nationalism and, as such, furbish political analysts and social scientists alike with a detailed picture of the possible long-term effects of the MHP's increased parliamentary involvement between 1999 and 2002.

WHY RADICAL TURKISH NATIONALISM AND HOW TO APPROACH IT?

The negative image of the Gray Wolves—an openly fascist youth branch of the MHP widely active during the 1970s—is still alive and well among European political observers. The MHP movement, which started under the leadership of Alpaslan Türkeş (1917–97) in the 1960s, has a long history of involvement with paramilitary insurgencies, organized political violence and state-centric totalitarian political scenarios. Furthermore, although the 1980 coup caused a temporary silencing of both the organizational cadres and the leadership, the MHP bounced back with renewed vigor soon afterwards. Developments that took place after the death of the movement's leader, however, led to noticeable changes in Turkish radical nationalists' self-perception and self-presentation. These alterations were further accentuated by the subsequent increase in the movement's parliamentary power and its new role in Turkish politics.[1]

It is generally agreed that, following the 1999 elections, the MHP's newly acquired position as a senior coalition partner with 18 percent of the vote was of great significance—both for Turkish politics and for Turkey's international relations. The post-cold war environment dictates that Turkey is no longer just a critical buffer zone. Instead, it is gradually maturing into a regional power, providing linkages between southeastern Europe, the Middle East and Central Asia. As such, its internal order became an increasing concern for the world at large.[2] In this context, the MHP's rise to power led to fears that Turkey could assume unnecessarily defensive, nationalist or even expansionist gestures and thus challenge the new dynamics of regional stability and security beyond repair. Skeptics refer to the MHP's involvement in the 1974 invasion of Cyprus and in the long history of diplomatic skirmishes with Greece as early signs of such an impending danger. The response of MHP leaders to the Kurdish insurgent leader Abdullah Öcalan's capture and imprisonment is also addressed as a case in point. MHP cadres continue to insist on carrying out the death penalty Öcalan was sentenced to, seeing it as a matter of "national pride." Similarly, the issue of Cyprus' accession to the EU is heavily criticized by leading figures in the movement as an attempt to complete the Greek *Megali Idea* and to turn Cyprus into yet another Crete cleansed of its Muslim Turkish heritage. In these and other related areas—such as the acceptance of a repentance law for Kurdish militants and the reformation of the State Security Courts (*Devlet Güvenlik Mahkemeleri*) that function above and beyond the Turkish judiciary system—the MHP indeed appeared to be a major obstacle for the long-awaited reforms towards democratization of the Turkish political system and the anticipated new phase of peaceful regional conduct with countries such as Greece.

Whether the MHP is indeed a powerful actor in Turkish politics and destined to raise its position to hegemonic heights despite its disappearance from the Parliament with the November 3, 2002 elections, is a difficult question to answer due to the fluctuating nature of the Republican political system. Still, the fact that Turkish politics epitomizes a long tradition of identification of a strong nation with a combination of extensive state power and strong military might provides the movement with a relatively more acceptable ideological entry-point to the system—especially compared with Marxist or Islamist parties and movements. As the profiles of Türkeş and other key figures of the movement suggest, the radical nationalist political elite even wanted to act in the name of the state in order to salvage the national polity. That is why in recent Turkish history radical nationalist cadres exhibited such a strong tendency towards the orchestration of paramilitary actions. Another aspect of this tendency is insistence on the heavy-handedness of state policies, especially in the area of minority and group rights. As the MHP traditionally envisions itself as an organization with a mission to protect the Turkish state in the name of the Turkish nation and visa versa, the party line wishes to target swiftly any perceived challenge to state security. An equally important issue concerning the MHP's influence in Turkish politics is the vision it provides for Turkish society. The presentation of an overall political program that includes mechanisms of implementation for charted political objectives and restructuring of the party as a bureaucratic, democratic body are some of the recent inventions of the younger, and seemingly tamer, cadres of radical nationalists. These developments suggest that the MHP might have begun to accept the rules of pluralistic democracy. However, whether these are only superficial changes remains a disturbing question. Parliamentary speeches regarding the November 3, 2002 elections indicated that radical nationalists still experience great difficulties in sharing power or negotiating with present or possible future allies. The foundations of this tendency are two-fold. First, such an attitude might stem from the assumption that the center-right support for the party in the 1999 elections under the leadership of ex-academic Devlet Bahçeli was for the traditional line the MHP followed and there is, therefore, little need for compromise, innovation or collaboration. Second, the movement's self-claimed status of representing the whole of the nation leaves very little room for negotiating with other movements or parties for the attainment of goals regarding the "common good." In this regard, how far the MHP's new political idiom transcends the boundaries of its party offices and can be translated into active politics is an issue that requires critical examination.

Finally, there is the deep-seated problem of racism and fascism that colors the entire history of the radical Turkish nationalist movement. In the past, its elevation of pure Turkish blood fed into political violence against various minorities, particularly against the Alevi population of Turkey.[3] The MHP's official line has since embraced these Asia Minor Shiites as "true Turks of Anatolia." However, issues concerning the Kurds of Turkey and various small religious minorities remain unresolved. The repercussions of Turkist racism are also felt in issues related to the Turkish state's involvement with Muslim and Turkish speaking or Turkic minorities outside the borders of Turkey. This includes the Cyprus problem and relations with Greece which, to say the least, has almost always elicited hawkish reactions from the leaders of the movement. The following pages trace the origins of this attitude of radical and uncompromising difference within the larger spectrum of political ideologies and intellectual traditions in Republican Turkish history. As such, we hope to situate the relevance of Turkish radical nationalism beyond the bounds of calculations of parliamentary gains and losses. Such an approach allows the examination of the notion of Europeanness in modern Turkish society as an ongoing phenomenon rather than a singular or extraordinary event. In this regard, without understanding the extent of the rootedness and connectedness of the radical nationalist ideology in Turkey, it is futile to try to reach informed conclusions regarding the sphere and character of its wider influence.

ORGANIZED RADICAL NATIONALIST POLITICS IN TURKEY:
HISTORICAL BACKGROUND

Radical Turkish nationalism has a long history that extends beyond the confines of the Republican regime. Meanwhile, in its current form, this populist political movement is heavily intertwined with the leading ideologies of Kemalism and political Islam. As such, it constitutes an important part of the *status quo* in Turkish politics.

Republican Turkish politics represent a relatively high degree of institutionalization of political parties, despite the fact that it also suffers from chronic fragmentation, ideological polarization and electoral volatility.[4] This unique combination of organizational grandeur and lack of stable and reciprocal relations between Turkish political parties and their constituencies often leads to sudden and significant changes in the results of consecutive elections. Interestingly, at least up until 2002, the parliamentary representative of radical Turkish nationalists—MHP—has traditionally benefited from these oscillations. Since 1960s, accentuated by the context of successive short-lived and ideologically incompatible coalition governments, MHP cadres gradually increased their grip over Turkish politics. In addition, they became a considerable force located within the state apparatus by occupying significant long-term posts in the ministries and the bureaucracy.[5]

The continual influence of radical nationalism in Turkish politics can be attributed to several factors, among which one must first and foremost list the set of large-scale socio-economic changes that affected Turkish society particularly between 1950s and 1970s, the kind considered foundational to the birth of nativist fascist movements—such as massive rural-urban migration and peripheralization of the national economy.[6] A more recent interpretation of events points to the post-1980s erosion of the legacy of center-right politics and hence the swing to radical nationalism. Although both factors are worthy of attention, there is also a third and more structural reason behind the MHP's gradual but steady rise to prominence. That is, since the 1960s there has been a marked relationship in the making that brought state-sponsored Kemalism and radical Turkish nationalism close enough to be considered as allied ideologies in certain areas, such as regulations related to citizenship, cold-war anti-communism, migration policies and the cultural politics of the Republic.

The MHP belongs to a political tradition equating the Turkish nation state with the Turkish nation as opposed to following a pan-Turkist path. The party was founded by the generation of Turkists who initiated the multifaceted radical nationalist political activities during the years 1945–70. There were several attempts at total state control over "grass-roots" radical Turkish nationalism up until the Second World War years, culminating in the famous 1944 trials targeting the ideologues of the Turkish nationalist right. However, in the post-war environment the "Soviet threat" opened the doors for new alliances, leading to the establishment of *Türk Kültür Ocağı* (The Fraternity of Turkish Culture) in 1946.[7] In this new phase of establishing alliances between variant forms of Turkish nationalism, the tenets of radical Turkish nationalism were redefined as Turkey-based Turanism, racism and the cleansing of alien blood from the Turkish race within the borders of the Turkish nation state (targeting the remaining Christians as well as Jewish communities of Turkey), promotion of an ethnically pure state, militarism and anti-communism. In turn, its new make-up rendered the movement more eligible for open or semi-legal partnerships in mainstream politics. Particularly after the victory of the Justice Party (*Adalet Partisi*—AP) in 1965, the ultra-nationalist circles began to receive increasing support from the government as a useful force to suppress the oppositional and revolutionary left-wing movements. In some circles they were even identified as auxiliary forces of the state.[8]

This aforementioned period of state-induced tolerance for radical nationalism coincided with the adoption of a militant vision by the MHP. During the 1970s, a grass-roots fascist movement flourished in its youth branches, particularly through the wide network of the *Ülkü Ocakları* (Idealist Associations) active in different sectors of the economy, schools, neighborhood units, etc. Meanwhile, the critical factor leading to the recent popular appeal of radical Turkish nationalism did not emerge until the aftermath of the 1980 coup. During the 1980s, the militant branch of the movement gradually embraced the ideological formulation of the synthesis of Turkism and Sunni Islam (*Türk-İslam sentezi*—TIS).[9] In addition, the once-exalted mottoes of the radical nationalists—such as absolute obedience to the party, explicit exhibits of military discipline and fighting spirit, glorification of the movement's leader to almost cult status, self-sacrifice for the "state" and adherence to strict hierarchy—seem to have been shuffled to the background of the movement's agenda. As a result, since the 1990s radical Turkish nationalism is, more often than not, included in Turkish politics not as an extremist side element but as a relatively central force. As such, it represents a successful cross-fertilization of select elements of the state-sponsored Kemalist nationalist program with grass-roots nationalist and conservative politics.[10] Ultimately, establishing alliances around this particular amalgam of themes not only strengthens the political position of radical Turkish nationalists, it also elevates the mental of patriotic Turkish nationalism beyond the auspices of state-sponsored research institutions, the bureaucracy and the army by openly addressing the concerns of Islamist and conservative camps in Turkish politics within the limits of parliamentary politics. Needless to say, radical nationalists had to share the stage with left-wing patriotic nationalists during the 1970s, market-oriented liberalist political parties during the 1980s and the pro-Islamist camp, as well as Republican nationalists, since mid-1990s. In this sense, it would be hasty to suggest that the MHP is the only source that reveals the true colors of nationalism in Turkey. However, it would be equally erroneous to argue that the kind of nationalism, xenophobia and protectionism honored by the radical nationalists occupies only a marginal position in Turkish politics. As the remainder of this essay reveals, the current radical nationalist stance signifies the culmination of the intertwining of several trends in Turkish politics that traditionally lie at the right of center. In this sense, its influence appears to be related to more than just the success of a relatively minor political party.

EUROPE, EUROPEANNESS AND TURKISH NATIONAL IDENTITY: CONTRIBUTIONS OF MHP TO THE DEBATE

Europe constitutes a key part of Turkey's relations with the outside world. However, it would be a mistake to reduce the Turkish society and state's relations with Europe to the issue of inclusion in the European Union. Turkey has a long history of opposing, admiring, copying, denying, naming and judging things European. In this regard, the Turkish modernization project and its defenders as well as its critics have a complex relationship with the idea of Europe and what constitutes European identity. The current state of relations between European states and Turkey, revolving primarily around the issue of inclusion in the EU, thus has to be examined in light of this cultural background and the political debates that lie beyond the accession debate.

Notwithstanding these introductory observations, particularly between 1999 and 2002, MHP leaders and ideologues seem to have taken over the spokesmanship of Turkey's "national interests versus European impositions" controversy. Following their electoral success in 1999, MHP leaders claimed that they represented not just the interests of a party but the Turkish nation itself. One area that the degree of accuracy of such statements could be examined is non-MHP-related appropriation and usage of similar concepts, ideals and policies in Turkish politics regarding Turkey's relations with Europe. This task is relegated to the last two sections of this essay. However, in order to establish a frame for comparative analysis, in this section we examine the official MHP discourse on Turkey's relations with Europe and what Europeanness stands for.

Patriotic Turkish nationalism always spoke in the language of mass resistance and salvation from imperial incursions and dominance. Over the years, the authoritarian tendencies of Kemalist bureaucrats and politicians tended to reduce the credibility of these claims. Still, apart from the Republican Turkish Army, which traditionally acted as the bastion of protection for the Republican State[11] and the original fortress of Kemalism—*Cumhuriyet Halk Partisi* (Republican People's Party—CHP)—significant sectors of modern Turkish society also embraced at least some of the founding myths of the Turkish nation state and the accompanying history of Turkish nationhood. In effect, recent developments in radical nationalist politics suggest that the propagation of the *Official Turkish History Thesis*, which elevates the Turkish people to the status of one of the founding members of the privileged clan of ancient civilizations, is far from dead. Instead, it is re-appropriated and reactivated in order to fuel large-scale popular reactions to European expectations of changes in Turkish legal, political and economic affairs.

Initially the second largest party in the Turkish parliament—between August and November 2002—the MHP enjoyed the position of first seat due to ongoing governmental crisis. As such, the stance taken by the party officials *vis-à-vis* European Union, and in general the standards set by international bodies, mattered as gestures reflecting the opinions of more than just the dedicated nationalists. As already mentioned, it is now the common assumption that the MHP's 1999 electoral success was due to the shift of votes from the nationalist-conservative segments of the center-right *Anavatan Partisi* (Motherland Party—ANAP) and *Doğru Yol Partisi* (True Path Party—DYP), as well as the Islamist *Refah Partisi* (Welfare Party—RP) and its continuation *Fazilet Partisi* (Virtue Party—FP).[12] During the 1990s, at least the founding leaders of all these parties mentioned above were by and large critical of dependency on Europe and in favor of further assertion of Turkish traditions and values in society. In this regard, the MHP's ambivalent attitude towards Europe complied with much of its wider constituency. However, the latest MHP involvements for reversing the newly established ban on capital punishment in Turkey suggest that there are limits to MHP cadres' desire to please a larger section of the electorate. Indeed, the MHP Party Program of 1999 defines the unified Turkish nation as the sole social and cultural basis of the country's existence. Even the emphasis on the importance of freedom of expression is constricted by the clause that it is possible to sustain such freedoms as long as the national unity of the country, the public good and the moral values of the Turkish nation are not harmed. In a similar vein, although the MHP's former leader, Devlet Bahçeli, made repeated claims that his party has "no enmity against Europe" and that it has "no intention of making Turkey a closed society," he is quick to underline the importance of preserving one's national character, unity and sovereignty.[13] Similarly, whichever changes have to be made to improve the Turkish state's record on human rights, Bahçeli insisted that it had to be done in a way that respects the sensitivities of the Turkish nation and in response to global changes, not just in accordance with demands from European countries.[14] In effect, the world map within which MHP leaders situated Turkey includes the regions of the Caucasus, the Middle East and the

Balkans, and does not really include Europe.[15] The center of this map is identified as Eurasia, the landmass critical for the wellbeing of the "Turkish World." Within these parameters, Europe and the EU are accused of maintaining a hostile and alienating attitude towards Turkish people and are called upon to correct their actions and keep the agreements signed in the past. The EU is particularly frowned upon for acting with prejudice in regard to the Cyprus issue and for blaming the Turkish people of Cyprus for their own suffering. Recent developments that took place at the 2002 Copenhagen summit only furthered these assumptions, although the MHP is no longer an actor in the Turkish Parliament.

Highlighting all these concerns about what Europe and the Europeans want from Turkey, the MHP party press published a special edition of their bi-monthly journal *Türkiye ve Siyaset* [Turkey and Politics] in April 2002 on Turkey-EU relations. Many of the key figures of the party organization took part in this endeavor and published essays on special aspects of Turkey's EU membership process. Among these, four are worth mentioning here. The opening essay, carrying the signature of Devlet Bahçeli himself, once again reminds the public of the precious geopolitical and geo-cultural position of Turkey and, as such, Turkey is needed more than Turkey needs others in the region, including European countries.[16] He then states that EU-Turkey relations are heavily tainted with prejudice on the part of the Europeans, only some of which were possible to eradicate thanks to the active approach taken by the fifty-seventh Turkish government, of which the MHP was a coalition partner. Bahçeli mentions three "critical points" that will determine the future of EU-Turkey relations: the handling of the Cyprus problem, EU perspectives on terrorist organizations that threaten political peace and the territorial integrity of Turkey—that is, the Kurdish movement—and the remedy of the continual delays in the delivery of promised financial aid packages. Bahçeli concludes his essay by pointing out the futility of, and self-defeatism stemming from, the constant questioning of what more Turkey needs to do to in order to qualify for EU membership. He suggests Turkey should turn the tables and question what European countries need to do in order to make it acceptable for Turkey to become a full member of the EU.[17] Bahçeli also questions the local trend of apologizing for what he considers to be "unjustifiable behavior" on the part of European countries concerning such issues as their refusal to list the PKK in Turkey as a terrorist organization and their denial of the "national importance" of Cyprus for Turkey.[18] In his view, if Turkey's membership to the EU is to happen it must be regarded as a matter of the meeting of great (equal) civilizations, rather than Turkey learning to be European. Bahçeli states that the current slogan of "EU membership is the only choice for Turkey" is disgraceful and degrading for the Turkish nation. Accordingly, a great nation will always have choices and should never give up its right to negotiate for its own ends.[19]

The works of Ahmet Selçuk Can, Osman Karacakurt and Selim Kuzu (in the same volume) take some of the issues mentioned by Bahçeli further.[20] In Can's essay, Ankara-Brussels relations are reassessed from the point of view of inconsistencies in EU politics in terms of guarding Turkish interests. Can argues that the unilateral imposition of "membership regulations" on Turkey should be regarded as an infringement on Turkey's internal affairs in the areas of national security, politics and economics. He then raises the issue of Armenian genocide and regards the European recognition of it as a highly unfriendly act that has no justification. He suggests this act alone signifies the lurking of Europe's racist prejudice against Turkey once more. The attitude of the European Parliament "against Turkey" is to be regarded as a mirror for European sentiments regarding Turkey *in toto*. In this context, the European Parliament is characterized as a chaotic and prejudiced platform of debate lacking basic principles of ethical conduct.[21] Karacakurt, on the other hand, proposes that the pro-EU camp in Turkish politics is tainted by the over-representation of the PKK and the representatives of fundamentalist Islam. Both groups are to be regarded as targeting the unity of the Turkish state and as awaiting the downfall of the Republican political regime. He also points out Greek involvement in the membership negotiations and warns that the Greek government will support the Turkish application only in exchange for a settlement of both the Cyprus question and the "Aegean problem" to Greek benefit.[22] Finally, Selim Kuzu presents a survey of references in Greek newspapers to the EU debate in Turkey and states that editorials such as those published on the subject in *Cumhuriyet* created the impression that Turkey had no other choice but to comply with European norms in order to survive as an independent nation state.[23] All in all, these four essays provide a succinct summary of the MHP's pre-November 2002 election understanding of Turkey's relations with the EU and the points of contention that the MHP raises at the political platform. The next task is to examine whether such concerns are brought to debate solely by the radical nationalist cadres and, if not, in which other circles they are considered important issues.

THE NATIONALIST-CONSERVATIVE TRADITION AND EUROPE

From the early days of the Republican regime onwards—among some circles of opposition politics in Turkey—Kemalist mono-party rule and its modernist cadres were typically characterized as blindly Western-oriented and detached from their own roots. Furthermore, they were pitied as being incapable of discerning the hidden desires of the Turkish people and the incessant plans for its abuse, believed to have been devised by "old and calculating Europe."[24] In response to such accusations, the "new Turkey" rhetoric of republicans of the past as well as new generation republicans proposes that the Turkish nation is more than capable of fulfilling the requirements of being "civilized" without copying Europeans verbatim. A classical trend on the "oppositional" side of this debate is set by the nationalist-conservative camp, which over the years combined the strongest aspects of radical nationalist, conservative and Islamist discourses in an effort to produce a counter-narrative to Republican iterations of post-Ottoman Turkish history.[25] An early representative of this trend is the author of the Turkish National Anthem, Mehmet Akif, a poet and thinker of dedicated conservative and Islamic beliefs. In his words, Western civilization is nothing but a monster with a single remaining tooth (*medeniyet denen tek dişi kalmış canavar*). In a similar vein, when referring to the ingenious creation of the Sun-Language Theory of early Republican years that glorified the history of Turks as being ahead of all other civilizations in the Bronze Age, the nationalist ideologue of early Republican years and well-known journalist Yunus Nadi suggests that "Although Renaissance brought about significant changes that helped the veil of ignorance to be removed in European societies, Christianity and the piousness and superstitions that came with it have never left the European psyche fully."[26] Indeed, even the group of Republican intellectuals—nicknamed "those dedicated to 'Humanist Anatolia'"—did not hesitate to raise the issue of European double-standards, the kind that neglect historical achievements of non-European peoples across the Mediterranean basin and the fertile crescent while glorifying the Greco-Roman heritage of the Europeans.

However, the sincere yearning for the title "civilized" always stopped the Republican ideologues short of denying European values and norms. Instead, the nationalist elite with Kemalist and/or modernist inclinations tend to aspire to the political and historical trajectories of change that are characteristic of European nation states. In this sense, the novelty of the nationalist-conservative tradition is its qualified and persistent denial of all things European except select developments in the areas of science and technology. This intellectual attitude is certainly some steps ahead of the traditional Islamist critique of the West en bloc in the sense that nationalist-conservative anti-Europeanism is directly related to the perception of what modern-day Turkey is and ought to be, rather than yearning for a lost golden age of imperial grandeur. According to the conservative ideologue Nihad Sami Banarlı, for instance, the process of westernization is described as a deliberate act of weakening targeted states, followed by forceful imposition of norms and values that benefit Europe alone.[27] To quote:

> We had two choices: either to achieve an unforeseen miracle on the basis of making the West like our national characteristics and genuine intellectual capacity, and to reintroduce ourselves with our original costumes, traditions, alphabet, literary and art works and civilization in order to make them accept us and overcome their prior negative perceptions, or, to become totally conversant in the idiom Western civilization ... in order to use it to prove that we are far from being the dark and backward nation as they have long imagined and to insert that we have been one of the brightest success stories in the history of all nations. The second route is the one to be taken by the realist idealist.[28]

Banarlı's main worry, shared by many other nationalist-conservative thinkers, is the loss of the true character and values of what he identifies as the Muslim Turkish society and civilization. Still, his line of thought could best be classified as modernist and therefore is not fully representative of the nationalist-conservative tradition. The latter produced much more vehement critics of European history and society. According to the majority of its ideologues during the 1960 and 1970s, the heyday of the radical nationalist movement at the grass-roots organization level and its formulation of a new political rhetoric—westernization—and especially the willing espousal of European civilization, are to be regarded as a shameful loss of self, born out of the unfortunate circumstances of the decline of the Turkish people in the arena of world politics.[29] It is possible to detect a certain degree of *cultural pessimism* regarding the interaction between different societies and civilizations. It is as if such an interaction was to take place only in the context of a defeat and at the mercy of the winning party. One way to diffuse this sentiment has been to emphasize the achievements of Turkish people throughout history with direct reference to European sources themselves. This is also a strategy devised to take action against the Orientalist trend that reduces "eastern peoples" to a herd incapable of producing or enjoying civilization. Typical examples of such an undertaking are produced by the literary figure İsmail Hami

Danişmend.³⁰ According to his analysis, from democracy to science—and even in the spheres of theatre and the arts, Turkish influence has been paramount in the formation of what we know as the Western civilization today. This insistence on the intrinsic value of all things Turkish is the second theme that brings nationalists—in some instances this categorization includes Kemalists—and conservatives closer in the creation of a new, hybrid idiom with an ever-expanding following.

Meanwhile, there remain a few weak points in this alliance. For instance, the nationalist-conservative idiom has a real problem with the cultural as well as political reforms of the Kemalist regime during the founding days of the Republic. Seen as a continuation of the "infamous" Tanzimat tradition of "mimicking the West" during the late Ottoman era, these reforms are regarded as fundamentally flawed due to their imitationist nature.³¹ Based on a barren reproduction of the founding father of Turkish nationalism Ziya Gökalp's dichotomous formulation of culture-civilization, nationalist-conservative ideologues are rather keen on caricaturizing the weaknesses and personal obsessions of those who paved the way for the wholesale modernization of Turkish society. Accordingly, these elite bureaucrats forgot their own culture while running after someone else's civilization. In contrast, the authentic Muslim Turk is portrayed as the epitome of resistance to alienation, loss of one's true identity and to what is called by the Islamist poet-thinker Sezai Karakoç "auto-colonization."³² Westernization, in this regard, is equated with giving up one's status as a member of a worthy and powerful nation with a proud history. In its name, Turkish people were forced to face the disgraceful lifestyle of "living like the French while being ashamed of even mentioning one's Turkishness."³³ Cosmopolitan and Europeanized forms of identity are thus considered as something that Turkish society could admire only at the expense of its own authentic identity.³⁴ Here, the transposition of communal and national identities in the formulation of Turkishness is noteworthy. By doing so, the nationalist-conservative tradition leaves hardly any space for even a minimal dose of "difference" among the members of what is deemed as Turkish society. In this framework, the arch-enemy is identified as the westernized, Europeanized and therefore "alienated" Turkish elite and intelligentsia, regarded as deserters of their own culture, heritage and religion in their attempts for achieving similitude with the West through servitude to it.³⁵ Islamist conservative writers such as Ahmet Kabaklı goes as far as to describe this presumed process as "reverse levying" (*tersine Yeniçerileşme*) in the sense that the West is portrayed as now being in the position of assimilating Muslim Turks for its imperial gains. Interestingly, similar depictions of the alienation of the Turkish intelligentsia can sometimes be located in the writings of leftist Kemalist thinkers. It is true that this latter group's main concern is related to the Marxist construct of the "working people" of the country who are exploited to further enrich Western capitalists. On the other hand, this example proves that the theme of "selling the country" for closer relations with Western powers in the name of Europeanization is an old and weathered one in Turkish political thought.

Some of the earliest examples of these characterizations are found in the Turkish literary tradition of the late Ottoman era, such as the Felatun Bey of Ahmet Mithad or the ethically degraded evil figures of Peyami Safa's novels. These fictitious figures were all deformed beyond recognition and salvation in the name of their blind admiration of the West, and Europe in particular.[36] This trend of caricaturizing and externalizing Western-oriented groups and classes is symptomatic of a marked inability to come to terms with the transformations that affected the whole imperial socio-political system as well as related networks of economic relations. Instead, the nationalist-conservative tradition opts for totalitarian scenarios bordering on fascism and aiming at either the preservation of the "old order" or a totally regulated scheme of change in Turkish society. In this context, radical nationalist insistence on the protection of the Turkish state and nation to the degree of not complying with democratic norms and regulations affecting both individual and group rights with the pretext of resisting to what is imposed by the EU can hardly be regarded as a singular or even original gesture in Turkish political and intellectual history. Classical works produced in the nationalist-conservative tradition such as D. Mehmet Doğan's manifesto *Batılılaşma İhaneti* [The Treachery of Westernization] have already pointed out the dangers of alliances with Europe and admiration of European ways, norms and values.[37] Similarly, conservative thinker Nurettin Topçu had long theorized about the problem-laden issue of "not taking after the West" and cherishing one's original, superior culture.[38] For Topçu, this is matter of saving one's spirit and soul in the face of the impending danger of total, albeit informal, colonization. In his words, "While the others have their vision stuck in [conquering] the universe, we should look within ourselves."[39] Another thinker worth mentioning in this context is Cemil Meriç, who is keen to emphasize the difference between "us" and "Westerners" at the level of essences. According to Meriç, the Western, particularly the European, "success story" has come about thanks to pitiless barbarian and tyrannical acts of destruction and occupation of other nations.[40] Furthermore, he describes Westerners as those who lack ethical principles, who shamelessly engage in double-dealings and, worst of all, as those capable of hiding their true aspirations and feelings under the mask of self-control.[41] Such marked anti-European sentiments are readily reproduced in the public addresses and ideological statements of radical nationalists.

IMPERIALISM, CRUSADES, COMMUNISM AND OTHER "WESTERN ILLS"

In nationalist-conservative political discourse, Europe is regarded first and foremost as a threat ready to inflict a multitude of incurable ills upon "non-Western" societies. It is thus described as a pollutant that cannot be tackled via rational or pragmatic means. Furthermore, this presumed contaminating effect of all things European is deemed to be not contextual but absolute. And what lies at its roots is Christianity. The political culture of Christianity, best observed in the bloody history of the Crusades, is described as obsession with the annihilation of the Turks, the flag-bearers of Muslim civilization. The dynamics of imperialism, as well as the dynamics of what we know as the modern civilization, are thus to be interpreted in the light of this ancient antagonism.[42] Even among the secular Kemalist reactionaries there are some who prescribe to this satanization of Western history if and when things go wrong regarding Turkish national interests at the international level. The theme of ancient and unresolved feuds therefore constitutes yet another line of thought that strengthens the position of nationalist-conservative idiom in Turkish politics.

A pamphlet prepared at the İzmir branch of the key MHP grass-roots organization *Ülkü Ocakları*, dated 1970, is symptomatic of such fears of annihilation hidden under the disguise of modernization.[43] Its main theme is the "true nature" of the annual culture and arts festival in the ancient Aegean site of Ephesus: "Yesterday, the imperialism of the Crusades came and occupied our lands with their knights in armour, their dukes, their armies. Today, they come with their missionaries, foreign schools, and peace workers."[44] Turkish radical nationalists, while existing under the right wing of the United States in the name of the fight against the "Red Peril," were thus cleansed of their sins by attacking the "cultural imperialism" of the Europeans. In this context, with a strange twist, Communism is also associated with Europe and cosmopolitanism. It is regarded as part and parcel of departing from traditional values and losing the sense of one's community of origins.[45] In turn, this loosely defined horror of losing one's "cultural independence"—a discursive characteristic of 1970s—was transformed into anti-EU attitudes during the 1980s and 1990s. Needless to say, the fundamentalist Islamist trend of denying European influences solely by virtue of their foreignness contributed further to this trend.

In summary, the nationalist-conservative tradition assumes the existence of "natural ties" between alienation due to infatuation with the West and left-wing politics. To this end, Islamist conservative ideologue Ahmet Kabaklı argues that "Hammer and sickle, the star of David and the Cross are all symbols of Western imperialism."[46] The fact that the nationalist-conservative idiom oversees the Marxist critiques of both capitalism and imperialism could only be explained by the categorical rejection of "all Western ideologies" as foreign. In effect, political Islam's traditional leader Necmettin Erbakan spelled this strategy out in many of his public addresses.[47] Accordingly, being exposed to Western and, in particular, European traditions of thought makes one vulnerable to the damaging influence of extremisms of all kinds, Communism being the most obvious.[48] In turn, the nationalist-conservative conviction that Turkish socialists and communists are the worst kind of traitors—as they come from within—is readily appropriated by the radical nationalist cadres. Similar worries include the existence of hideous foreign plans of destruction of the Turkish nation to be carried out by native informers and agents of outside forces. Europe, in this regard, is regularly cited as the site where evil comes from and around which Turks should always have their wits about them.

CONCLUSION

In the aftermath of the general elections held on November 3, 2002, there are at least some signs of the adoption of a more civic and democratic political culture in Turkey and a more accommodating definition of Turkish national identity. A major case in point is the continual parliamentary approval of the legal adjustments required by the EU accession plans. However, with the continuation of the Kurdish problem in the southeast, the ongoing debate around Turkey's entry into the Union— especially regarding the issue of whether Europe wants or respects Turks and their national interests—and the unresolved Cyprus dispute, in addition to recurrent waves of political violence targeting Muslim minorities in the Balkans and the Caucuses, the appeal of radical Turkish nationalism is likely to remain even if they are no longer represented in the Turkish Parliament. In this contribution, we presented the argument that the *roots* of the MHP's political rhetoric lie deep in Turkish society and political culture. Its political promise, therefore, cannot be regarded as a momentary success resulting from opportunistic calculations of select political leaders. The movement's political idiom, although lacking a clear-cut vision, certainly conveys a strong sense of pride and self-sufficiency as a distinct nation. Europe, in this context, is defined just as *one of many* sites from which Turkish society can draw benefits. In line with many of the key thinkers and ideologues within the nationalist-conservative tradition, MHP cadres ridicule the desire to comply with European norms and regulations as a pitiful gesture of alienated intellectuals and self-interested politicians. Accordingly, Europeanness is by no means deemed as an objective to be honored by modern Turkish society. Instead, relations with Europe are defined as a matter of primarily economical and security-related alliances. As discussed in the previous sections, both the former party leader Devlet Bahçeli's public addresses on the issue and internal party documents and debates point to this end.

Considering the fact that the rhetoric traditionally entertained by radical Turkish nationalists has come dangerously close to totalitarian fanaticism more than once during the 40-year history of the movement, their current tactic of convincing the public that Turkey is not *obligated* to follow the model of an open and democratic society—as defined by the Europeans—may well be alarming. This is all the more so as the movement successfully defines an ethically charged communitarian identity. In other words, it does offer a powerful alternative to being classified as a "developing country" with second-class politics and a second-class economy. MHP cadres openly claim to speak for the Turkish people who wrongfully suffer from anxieties related to being ridiculed or looked down upon by Europeans in particular and Westerners in general. In this context, the more Europeanness is presented as an ideal state of human civilization that Turks are yet to reach, the more ammunition becomes available to the ideologues and leaders of radical Turkish nationalism. In addition, their motto of reinserting the "Turkish nation" as an "honorable, successful, strong and self-sufficient people" in history can resonate with groups that are not necessarily of a radical nationalist dedication. Their loss of seats at the November 2002 elections could perhaps bring forward some changes in their rhetoric, although the party organization is yet to come to terms with what happened and why. At present their tendency is to radicalize their discourse rather than tame it.

As the history of the nationalist-conservative trend in Turkish politics proves, radical Turkish nationalists are far from having to reinvent the wheel. Rather, they are the beneficiaries of a long tradition of Europhobia which identifies Europe and other Western societies as forces of evil that violate the true, authentic identity of Muslim Turks while stealing away their self-confidence. This phenomenon, in a way, can be categorized as the "Oriental" re-enactment of the known Huntingtonian thesis on the clash of civilizations.[49] Like its Occidental version, it shields the true nature of the problems of socio-political transformation and economic globalization and manages to divert the attention to sanctified cultural essentials instead. Perhaps, in this regard, anti-European sentiments reproduced by the MHP—and the intellectual tradition that it relies upon—can be regarded as part and parcel of the *status quo* in a world where fundamentalist, revivalist and nativist movements are as much in demand as those dreaming of change, interaction and the establishment of new systems of governance above and beyond the nation state unit. If so, radical Turkish nationalists characterize Turkish society only as much as Le Pen does the French or Haider did the Austrian. In other words, as much as one should not minimize the role played by radical nationalism, its parliamentary potential and the rich tradition of nativist critique it benefits from, one should refrain from being alarmed about their presence to the extent of making generalizations that encompass the whole of modern Turkish society.

This cautionary observation notwithstanding, Turkish radical nationalists are to be separated from their European counterparts due to the fact that extreme right parties across the Continent are by and large in agreement with the existence and exhalation of a common, and presumably superior, European heritage.[50] Even though the core ideological stance of the MHP and European radical nationalist parties such as *Die Republikaner* and *Deutsche Volksunion* in Germany, *Vlaams Blok* in Belgium, or *Centrumdemocraten* and *Centrumpartij '86* in the Netherlands seem to exhibit common features, the issue of Europeanness remains an "alien" concept for the Turkish radical nationalists whereas for the others it is a matter of cultural rootedness. In this sense, it would be apt to suggest that radical nationalism acts as a restricting force on Turkish politics *vis-à-vis* Europe in comparison to parties and movements of a similar kind within Europe. It would, of course, be a much more rewarding exercise to look into the attitudes of fascist and/or radical nationalist parties in countries surrounding Europe such as Poland, Russia and the Balkans. Only then can one observe an accurate picture of how idiosyncratic the MHP is in its definition of what Europe is and what Europeanness stands for. This, however, remains the task of the comparative analyst.

NOTES

1. A select number of works in the literature on radical Turkish nationalism indicate a decided change towards a more complex, comparative and interdisciplinary understanding of right-wing nationalist movements in Turkish society. However, the bulk of the research done on the issue belongs to other genres—such as journalism and popular history—and possesses a highly polemical character. Of the scholarly works that pay attention to radical nationalism, the majority do so in the larger context of political, social and economic changes in Turkey during a specified time-period. See Çiğdem Balım-Harding (ed.), *Turkey: Political, Social and Economic Challenges in the 1990s* (Leiden: E.J. Brill, 1995); Atilla Eralp, Muharrem Tunay and Birol Yesilada (eds.), *The Political and Socioeconomic Transformation of Turkey* (Westport, CT: Greenwood, 1993); Larry Diamond (ed.), *Political Culture and Democracy in Developing Countries* (Boulder, CO: Lynne Rienner, 1993); Clement Dodd, *Crisis of Turkish Democracy* (London: Prometheus Press, 1983). In addition, a number of contemporary authors investigate the movement from the perspective of party politics and emphasize voting patterns, party programs, etc. See Ergun Özbudun, *Contemporary Turkish Politics* (Boulder, CO: Lynne Rienner, 2000); Metin Heper and Ahmet Evin (eds.), *Politics in the Third Turkish Republic* (Boulder, CO: Westview Press, 1994); Metin Heper and Ahmet Evin (eds.), *State, Democracy and Military: Turkey in the 1980s* (Berlin: Walter de Gruyter, 1988); Metin Heper, "The State, Political Party and Society in Turkey," *Government and Opposition*, Vol.25, No.2 (Summer 1990), pp.321–33. The radical nationalist movement also finds some mention in the literature on the history of democracy and democratic institutions in Turkey. However, by and large, radical Turkish nationalism has not been studied as a subject in its own right. Even in the area of historical studies there are only a few key works on the history and characteristics of the movement. See Jacob M. Landau, *Pan-Turkism in Turkey: A Study of Irredentism* (London: Hurst, 1995); Jacob Landau, "The Nationalist Action Party in Turkey," *Journal of Contemporary History*, Vol.17, No.1 (1982), pp.587–606; Jacob Landau, "Main Trends of Turkish Nationalism in the Late Nineteenth and Early Twentieth Centuries," *History of European Ideas*, Vol.15, Nos.5–6 (1992), pp.567–9; Tanıl Bora, *Türk Sağının Üç Hali* [Three States of the Turkish Right] (Istanbul: Birikim Yayınları, 1999); David Kushner, *The Rise of Turkish Nationalism* (London and Portland, OR: Frank Cass, 1977). Others mention the radical nationalists largely in passing as one of the many actors in Turkish Republican history. This is true even for writers working directly on Turkish nationalism. See Taner Timur, *Türk Devrimi ve Sonrası* (Ankara: İmge, 1997); Ali Engin Oba, *Türk Milliyetçiliğinin Doğuşu* [The Birth of Turkish Nationalism] (Istanbul: İmge Yayınevi, 1995); Taha Parla, *Türkiye'de Siyasal Kültürün Resmi Kaynakları*, Cilt 3: *Kemalist Tek-Parti İdeolojisi ve CHP'nin Altı Ok'u* [The Official Sources of Political Culture in Turkey, The Kemalist Single Party Ideology and CHP's Six Arrows] (Istanbul: İletiş im Yayınları, 1992); Speros Vryonis Jr., *Turkish State and Society: Clio Meets the Grey Wolf* (Thessalonike: Institute of Balkan Studies, 1991); Alev Er, *Türk Milliyetçilişinin Kökenleri* [The Roots of Turkish Nationalism] (Ankara: Yurt Yayınları, 1986); Baskın Oran, *Atatürk Milliyetçiliği: Resmi İdeoloji Dışı Bir İnceleme* [Atatürk Nationalism: An Unofficial Inquiry] (Ankara: Dost, 1988). There is thus a marked need for work that weaves together the party political and socio-historical perspectives for the examination of the movement. Partially fulfilling this need, for the most current academic debates on MHP's role in Turkish politics, see Ayşe Güneş Ayata, "Ideology, Social Bases and Organizational Structure of the Post-1980 Political Parties," in Eralp (1993), pp.31–49 and Burak Arıkan and Alev Çınar, "The Nationalist Action Party: Representing the State, the Nation, or the Nationalists," *Turkish Studies*, Vol.3, No.1 (Spring 2002), pp.25–40.
2. See Kemal Kirişci and Barry Rubin (eds.), *Turkey in World Politics: An Emerging Multi-Regional Power* (Colorado: Lynne Rienner, 2001), and Andrew Mango, *Turkey: The Challenge of a New Role*, Washington Papers No.163 (Westwood: Praeger, 1994).
3. Nergis Canefe, "Tribalism and Nationalism in Turkey: Reinventing Politics," in Kenneth Christie (ed.), *Ethnic Conflict, Tribal Politics: Global Perspectives* (London: Curzon Press, 1998), pp.112–36.
4. See Yılmaz Esmer, "At the Ballot Box: Determinants of Voting Behavious in Turkey," in Yılmaz Esmer and Sabri Sayarı (eds.), *Politics, Parties and Elections in Turkey* (Boulder,

CO: Lynne Rienner, 2002); Ali Çarkoğlu, "The Turkish Party System in Transition: Party Performance and Agenda Change," *Political Studies*, Vol.46, No.3 (1998), pp.544–71; Ergun Özbudun, *Contemporary Turkish Politics: Challenges to Democratic Consolidation* (Boulder, CO: Lynne Rienner, 2000); Ersin Kalaycıoğlu, "Türkiye'de Köktenci Sağ Partiler ve Seç men Tercihleri" [Radical Right Parties and Voter Preferences in Turkey], *Dünü ve Bugünüyle Toplum ve Ekonomi*, Vol.7 (Oct. 1994), pp.65–84.
5. Mustafa Çalık, *MHP Hareketi—Kaynakları ve Gelişimi, 1965–1980* (Ankara: Cedit Nesriyat, 1995).
6. See Daniel Bell, *The Radical Right* (New York: Transaction, 2001) and Paul Hainsworth, *The Politics of the Extreme Right: From the Margins to the Mainstream* (New York: Pinter, 2000).
7. This new organization had the mandate of defending "Turkish culture" against both internal and external enemies. See Hugh Poulton, *Top Hat, Grey Wolf and Crescent: Turkish Nationalism and the Turkish Republic* (London: Hurst, 1997) and Landau (1995).
8. Tanıl Bora and Kemal Can, *Devlet, Ocak, Dergah* (Istanbul: İletisim, 1994).
9. The definitive formulation of the synthesis was announced in 1984 by the nationalist-conservative organization *Aydınlar Ocağı* (The Guild/Fraternity of Intellectuals).
10. Bora and Can (1994) and Parla (1992).
11. See Zafer Üskül, *Siyaset ve Asker: Cumhuriyet Döneminde Sıkıyönetim Uygulamaları* [Politics and Military Practices of Emergency Law during the Republican Period] (Istanbul: Afa Yayınları, 1996) and William Hale, *Turkish Politics and the Military* (New York and London: Routledge, 1994).
12. Ali Çarkoğlu, "The Geography of April 1999 Turkish Elections," *Turkish Studies*, Vol.1, No.1 (2000), pp.149–71; Ersin Kalaycıoglu, "The Shaping of Political Preferences in Turkey: Coping with the Post-Cold War Era," *New Perspectives on Turkey*, Vol.20, No.1 (1999), pp.47–76.
13. *Turkish Daily News* interview, no author (headline), April 27, 1999.
14. MHP Party website (<www.MHP.org>), Press Report dated June 25, 2002.
15. Devlet Bahçeli, "Türkiye-AB İliskilerinde Kırılma Noktaları," *Türkiye ve Siyaset*, No.7 (2002), pp.1–14.
16. Bahçeli (2002), pp.1–14.
17. Ibid., p.14.
18. Ibid., pp.9–10.
19. Ibid., p.13.
20. Ahmet Selçuk Can, "Avrupa Birliği Yetkililerinin Türkiye'ye Yaklaşımları," *Türkiye ve Siyaset*, No.7 (2002), pp.15–22; Selim Kuzu, "Güncel Tartısmalar Isığında Türkiye-AB İlişkileri, Basın ve MHP," *Türkiye ve Siyaset*, No.7 (2002), pp.72–84; Osman Karacakurt, "Türkiye AB Ilişkilerinde Kritik Yol Ayrımı," *Türkiye ve Siyaset*, No.7 (2002), pp.45–58.
21. Can (2002), pp.18–21.
22. Karacakurt (2002), p.49.
23. Kuzu (2002), p.73.
24. Agah Sırrı Levend, *Halk Kürsüsünden Akisler* (Istanbul: Burhaneddin Matbaası, 1941), p.63.
25. See Niyazi Berkes, *Türk Düşününde Batı Sorunu* (Ankara: Bilgi Yayınevi, 1975).
26. In Mehmet Kaplan (ed.), *Atatürk Devri Fikir Hayatı* (Ankara: Kültür Bakanlığı, 1992), p.298.
27. Bora (1999), pp.88–9.
28. Nihad Sami Banarlı, *Devlet ve Devlet Terbiyesi* (Istanbul: Kubbealtı Nesriyat, 1985), pp.217–18.
29. Ahmet Kabaklı, *Temellerin Duruşması* (Istanbul: Tü rk Edebiyatı Vakfı Yayınları, 1990), p.15.
30. Ismail Hami Danismend, *Garp Menba'larına Göre Eski Türk Demokrasisi* (Istanbul: Sucuoglu Matbaası, 1964).
31. Mehmet D. Doğan, *Batılılaşma İhaneti* (Ankara: Birlik Yayınları, 1979), p.15.
32. Cited in Ismail Kara, *Türkiye'de İslamcılık Düşüncesi* (Istanbul: 3 Pınar Yayınları, 1994), p.383.
33. Doğan (1979), p.46.
34. Osman Yüksel Serdengeçti, *Bu Millet Neden Anlar?* (Konya: Milli Ülkü Yayınevi, 1986), p.59.
35. Kabaklı (1990), pp.361–2.

36. Berna Moran, *Türk Romanına Eleştirel Bir Bakış* (Istanbul: İletişim Yayınları, 1983), pp.219–26.
37. Doğan (1979).
38. Nurettin Topçu, *Kültür ve Medeniyet* (Istanbul: Dergah Yayınları, 1998), p.11.
39. Ibid., pp.119–26.
40. Cemil Meriç, *Kültürden Irfana* (Istanbul: Insan Yayınları, 1986), p.385.
41. Cemil Meriç, *Jurnal-2* (Istanbul: İletişim Yayınları, 1992).
42. Nurettin Topçu, *Yarınki Türkiye* (Istanbul: Dergah Yayınları, 1972), p.148.
43. Izmir Ulku Ocakları Birligi, *Efes Festivalinin İçyüzü* (Izmir, 1970).
44. Ibid., p.1.
45. Tahsin Banguoğlu, *Kendimize Geleceğiz* (Istanbul: Derya Dagıtım, 1984), p.116.
46. Kabaklı Ahmet, *Müslüman Türkiye* (Istanbul: Toker Yayınları, 1970), p.130.
47. Necmettin Erbakan, *Türkiye'nin Meseleleri ve Çözümleri* (Ankara: Birlik Yayınları, 1991).
48. Ekrem Hakkı Ayverdi, *Makaleler* (Istanbul: Istanbul Fetih Cemiyeti, 1985), p.370.
49. Samuel Huntington, *The Clash of Civilisations* (New York: Simon and Schuster, 1996).
50. Cas Mudde, *The Ideology of the Extreme Right* (Manchester: Manchester University Press, 2000), pp.172–8.

9

Turkey's Slow EU Candidacy: Insurmountable Hurdles to Membership or Simple Euro-skepticism?

GAMZE AVCI

Public opinion polls in Central and Eastern European candidate countries point to a mixed picture when it comes to supporting European Union (EU) membership.[1] However, the data in Turkey suggests that the Turkish public has been continuously supportive of its country's bid for membership. Over 60 percent of the Turkish people think that EU membership is a good thing.[2] Yet despite public support and the initiation of Turkey's EU candidacy, the required reform process that would accompany and ultimately induce membership has been relatively slow, or at best sporadic. Thirty-nine percent of the Turkish public characterize the EU accession process as "standing still," and perceive it to be much slower than they would like it to be.[3]

The coalition government, which has been in place since June 1999 and has presided over the initiation of the candidacy status in December 1999, has not succeeded in passing the necessary reforms in order to meet at least the political aspect of the Copenhagen European Council required criteria needed to initiate negotiations. Early elections in Turkey are now scheduled to take place on November 3, 2002, and whether the latest reform package, which was passed on August 3, 2002, will suffice and negotiations will begin will be decided in December 2002. It is clear that as time passes and debates intensified the EU has increasingly become central in Turkish politics. This has become even more visible on the eve of the most recent political crisis surrounding the frail health of Turkish Prime Minister, Bülent Ecevit. Indeed, the EU is so critical a factor in domestic politics that early elections in Turkey, prior to the European Council's Copenhagen summit in December 2002, will be considered a referendum on EU accession.[4]

This contribution will focus on how the issue of EU membership has affected domestic political debates in Turkey in the context of the Copenhagen criteria.[5] In particular, it will try to reveal possible impasses within the coalition government concerning the political issues within the

Copenhagen conditions. After presenting a background and history of recent EU-Turkish relations, the essay will evaluate the progress reports of the EU and subsequently the political discourse in Turkey since 1999. The essay will conclude by linking this Turkish discourse to discussions within the EU and other candidate countries.[6]

THE HELSINKI DECISION AND BEYOND

The Helsinki decision of 1999 granted "candidacy status" to Turkey, which has been knocking on the EU's door since 1987 and has been associated with the EU since 1963. Consequently, Turkey would be treated in the same way as all other countries waiting to join the Union. The Helsinki decision stood in harsh contrast to decisions reached two years before at the EU's Luxembourg summit, where Turkey's application was simply acknowledged.[7] Relations between the EU and Turkey suffered a serious setback as a result of this as Turkey considered it an abrasive rejection. Furthermore, many believed that the reason behind this decision was that the EU is a Christian "club" that would never accept a country of 65 million Muslims.[8] The Helsinki summit became an opportunity to rectify the situation and "restart" relations. In German Chancellor Gerhard Schröder's words, "The damage caused in Luxembourg was repaired in Helsinki."[9] Much of this change also had to do with shifting political constellations in Europe, such as the election of the Schröder government. In addition, the EU did not have much to lose. The candidacy status grants no special rights to the candidate. The candidate must still meet all of the EU membership criteria before it can actually be admitted to the Union.

The EU has couched the developments after the Helsinki Council meeting in rather positive terms. Thus, the Gothenburg European Council (June 15–16, 2001) asserted that "the decisions in Helsinki have brought Turkey closer to the EU and opened up new prospects for her European aspirations."[10] This statement followed the Turkish government's adoption of the National Program for the Adoption of the Acquis (NPAA), announced on March 19, 2001. The same Council considered the adoption of the NPAA "a welcome development."[11]

NPAA adoption followed the beginning of the EU's Accession Partnership (AP) on March 8, 2001. This Accession Partnership was of great consequence because it set out the short- and medium-term measures necessary to ensure that Turkey meets the criteria for membership. Measures to be adopted in the short term were "selected on the basis that it is realistic to expect that Turkey can complete or take them substantially forward by the end of 2001."[12] Medium-term measures were not expected to be completed within one year, but it was hoped that work on these would begin during 2001. Taking the AP into account, the NPAA stated the manner in which Turkey will aim to meet the requirements. However, critics have described the NPAA as lacking clear commitment and containing vague statements, making it a weak foundation for such an endeavor.[13] They have argued that, compared to what is expected from Turkey in the AP, the NPAA remains relatively unsatisfactory and does not live up to the targets set in the AP.

Despite such criticism, during the Laeken meeting (December 14–15, 2001) the European Council stated that:

> Turkey has made progress towards complying with the political criteria established for accession, in particular through the recent amendment of its constitution. This has brought forward the prospect of the opening of accession negotiations with Turkey.[14]

The EU acknowledged steps taken towards reform and indicated that, if Turkey continues on this path, there is light at the end of the tunnel. Accordingly, in Seville (June 21–22, 2002) the Council's reaffirmed that:

> the implementation of the required political and economic reforms will bring forward Turkey's prospects of accession in accordance with the same principles and criteria as are applied to the other candidate countries.[15]

But the most significant statement that emanated from Seville was that:

> New decisions could be taken in Copenhagen (in December 2002) on the next stage of Turkey's candidature in the light of developments in the situation between the Seville and Copenhagen European Councils, on the basis of the regular report to be submitted by the Commission in October 2002 and in accordance with the Helsinki and Laeken conclusions.[16]

This statement has given rise to expectations and hope in Turkey. Increasingly, Ankara expects the European Commission to clearly indicate a date on which formal accession negotiations will begin. Such a "green light" would greatly help to allay doubts regarding EU intentions and would further motivate and speed-up the reform process.

THE COPENHAGEN CRITERIA AND CONDITIONALITY

Turkish "exceptionalism" stems largely from the fact that Turkey remains the only candidate country that does not satisfy the political aspects of the

Copenhagen criteria. This is based on official Commission opinions on the Turkish application for membership. The Commission has continuously noted that Turkey so far does not satisfy the political conditions laid down by the European Council in Copenhagen.[17] It is therefore important to state the criteria precisely:

> Membership requires that the candidate country has achieved stability of institutions guaranteeing democracy, the rule of law, human rights and respect for and protection of minorities (condition 1), the existence of a functioning market economy as well as the capacity to cope with competitive pressure and market forces within the Union (condition 2). Membership presupposes the candidate's ability to take on the obligations of membership including adherence to the aims of political, economic and monetary union (condition 3).[18]

The Commission's assessments so far have presented a major *problematique* for Turkey since the political criteria for membership (condition 1) have to be satisfied *before* accession negotiations can begin. This use of conditionality in relations with third countries is fairly common for the EU.[19] The idea is to show the "carrot" rather than the "stick" in enlargement matters. The Danish Presidency most recently reminded Turkey of this conditionality. Addressing members of the European Parliament on July 3, 2002, Danish Prime Minister Anders Fogh Rasmussen said Ankara should not expect any departure from membership criteria and stated that:

> Turkey does not fulfill the criteria for getting a date for the start of accession negotiations. So, at the end of the day, it is more or less up to Turkey herself when such a date can be presented because if and when Turkey fulfills the political criteria, we can start accession negotiations.[20]

Denmark, which took over the EU's rotating presidency from Spain on July 1, faces the difficult task of selecting the candidates that will be invited to join the EU in 2004 as part of the first wave of enlargement. This is a decision that is likely to be announced at the EU's Copenhagen summit in December 2002. This "pressure" has led to some landmark changes in Turkey in August 2002. The Turkish Grand National Assembly passed a package of human rights reforms (including the abolition of the death penalty in peace time). The EU's official reaction is expected in the fall with the publication of the new Progress Report.

THE PERCEPTIONS OF PROGRESS REPORTS

As mentioned before, the criteria set by the Copenhagen European Council in 1993 require that applicant countries achieve "stability of institutions guaranteeing democracy, the rule of law, human rights and respect for and protection of minorities."[21] The political reform requirements are thus in the fields of human rights, rule of law, and protection of minorities. The perceptions of Turkey's readiness or progress are conditioned by the Commission's Regular Reports issued in the fall of each year.[22] Turkey has been evaluated in four reports from 1998 to 2001. Of these, the 1998 and 2001 reports stand out most. The first report is significant as it sets the tone for subsequent reports. The latter's importance lies in its being the most comprehensive evaluation of Turkey's progress so far and also as it coincided with the period when the most extensive steps towards reform were taken and critical debates were waged within Turkish society. The reports have many overt, but also some embedded, requests. The individual reports and the perceived weak issues in Turkish politics they point out will now be summarized.

The 1998 Report was issued prior to the Turkish candidacy and can serve as a framework for the subsequent reports, which are more detailed. It touches upon the critical issues that the later reports follow up. The report states that despite progress, the human rights situation and the respect for the identity of minorities have not yet reached a satisfactory level. Furthermore, "there are ambiguities in the Turkish legal system with regard to civilian political control of the military."[23] The National Security Council is considered to be the prime example of this. The dissolution of the *Refah Partisi* (Welfare Party—RP) by the Constitutional Court in 1998 is mentioned as having implications for democratic pluralism and freedom of expression. Although the Turkish administration is viewed as functioning properly, problems concerning corruption, favoritism and influence peddling are noted. The need to make the judicial system more impartial and to eliminate cases of corruption is highlighted. Emergency courts (state security courts) are considered to be undemocratic and counter the principles of the European Convention on Human Rights. Civil and political rights of Turkish citizens are not upheld satisfactorily. The report lists specific problems in detail and refers to issues of torture, disappearances, extra-judicial executions, freedom of expression, freedom of association and freedom of the press. Conditions in prisons are described as not meeting accepted standards. Capital punishment, though not implemented, is cited as violating the European Convention on Human Rights. The status of women is regarded as satisfactory yet somewhat insufficient. Restrictions, particularly concerning trade unions, still exist. Freedom of religion is only granted to religious communities that were recognized in the Lausanne Treaty. Economic, social and cultural rights are evaluated as well. Reference is made to the Turks of Kurdish origin and their problems. The need to create outlets for the recognition of their cultural identity is emphasized. Kurdish cannot be used in "political" communication nor can it be used in radio and television broadcasting. Furthermore, the state of emergency and the consequences thereof are cited as problems. The lack of the right of asylum for refugees from outside of Europe is mentioned. Finally, the report refers to the issue of Cyprus (although Cyprus is not part of the Copenhagen criteria, it has been included as an item) and the need for a settlement is underlined. The general evaluation adds that Turkey must make an effort to resolve its disputes with neighboring countries.

Progress made since the 1998 Regular Report is examined in the 1999 Report. The report points out that the Political Parties Law has been amended and that it is more difficult to close parties down and ban members of that party to engage in political activities.[24] Nevertheless, it is also noted that the April 1999 elections—with the national threshold of ten percent—effectively excluded about 5 million voters. The reform of the State Security Courts and, in particular, the removal of the military judge from these courts, was welcomed. The lack of progress dealing with corruption and the continued influence of the National Security Council was noted. In terms of human rights, problems remained largely untouched. No major changes are observed concerning the issues of minorities, women, civil and political rights, as well as economic, social and cultural rights. Turkey was reminded once again of its commitment to assist in resolving the Cyprus issue.

The end of the first year of the Bülent Ecevit-Yılmaz-Bahçeli coalition government coincided with the publication of the 2000 Report.[25] The report draws attention to the wide debate initiated by the reforms required for EU accession. The initiatives accompanying these debates are praised. No major changes were noted in the sections covering the functioning of the parliament and the executive except for the strengthening of internal coordination on EU matters. The examination of the judiciary system revealed a mixed picture. For example, the increase in the number of judges is commended but the lack of progress on enhancing the efficiency of the judicial system is criticized. The issue of the State Security Courts is highlighted once again. Minor changes in some legal provisions and the launching of some legal training programs were mentioned. According to the 2000 Report, corruption was still of major concern as was the functioning of the National Security Council. In terms of human rights, the problems remained largely the same as in the previous report. Finally, developments and problems in Cyprus were presented.

Important changes can be detected in the 2001 Report when compared to the first three reports.[26] Central to this was the passage of a legislative package containing 34 amendments to the 1982 Constitution, adopted on October 3, 2001 (shortly before the publication of the report). The report gave a preliminary analysis of these changes and its implications. A number of changes and initiatives were reported, some targeting the judicial system *per se*, its efficiency and staff training. The report highlighted these steps but also expressed concern regarding areas where there has been little or no progress. Anti-corruption initiatives and measures were praised. The issue of Turkey's involvement in the European Security and Defense Policy (ESDP) was mentioned for the first time. The report took into account the severe financial and economic crises in November 2000 and February 2001. In addition, the report noted that on June 2001 yet another party, the Virtue Party (*Fazilet Partisi*—FP), was closed down. The 2001 Report remarked that some restructuring of the bureaucracy on the basis of EU affairs had been carried out. The report stated that overall, between October 2000 and June 2001, 117 laws (relevant to the EU) were passed.

In sum, repeatedly and throughout its four reports, the Commission stated that, "although the basic features of a democratic system exist, Turkey still does not meet the Copenhagen political criteria."[27] The progress on human rights was considered insufficient. This is very important because "The EU does not start membership negotiations with countries who do not consider human rights issues."[28] The report for 2002 is expected to be published in November. It remains to be seen whether the Commission will see the latest reforms as sufficient to recommend starting accession talks.

THE POLITICAL DISCOURSE IN THE POST-HELSINKI PERIOD

Up until the Helsinki summit (1999), Turkish political discourse on the issue of EU membership was relatively uncomplicated. This was largely due to a consensus among the major political parties, groups and elites that Turkey should pursue EU membership. Although there were clearly varying degrees of enthusiasm and nuances in their different approaches, no major Turkish political grouping or actor questioned the objective of EU membership in a substantial manner. After all, Turkish EU membership had been one of the major pillars of Turkish foreign policy since the 1960s. Nonetheless, very often this did not really lead to a deliberate and well thought-out assertion of support and public backing for EU membership. However, over the last couple of years, it appeared that the choice in favor of joining Europe, at least for some, is, in reality, built on somewhat weak foundations. In the past, there was very little serious debate about what EU membership actually entailed. Changes, prospective costs and benefits of accession were not pondered. Consequently, the issue was practically insignificant in everyday political discourse in Turkey and, as a result, had little effect on the daily lives of individual Turkish citizens. The Turkey-EU debate was couched in very abstract and broad geopolitical or historical terms relating to general notions such as "becoming part of Europe" or "becoming European." Furthermore, given the apparent consent among political elites, many Turkish Euro-skeptics were probably hesitant to deplore EU membership. Given that, one could possibly argue that past polling data on EU membership support in Turkey may have overstated the real levels of public support. This "shallow" consensus on EU membership was critically shaken with the initiation of the required reform process in Turkey. The process received its official start when Turkey was formally accepted as a candidate at the Helsinki summit in 1999.

Before Helsinki, Turkey's focus was how to become an official candidate without any particular strings attached and on an equal footing with the other 12 candidates.[29] Naturally, after the Helsinki summit—with the granting of candidacy—the issue of EU membership acquired a somewhat higher profile. The pending short- and medium-term deadlines have increasingly divided the political spectrum and EU membership has moved up on the political agenda as time for reform became short. Furthermore, some politicians and media presented the "homework" needed for EU membership in an increasingly negative way. Thus, EU membership emerged as a focal point for controversy and opposition. The sheer scale of the problems in Turkey has not made the tasks ahead easier. Although many groups have continued to state their support, politicians have not been as committed to carry out the necessary reforms. The lack of commitment has been exacerbated by doubts that the EU will never admit Turkey.[30]

To a certain degree, intense soul-searching was inevitable. Undoubtedly, Turkey will be a difficult new member for the EU to accommodate. At the same time, having to conform to the requirements of membership will bring painful political, economic and social consequences for Turkey. Hence, as the prospect of negotiations has become a more realistic possibility, the discussions have become increasingly polarized. The difficult issues that need to be tackled, not surprisingly, focus to a large extent on the concessions that will have to be made by Turkey. As a result, the Turkish public and politicians are realizing that potential EU accession is a costly process that will generate losers as well as winners with difficult issues needing to be tackled, such as restructuring the political system. Parallel to these changing perceptions, the EU has become a convenient "scapegoat" for Turkish politicians, enabling them to shift the blame for the negative consequences of reform by claiming that these were forced upon Turkey by EU membership requirements. To the extent that these reforms are linked to potential EU accession in the public awareness, there is likely to be a rise in Euro-skepticism and EU membership (that is, the reforms it entails) will emerge as an issue that divides Turkish politics. In sum, the period since the beginning of candidacy status has seen a marked politicization of the debate on Turkish EU membership, not so much about whether or not the country should join *per se* but more concerning the actual terms of accession.

Turkey's political parties, in particular, have been wrangling over details of what the government is ready to concede to the EU.[31] Very frequently, the political debates around EU membership turned into "ideological" confrontations between the nationalists and the rest of the parties. The *Milliyetçi Hareket Partisi* (Nationalist Movement Party—MHP) has been the primary source of nationalist opposition. But the military's elite, left-wing nationalists and extremists have also repeatedly voiced their concern or opposition on certain EU issues. Though, despite its reservations, the military is careful to distance itself from an "anti-EU" label overall since it believes NATO member Turkey's economic and political destiny lies in Europe, one way or another.

On the other hand, support for EU membership has come more from business circles, liberals and, somewhat inconsistently, from the mainstream right parties (the True Path Party, *Doğru Yol Partisi*—DYP—and the Motherland Party, *Anavatan Partisi*—ANAP).[32] Occasionally, pro-Islamists have voiced support for this step when it fitted their purposes.[33] It is also worth mentioning that nationalist overtones have been heard occasionally from all parties.[34] Finally, NGOs have been very outspoken and generally very supportive of the EU.[35]

In the discussion since 1999, the MHP's role has become overly evident because it was part of the government and critical in passing reforms. Incidentally, the first three years of Turkey's EU candidacy have been under the governance of the coalition government led by Ecevit.

Ecevit's *Demokratik Sol Parti* (Democratic Left Party—DSP) received 22.3 percent of the votes in 1999 and his coalition partners MHP and ANAP received 18.1 and 13.3 percent respectively. This reflected, to a certain extent, the ongoing fractionalization of the Turkish political system. For the second consecutive election, six parties scored between eight and 22 percent of the vote. In addition, smaller parties faced the electoral threshold of ten percent, which failure to exceed prohibits them from entering the parliament. The election itself also demonstrated the decline of the secular center-right in Turkey. The government grouping that emerged was widely seen as virtually the only plausible coalition possibility given Ecevit's known desire to work with Yılmaz, Yılmaz's objection to working with Çiller (DYP), and the pro-Islamist FP's unacceptability to the military.

On March 18, 2000, the government announced that the three coalition partners had finally reached a compromise on the commitments Turkey would make to the EU. The NPAA of short- and medium-term reforms announced 89 new laws and forthcoming amendments to 94 existing laws, and proposed a massive overhaul in Turkish politics. This occurred only after long deliberations and much struggle. The NPAA appeared to be a joint declaration of the three coalition partners but also, in a way, symbolized the difficulties the coalition partners had when attempting to agree on sensitive issues. Many of the requested and listed reforms were watered down versions of what was truly needed. Despite the commitment made in the national program, progress was inconsistent, particularly in some of the substantial areas. Most of the delay in the NPAA was caused around discussions of the "national interest." Once more, although nationalist tendencies exist in all three coalition parties, these tendencies tended to be more pronounced in the MHP. Thus, the MHP acquired a pivotal role in the coalition when it came to EU reforms. Its resistance to certain reforms set the agenda for discussion. Parties either responded to the MHP's objections or compromised their protest. Frequently, MHP's attitude led to deadlocks within the fragile coalition. This situation may have been predictable given the MHP's ideological standing but it was delayed due to the streamlining effect of being in government and became more pronounced over time.[36] The MHP's attitude narrowed the parameters of the EU discussions for the other parties on the already sensitive and difficult issues.[37] Looking at the MHP's attitude towards the EU and particular EU-related issues, this will become obvious.

The MHP itself acknowledges that it had a more reserved attitude towards the EU until the early 1990s but that it adopted a more "cool-headed" and multi-dimensional attitude thereafter.[38] Yet, when referring to the (then) upcoming Accession Partnership Agreement, which set out the reforms needed in order to join the Union, the leader of the MHP and Deputy Prime Minister, Devlet Bahçeli, stated that it was the party's right to expect that the interests of the Turkish nation and people be taken into account.[39] When the EU membership plan was first proposed in November 2000, it angered the MHP as well as the military by referring to sensitive issues such as Cyprus and Kurdish separatism, among others.[40] In all of these critical issues, the MHP accused the EU of being inconsistent and indeterminate.[41] The progress reports were also perceived as problematic. Responding to Deputy Prime Minister Mesut Yılmaz's statements that the EU progress report is objective, Bahçeli said that "Supporting the EU's stance or calling it 'objective' ignores the EU's insincerity in its policies towards Turkey."[42]

Bahçeli, moreover, has said in the past that the MHP is falsely portrayed as an EU enemy and that the journey towards joining the EU has been overly beautified and seen as a journey to heaven.[43] As Turkey's deadline for meeting short-term EU requirements approaches, resentment of the EU has grown within the MHP. However, joining the EU is seen as a potential option open to Turkey. Bahçeli has stated that "we want to take part in this union," but in the same breath he also noted "this participation should be in compliance with the magnitude, history and potential of our country." He asserted: "it is hard to claim that EU administration is quite aware of Turkey's efforts and contributions to the Union so far."[44] Evaluating the period since Helsinki, Bahçeli noted that there have been some positive developments but that the relationship is not sufficiently transparent and understandable. He has pointed to the geopolitical and geo-economic nature of the partnership and that there are factors which are way beyond (and more powerful than) the attitude which requires that one does one's homework at once and become a member immediately.[45]

When it comes to the EU, the prime issue for the MHP is Cyprus' bid to join the Union. The bid itself and its implications are considered to be problematic.[46] Bahçeli believes that the EU would like to create a *fait accompli* in Cyprus and supports the Greek position as well as the Greek-Cypriots. He has announced that no concessions will be made concerning Cyprus and that the MHP will support Rauf Denktaş until the end.[47] When examining the Cyprus issue, there is little difference between the MHP and the other parties. It remains a "national" priority and, in Mesut Yılmaz words, "we witness that the EU has given guarantee to the Greek Cypriot side, and put pressure on us."[48] Ecevit has complemented such statements by saying, "as long as the Greek Cypriot side depends upon the EU, it hardly seems possible that it will follow a conciliatory path."[49] On other occasions, Yılmaz said that Turkey needs to be more active about Cyprus and take the initiative, and that, if Denktaş wants to help Turkey, he should be more open to compromise.[50]

Another critical issue for the MHP is the abolition of the death penalty, as this has direct implications for the Öcalan issue. Abdullah Öcalan, the former leader of the now-defunct Kurdistan Workers Party (*Partiya Karkaren Kurdistan*—PKK), has been found responsible for the death of an estimated 35,000 people in the guerrilla warfare that pitted government forces against Kurdish separatists between 1984 and 1999; he was sentenced to death for high treason after his capture in 1999. Turkey has maintained a moratorium on the use of capital punishment since 1984. The abolition of capital punishment is a touchy political issue, mainly because the MHP and other nationalists within the government coalition wish to retain the right to order the execution of Öcalan, who is currently in prison. In October 2001, an amendment to the Constitution abolished capital punishment except for cases in time of war, under the imminent threat of war and for terrorist crimes. The first two exceptions are permitted under Protocol 6 of the European Convention on Human Rights, but the third—concerning terrorist crimes—is not. It is this third exception, however, which is particularly important for those who wish to retain the right to order the execution of Öcalan. Conversely, by refraining from executing Öcalan, Turkey will advance its EU candidacy. Hence, Bahçeli stated that Turkey wants to unite with Europe in an honorable, fair and full membership. However, there would be "no bargaining concerning Öcalan."[51]

Bahçeli's view has been in direct contrast to Prime Minister Ecevit's position, which is very much in favor of abolishing Turkey's death penalty. Ecevit has repeatedly stated that he would like to see the abolition of the death penalty as soon as possible.[52] Ecevit has claimed that it is not in Ankara's interests to execute Öcalan.[53] He says Turkey is bound by international obligations, to obey the European Court of Human Rights' call to delay the Kurdish leader's execution until it has considered an appeal lodged by his lawyers. The MHP is being pressured greatly by its grassroots because of its acceptance to hold the death penalty file of Öcalan at the Prime Ministry and not sending it to parliament for debate. Naturally, should the MHP accept the lifting of the death penalty by a government in which it is a coalition partner it would be very harmful for the party. One of the MHP's election pledges in 1999 was that, if it came to power, it would assure the execution of Öcalan.[54] The MHP did suggest at some point that it would not oppose abolishing the death penalty if the

DSP and ANAP legislated it through parliament with the support of the opposition, but it has changed its position during the course of the discussion.[55] The DSP and ANAP asserted their shared position that the death penalty should be replaced with lifetime imprisonment with no chance of parole.[56] The pro-Islamist parties—the AKP (*Adalet ve Kalkınma Partisi*—Justice and Development Party) and the SP (*Saadet Partisi*—Felicity Party)—have stated that the death penalty should be lifted through a constitutional change because legal changes are susceptible to being reversed in the future.[57] However, their views on this issue have frequently changed.[58] The Turkish parties' dilemmas are actually summarized in the DYP attitude, which has stated that the party will not oppose the lifting of the death penalty—but only after Öcalan is executed. Using this attitude, the DYP is trying to lure voter support from the MHP.

The use of Kurdish in education and on television poses another dilemma in the coalition government. The problem with extending rights to the Kurdish minority has much to do with the violent struggle between the PKK and the Turkish army. Hence, very often the extension of rights to Kurds is seen as rewarding terrorism or approving violence. In that context, Bahçeli calls the EU's attitude concerning terrorism "double-faced and not serious."[59] He argues that "most European countries continue to embrace terrorists who are the enemies of Turkey. This demonstrates these European countries' failure to learn any lessons from the September 11 attacks, while it also proves how justified Turkey is in its concerns."[60] Yılmaz does not sound much different when he states that "the EU has always been egoistical on the issue of terrorism ... Its exclusion of terrorist organizations such as the PKK and the Revolutionary People's Liberation Party-Front [*Devrimci Halk Kurtulus Partisi-Cephesi*— DHKP-C] from its list of terrorist organizations has revealed the fact that it tolerates terrorist organizations targeting Turkey unless they cause any damage to the EU."[61]

Bahçeli believes that allowing teaching, free broadcasting or publication in the Kurdish language would help separatism. Actually, the military has also expressed their reservations on this matter but has been open to some changes given it would be under strict governmental control.[62] The MHP is strictly against allowing education in Kurdish—not even as elective courses—and claims it is a new strategy by the outlawed PKK.[63] ANAP leader and Deputy Prime Minister Mesut Yılmaz urges tolerance for Kurdish education demands but adds that making such a move would be impossible under the current laws.[64] Yılmaz's attitude has caused an open rift between ANAP and the MHP.[65]

The MHP also is dissatisfied with the discussions surrounding Article 312 (banning incitement to religious and ethnic hatred). Speaking at the MHP's parliamentary group meeting, Bahçeli said that the proposed amendments to Article 312 would neither save nor punish anyone. He said that his party was against both the total lifting of the article and making radical amendments to it in a manner that would "make it an empty shell."[66] Bahçeli stated that exempting provocative speech or behavior from punishment could not be reconciled with democracy or the notion of freedom of speech. "For us, propagating separatism [and] instigating unrest have nothing to do with freedom in a democratic, pluralist society," Bahçeli said.[67]

The European Security and Defense Identity (ESDI) has also become an intractable problem.[68] Turkey has made it known that it would like to participate in the decisionmaking process of the ESDI. The problem is that for many "The ESDI cannot be without Turkey as Turkey is Europe's strategic partner."[69] The United States, which has made no secret of Turkey's EU bid, also believes that Turkey should be included in emerging EU defense structures.[70] The problem here is that Turkey, with the second largest army in the Atlantic alliance, does not want to give its approval to this force because it fears that one day it may operate in Turkey's own backyard. EU governments cannot go ahead without NATO's approval, in part to avoid undermining it and partly because they will need to borrow its weapons and equipment. Ankara refuses to drop its opposition to the EU's rapid reaction force (RRF)—intended to mount limited operations when NATO is not involved. An agreement (the so-called Ankara document) concerning the ESDP was reached between the US, Britain and Turkey in December 2001 but has been vetoed so far by Greece. The MHP has indicated that leaving Turkey outside the ESDP mechanism sheds an interesting light on the EU's true intentions.[71]

The latest issue dividing parties along the EU issue was early elections. Bahçeli wanted to call for early elections to end the political uncertainty that has grown in recent months as Ecevit's illness kept him from work while coalition members clash over EU reforms. Ecevit's DSP, which has seen its parliamentary presence halved in July 2002 after defections by his members of parliament, feared it could suffer at the polls. Voters are expected to punish a government which has presided over Turkey's worst recession since the Second World War. The third coalition partner, the Motherland Party, also backed a November 2002 election but wanted to complete the EU reforms first to strengthen its hand in the election campaign. On the other hand, Bahçeli claimed that debating the reforms will take too long, leaving insufficient time to prepare for November polls. He also stated that his party favors a discussion of individual reform items rather than passing a comprehensive EU reform package.[72] The SP supported ANAP's bid,[73] whereas the DYP exhibited a mixed attitude and remains non-committal.[74] *Yeni Türkiye Partisi* (New Turkey Party—YTP), a new party established by former foreign minister İsmail Cem—the most prominent member of the government to abandon Ecevit, says that it will support the EU reforms.[75] Cem's New Turkey Party has regrouped the defectors around a pro-EU platform and has immediately become the fifth-largest party in parliament. During these discussions, an important development was that Kemal Derviş, the economy minister and architect of the government's recovery program, resigned and joined the *Cumhuriyet Halk Partisi* (Republican People's Party—CHP). Both Derviş and the CHP are seen as supportive of Turkey's EU bid. The CHP, which is currently not represented in parliament, is expected to make a comeback in the next election. Finally, AKP, the pro-Islamist party, supported early elections and appeared supportive of EU reforms. AKP is ranked first in recent election polls. Thus it became apparent that the deadlock over EU reforms within the coalition, Ecevit's waning health and the issues surrounding early elections have facilitated the emergence of new political actors focusing primarily on support for Turkey's EU membership.

The discussions on early elections have overlapped with discussions on a final attempt to pass necessary EU reforms. The parliament has approved elections to be held on November 3, 2002. At the same time, on August 3 the parliament voted to approve a package of human rights reforms it hopes will clear the way for Ankara to join the Union. The package was adopted after an overnight marathon session. It includes the abolition of the death penalty in peacetime, which is to be replaced with life imprisonment with no possibility of parole. It also legalizes broadcasting and education in languages other than Turkish, notably Kurdish. Furthermore, the package did away with penalties for criticizing state institutions, including the military, eased restrictions on demonstrations and associations, and allowed non-Muslim religious foundations to buy and sell real estate. The package was presented by Yılmaz's ANAP and was passed despite the opposition of the MHP (on all reform items in the package), with the votes of the DSP, ANAP and opposition parties. The MHP has voted "no" en bloc. The other parties—despite their various talks—have supported the package. There have been defections from all of the other parties (government and opposition) but no consistent resistance to the package as a party line. In remarks made on August 4, Bahçeli said that the MHP would appeal to the

Constitutional Court in a bid to force parliament to reverse its decision regarding the death penalty and minority rights.

Finally, the military's attitude towards the EU has also been ambivalent. In issues like the death penalty (especially the Öcalan issue) and legalizing the use of Kurdish, the military has been particularly hesitant. During the post-Helsinki period, one of the most controversial statements came from General Tuncer Kılınç on March 7, 2002. Speaking at an Istanbul conference on foreign policy, Kılınç, the Secretary General of Turkey's National Security Council, told delegates that during the 40 years it has been knocking on Europe's door, "Turkey hasn't seen the slightest assistance from the EU."[76] While it should do nothing to compromise its relations with the United States, he argued, Turkey would do well "to begin a new search [for allies] that would include Iran and the Russian Federation."[77] The General argued that the EU held negative views on Turkey, has never assisted it, and agreed that "the EU is a Christian Club, a neo-colonialist force, and is determined to divide Turkey."[78] Though General Kılınç stressed that he was speaking in a personal capacity, his words shocked the Turkish establishment. First, because they differ sharply from the army's usual claims to be pro-European. Second, because it is common knowledge in Turkey that the army speaks with one voice.[79] Kılınç's statement received different responses from the coalition partners. Prime Minister Ecevit stated that, "We cannot be swayed by the obstacles and difficulties we have faced on the path to EU membership and [cannot therefore] look for other options."[80] Meanwhile, Deputy Prime Minister Mesut Yılmaz described a Turkish-Iranian-Russian link up as "a nightmare scenario."[81] Bahçeli remained silent.

CONCLUSION: THE "ELECTORAL CONNECTION"

The role of political parties is crucial in any polity. Euro-skepticism or, in the Turkish case, "nationalism in disguise," has become a powerful tool for Turkish parties in their quest for votes and has reshaped aspects of party competition.[82] Euro-skepticism is not a new topic in European Union studies. Paul Taggart and Aleks Szczerbiak, in their pioneering work on Euro-skepticism, point to differences and similarities in Euro-skepticism among both EU members and candidate countries (Central and East European countries only).[83] They make a critical differentiation between hard and soft Euro-skepticism. Hard Euro-skepticism is the "outright rejection of the entire European project and EU membership;"[84] soft Euro-skepticism is "qualified and contingent opposition, which does not imply the rejection of membership itself."[85] In their extensive study they conclude that hard Euro-skeptical parties are not central in any current European governments. Where governing parties are Euro-skeptical, they are almost invariably soft Euro-skeptics.[86]

Although the MHP does not clearly fit into the hard Euro-skeptic realm, it definitely has exhibited features of both hard and soft Euro-skepticism. This dilemma within the MHP has complicated its stance within the coalition and *vis-à-vis* the voter. Internal coalition battling caused by the MHP has hampered the EU reform process. The MHP is currently the largest party in the parliament—after resignations from the DSP following Ecevit's ill health and inner party strife—and plays a crucial role in the party system. Within the government, it was obliged to pay lip service to the principle of supporting EU membership but has been hesitant and unable to carry out its duty necessary for the reforms. This again confirms Taggart and Szczerbiak, who state that smaller, more extreme nationalist parties become unacceptable coalition parties for governments dealing with EU accession, which frees them up to take hard Euro-skeptic positions.[87] The MHP has stuck to its anti-EU platform even during the most recent and most critical discussions on EU reforms in August 2002. Although this has not broken up the coalition, the understanding has been that the coalition will break apart with the upcoming elections in November.

It remains to be seen whether the next parliamentary elections in Turkey will prove Taggart and Szczerbiak's finding that "parties at the 'core' of their party systems ... have high costs associated with expression of any sort of Euroscepticism," whereas for peripheral parties (that is, those unlikely to enter government) "Euroscepticism is a relatively costless stance."[88] The parties closer to the center—DSP, DYP and ANAP—have exhibited features of soft Euro-skepticism, when convenient. This was based on the understanding that "Speaking against the EU, and saying that the EU discriminates, creates credibility ... in domestic policy."[89] The pro-Islamist parties have very rationally supported the EU whenever it supported their cause but opposed it when it came to crucial matters. Overall, during the period since the Helsinki summit, the Turkish party elites have been inconsistent in exhibiting their unambiguous commitment to EU reform. Neither the left nor the right (nor the Islamists for that matter) are "true believers" in the EU. Yet, today, in the wake of early elections, the EU-card is pivotal for many, especially in the light of high support for the EU among the Turkish public. The last package passed in parliament signaled that most parties felt the need to "bow" to the EU demands of the Turkish electorate. Yet, one wonders how things would have proceeded if there were no immediate election upcoming in Turkey, a consideration that is not applicable to European Union member states. In Europe, the European integration process was very much elite-driven. Still, in all EU member states the elite is more in favor of European integration than the mass public.[90] Given that the picture is reversed in Turkey, Turkey's path to the EU will be much bumpier. Yet, the electoral connection may give the Turkish party elites the incentive to appear more pro-membership than they actually are.[91] They know that the voter will now decide on who is most credible concerning EU affairs. At the same time, the EU's credibility will also be put on test in December 2002. Despite the latest landmark legislation passed in August, the EU's reaction was cautious and lukewarm.[92] The Commission praised the progress but stated they would like to see how the reforms are implemented before assessing Turkey's progress towards achieving European standards of human rights.[93] Further, the EU probably wants to see what kind of government will emerge after the elections. According to current election polls, none of the coalition partners appears to be able to score above the electoral threshold. However, given the discrepancy in EU support between the Turkish public and the party elites, a perceived disappointment at Copenhagen in December 2002 would most definitely play into the hands of the party elites who like to (ab)use the anti-EU card.

POSTSCRIPT

On November 3, 2002 the Turkish government changed. The parties of Ecevit's coalition government were all wiped out and did not make it into the new parliament. The new government was formed by the AKP. The CHP became the only opposition party. Although the AKP was not elected on its EU agenda, it "responded" to Turkish public opinion. It vowed to strive for EU membership, as did the CHP. Immediately after its election to office, the AKP was faced with the EU's December Copenhagen summit. The new government, keen on gaining credibility and establishing confidence with the voter, lobbied intensively in many European capitals and even in the United States. Yet the results were not necessarily to the liking of many. The EU has postponed a real decision on opening negotiations until 2004 and the negotiations themselves can only be started in 2005 by an EU of 25 members. The AKP has committed itself to continue to working towards this date and accomplishing the necessary EU reforms. The pace of the reform process remains to be seen.

NOTES

1. See *Eurobarometer Candidate Countries* (Dec. 2001), <http://europa.eu.int/comm/public_ opinion/cceb_en.htm>. On average, six out of ten people across all the 13 candidate countries believe membership would be a "good thing." The general figures, though, mask sharp regional differences. For instance, only 33 percent of those questioned in Estonia and Latvia supported membership, and the figures were not much better in Lithuania and Slovenia. For a discussion of Poland, see Aleks Szczerbiak, "Polish Public Opinion: Explaining Declining Support for EU Membership," *Journal of Common Market Studies*, Vol.39, No.1 (March 2001), pp.105–22.
2. See *Eurobarometer Candidate Countries* (Dec. 2001), <http://europa.eu.int/comm/ public_ opinion/cceb_en.htm>. See also a public poll carried out by the Turkey Economic and Social Studies Foundation (TESEV) in June 2002 showing that some 64 percent of Turks would vote in favor of EU membership in a referendum if held today (<http://www.tesev.org.tr/ bltn/t1.html>). A poll carried out by Piar-Gallup in August 2000 (<http://www.inaf.gen.tr/ english/comment/20000922.htm>) found that 69 percent of respondents favored the idea, with only ten percent opposed (mainly for religious reasons) and the remaining 21 percent classified as "don't know." Research carried out by the Turkish-European Foundation in February 2002 confirmed that 68 percent of the Turkish public supported the goal of EU entry (<http://www.csis.org/turkey/TU020308.htm>).
3. *Eurobarometer Candidate Countries* (Dec. 2001), <http://europa.eu.int/comm/public_ opinion/cceb_en.htm>.
4. Statement by Mesut Yılmaz, leader of *Anavatan Partisi* (Motherland Party—ANAP), television interview on NTV, July 9, 2002.
5. For earlier studies, see David Barchard, *Building a Partnership: Turkey and the European Union* (Istanbul: Turkish Economic and Social Studies Foundation, 2000); Christopher Brewin, *Turkey and Europe After the Nice Summit* (Istanbul: TESEV Publications, 2002); Barry Buzan and Thomaz Diez, "The European Union and Turkey," *Survival*, Vol.41, No.1, (Spring 1999), pp.41–57; Bruce Kuniholm, "Turkey's Accession to the European Union: Differences in European and US Attitudes and Challenges for Turkey," *Turkish Studies*, Vol.2, No.1 (Spring 2001), pp.25–53.
6. For discussions of Euro-skepticism, see Aleks Szczerbiak and Paul Taggart, *Opposing Europe: Party Systems and Opposition to the Union, the Euro and Europeanisation* (Brighton: Falmer, Sussex European Institute Working Paper No.36 and Opposing Europe Research Network Working Paper No.1, Oct. 2000); Paul Taggart and Aleks Szczerbiak, *Parties, Positions and Europe: Euroscepticism in the EU Candidate States of Central and Eastern Europe* (Opposing Europe Research Network Working Paper No.2, May 2001); Paul Taggart and Aleks Szczerbiak, *The Party Politics of Euro scepticism in EU Member and Candidate States* (Opposing Europe Research Network Working Paper No.6, April 2002); all papers are available online at <http://www.sussex.ac.uk/Units/SEI/oern/WorkingPapers/ index.html>.
7. At that time, the EU named six countries that would begin accession negotiations immediately (Poland, Hungary, the Czech Republic, Cyprus, Slovenia and Estonia) and five that would be official "candidates" but not begin negotiations yet (Lithuania, Latvia, Slovakia, Bulgaria and Romania).
8. Meltem Müftüler-Baç, "Through the Looking Glass: Turkey in Europe," *Turkish Studies*, Vol.1, No.1 (Spring 2000), pp.21–35; Kevin Robins, "Interrupting Identities: Turkey/Europe," in Stuart Hall and Paul du Gay (eds.), *Questions of Cultural Identity* (London: Sage Publications, 1996), pp.61–86; Nuri A. Yurdusev, "Avrupa Kimliğinin Oluşumu ve Türk Kimliği" [The Formation of European Identity and the Turkish Identity], in Attila Eralp (ed.), *Türkiye ve Avrupa* [Turkey and Europe] (Ankara: İmge, 1997), pp.17–87.
9. *Sabah*, Dec. 17, 2002.
10. European Council Meeting in Gothenburg: *Presidency Conclusions*, June 15–16, 2002, para.10.
11. European Council Meeting in Gothenburg: *Presidency Conclusions*, June 15–16, 2002.
12. Quoted from <http://www.mfa.gov.tr/grupa/ad/adc/Accession.partnership.pdf>.
13. Ayşegül Uzun, "Siyasi Kriterler Çerçevesinde Katılım Ortaklığı ve Ulusal Program 'ın

Karşılaştırılması" [A Comparison of the Accession Partnership and the National Program on the Adoption of the Acquis in the frame of the Copenhagen Criteria], in Cengiz Aktar (ed.), *Avrupa Birliği'nin Genişleme Süreci* [The Enlargement Process of the EU] (Istanbul: İletişim, 2002), pp.77–100.
14. European Council Meeting in Laeken: *Presidency Conclusions*, Dec. 14–15, 2002, para.12.
15. European Council Meeting in Seville: *Presidency Conclusions*, June 21–22, 2002, para.25.
16. Ibid.
17. The European Commission's 1998 *avis* and its subsequent progress reports in the fall reports of 1999, 2000 and 2001 are available at <http://www.europa.eu.int/comm/enlargement/turkey/docs.htm>.
18. European Council in Copenhagen: *Presidency Conclusions*, June 21–22, 1993.
19. For a discussion of European Union conditionality and its constraints, see Heather Grabbe, "European Union Conditionality and the Acquis Communaitaire," *International Political Science Review*, Vol.23, No.3 (July 2002), pp.249–68.
20. Cited in Jean-Christophe Peuch, "Turkey: Ecevit's Illness puts reforms, EU bid into balance," Radio Free Europe, July 4, 2002, <http://www.rferl.org>.
21. European Council in Copenhagen: *Presidency Conclusions*, June 21–22, 1993.
22. For an in-depth discussion of how the progress reports are composed and what they contain, see Graham Avery and Fraser Cameron, *The Enlargement of the European Union* (Sheffield: Sheffield Academic Press, 1999), pp.34–92.
23. Quoted from <http://www.europa.eu.int/comm/enlargement/turkey/docs.htm>.
24. Ibid.
25. Ibid.
26. Ibid.
27. Ibid.
28. Statement by Guenther Verheugen, the EU Enlargement Commissioner, cited in *Cumhuriyet*, Jan. 13, 2000.
29. For a discussion of Turkey's candidacy and its characteristics, see Gamze Avcı, "Putting the Turkish EU Candidacy in to Context," *European Foreign Affairs Review*, Vol.7, No.1 (Spring 2002), pp.91–110.
30. House of Commons, *Select Committee on Foreign Affairs. 6th Report: Turkey*, <http://www.parliament.the-stationery-office.co.uk/pa/cm200102/cmselect/cmfaff/606/60602.htm>, prepared May 30, 2002, available as of July 17, 2002.
31. For a discussion of the various "turbulences" caused by the democratization process after Helsinki, see Panayotis J. Tsakonas, "Turkey's Post-Helsinki Turbulence: Implications for Greece and the Cyprus Issue," *Turkish Studies*, Vol.2, No.2 (Autumn 2001), pp.1–40.
32. For example, see the statements of Mesut Yılmaz, ANAP party leader, in *Hürriyet*, July 19, 2000, *Turkish Daily News*, Sept. 11, 2000, and *Cumhuriyet*, Oct. 10, 2000.
33. Past and present Islamist parties include *Refah Partisi* (Welfare Party—RP, banned by the Constitutional Court in 1998), *Fazilet Partisi* (Virtue Party—FP, banned in 2000), *Saadet Partisi* (Felicity Party—SP) and *Adalet ve Kalkınma Partisi* (Justice and Development Party—AKP).
34. See, for example, the discussions surrounding the customs agreement between Turkey and the EU: Mine Eder, "Becoming Western: Turkey and the European Union," in Jean Rugel and Will Hout (eds.), *Regionalism Across the North-South Divide: State Strategies and Globalization* (London: Routledge, 1999), pp.79–95.
35. TÜSİAD (*Türk Sanayicileri ve İşadamları Derneği*—Turkish Industrialists and Businessmen Association) and İKV (*İktisadi Kalkı nma Vakfı*—Economic Development Foundation) are the leading organizations favor of the EU. The İKV has frequently acted as an umbrella organization for other NGOs when gathering support for the EU movement. It has garnered the support of as many as 200 NGOs when appealing to the government to focus on and speed up EU affairs. TESEV (*Türkiye Ekonomik ve Sosyal Etüdler Vakfı*—Turkish Economic and Social Studies Foundation) and the European Movement 2002 have also played a critical role with their activities geared towards educating the public and mobilizing EU supporters.
36. For a recent discussion of the MHP's nationalism, see Alev Çınar and Burak Arıkan, "The Nationalist Action Party: Representing the State, the Nation or the Nationalists?," *Turkish Studies*, Vol.3, No.1 (Spring 2002), pp.25–40.

37. In Mesut Yılmaz's words, "the MHP had some concerns pertaining to the preparation and implementation of the National Program. They have stated those views. We made changes on many issues by taking their views into consideration. We had the same difficulties when time came for the final arrangements." *Anadolu Agency*, March 21, 2002.
38. Devlet Bahçeli's speech at the MHP's Sixth Regular Congress Meeting, Oct. 6, 2000, <http://www.mhp.org.tr>.
39. Ibid.
40. For a sample of Turkish armed forces reaction see *Sabah*, Nov. 27, 2000.
41. Devlet Bahçeli's group speech at the National Assembly, June 11, 2002, <http://www.mhp.org.tr>.
42. Quoted in *Cumhuriyet*, Nov. 21, 2001.
43. Ibid.
44. *Anadolu Agency*, June 18, 2002.
45. Devlet Bahçeli "21. Yüzyılın Zorlukları ve Fırsatları Karşısında Türkiye ve Türk Dünyası Gerçeği" [The reality of Turkey and the Turkic world vis-à-vis the difficulties and opportunities of the 21st century], *Türkiye ve Siyaset*, July–Aug. 2002, available at <http://www.türkiyevesiyaset.com>.
46. Devlet Bahçeli's group speech at the National Assembly, Nov. 13, 2001, <http://www.mhp.org.tr>.
47. NTV news, July 21, 2002, <http://www.ntvmsnbc.com/news/165061.asp>.
48. *Anadolu Agency*, March 21, 2002.
49. Quoted in *Turkish Daily News*, March 22, 2002.
50. *Hürriyet*, May 11, 2002.
51. Quoted in *Türkiye*, Dec. 1, 1999.
52. See, for example, the mention in Jolyon Naegele, "Turkey: Party Leaders Agree To Postpone Ocalan's Execution," Radio Free Europe, Jan. 13, 2000, <http://www.rferl.org>.
53. *Guardian*, Jan. 13, 2000.
54. *Sabah*, Dec. 6, 1999.
55. *Turkish Daily News*, May 24, 2002.
56. <http://www.abhaber.com>, June 26, 2002.
57. Ibid.
58. *Zaman Gazetesi*, June 25, 2002.
59. Bahçeli (July–Aug. 2002), <http://www.türkiyevesiyaset.com>.
60. Quoted in *Cumhuriyet*, Nov. 21, 2001.
61. *Anadolu Agency*, March 21, 2002.
62. Jean-Christophe Peuch, "Turkey: Frustration Mounting Over EU Demands For Reform," Radio Free Europe, March 15, 2002, <http://www.rferl.org>.
63. *Turkish Daily News*, Jan. 27, 2002.
64. Ibid.
65. Jean-Christophe Peuch, "Turkey: Coalition Partners Cross Swords Over EU Reforms, But Is It All About Human Rights?," Radio Free Europe, Sept. 12, 2002, <http://www.rferl.org>.
66. *Sabah* and *Hürriyet*, Jan. 23, 2002.
67. *Hürriyet* and *Cumhuriyet*, Jan. 23, 2002.
68. For a more detailed discussion see Chris Brewin, *Turkey and Europe after the Nice Summit* (Istanbul: TESEV Publications, 2002), pp.17–19. The MHP accuses the EU of being inconsistent and indeterminate concerning each of these important issues.
69. Italian Minister of Foreign Affairs, Lamberto Dini, quoted in *Türkiye*, Dec. 8, 1999.
70. *Akşam*, Dec. 2, 1999.
71. Devlet Bahceli, "Dış İlişkilerimizde Yeni Gelişmeler, Sorunlar ve Temel Yaklaşım Biçimimiz" [New Developments, Problems and our Main Attitude in our Foreign Relations], *Türkiye ve Siyaset* (Jan.–Feb. 2002), <http://www.türkiyevesiyaset.com>.
72. "Bahçeli: paket bölünü rse destekleriz" [Bahceli: We will support the package if it is split], <http://www.ntvmsnbc.com.tr>, July 28, 2002.
73. "ANAP–SP 'den 'önce AB' önergesi" [ANAP and SP propose to put EU first], <http://www.ntvmsnbc.com.tr>, July 25, 2002.
74. "DYP: Yılmaz'ın sözleri esef verici" [DYP: Yilmaz's statement is appalling], <http://www.ntvmsnbc.com.tr>, July 25, 2002; "Çiller: AB konusunda elimizden geleni

yaparız" [Çiller: We will do what we can about the EU], <www.ntvmsnbc.com.tr>, July 26, 2002.
75. "Cem' den AB'ye koşulsuz destek" [Unconditional EU support from Cem], <http://www.ntvmsnbc.com.tr>, July 25, 2002.
76. Quoted in "Turkish general causes controversy with call for Turkey to stop seeking EU membership," *Eurasia Insight*, March 13, 2002.
77. Ibid.
78. Ibid.
79. "A general speaks his mind," *Economist*, March 16, 2002.
80. *Turkish Daily News*, March 9, 2002.
81. Television interview on CNN–Turk, March 14, 2002, <http://www.anap.org.tr/anap/genelbaskanlar/YILMAZ/basin/2002-03-14_egrisidogrusu.htm>.
82. For discussions on other candidate countries see, for example, Agnes Batory, *Hungarian Party Identities and the Question of European Integration* (Opposing Europe Research Network, Working Paper No.4, Sept. 2001); Karen Henderson, *Euroscepticism or Europhobia: Opposition attitudes to the EU in the Slovak Republic* (Opposing Europe Research Network, Working Paper No.5, Sept. 2001). Both papers are online at <http://www.sussex.ac.uk/Units/SEI/oern/WorkingPapers/index.html>.
83. Paul Taggart and Aleks Szczerbiak (2001).
84. Ibid.
85. Ibid.
86. Paul Taggart and Aleks Szczerbiak (2002).
87. Paul Taggart and Aleks Szczerbiak (2001).
88. Ibid.
89. *Anadolu Agency*, March 21, 2002.
90. See Simon Hix, *The Political System of the European Union* (New York: St. Martin's Press, 1999), pp.158–65. For example, 94 percent of all elites see EU membership as a good thing, compared to only 48 percent of the general public.
91. The reverse is true in the EU: elites appear less pro-European in order to please the voter.
92. Jean-Christophe Peuch, "Turkey: Reforms Raise Hopes For EU Membership, But Brussels Remains Cautious," Radio Free Europe, Aug. 6, 2002, <http://www.rerl.org>.
93. Ibid.

10

Who Wants Full Membership? Characteristics of Turkish Public Support for EU Membership

ALİ ÇARKOĞLU

The preferences of the Turkish public at large form the very background of and constitute the moving force behind Turkey's relations with the European Union. At different levels of interaction, ranging from the official diplomatic level to the unofficial and informal interactions between players of civil society on both sides, the intensity and direction of relations are molded by the legitimizing force of the public opinion about Turkey's bid for full membership of the EU. At the diplomatic level, the limits of various concessionary moves or possibilities of cooperation on different issues are determined and decided upon by referring to the preferences reflected in public opinion about the issues involved. At the grass-roots level of civil society, interaction efforts ultimately aim to influence the choices of various opinion constituencies. Looking at domestic or foreign policy issues, these opinion constituencies are quite heterogeneous and may hold quite a variety of preferences concerning the policy options available. Whether attempting to gather support for a policy or to counteract the legitimacy of a policy decision by using an unfavorable public opinion poll, the preferences of these different opinion constituencies must be carefully analyzed.[1]

Turkey's candidacy for EU membership requires an extensive set of policy adjustments and legal, as well as institutional, changes—all of which ultimately derive their legitimacy from the support of various constituencies. Most of the issues involved are too technical and sophisticated for laymen to actually form an opinion about. However, they also constitute the basis of many highly sensitive issues that are debated in the public agenda. Politicians and other opinion leaders simplify and somewhat distort these issues for their convenience and present them for public consideration, ultimately using the resulting preferences for or against a given policy.

There are a number of critical points that need clarification in this process. Who might these opinion constituencies be? How can these constituencies be determined and their preferences diagnosed? How extensively can the policy issues be presented to the opinion constituencies? To what extent can their deliberations in the reality of the political world be duplicated within the superficial context of the public opinion measurement exercise? Once these questions are adequately addressed, a second set of questions concerning the linkage between public opinion and the actual policy carried out can be answered.

The results of an attempt to answer some of this first set of questions through a measurement experiment in a survey setting are presented below. The nationwide representative sample survey, from which the data analyzed below comes from, was conducted between May 18 and June 4, 2002.[2] The survey consisted of face-to-face interviews with 3,060 voting-age citizens living in rural as well as urban dwellings. The respondents were asked whether they would vote for or against Turkey's bid for full membership in the EU if a referendum were to be held. The answers to this simple question form the center of attention in the ensuing sections. In order to determine variations across different public opinion constituencies I have devised various variables which help one to differentiate individuals on the basis of their political preferences, attitudes towards Europe in general, their religiosity and faith, and their degree of nationalism in their perceptions of various issues. Similarly, I have tested whether conventional demographic characteristics such as sex, age, geographic location, ethnicity, socio-economic status and economic wellbeing help one diagnose significant public opinion constituencies that differ from the population at large.

The following sections first describe EU support across different public opinion constituencies.[3] The essay moves on to provide a multivariate statistical analysis of the support for EU membership followed by a series of interpretations and commentary for their implications concerning EU-Turkey relations.

PUBLIC OPINION AND THE EU

General Observations

Despite long and arduous relations between Turkey and the EU, beginning with the 1959 application for associate membership of the European Economic Community, the bases of mass support for this relationship have not attracted much academic attention. Yılmaz Esmer reports results in provincial surveys conducted in 1993 for Istanbul (sample size of 434) and another in 1994 for Konya and Istanbul (sample sizes [N] of 364 and 570 respectively).[4] Although these samples are not representative of the country at large, they nevertheless provide first clues as to the bases of support for EU membership. Esmer notes that the percentage of those in Istanbul who prefer Turkey to be part of Europe are more than double those who prefer the Turkic or Islamic world. Esmer also reports in bivariate analyses that, while increasing education level has a positive impact, increasing religiosity has a negative impact on choice for Turkey to be part of Europe, which also significantly varies with respect to party choice.[5]

Another exception to the general neglect of this issue is the series of surveys conducted since 1994 by Necat Erder and associates.[6] In these nationwide representative surveys the respondents were asked in 1996 (N=2,396) and 1998 (N=1,800) whether they "would like Turkey to be a member of the EU." Those who indicated that they would like EU membership were found to constitute 61.8 percent in 1998, up from 54.8 percent in 1996.[7] For both surveys, cross tabulations with respect to education level, religiosity as reflected in support for a Shari'a rule (şeriat) in Turkey and left-right ideological self-placement are given. Similar to Esmer's previous analyses, the Erder study observes that as education level increases support for EU membership increases. Approval of EU membership is significantly higher among those who do not support şeriat in Turkey than among those who do. Along the conventional left-right ideological divide those who consider themselves to be leftists are significantly more inclined to support EU membership.[8]

These findings reflect supportive evidence regarding the character of support for EU membership in Turkey. More educated, thus less religious, and—not surprisingly—more leftist constituencies are supportive of EU membership. However, since all of these explanatory factors are correlated, it is unclear which one (or ones) constitutes the dominant and significant factor influencing the preference for EU membership. Answering such a question requires a multivariate analysis, to which I will turn following a description of the responses obtained in the sample survey that forms the basis of the ensuing analyses.

Support for EU Membership and Basic Demographic Characteristics

Table 1 demonstrates that those who would vote in favor of full EU membership at a referendum comprise 64 percent of the sample while 30 percent indicate they would vote against EU membership and six percent did not provide an answer or did not have an opinion. We observe from Table 1 that males, rather than females, are more supportive of joining the EU. While age differences do not seem to be of significance, as the number

TABLE 1
IF THERE WERE TO BE A REFERENDUM ABOUT TURKEY'S FULL MEMBERSHIP TO THE EU, WOULD YOU VOTE IN FAVOR OF OR AGAINST FULL MEMBERSHIP?*

		I would vote in favour of Turkey's full membership in the EU	I would vote against Turkey's membership in the EU	DK/NA
Sex	Male	66	29	5
	Female	62	30	8
Age	18–24	65	30	4
	25–34	63	31	6
	35–44	64	30	5
	45–54	64	27	8
	55 +	63	27	10
Education	No formal schooling	56	29	15
	Primary + Junior high	60	33	7
	High school	68	27	4
	University +	74	20	6
Dwelling type	Shantytown dwellings	62	31	7
	Non-shantytown middle-range dwellings	64	30	6
	Non-shantytown luxurious dwellings	71	22	7
Urban-rural	Province center	65	29	6
	District center	67	27	6
	Village	61	32	7
Socio-economic status	Low	60	33	8
	Middle	65	30	5
	High	74	21	5
Knowledge of Kurdish	Yes	71	24	4
	No	63	30	7
Party preferences	ANAP	77	19	4
	CHP	79	17	3
	DSP	77	22	1
	DYP	65	28	7
	Saadet Partisi (SP)	38	58	3
	MHP	68	28	3
	HADEP	85	13	2
	Ak Parti	52	41	7
	Would not vote	70	26	4
	Would not vote for any one of the existing parties	61	31	7
	Undecided	63	23	14
	Would vote for one of the other minor parties	63	37	1
Total		64	30	6

Notes: DK/NA = Don't know/Not available.
 * All entries are row percentages.

of years under formal schooling increases the level of support for EU membership also rises. Poverty in general terms—as reflected in shanty town dwellings, low socio-economic status and rural habitation—brings about relatively low levels of support for EU membership. One exception to this observation comes with knowledge of Kurdish. Those who can speak Kurdish have significantly higher levels of support for joining the EU.

Geography of EU Support

Figure 1 shows the distribution of support for EU membership across clusters of provinces used in our sampling procedure.[9] The respondents from Cluster 4, which comprises Eastern and Southeastern provinces, show the highest level of support, with about 72 percent of the respondents indicating they would vote for EU membership. The next highest support comes from the metropolitan cities, with approximately 71 percent supporting EU membership. Clusters 1 and 2, which comprise mostly the coastal provinces, plus the inner Aegean and a few central Anatolian provinces, have about the same level of support: approximately 60 percent favor EU membership. The lowest level of support for EU membership comes from Cluster 5, with only 52.5 percent supporting such a step.

There are a number of striking observations resulting from this picture. First, none of the clusters of provinces present a majority indicating they would not vote for EU membership if a referendum were to be held. Second, there are clues as to where the geographic bases of anti-EU sentiments might lie. Third, these province clusters largely reflect electoral patterns, which means that not only do we have a geographical pattern here but one that also reflects political predispositions.

The largest number of provinces in this map lies at the western, coastal and inner Aegean and at some central Anatolian provinces where, again, a comfortable majority of about 60 percent back EU membership (Clusters 1 and 2). Together with the metropolitan cities, these EU support clusters reflect high degrees of electoral fragmentation and levels of competition in the provincial party systems, reflected in a high number of effective parties—of mainly centrist ideological tendencies—and relatively low levels of volatility (see Table 2). The Southeastern provinces of Cluster 4 have high degrees of electoral fragmentation (a high number of effective parties), quite low electoral volatility and a high degree of ideological polarization. Since this region is dominated by the People's Democracy Party (*Halkın Demokrasi Partisi*—HADEP), which remains unrepresented in parliament for being below the nationwide electoral support threshold of ten percent, it also has the largest gap between mass preferences and parliamentary representation.

FIGURE 1
LEVEL OF SUPPORT FOR FULL EU MEMBERSHIP ACROSS CLUSTERS OF PROVINCES

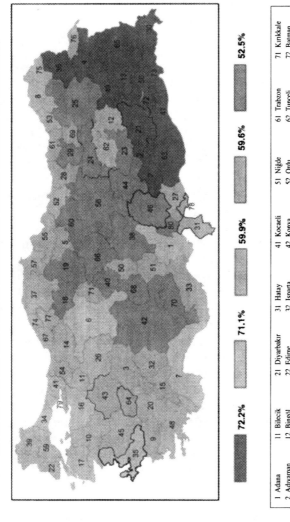

Who Wants Full EU Membership? 177

TABLE 2
PARTY SYSTEM CHARACTERISTICS IN DIFFERENT PROVINCE CLUSTERS

	Number of provinces	Population share (%)	ENP	Volatility	Center-right	Center-left	Pro-Islamist	Nationalist	Ethnic Kurdish
Cluster 1	22	16.6	3.3	21.1	32.5	35.9	8.6	15.5	2.5
Cluster 2	21	19.2	2.9	24.5	27.9	23.6	15.6	24.7	3.6
Cluster 3	7	35.5	3.2	23.0	24.2	37.3	14.0	17.8	3.5
Cluster 4	13	11.8	4.3	18.3	28.1	11.5	15.1	7.8	27.9
Cluster 5	17	16.9	2.6	26.6	20.5	18.3	21.3	32.4	1.8
	80	Country Average =	3.2	22.9	27.3	25.1	14.7	20.4	6.9

Notes: Center-right = ANAP, DYP.
Center-left = CHP, DSP.
Pro-Islamist = FP.
Nationalist = BBP, MHP.
Ethnic Kurdish = HADEP.

The *volatility index* (V) is calculated by using i=1,...N parties in the following formula:

$$V = \{(1/2)\Sigma_N(|Vote\%_{i,t} - Vote\%_{i,t-1}|)\}$$

The index lies between 0 and 1. V=1 represents a completely unstable system whereas V=0 represents one where all parties obtained the same vote shares as they did in the previous election. (See Mogens N. Pedersen, "The Dynamics of European Party Systems: Changing Patterns of Electoral Volatility," *European Journal of Political Research*, Vol.7, No.1 (1979), pp.1–26.

The *fractionalization index* (F) is calculated by using election outcomes for i=1,...N parties in the following formula:

$$F = \{1 - \Sigma_N (Vote\%)^2\}$$

F also varies between 0 and 1. The fractionalization index reaches a minimum of zero when one party receives all of the popular vote. When too many parties receive relatively small electoral support the index will approach to zero; i.e. extreme vote concentration corresponds to zero fractionalization. As the number of parties with small shares of electoral support increases the index approaches 1. See Douglas Rae, *The Political Consequences of Electoral Laws* (New Haven, CT: Yale University Press, 1967).

The effective number of parties (ENP) is calculated by using the fractionalization index N=[1/(1-F)]. See Rein Taagepera and Matthew S. Shugart, *Seats and Votes: The Effects and Determinants of Electoral Systems* (New Haven, CT: Yale University Press, 1989).

The core of resistance forces is likely to lie in Cluster 5 provinces where only a slim majority is supportive of EU membership. These provinces are typically the hotbeds of nationalist and pro-Islamist ideology. As Table 2 indicates, both nationalists as well as pro-Islamists receive the highest percentage of electoral support in Cluster 5. Electoral fragmentation and thus the level of competition—as reflected in the number of effective parties—are lowest compared to other clusters, but volatility of electoral support is highest while ideological polarization is also relatively low. In short, the MPs from this cluster are more likely to be subjected to constituency pressures, which might not be too supportive of EU membership. The centrist parties in this region have little political clout and, accordingly, the competition is between the parties to the right of the center. Since the ideological and (for our purposes) anti-European predispositions of the electorate in this cluster of provinces are unfavorable towards the EU at large, any move that might be portrayed as being concessionary by the competitor might cost the other side dearly in this cluster. Moreover, the electorate is quite volatile here, thus the right-of-center parties need to be wary of the easily shifting support in case they find themselves at odds with the expectations of the electorate. Thus, the party system characteristics of the province cluster where EU support is lowest do not allow for a cooperative leadership on the part of political party elites towards the EU membership issue. Right of center elites cannot push the pro-EU argument in their core constituencies of Cluster 5, which most likely is going to hurt them in the next elections. For an in-depth understanding of the political considerations I now turn to party constituencies' perceptions of the EU membership issue.

Party Preferences and Support for EU Membership

Perhaps most interesting among the results presented in Table 1 concerns the levels of support for EU membership across different party constituencies. Among all major political parties only the pro-Islamist Felicity Party (*Saadet Partisi*—SP) has a majority of its voters against full membership in the EU. SP's major pro-Islamist contender, the Justice and Development Party (*Adalet ve Kalkınma Partisi*—AKP), has a slight majority (52 percent) in favor of full EU membership. All other parties have clear majorities in favor of EU membership. It is interesting that the highest level of EU support comes from the Kurdish HADEP. Despite much open resistance by the party elite, the Nationalist Action Party (*Milliyetçi Hareket Partisi*—MHP) voters are also in clear support of the EU membership (68 percent). However, when one looks at the MHP voters in Cluster 5 (Table 2), it is clear that support for EU membership drops there to about 59 percent while its biggest competitors, the pro-Islamist SP and AKP—who resist membership in EU, are more numerous. Accordingly, in Cluster 5, the most volatile, not only does the MHP find its lowest level of support for EU membership but also observes that its most serious competitors for that cluster—that is, AKP and SP—have most of their constituencies against EU membership. Finally, while those who declare that they will not vote in the next election are clearly supportive of the EU membership (70 percent), those who are uncertain or alienated from the existing parties remain somewhat below the national average level of support, but still about 60 percent advocate EU membership.

Socio-Economic Status and Support for EU Membership

Among the variables in Table 1, those covering socio-economic data require slightly more detailed explanation. The three categories of social status are created by applying a series of statistical techniques.[10] These categories primarily reflect a relative ranking of individuals' ownership of certain household items, their income, level of education, dwelling type, number of adults living in the household, employment status, whether or not they own their residence or simply pay rent and whether they would consider migrating to EU countries even if Turkey catches up with Europe in terms of living standards. We observe that EU membership is being supported by 60 percent of the low socio-economic status group while the countrywide support is 64 percent. As we move up the socio-economic status ladder, we observe that support for EU membership in these two higher socio-economic status groups also rises.

Nationalist/Patriotic Values and Support for EU Membership

Several other conceptual variables are expected to be of significant influence over the expressed support for EU membership. One such variable revolves around the nationalist and patriotic rhetoric in Turkey. Both of these concepts are quite complicated and present a difficult measurement challenge due primarily to conceptual lack of clarity and consensus as to their meanings. The simple measurement framework used in the ensuing sections relies on a mixture of the more emotional nature of patriotism and the more cognitive meaning attached to nationalism. I take *patriotism* to mean "love of country" or simple attachment to one's homeland. *Nationalism*, however, is taken as a relative evaluation of one's country with respect to other countries or international groups. Obviously, the two concepts are intensely related to one other. Emotional attachment or affection is certainly a significant component of nationalism. However, patriotism does not necessarily involve a belief in the natural superiority of one's country over others.[11] The nationalist on the other hand, unlike a typical patriot, advocates international policies in support of his or her country. The attitudes toward EU membership specifically may be inversely related to nationalism but need not necessarily have a significant relationship—inverse or positive in direction—with patriotism.

Although the two concepts differ from one another, the efforts to measure them may not always perfectly reflect the inherent conceptual differences. The measurement adopted here reflects traits of both of these concepts in a single dimension since the main objective here was to define sub-groups of public opinion constituencies that significantly differ with respect to their preferences towards EU membership and related policies. The overlapping segments of patriots and nationalists were thus targeted here rather than the aspects differentiating one from the other. My expectation was that Turkish national interest advocates and those who promote love of the country on the basis of ethnic identity of the Turk (as opposed to ethnic separatists in Turkey) would, on the whole, be one and the same. In this case, the increased nationalist/patriotic attitudes would correlate negatively with support for EU membership. Obviously, this is not out of conceptual necessity but rather due to contextual circumstances in Turkey, where EU membership advocacy necessarily means acceptance of ethnic minority rights and concessions in the Aegean and Cyprus disputes—which obviously are not easily acceptable to nationalists. Patriots could accept concessions on these issues on grounds of love of country, perhaps seeing the fulfillment of possible long-term interests following these polices. However, in the Turkish context, high casualties—both in Cyprus and the Southeastern conflict—impede any differentiation between the nationalist and patriotic constituencies.

The idea of a united Europe free of national boundaries and united, not by shared cultural values, but by greater universal democratic ideals and shared interests in creating a cooperative transnational environment has not fared well with Turkish nationalist/patriotic circles. These circles have long taken the adversary of foreigners as the basis for mobilizing their support base. Traditionally, Turkish nationalists have used the communist threat of the cold war era as a mobilizing force for their supporters. In the aftermath of the cold war, the search for a mobilizing enemy was conveniently found in the ethnic separatist conflict in the southeast of the country. The open moral or material support of EU member states for ethnic separatism in Turkey was, in a sense, welcomed by the nationalists as a complement to the much needed evil "other" for building not only a sympathizer group but also a formidable electoral support base as proven in the 1999 elections.[12]

As Table 3 demonstrates, the composite scale of nationalist/patriotic attitudes conforms well to our a priori expectations. Those respondents who hold relatively more intense nationalist/patriotic attitudes towards others have a relatively low degree of support for EU membership whereas those who are relatively less nationalistic and patriotic tend to support EU membership well above the overall national levels of support. However, as previously observed with the nationalist MHP constituencies, even within the highest nationalist/patriotic attitudes group those who would vote for

TABLE 3
IF THERE WERE TO BE A REFERENDUM ABOUT TURKEY'S FULL MEMBERSHIP TO THE EU, WOULD YOU VOTE IN FAVOR OF OR AGAINST FULL MEMBERSHIP?*

		I would vote in in favour of Turkey's full membership in the EU	I would vote against Turkey's full membership in the EU	DK/NA
Nationalist attitudes	Relatively low	77	20	3
	Middle	66	28	6
	Relatively high	57	36	7
Euro-skepticism	Relatively low	74	22	4
	Middle	68	27	6
	Relatively high	56	39	6
Pro-EU attitudes	Relatively low	39	53	8
	Middle	63	30	6
	Relatively high	86	12	2
Religiosity	Relatively low	80	16	4
	Middle	65	31	4
	Relatively high	51	42	7
Anti-democratic attitudes	Relatively low	75	22	4
	Middle	64	30	7
	Relatively high	55	41	5
Total		**64**	**30**	**6**

Note: * All entries are row percentages.

EU membership are in a clear majority. Therefore, it is hard to claim that the nationalist/patriotic predispositions of individuals act as a barrier against EU membership.

Euro-skepticism, Pro-EU Attitudes and Support for EU Membership

Skepticism towards the EU and Europeans in general is summarized in the *Euro-skepticism* variable.[13] This variable is a weighted summary of attitudes on EU policy towards the Turkish bid for membership, Europeans' general failure to understand Turks, the perceived bias in the EU's evaluation of the Turkish application and the perceived threat of losing national identity when a country becomes a full member. The variable of pro-EU attitudes and predispositions is also a weighted scale of responses to questions concerning the EU's ability to resolve conflicts in the Aegean and Cyprus, whether one supports having Europeans work in Turkey, having a European marry one's daughter, or having Europeans as neighbors. Additional factors considered were whether one evaluates the Customs Union favorably and whether one approves of the policy adjustments and legal changes undertaken in order to conform to EU standards and satisfy the Copenhagen criteria.

As expected, Table 3 indicates that when the degree of skepticism towards EU and Europeans increases, the tendency to support EU membership declines. Similarly, when the degree of positive predispositions and supportive attitudes towards EU policies increase, the tendency to support EU membership rises. These categorizations of low, middle and high degrees of skepticism or pro-EU attitudes are all relative. Therefore, what is more important to note here is not the size of these groups within the sample but rather the changing character of support levels across them. In other words, do we observe the support level to be the lowest (highest) for the lowest category in a relationship that is expected to be positive (negative)? The expected tendency to support EU membership can be observed in both Euro-skeptics and those who have pro-EU attitudes. As we observed in previous sections, within the group considered the most skeptical of the EU, a majority of the respondents are not against EU membership for Turkey and the level of support rises as we move to lower levels of Euro-skepticism. However, in the group portraying the lowest pro-EU attitude, we observe that 53 percent oppose EU membership. As we move into the middle category and upwards on the pro-EU attitude scale, we observe clear majorities in support of EU membership.

Religiosity and Support for EU Membership

As previous works have already shown, there is a general expectation that support for EU membership will be inversely related to an individual's level of religiosity. Similar to previous measurement exercises, the religiosity variable used in Table 3 is based on a composite index of people's attitudes on certain issues of religious significance, such as the headscarf and turban ban, the necessity to provide freedom of conscience and religion, religious practices and the choice of using "Muslim" as a primary identity together with the perception of the EU as a "Christian club." We observe that religiosity is indeed inversely related with support for EU membership. However, once again—even in the highest religiosity group—a majority supports EU membership.

Attitudes toward Democracy and Support for EU Membership

Democratic principles are an integral part of the EU accession process. Many of the programmatic implications of the Copenhagen criteria for Turkey concern policy and legislation changes to ensure development of a democratic environment in the country. An extensive set of questions in our survey involved obtaining respondents' reactions to many assertions concerning democracy's ability to deal with various problems and whether certain freedoms could be banned depending on circumstances or should be available under any conditions. The summary measure of all these evaluations about freedoms and democracy at large is grasped by the variable anti-democratic attitudes. As expected, those who are skeptical about democracy's ability to resolve pressing problems in Turkey approve of somewhat curtailing basic rights and freedoms—depending on circumstances—and have the lowest tendency to approve of full membership in the EU. As this skepticism towards democracy declines, support for EU membership increases (see Table 3).

An important observation at this juncture is that despite variation in the level of support for EU membership across different sub-groups of our sample in the expected direction, almost all sub-groups display clear majorities supporting the EU cause. Only among the supporters of SP and in the sub-group where pro-EU predispositions are lowest do we detect a majority opposed to EU membership. Given the fact that these sub-groups are not large, the hypothetical referendum result should be clear: the Turkish public at large approves of EU membership. However, since there is an undeniably influential resistance to the fulfilling of all of the Copenhagen criteria and even to beginning the accession negotiations, the real question should be how to discern the factors most influential in determining support for EU membership. Many of the variables used in the analyses above are correlated to one another, making it impossible to determine whether their singular impact on EU membership support would actually continue once the influences of various other variables are controlled for in a multivariate test. Once these tests are carried out, one would be able to analyze intervening factors that might be responsible for the obvious referendum paradox we might be faced with. The paradoxical nature of the problem is that despite clear majorities supporting the EU membership in sub-groups as well as within the electorate at large, representatives in parliament are reluctant to pass the necessary legislation for fulfilling the Copenhagen criteria and to unambiguously support Turkey's bid for membership in the EU.[14]

A MULTIVARIATE ANALYSIS OF SUPPORT FOR EU MEMBERSHIP IN TURKEY

Table 4 reports the results of a binary logistic regression using the referendum question as the dependent variable, which is coded as 1 for those who indicated that they would vote for Turkey's full membership in the EU and 0 for those who would vote against it.[15] Since the estimated model involves a number of categorical dummy variables as well as regular interval ratio variables, it is necessary to note the reference category that is grasped by the model's constant term. The reference category here is the joint complement of all dummy variables in the equation. It represents women with no formal schooling, who do not know Kurdish, and who live in urban Metropolitan cities. These women are also undecided about their party of choice, did not have to take loans or use past savings in the past year and are also optimistic about the economic conditions of their families over the next year. The negative sign of the constant term implies that these women have a bias against voting in favor of Turkey's full membership in the EU. We see that party choice variables are all insignificant except for those who indicate they would vote for marginal parties not included in the list of parties; these marginal voters have a lower tendency to support membership in the EU. It is interesting to note that, disregarding SP voters, when the impacts of attitudinal, demographic and other variables are controlled, party choice ceases to be of significance in explaining vote choice in the EU referendum. This is despite the above observation of comfortable majorities in support of the EU in all party constituencies. In other words, if one does not control for the influences of other variables, the party choice might be taken to be of significance in explaining the referendum vote.

Attitudinal indicators discussed above appear to be the most influential of all variables in the model. As expected, the degree of Euro-skepticism has a significant negative impact while pro-EU attitudes have a significant positive impact on the likelihood of voting in support of EU membership. As an individual becomes more religious or more in support of anti-democratic assertions their likelihood of being supportive of the EU membership declines. Despite the fact that, in a categorical treatment, nationalistic/patriotic attitudes yielded an expected impact on EU support levels in the above analysis, when used in a multivariate setting this variable also ceases to be significant. This might be a reflection of the fact that in our measurement of this complex phenomenon of nationalist/patriotic attitudes it is the patriotism rather than nationalism that dominates our measurement. Being patriots rather than nationalists, Turkish voters are not negatively predisposed against the EU, so this factor is not influential in explaining their choice of support for EU membership.

Besides pro-EU attitudes, evaluations of individuals concerning the impact of EU membership on their personal lives and the likelihood of Turkey becoming a full EU member have the largest positive impacts on individuals' decisions concerning EU membership. In other words, as individuals become more convinced that they will personally benefit from membership and that it is more likely that Turkey will become a member

TABLE 4
DETERMINANTS OF SUPPORT FOR EU MEMBERSHIP IN A REFERENDUM

	Coefficients	Standard Error	Significance level
Constant	**-2.72**	**0.55**	**0.00**
Political preferences			
ANAP	0.40	0.43	0.34
CHP	0.01	0.31	0.97
DSP	0.10	0.43	0.81
DYP	0.10	0.33	0.76
SP	-0.74	0.47	0.12
MHP	0.07	0.33	0.83
HADEP	-0.01	0.46	0.98
AKP	-0.01	0.26	0.98
Not going to cast a vote	-0.06	0.33	0.85
Will vote for none of the presently available parties	-0.10	0.25	0.68
Will vote for other smaller parties	**-0.80**	**0.40**	**0.04**
Attitudinal Indicators			
Nationalist/patriotic attitudes	-0.02	0.08	0.84
Euro-skepticism	**-0.21**	**0.07**	**0.00**
Pro-EU attitudes	**0.49**	**0.08**	**0.00**
Religiosity	**-0.24**	**0.08**	**0.00**
Anti-Democratic attitudes	**-0.21**	**0.07**	**0.00**
Not satisfied with the way Turkish democracy works	0.38	0.23	0.10
Evaluation of the way personal life will change in case Turkey becomes a member in EU	**0.46**	**0.03**	**0.00**
Evaluation of the possibility that Turkey becomes a full member in EU over the next ten years	**0.06**	**0.03**	**0.01**
Various Demographic Indicators			
Age	**0.01**	**0.01**	**0.03**
Male	0.09	0.14	0.49
Knows Kurdish	0.38	0.22	0.09
Living in a rural area	-0.08	0.15	0.58
Number of adults working in the household	-0.05	0.06	0.42
Cluster 1	**-0.56**	**0.21**	**0.01**
Cluster 2	**-0.54**	**0.18**	**0.00**
Cluster 4	0.12	0.26	0.64
Cluster 5	**-0.45**	**0.19**	**0.02**
Primary + junior high school graduate	0.37	0.31	0.23
High school graduate	0.42	0.35	0.22
University + graduate	0.68	0.41	0.10
Economic wellbeing and expectations			
Socio-economic status	-0.09	0.09	0.31
Pessimistic expectations for the family's economic situation over the next year	-0.19	0.13	0.15
Condition of family's economic situation over the past year (had to take loans or used past savings)	-0.02	0.13	0.87

		Predicted		
		Yes to EU	No to EU	% correctly predicted
Observed	Yes to EU	332	254	56.7
	No to EU	115	1180	91.1
			Overall	80.4
Nagelkerke R-square	0.45			

over the next ten years, they tend to support EU membership in a referendum setting.

Surprisingly, as people become older they tend to vote for EU membership. In other words, being younger does not mean that individuals will be more supportive of the EU membership. Although knowing Kurdish has a somewhat positive influence over the EU vote, it is not significant at the conventional levels. Neither does the urban/rural divide appear to be significant, nor the level of education. The fact that the level of education ceases to be significant is also surprising. Together with age being significant, this finding points to the fact that younger generations who are typically more educated are not inculcated with a pro-EU predisposition. In fact, after controlling for the influences of attitudinal variables, education level alone no longer significantly differentiates EU supporters from the rest.

Geographic location (as depicted in Figure 1) continues to remain significant in the multivariate model. Individuals living in the metropolitan provinces, the East and the Southeastern provinces are not significantly different from each other regarding their likelihood of support for EU membership. Individuals in all remaining clusters have a lower tendency to support EU membership. It is also worthwhile to note that having controlled for their nationalist/patriotic and anti-democratic attitudes together with their Euro-skepticism, individuals in Cluster 5 are not more likely to be against EU membership compared to Clusters 1 and 2.

The voting preference for EU membership in a referendum setting does not seem to be influenced by socio-economic status or retrospective or prospective evaluations of economic conditions. Overall, the multivariate model predicts 80 percent of the vote correctly.

CONCLUSIONS

The results of the above analyses are somewhat surprising. Despite increasingly polarized debates in public by the political elite of major parties, there exists very little significant difference in their constituencies' preferences concerning Turkey's bid for membership in the EU. In all major parties, except the pro-Islamist Felicity Party (SP), a clear majority supports Turkey joining the EU. However, general attitudinal bases of resistance to EU membership—religiosity, anti-democratic attitudes and Euro-skepticism—do form sources of EU refutation. The Turkish electorate at large has very high expectations from membership and as their expectations and optimism about the possible membership grow, their tendency to support membership also grows. Geographic position and generation gap also seem to inhibit consensus on EU membership.

From a policy perspective, there exist many so-called "sensitive" issues that can easily be used by groups and parties who choose to oppose EU membership. These issues are more likely to be publicly expressed, and thus conveniently exploited, within a nationalistic, Euro-skeptic and religious rhetoric so as to make them more palatable to the largely EU-supportive Turkish public. The choice of the rhetoric adopted may significantly change the level of support for or against policy modifications necessary for the fulfillment of the Copenhagen criteria. A significant reason for such fragility of EU support in some constituencies is expected to be lack of information about the EU membership process and policy requirements of full membership. Accordingly, despite mass public support for EU membership, the polarized elite resistance to membership finds ample opportunities to manipulate the public agenda. Segments within the political elite can easily accomplish their objective of melting mass support for EU membership by providing misinformation to the public and strategically shaping their rhetoric around the sensitive issues; this is especially the case concerning the cultural rights of citizens of Kurdish origin and the abolition of the death penalty, which is linked to the Kurdish issue due to the fact that Abdullah Öcalan, the PKK leader, is currently on death row.[16]

Another surprising result derives from the fact that in all of the sub-constituencies devised to test EU support, excluding the segment of the electorate holding a low degree of pro-EU predispositions, a clear majority supports EU membership. How, then, is it possible that political elites manage to resist policy changes without losing electoral support or endangering their legitimacy within the Turkish political system? This question might be seen as somewhat unnecessary given the surprising passage of the EU package that lifted the ban on education in languages other than Turkish and the broadcasting of such languages (the most problematic being Kurdish) on television and radio and abolished the death penalty in the Turkish penal system along with many other pieces of sensitive legislation. However, since the implementation of these new legislative frameworks of cultural rights will now be the focus of attention, there is still room for political resistance and maneuvering that merits explanation. Moreover, since these pieces of legislation were passed when parliament had already decided on early elections, the resistance to EU membership is more likely now to take the form of a campaign issue by the nationalist parties and cadres.

One possible explanation of the persistent resistance of the political elite to policy changes necessary for EU membership could be the very nature of the Turkish representation system. Once the constituent bases of representation are defined, it may so happen that while the majority at large in a referendum prefers to become a full member of the EU, without changing anybody's preferences sub-groups or sub-constituencies may be so distributed that a majority of them may contain majorities preferring the option of Turkey staying out of the EU, hence a referendum paradox may arise. Defined in either geographical or other functional or attitudinal terms, almost all sub-constituencies in Turkey have a majority that supports EU membership. The paradox, therefore, may lie in the Turkish representation system, which allows for the political elite to ignore and/or manipulate the preferences of the masses they face. Given the recent passage of the so-called "EU adjustment" legislation at the beginning of August 2002, it seems that a possible referendum paradox can be avoided in the Turkish system. However, pockets of resistance within the representation system will continue to be serious forces that will repeatedly surface as Euro-skepticism flares up in the country for many different reasons.

The potentially paradoxical nature of the Turkish representation system dissolves if one diagnoses that EU membership and related issues evolving around the process of accession to full membership are simply unimportant for the masses at large and thus politically non-salient, if not irrelevant. Such a diagnosis is quite difficult to produce. It is quite true that the layman in the street in Turkey cares more about daily economic difficulties than about complicated policy changes or legislation concerning cultural minority rights, especially within the context of the deep economic crisis that has gravely shaken the country. On the other hand, it is also clear that, before the summer of 2002, there had not been a single political leader from any of the political parties who supported EU membership openly and without reservations concerning the Copenhagen criteria. None of these leaders, therefore, linked the "bread-and-butter" issues of the current economic crisis to the prospect of EU membership or, more significantly, to the prospect of failing to meet the Copenhagen criteria before the end of the year 2002. It is understandable that such a cautionary position might not be easily adopted by the ruling party elites, nor would such a stand be credible, since the ruling parties have both the power, as well as the duty, to act if some precautionary measure needs to be taken. However, even the opposition parties that consistently repeat their support for EU membership did not link the likely failure to meet the Copenhagen criteria to a deepening economic crisis.

Besides the link to economic crisis there exist a number of other issues that could also be linked to EU criteria, thus helping to make the salience of the EU topics even greater. These include issues such as insufficient public services and vast corruption. With the resignation of the largest partner in the DSP ruling coalition in summer 2002 and the resulting New Turkey Party (*Yeni Türkiye Partisi*—YTP) under the leadership of former Minister of Foreign Affairs İsmail Cem, EU and EU-related issues seem to be pushed to the forefront of political debate in the country. However, it remains to be seen how other political party leaders will deal with this issue in front of the electorate. Although, besides Cem, ANAP leader Mesut Yılmaz seems ready to use this issue in his campaign, the MHP leadership now openly questions the worth of EU membership. In short, if the EU issue is going to shape the electoral agenda in the next general elections, the willingness of the political elites to raise the salience of the EU issues will be a major factor behind this development.

Another possible explanation for the failure of the political elites to meet mass preferences concerning EU membership pertains to the functioning of the Turkish party organization. A small ruling elite that keeps any opposition, together with any civil society influence, out of their parties, dominates the Turkish parties. Hence, it is not surprising that civil society preferences for EU membership has failed to penetrate the parties and thus pressure the party organizations and their leaders to reformulate their positions in support of the EU membership. Unless the parties open up to pro-EU interest groups' influence, their pro-EU reactions will remain limited in the future.

Alternatively, the answer may lie more in the geographical support bases of the parties and the distribution of support for membership in the EU. As noted above, while the highest degree of support for membership is observed in the metropolitan provinces as well as the Eastern and Southeastern provinces, the lowest level is observed in the central Anatolian provinces. The party system characteristics of these regions of EU support are such that they do not allow the dominant parties of these regions to push for much pro-EU policy initiatives if they want to maintain or build upon their previous levels of electoral support. More specifically, the nationalist and pro-Islamist parties compete for the core of their electoral support in the same provinces where we observe the lowest level of support for EU. These provinces also have the highest level of volatility and lowest effective number of parties; that is, the lowest levels of competition in their provincial party systems, which allow for 2.6 effective parties appearing within a highly volatile context. If they adopt an openly pro-EU stand they risk facing harsh opposition in these provinces by the only other real competitor. Since the volatility of electoral support is also the highest in the country, for these provinces the likelihood of serious electoral losses is quite high. In consequence, both the nationalists and the pro-Islamists would be very timid in welcoming pro-EU changes if they act simply as rational representatives of their core constituencies and in expectation of campaign tactics that might be followed by their competitors. Such an explanation would not be valid, of course, if the pro-Islamist and nationalist parties can rationally hope to gain more votes somewhere else than the sums they lose in their core provinces. Such an expectation is perhaps more valid for the pro-Islamists than for the nationalists, since the most prominent pro-Islamist party (the Virtue Party, *Fazilet Partisi*—FP) has recently been split in two. Such divisions always have the potential to bring about the shifting basis of electoral constituencies and more entrepreneurial political spirit. The MHP has been in office for approximately the last three years and in the process has either committed itself more solidly to certain stands or chosen not to act on certain policies. The AKP, for instance, may feel less pressure against adopting a more liberal pro-EU stand than the MHP since such a position may attract more of the floating voters. In addition, on a cautionary note, one should keep in mind that no party is fully flexible in adopting certain policy stands due to past ideological commitments. From this perspective, being newly formed allows the AKP more flexibility. However, it is unclear as to what degree any of the new parties are truly new and thus less constrained.

I have consciously refrained from commenting on the ideological commitments of the parties concerning the EU membership issue. Obviously, parties' ideological predispositions effectively shape their stands. Given the fact that sovereignty as well as minority rights together with many commercial interests are at stake here, ideological baggage is likely to grow heavier as electoral pressures grow. However, the first round of battle seems to have been lost by the Euro-skeptic forces. The Turkish parliament avoided falling into the trap of a referendum paradox and pushed ahead with fulfilling the Copenhagen criteria necessary for the commencement of negotiations for full membership. However, the institutional shape of the Turkish party system and political dynamics of November 2002 general elections continue to feed significant resistance to EU membership. It remains to be seen whether such resistance will gain momentum in the heat of electoral campaign, as a result of developments in the Cyprus negotiations, or any other likely event that would flare up if terror began in Southeastern Turkey (for example, due to US intervention in Iraq). All of these necessitate a continued focus of attention on the popular bases of support for or opposition to EU membership among Turkish voters and elites.

POSTSCRIPT

Since the completion of this essay a number of important developments have taken place that deserve evaluation in light of the arguments made earlier. One such evaluation concerns the role of the EU related issues in the general elections of November 3, 2002.

Looking back, one suspects that it was the economic crisis, the consequent incompetence of the incumbent coalition, as well as the main opposition, that proved responsible for the defeat of almost all of the Turkish party establishment. However, elections are always more about the future than about the judgements of the past. From this perspective, only two parties, CHP (Republican People's Party—*Cumhuriyet Halk Partisi*) and AKP seem to have convinced the institutionally relevant portion of the electorate—that is, more than ten percent of the nation-wide electorate—of their credibility.

To what degree then does the EU membership and the related reform process relate to the core economic worries of the electorate? Leaders of the major parties seem to have largely ignored EU-related discussions in their campaigns. However, short of a systematic evaluation of issues discussed during the 2002 elections, a reading of the election manifestoes of both AKP and CHP leads one to observe that EU-related issues played a critical role.[17] In its election manifesto the AKP portrayed the EU as a catalyst of many different issues ranging from the obvious foreign policy discussions about Cyprus and Turkish-Greek relations to reform of the judicial system, expansion of basic citizens' rights, economic policy, municipal reform, foreign direct investment policies and transportation policy. The CHP's emphasis was more on the membership aspect of the debate. However, in a similar fashion to AKP's argument, the CHP manifesto intricately linked EU issues to a large number of policy areas. In short, economic crisis formed the backbone of election issues and prepared a fertile ground for the emphasis of reform in public policy. Reform discussions provided a convenient linkage to the debate about EU membership and the policy transformations that this necessitates.

Another observation worthy of note is the presence of two staunchly nationalistic, and thus Euro-skeptic, parties in the campaign, the Young Party (*Genç Parti*—GP) and the MHP. Although both parties had a majority of their supporters in favor of the EU, their rhetoric were potentially inflammatory and carried high doses of anti-Europeanism. Both seemed to prefer to be the only party of the Euro-skeptics and thus carry high enough support behind them to pass the ten percent threshold.

Ex-post facto, the support bases of GP and MHP is seen not to overlap.[18] GP was a real threat to the centrist-left and -right establishments in the coastal provinces, whereas MHP was a force to be reckoned with in the central Anatolian provinces where AKP got most of its support. GP received around seven percent whereas MHP got about nine percent of support nationwide; enough to provide a serious threat since a slight increase in either one could have pushed them above the ten percent threshold and changed the seat distribution in the parliament substantially. In short, neither CHP facing GP, nor AKP facing MHP in their core constituencies in coastal or central Anatolian provinces respectively, could afford to push EU-related issues beyond subtle linkage to various reform debates. In consequence, the anti-European front was not confronted in any public debate and the two largest parties kept the EU issues at low salience. At the same time, the Euro-skeptic front was conveniently kept divided into smaller party constituencies, thus helping to waste their representation by keeping them out of the parliament since they were below the ten percent threshold.

NOTES

1. Putnam gives a well-rounded account of the dual nature of the policymaking context that involves many intricate sets of relations between the diplomatic negotiators (Level I) and the grass-roots interactions between non-official players like businesses, NGOs and other civil society groups (Level II). See Robert Putnam, "Diplomacy and Domestic Politics: The Logic of Two-Level Games," *International Organisation*, Vol.42, No.3 (1988), pp.427–60. For a more extensive treatment of the two-level games concept, see Peter B. Evans, Harold K. Jacobson and Robert D. Putnam (eds.), *Double-edged Diplomacy: International Bargaining and Domestic Politics* (Berkeley and Los Angeles, CA: University of California Press, 1993).
2. The survey was undertaken by a team of Boğaziçi University scholars including the author, Refik Erzan, Kemal Kirişci and Hakan Yılmaz. The Turkish Economic and Social Studies Foundation (*Türkiye Ekonomik ve Sosyal Etüdler Vakfı*—TESEV) graciously provided the financial support. For details of the results, see <http://www.tesev.org.tr/eng/>.
3. A description of the sampling procedures followed can be found on the TESEV website (<http://www.tesev.org.tr/eng/>) or may be obtained from the author.
4. Yılmaz Esmer, "Türk Kamuoyu ve Avrupa" [Turkish Public Opinion and Europe], in *Türkiye Avrupa Birliğinin Neresinde? Gümrük Birliği Anlaşmasının Düşündürdükleri* [Where is Turkey in Europe? Thoughts on Customs Union with EU] (Ayraç Yayınevi, 1997), pp.124–35.
5. Ibid., pp.134–5.
6. TÜSES (Turkish Social Economic and Political Studies Foundation), *Türkiye'de Siyasi Parti Seçmenleri ve Toplum Düzeni* [Political Party Constituencies and Social Order in Turkey] (Boyut Matbaacılık Aş, 1999).
7. Ibid., p.79.
8. Ibid., pp.79–83.

9. First, provinces were divided into clusters according to socio-economic characteristics and political preferences. Balıkesir, Denizli and Sinop were selected from Cluster 1, which comprises the coastal provinces of the Black Sea, Marmara and Aegean regions. Gaziantep, Samsun and Burdur were selected from Cluster 2, which comprises mostly the inner Aegean and some Black Sea and Southeastern provinces. Adana, Bursa, İzmir, Ankara and Istanbul were selected from the metropolitan provinces of Cluster 3. Diyarbakır, Kars and Şanlıurfa were selected to represent the Southeastern and Eastern provinces of Cluster 4. Finally Erzurum, Konya and Malatya, were selected to represent the Central and Eastern Anatolia provinces of Cluster 5. The EU membership support levels plotted on Figure 1 represent the percentage support observed in these provinces grouped according to their cluster membership and generalized across all provinces in their clusters.
10. First a factor analysis was applied to create a composite index of socio-economic status, then the factor scores that reflect a summary measure of all values of the index components for every individual are used in a cluster analysis. As a result, those individuals who belong to low socio-economic status can be differentiated from the middle and higher levels. A similar path of analysis was followed in all variables created below for analyzing nationalist/patriotic attitudes, Euro-skepticism, religiosity and attitudes toward democracy. The details of these analyses can be obtained from the author.
11. R. Kosterman, and S. Feshbach, "Toward a Measurement of Patriotic and Nationalist Attitudes," *Political Psychology*, Vol.10 (1989), pp.257–74.
12. See Ali Çarkoğlu, "Geography of April 1999 Turkish Elections," *Turkish Studies*, Vol.1, No.1 (2000), pp.149–71 and Ersin Kalaycıoğlu, "The Shaping of Political Preferences in Turkey: Coping with the Post-Cold-War Era," *New Perspectives on Turkey*, Vol.20, No.1 (1999), pp.47–76.
13. Discussions of Euro-skepticism have recently attracted intense academic interest. For a taste of the issues involved in these discussions, see Paul Taggart, "A Touchstone of Dissent: Euroscepticism in Contemporary Western European Party Systems," *European Journal of Political Research*, Vol.33 (1998), pp.363–88; Aleks Szczerbiak and Paul Taggart, *Opposing Europe: Party Systems and Opposition to the Union, the Euro and Europeanisation* (Falmer, Brighton: Sussex European Institute Working Paper No.36. Opposing Europe Research Network Working Paper No.1, Oct. 2000); Paul Taggart and Aleks Szczerbiak, *Parties, Positions and Europe: Euroskepticism in the EU Candidate States of Central and Eastern Europe* (Falmer, Brighton: Opposing Europe Research Network Working Paper No.2, May 2001); Paul Taggart and Aleks Szczerbiak, *The Party Politics of Euroskepticism in EU Member and Candidate States* (Falmer, Brighton: Opposing Europe Research Network Working Paper No.6, April 2002).
14. Hannu Nurmi defines the referendum paradox in the following way: "Suppose that a consultative referendum is arranged on an issue, say ... joining the European Union ... Suppose that 'yes' wins by a handsome margin. Then the issue is brought to the parliament, which makes the final decision. It may happen that the latter decision is 'no' despite the results of the referendum." See Hannu Nurmi, *Voting Paradoxes and How to Deal with Them* (Berlin-Heidelberg: SpringerVerlag, 1999), p.76. See also Hannu Nurmi, "Referendum Design: An Exercise in Applied Social Choice Theory," *Scandinavian Political Studies*, Vol.20 (1997), pp.33–52; Hannu Nurmi, "Compound Majority Paradoxes and Proportional Representation," *European Journal of Political Economy*, Vol.13 (1997), pp.443–54. The referendum paradox occurs whenever the majority of a representative body reverts the majority decision of a referendum because the majority of the representatives may observe that a majority in the constituency they represent prefer the option against the majority decision of a referendum. Obviously, such an outcome depends on how constituencies in a representative body are defined—either in geographic terms, as it is usually done, or even non-overlapping functional bases of representation, which I use in some of the analyses below.
15. Since the dependent variable is a binary dummy variable the conventional regression

methods are not appropriate here. For an accessible review of the methods used here, see John H. Aldrich and Forrest D. Nelson, *Linear Probability, Logit and Probit Models* (Newbury Park, CA: Sage, 1984) and Alfred Demaris, *Logit Modelling, Practical Applications* (Newbury Park, CA: Sage, 1992).

16. Due to lack of space, a detailed analysis of these sensitive issues will have to be tackled elsewhere. However, the same survey from which the data used here originates contains questions that deal with these issues. This, and a descriptive analysis, can be found at <http://www.tesev.org.tr/eng/>.

17. AKP's election manifesto, *Herşey Türkiye İçin* [Everything is for Turkey], is available at <http://www.akparti.org.tr/>. CHP's election manifesto, *Güzel Günler Göreceğiz!* [We'll See Good Days!], is available at <http://secim2002.chp.org.tr/bildirge.asp>.

18. See Ali Çarkoğlu, "The Turkish General Elections of 2002," *South European Society and Politics* (forthcoming).

Turkish Parliamentarians' Perspectives on Turkey's Relations with the European Union

LAUREN M. McLAREN
and MELTEM MÜFTÜLER-BAÇ

Turkey is currently one of the 13 candidates for European Union (EU) membership. Among these candidates, it has a long association with the EU (since 1963) and the oldest standing application for membership (since 1987). Despite this history, when the EU embarked on its enlargement process in the 1990s it did not include Turkey in its list of prospective candidates. During the Luxembourg summit of December 1997, the European Council decided to clear the path for the Union's enlargement towards the Central and Eastern European countries and Cyprus, basing its decision upon the European Commission's proposal in its Agenda 2000 of July 1997.[1] However, it was only quite recently, during the Helsinki summit of the European Council of December 1999, that the EU included Turkey in this process of enlargement by granting it candidacy. Officially, the major obstacle to Turkey's accession is the need to meet the Copenhagen criteria adopted in 1993,[2] but there are other important obstacles that are not part of the Copenhagen criteria which still play a significant role in the accession process, such as Turkey's relations with Greece—a member of the EC/EU since 1981. Particularly important within the general framework of Turkey's relations with Greece is the Cyprus problem. The EU's Accession Partnership Document (APD) of November 2001 has included the resolution of the Cyprus issue among the medium term objectives that Turkey must meet. Thus, Turkey's adherence to the Copenhagen criteria will officially determine when and under what conditions the EU will begin accession negotiations with Turkey, but the resolution of the Cyprus conflict is likely to be an equally important factor in determining the opening date for Turkey's accession negotiations. It is, therefore, important to assess the extent to which the Turkish public and its representatives are aware of the critical importance of these factors.

Throughout this often turbulent history of relations between the EU and Turkey very little was known about how Turkish citizens view these relations. This analysis begins by briefly reviewing Turkish-EU relations in terms of the obstacles to Turkey's accession, and then presents the results of a survey that was conducted among a rather important portion of the Turkish citizenry, deputies in the Turkish parliament—namely the Turkish Grand National Assembly (*Türkiye Büyük Millet Meclisi*— TBMM). These individuals are important not only as representatives of public opinion related to the EU but also as decisionmakers in the adoption of new legislation which is required to meet EU standards. Specifically, Turkish members of parliament (MPs) must give final approval to the government's EU-related proposals, many of which touch upon extremely controversial issues such as minority rights and privatization of industries. The MPs' perceptions of the EU are, to a great extent, shaped by their party line and affiliations. Nevertheless, it is important to assess their individual perceptions as they are representatives of the mass public.

Our survey of 61 MPs was conducted in April/May 2000. The results indicate that, despite the ups and downs in Turkish-EU relations and some fears that cultural/religious issues might prevent Turkey from one day becoming a full EU member state, most members of the Turkish Parliament are rather hopeful about Turkey joining the EU in the relatively near future. The results that address the perceived obstacles facing Turkey, the benefits to be gained from membership and the attitudes towards one of the specific issues involved in Turkish-EU relations—the Cyprus issue—are the focus of the current analysis.

We believe that in terms of the Turkish political elite's perceptions of EU membership and Turkey's position in the EU's enlargement process the findings of this contribution will shed light on Turkey's negotiations with the EU and its future prospects. Specifically, should the results indicate a lack of consensus regarding Turkey's accession to the EU or a lack of acceptance of the potential problems that must first be resolved this will not bode well for Turkey's future EU membership. The reforms that must be made in order to meet the EU's Copenhagen criteria are extensive and some will be economically and politically painful. If there is no consensus regarding EU membership in the first place it will be quite difficult for the government to continue pushing through the necessary changes in the TBMM.[3] Similarly, results indicating a lack of understanding among the deputies concerning the significance of Cyprus in Turkey's relations with the EU—or no willingness to concede that that there is a problem in Cyprus—would not bode well for generating a domestic consensus on its resolution, even though the resolution of the Cyprus conflict is not part of the Copenhagen criteria. Thus, we believe an analysis of the attitudes of the Turkish political elite is important in order to assess the nature of Turkey's negotiations with the EU.

TURKEY'S RELATIONS WITH THE EUROPEAN UNION

At the end of the Second World War a new European order was created with the establishment of new institutions. Turkey became a member of several European and western organizations, such as the Organization for Economic Cooperation and Development (OECD [1948]), the Council of Europe (1949) and the North Atlantic Treaty Organization (NATO [1952]). The quest for external validation of its European credentials and a desire to participate in a community of Europeans eventually led leaders to apply for associate membership of the European Economic Community (EC) in 1959.[4] The Ankara Agreement, modeled according to the Greek Association Agreement—the Athens Treaty, was signed in 1963.[5] Article 28 of the Ankara Treaty stipulates that Turkey's full membership would be possible when both the EC and the Turkish political elite find that Turkey would be able to meet the obligations of membership. Thus, there was a great deal of encouragement for Turkey to continue on its stated path of becoming part of the community of Europe.

Turkey is one of two countries whose Association Agreement (AA) stipulated that it would be welcome to join the EC as a full member at a future date when able to fulfil the requirements of membership; the other country with a similar clause in its AA being Greece.[6] The Association Agreement was amended in 1970 with the signing of the Additional Protocol, which stated the ultimate goal as the creation of a customs union between Turkey and the EC by December 31, 1995. Relations between the two sides, however, were far from cordial between the time of the Additional Protocol and the establishment of the Customs Union.[7] This was partly as a result of perceived bad relations and partly because the prime minister at the time, Bülent Ecevit, was concerned about the negative effects of moving forward with the completion of the Customs Union and wanted to catch up to the EC countries before continuing with the tariff reductions.[8] Turkey then froze relations with the EC in 1978. To make matters worse, Turkey experienced a military coup in 1980 and, since the EC does not associate itself with non-civilian governments, the Association Agreement was frozen. However, in 1986, under Turgut Özal, a prime minister who believed that economic integration with the EC would be good for the Turkish economy, relations finally began to return to normal, and a year later Turkey applied for full membership of the EC.

By this time, Greece, Spain and Portugal had been accepted into the EC as full members, and the Commission's response to the Turkish application was that accession negotiations between the EC and any country could not feasibly begin until 1993 because of the need for further deepening of integration among the current members. The Commission recommended revitalization of the Association Agreement with the realization of a customs union as a short-term goal. In line with the Commission's recommendation, a customs union for industrial products was realized on December 31, 1995, as foreseen by the Ankara Treaty and the Additional Protocol. It should be noted that Turkey is the only country that realized a customs union with the EC prior to full membership.

Turkish hopes for full membership in the EU evaporated with the Luxembourg European Council summit meeting of December 1997, which delivered a major blow to Turkish-EU relations: it was decided that accession negotiations were open to all applicant countries except Turkey. The former communist countries, as well as Cyprus, appeared to have moved up in the queue, and many of these countries are likely to be included in the next wave of enlargement.[9] The period from 1997–99 was turbulent for Turkey's aspirations in the EU, with widespread expressions of hopelessness and hostility towards the EU. However, since 1999, there has been a major breakthrough in Turkish-EU relations. Somewhat unexpectedly, the EU opened the door for Turkish candidacy, relatively shortly after the aforementioned ominous Luxembourg summit. Apparently, within two years of the Luxembourg summit, EU preferences changed,[10] and by the December 1999 Helsinki summit the countries that had been the strongest holdouts on Turkey's membership, namely Germany and Greece, finally gave in and agreed to grant Turkey candidacy.

On November 8, 2000, the European Commission adopted its Accession Partnership Document for Turkey, which was approved in the General Affairs Council of December 4, 2000, and finally adopted by the Council on March 8, 2001. Turkey adopted its National Program for the Adoption of the *acquis* on March 19, 2001. Despite these positive developments, as of the summer of 2002, accession negotiations with Turkey have not begun.[11] Consequently, Turkey is the only candidate country that the EU did not include in its calculations of voting power and representation in the EU institutions made at the Nice summit in December 2000.[12]

As the above section illustrates, Turkey's relations with the EU have been an integral part of its foreign policy since the end of the 1950s and gained significant momentum in the 1990s with the EU's enlargement process. Although Turkish-EU relations date back to the 1950s, until quite recently very little has been known about Turkish public opinion regarding the European Union and, even with the conducting of public opinion polls on attitudes toward the EU within the last year, there has not been much focus on elite opinions. On the other hand, Turkish political leaders themselves do not seem to have a proper understanding of what EU membership entails. For example, Ecevit's perception of the EC in the 1970s and Özal's in the 1980s seem to be based solely on economic terms, most probably underestimating the political dynamics of European integration. Moreover, some of the constitutional reforms that have been proposed by these elites—especially related to the role of the National Security Council and to Article 159 of the Turkish Penal Code, which deals with punishments for criticizing the state—indicate a fairly fundamental misunderstanding regarding the sort of reforms the EU is demanding. A few things, though, have been learned about non-political elites through a survey conducted by McLaren in 2000 with business people, journalists, academics and bureaucrats.[13] The results of that study indicate considerably favorable attitudes towards Turkey's potential EU membership as well as hope that it will indeed occur in the relatively near future. However, those in the position of law and policymaking regarding Turkey's adoption of the *acquis* have not yet been interviewed to assess their opinions on Turkish-EU relations. Thus, we aim to open the black box of the Turkish state by studying the attitudes of the political elites in Turkey towards the EU, or, at least, to gain some insights regarding it.

Similarly, very little research has been conducted in analyzing attitudes towards EU membership among the candidate countries. Recent work on this subject is mostly directed towards the Central and Eastern European countries and the publics of the Baltic states.[14] We believe studying public support in candidate countries towards EU membership is important in order to gain new insights into the much-neglected aspects of EU enlargement and the attitudes of the candidate countries. Using a survey conducted among a random sample of Turkish MPs in April and May 2000, we investigate deputies' views on whether Turkey will ever join the EU, what they perceive as the most important obstacles facing the country's membership and what they see as the largest advantages and disadvantages of joining the EU. One should keep in mind that the survey was conducted in spring 2000 and some of the MPs' perceptions might have changed since then.

THE SURVEY

The Turkish parliament comprises of 550 members. Because of resource limitations, we were able to select roughly ten percent of the entire assembly for an interview. A combination of stratified and systematic sampling was used to select the sample. In order to ensure adequate representation from the various parties in the assembly, we compiled a list of deputies sorted by party and then alphabetically by surname within the party list. We then systematically selected every ninth deputy, the first one being selected randomly by computer program. As the list was in order by party, this ensured that the party distribution in the sample would approximate the party distribution in the parliament. If a deputy could not be interviewed, then the person above him or below him on the list was chosen by a flip of a coin. Approximately ten percent of the sample had to be reselected in this manner.

Before discussing the substantive results of the survey, we will first describe the basic characteristics of the respondents. Almost all respondents in the sample were male (97 percent), but since only four percent of the entire TBMM is female, this overwhelmingly male response was expected. Most of the respondents (71 percent) held an undergraduate degree, with a small minority having received a Master's or Ph.D. (ten percent had either an MA or MS and seven percent had a Ph.D.) and another minority having finished school at the high school level or lower (five percent had finished primary or secondary school, while eight percent had finished high school). The percentages from each party were: Motherland Party (*Anavatan Partisi*—ANAP), 13 percent; True Path Party (*Doğru Yol Partisi*—DYP), eight percent; Democratic Left Party (*Demokratik Sol Parti*—DSP), 18 percent; Virtue Party (*Fazilet Partisi*—FP), 33 percent; Nationalist Action Party (*Milliyetçi Hareket Partisi*—MHP), 28 percent.

These percentages under-represent ANAP by about three percent, DYP by about eight percent, and DSP by approximately seven percent, but over-represents FP by approximately 14 percent and MHP by about five percent. It is well known from sampling theory that the smaller the sample size, the larger the likelihood of drawing an unrepresentative sample. A sample of 61 (which is the number of our respondents) is extremely small, and thus the fact that it does not represent the parties perfectly is not all that surprising. In our case, the political right—the Virtue Party and the Nationalist Action Party—is particularly over-represented. This could have implications for the opinions and preferences reported by our respondents. In order to check for this, we constructed a variable which weights the deputies according to the actual size of their party in the parliament, reducing the weight of the FP and MHP deputies and increasing the weight of the other deputies. However, the multivariate analyses are virtually identical whether the weighted or unweighted data is used. Thus, we report the unweighted results. On the other hand, the observations are weighted for the one analysis that includes a comparison across the parties so that we can make some speculation about the preferences of the governing coalition between 1999 and 2002 (see section on Cyprus below).

PERCEIVED OBSTACLES

What are the obstacles that Turkish MPs see facing Turkish full membership of the EU? The survey measures the perceptions of these obstacles and, in that manner, we hoped to unveil any discrepancies between the Turkish MPs' perceptions about the EU's reservations towards Turkey and the EU reality.

We expected the answers to this question to be based on a few different sources. One source is the reports of the European Commission on the problems facing Turkey's EU membership. Although Turkey was still not included in the list of candidate countries at the time of the June 1998 Cardiff Council, the EU attempted to bring Turkey back into the realm of the EU by suggesting that it should continue working towards full membership. To that end, the Council asked the European Commission to write a report on Turkey's candidacy. In fact, all of the candidate countries' progress in meeting the Copenhagen criteria has been evaluated by the European Commission on an annual basis since 1998. The objectivity of these criteria is best summarized by the Commissioner responsible for Enlargement, Guenther Verheugen, who contends that "negotiations should proceed on the basis of merit not on the basis of compassion."[15] Turkey, as a candidate country, is subject to this evaluation in terms of its ability to meet the Copenhagen criteria.

The first report on Turkey in 1998 emphasized the following political and economic problems.[16] The political problems are related to three important issues: human rights violations, including torture and lack of freedom of expression, mostly resulting from the conflict in the southeastern part of the country;[17] military (that is, National Security Council) independence from civilian control; and Turkey's handling of the Cyprus issue. The economic problems mentioned include: inefficiency in the agricultural sector due to small farm holdings; financial sector problems revolving around the problem of a small number of banks holding a large amount of assets; inflation; socio-economic problems like illiteracy, infant mortality and poor health care; regional disparities in GNP and socio-economic development; price setting in agriculture, energy and transport; and the domination of manufacturing by small firms which would likely have difficulty if they faced more competition from manufacturing companies in the EU.

Four more Commission reports have been issued since then, in October 1999, November 2000, November 2001 and October 2002, all of which mentioned the same problems. Thus, after repeatedly hearing the same issues related to political and economic problems raised by the Commission, it seems likely that Turkish members of parliament will themselves emphasize many of these problems. The Progress Reports of 1998 and 1999 and the Commission's 1989 Opinion on Turkey's application preceded the survey, thus we expected the MPs to raise these problems.

In addition to Turkey's ability to meet the Copenhagen criteria, we expected the deputies to emphasize Turkey's religious differences and large population size as other major obstacles to its membership. These problems are not stated officially by the EU, in line with maintaining the ostensible objectivity of Copenhagen criteria. Particularly after the implicit rejection of Turkish candidacy during the Luxembourg summit, many Turks began to believe that the problem with Turkey was not the economy or the political system but that the EU rejected Turkey's candidacy for religious and cultural reasons. This feeling is substantiated by the fact that other prospective members have had similar problems (Romania, for example) and were still granted candidacy. By the mid-1990s, based on comparative measures such as Freedom House scores, Romania and Turkey were roughly equivalent in terms of democratic development.[18] Moreover, Romania's GDP/capita was approximately half that of Turkey.[19] Although Romania's political situation improved rapidly between 1996 and 1997, from the Turkish point of view it might have seemed rather odd (and suspicious) that the country would be accepted as a candidate for full membership so quickly, even after such improvements. The fact that another politically and economically backward country was accepted into the EU circle fairly easily, whereas Turkey was not, led to speculation regarding why this might be the case. Such speculation was that the real problems for Turkish membership are the rather unmentionable factors of religion and culture.[20]

Until the Helsinki summit there was a great deal of pessimism and a belief that "they will never let us in" because of these cultural and religious factors, and that the Europeans were simply hiding their cultural prejudice by emphasizing human rights problems in Turkey. As one scholar contends, "There often seems to be an air of unreality—not to say disbelief—in Brussels and the Community at large about the very idea of Turkish membership."[21] Former Turkish prime minister Mesut Yılmaz accused the EU of erecting another Berlin Wall in Europe around cultural identity with the Luxembourg decision.[22] Some of the declarations coming from the EU front did not help matters either as seen in the example of the European People's Party (the Europe-wide Christian Democratic group) declaration of March 4, 1997: "The European Union is a civilization project and within this civilization project, Turkey has no place."[23] Thus, while we expect that the Helsinki summit should have dispelled much of this belief, there might be some lingering doubt about these issues in the minds of the Turkish elite.

Similarly, we expected the deputies to emphasize the population factor and the difficulty of incorporating Turkey into the EU structure. With a relatively poor population of approximately 68 million,[24] there are also concerns of mass migration from Turkey to the EU, redistribution of regional development funds and allocation of votes and seats in EU institutions such as the Commission, Council of Ministers and European Parliament. The impact of this concern was illustrated with the Nice Council's decision to omit Turkey from the calculations of voting power in an enlarged Union. Turkey's population is larger than all member states except Germany, as well as the candidate countries; in this context, one should note that the second most populous country among the candidates is Poland, with only 39 million people. The population factor is, of course, not part of the Copenhagen criteria but nonetheless it would be an important factor impacting on Turkey's membership to the EU.[25]

We posed the question about obstacles facing Turkey in two different ways.[26] In the first question, we simply asked "In your opinion, what is the most important obstacle that must be overcome before Turkey will be admitted to the EU as a full member?" The MP was allowed to answer this question freely, giving multiple answers. The summary of responses to this question appears in Table 1. These findings indicate that the deputies in the parliament overwhelmingly emphasize the political difficulties facing Turkey: problems of democratization, human rights improvement, and even improvement of the legal structure. There is also, however, some emphasis on socio-economic problems, including general economic problems, as well as specific human development problems, but it appears that—according to the MPs in TBMM—the most important issues that must be resolved are political.

TABLE 1
MOST IMPORTANT OBSTACLE FOR TURKISH MEMBERSHIP OF EU
(OPEN-ENDED)

Obstacle	Percent
Political problems: human rights violations, democratization	43
Socio-economic problems: economic development, infrastructure, education	27
Other*	17
Legal structure	7
Cultural differences	5
Size of the Turkish population	1
Number of responses**	82

Notes: * This category includes responses such as problems in the Southeastern part of the country, the bureaucracy, and prejudice/hostility from the west.
　　** Multiple responses were allowed.

The second way in which this question was asked was by presenting the deputy with a list of potential obstacles facing Turkish membership of the EU and to ask him/her to rank these in terms of importance. The obstacle list appears in Table 2, along with the percentage of respondents who indicated each of these as the first—most important—obstacle. The percentages in this table mostly mirror those in Table 1. We find a rather large emphasis on political problems, mostly democratization and human rights development, with some acknowledgement of the importance of the role of the military in politics, but a reduced emphasis on problems of economic development. Furthermore, while very few deputies mentioned problems of religion in the open-ended question (Table 1), when presented with it in a list of potential obstacles 13 percent of the sample pointed to this problem as the most important obstacle. Thus, we find some concern among political elites that this somewhat unmentionable (and unchangeable) factor will keep Turkey out of the EU. As for the population factor, we found very little emphasis on the role of population: only one percent of the MPs mentioned this factor as the most important obstacle in an open-ended format and seven percent in the prepared list of obstacles. We found this to be an interesting result given the current debate in the EU on institutional reform and voting and representation weight of the member states. It is also worthwhile to note that, while population is not openly identified by EU officials as an important obstacle for Turkey's accession negotiations, it is raised as an important consideration behind closed doors, threatening member states with unwanted immigration, loss of structural funds and increased contributions to the EU budget.

TABLE 2
MOST IMPORTANT OBSTACLE (PREPARED LIST)

Obstacle	Percent
Political problems: human rights violations, democratization	36
Lack of economic development	15
Turkey's being a Muslim country	14
Position of the military in politics	8
Large size of the population	7
Problems in the Southeastern part of the country	5
All or several of these are equally important	5
Cyprus	3
Young population	2
None of these are obstacles	2
Number of responses	59

Cyprus

Since 1993, the resolution of the Cyprus problem has become a foreign policy objective for the EU.[27] The EU opened accession negotiations with Cyprus following the 1997 Luxembourg summit, hoping that EU membership would provide an incentive to the Turkish and the Greek Cypriots to resolve their differences. The possibility of Cyprus' membership in the EU is becoming more concrete as EU members would like to see the first wave of entrants participate in the European Parliament elections to be held in 2004 and Cyprus will accede to the EU on May 1, 2004. The Cyprus problem clearly impacts on Turkey's negotiations with the EU as well as its pre-screening process. For example, during the preparations of the Commission's APD for Turkey, "Greece persuaded its 14 members in the Union to add resolving the division of Cyprus to the list of short-term actions that they (Turks) must carry out before the start of membership negotiations."[28] Currently, Greece is threatening to hold up the EU's eastern enlargement plans if Cyprus is not included in the next wave of enlargement.[29] Thus, the EU would like to see a settlement of the dispute over the island as soon as possible.[30]

The EU has made its views known clearly and firmly regarding the need to resolve the Cyprus issue before Turkey can enter the EU—although this issue was not included in the Copenhagen criteria. It is, therefore, rather surprising that in the questions regarding obstacles facing Turkey in its bid to join the EU there appears to be a severe de-emphasis on resolving the Cyprus issue among the MPs. Not a single deputy mentioned this as a problem for Turkey's candidacy in the open-ended format, and only three percent mentioned it when prompted with this option in a list of potential obstacles. As indicated above, this stipulation is repeated in the Commission Reports in 1998 and 1999, both prior to the survey.[31] The implication seems to be that if Turkey can resolve the other problems—democratization, human rights improvement and economic development—the Cyprus issue will not really be a major obstacle and that the EU would allow Turkey into the organization regardless of the fact that Cyprus remains divided. It should be noted that these results mirror those from the non-political elite survey, in which only one person mentioned problems with Greece as being an obstacle to Turkey's candidacy.[32]

The de-emphasis of this major conflict with Greece among all influential groups—political and non-political alike—could have its roots in a failure to fundamentally accept that there *is* a problem in Cyprus, and this, in turn, has its roots in a belief that the international community has taken the wrong side of the dispute. In other words, if you perceive that your side has done nothing wrong you are also likely to perceive that there is no problem to overcome. Indeed, statements from high-ranking state officials, including the former prime minister, make it clear that the resolution of this problem does not involve any change in Turkish policy with regard to Northern Cyprus. As Prime Minister Ecevit has stated, "During the Helsinki talks we underlined our sensitivity on the Cyprus issue. We stressed that we would not make a concession on that issue ... When clearing the path for us by giving us candidate status, the EU knew that there were two states in Cyprus. It would be out of the question for the EU to expect Turkey to change its well-known views now."[33]

In order to determine whether there is a consensus regarding the solution to this problem, we asked the deputies how they believe the issue will be resolved (see the Appendix for the exact wording). We expected that if the resolution of this dispute is taken seriously by the Turkish leadership there would be a general outline of the expected goals of the conflict resolution and, in turn, that MPs would know what those expected goals are. Instead, we found a very divided distribution of responses: 48 percent of the deputies claimed that the Turkish Republic of Northern Cyprus (TRNC) must be recognized as a sovereign state; 46 percent said that the two sides should be reunited in a federal state; and two percent stated that the problem will never be resolved.[34] Thus, roughly equal numbers of deputies argue for extremely conflicting outcomes for this dispute.

However, even the notion of following the party line on the issue of Cyprus is questionable. While it may seem as if there is actually a great deal of discussion of this issue and that parties are simply in conflict over how to resolve it, when we examine the responses to this question by the deputy's party affiliation we see that within the parties there is a great deal of dispute (see Table 3).[35] ANAP—a center-right party—appears to be most internally divided over how the Cyprus problem will be resolved, with the FP and its successor Felicity Party (*Saadet Partisi*—SP)—the religiously oriented party—following closely behind. Even within the nationalist MHP not all deputies take the expected view that Northern Cyprus must be recognized as an independent state.[36]

The findings presented in Table 3 also make it clear that if the parliament eventually becomes involved in resolving the dispute, reaching an agreement is going to be extremely difficult due to general disagreement that not only prevails across parties but within the parties themselves. For example, under the former governing coalition (DSP-MHP-ANAP), reaching a solution parliament would be able to digest would be nearly impossible: most DSP deputies lean towards reunification as a solution, most MHP deputies support recognition as an independent state as a solution, and ANAP deputies are quite divided, as indicated above.

TABLE 3
CROSS-TABULATION OF RESOLUTION OF CYPRUS ISSUE
BY PARTY AFFILIATION

	ANAP	DYP	DSP	FP–SP*	MHP
Northern Cyprus must be recognized as independent, sovereign state	40%	20%	20%	50%	71%
Northern and Southern Cyprus must be reunited in a federal state	50%	80%	73%	33%	29%
The issue will probably never be resolved	–	–	–	8%	–
Other	10%	–	7%	8%	–
Number of responses	10	10	15	12	14

Note: * The Virtue Party-FP was closed down with a Constitutional Court decision and its members resigned and joined SP-Felicity party and their parliamentarian status continued under a new party banner.

Furthermore, there appears to be a great deal of discrepancy between the prime minister's views on resolving the issue and those of his deputies in the parliament. As indicated, Ecevit, who was also the prime minister during the 1974 intervention, seems quite unwilling to make concessions on the Cyprus issue, insisting that there are (and presumably always will be) two different states on the island of Cyprus. As Ecevit clearly states, he believes that if the EU extends membership to Cyprus without an overall settlement on the island's internal political future, Ankara may take the drastic measure of annexing TRNC.[37] However, the responses of his party members in TBMM point to a very different position and indicate that they believe the dispute will end with the reunification of Northern and Southern Cyprus. Overall, the position of the prime minister is quite different from that of the parliamentary coalition supporting him.

We also asked the deputies if they believed that the EU favors the Greek side in Turkish-Greek relations. Eighty-five percent of the deputies believed this to be the case. Thus, part of the obstinacy related to the Cyprus issue on the part of the Turkish government might stem from the perception that there is an unwarranted bias against the Turkish side of the dispute.

SUPPORT FOR EU MEMBERSHIP AND PERCEIVED COSTS AND BENEFITS

Regarding hopes about Turkey eventually joining the EU as a full member, we expected the Helsinki summit to have produced elites who are quite favorable and hopeful about Turkey's EU membership. However, this summit did not erase all negative feelings and there remain skeptics who voice statements such as "the EU would never allow a situation that would upset its own social, economic and cultural balances to develop. As the EU is working out how to delay the entry of the other 12 candidate countries, the terrifying cost of Turkey's entry positively precludes her from ever becoming a full member."[38] Thus, we expected some degree of skepticism from political elites with regard to the question of Turkish membership of the EU. In fact, we find that all but one deputy responded that they were either strongly in favor or in favor of Turkey joining the EU as a full member. Moreover, an overwhelming 64 percent of the sample claimed to be strongly in favor of full EU membership for their country. Regarding the time frame for joining, we find only a slight amount of the same sort of skepticism expressed above, with five deputes (eight percent) arguing that Turkey will never be able obtain full EU membership. A small minority (12 percent) of deputies believed that Turkey would be able to join the EU within the next five years, but the rest of the deputies were not quite as hopeful about a short time frame: 30 percent believed full EU membership was possible within the next ten years; 16 percent thought it could happen in the next 15 years; and 12 percent believed EU membership would occur within the next 20 years. In addition, seven percent argued that the process will take longer than 20 years and 15 percent thought that the time frame is difficult to estimate. Thus, while skepticism and hopelessness regarding Turkey's realistic chances for someday joining the EU are evident, we find a great deal of hope that full EU membership is indeed possible in the relatively near future. These results are quite similar to the findings of a non-political elites survey in which 86 percent were reported to be in favor of Turkey becoming a full EU member and 52 percent thought that membership would be granted to Turkey within ten years.[39] Note that the non-political elites survey was conducted in the spring of 1999, several months before the landmark Helsinki summit (and still in the shadow of Luxembourg), and so we contend that the results of the deputies survey do not merely reflect the jubilance of the Helsinki summit results. Thus, overall, we can confidently claim that Turkish elites are supportive of Turkey's membership in the EU but are not overly optimistic about the realization of this project in the near future.

What do the political elites see as the major benefits and costs of full EU membership? As was the case when asked about obstacles to full membership, the emphasis is on political development—such as improved democratization and more respect for human rights (see Table 4). That is not to say that socio-economic factors are unimportant. Indeed, this category comes in as a close second response to the political development response. We expected a great deal of concern for establishing European credentials or finally becoming part of Europe as a major benefit of EU

TABLE 4
MOST IMPORTANT ADVANTAGE OF BECOMING A FULL EU MEMBER

Advantage	Percent
Human rights violations, democracy will improve	33
Socio-economic development	27
Other*	14
Becoming part of Europe/the West	13
Free movement of goods, services, people	5
Legal reform	5
Number of responses**	82

Notes: * This category includes responses such as: cultural development, globalization and integration into the world system, the development of universal values, and the state will become more powerful.
** Multiple responses were allowed.

membership but, surprisingly, only a small minority (13 percent) of the responses of political elites point to the importance of this factor. Evidently, our respondents are mostly concerned with the political and economic development that will occur once Turkey is accepted into the EU. In contrast, with the non-political elites, the overwhelming response was that Turkey's socio-economic development would improve. The second most popular response was that Turkey's European credentials would finally be established. Emphasis on democratization and human rights came in a distant third.[40]

Finally, we wanted to observe whether the deputies are concerned about any major costs that would burden Turkey should it join the EU. The most frequent response to this question is that there will be no disadvantages to Turkey from full EU membership (26 percent). However, a similar number of parliamentarians (24 percent) were concerned that there would be some cultural degeneration or that there would be economic deterioration (23 percent) if Turkey joins the EU as a full member. As might be expected, based on the ideological stances of the parties, MHP and FP deputies emphasized the cultural degeneration issue more than other deputies. In fact, all but one of the deputies who mentioned this potential problem were from either the MHP or the FP. ANAP and DSP deputies mentioned the possibility of economic problems more, although some FP and MHP deputies discussed this issue as well. In addition, a minority of the deputies (17 percent) expressed concern that there would be a loss of power or loss of sovereignty as a result of EU membership. This was emphasized in relatively equal numbers across parties. When asked specifically if they thought Turkey's sovereignty would be decreased if the country were to become a full EU member, only 44 percent replied affirmatively. Thus, the potential loss of sovereignty does not appear to be a major concern of the deputies in the parliament. This finding illustrates that among the political elites—who should be concerned most about the probable loss of sovereignty for Turkey—there is a lack of comprehension as to what EU membership would entail. This brings us to the analysis of knowledge about the EU among the deputies. Given the fact that most of the conflict in the EU stems from balancing supranational authority with protection of national interests and state sovereignty, it is inevitable that Turkey during its negotiations will have to deal openly with this issue. The political elites' perceptions that this is not an absolutely important issue are partly explained by the general lack of knowledge as to what the process of European integration is about.

KNOWLEDGE ABOUT THE EU

Conventional wisdom about members of the Turkish parliament is that they are not very well informed about most issues, especially issues that are not directly related to domestic politics. We wanted to test this notion, but in a somewhat indirect manner in order to avoid offending the interviewees. To indirectly gauge knowledge of the EU, we asked the following two questions:[41] "Would any government change in an EU member state affect Turkey's prospects for joining the EU?" and "If Turkey joins the EU (meaning that it will already have accomplished the economic requirements), will it be able to comply with the requirements of the euro?" The first question was asked based on the assumption that deputies in the parliament should know that the German government which was in power at the time of the interview (a Social Democratic-Green coalition under the leadership of Gerhard Schröder) was much more favorable towards Turkey's candidacy than the previous Christian Democratic-led governments. Indeed, the change in the German government in 1998 was one of the key factors that paved the way for Turkey's candidacy for full EU membership. However, deputies in the parliament were mostly oblivious to the effect that changes in member state governments can have on external policy: only 12 percent of them thought that such a change might affect Turkey's prospects for joining the EU. From the answers to these questions, we gather that the MPs do not have a clear understanding of the decisionmaking procedures in the EU.

The second question was chosen because it was expected that the members of TBMM would have some idea as to what economic standards would have to be met in order to join the euro-zone. The euro requirements are beyond the economic requirements of accession to the extent to which even current members have difficulties in meeting them. Clearly, Turkey's economy does not come close to meeting these standards, and we expected deputies to acknowledge this fact. Participation in the euro-zone requires strict adherence to macroeconomic stability and realization of rigid rules on interest rates, public debt and budget deficit figures. Even though Turkey's macroeconomic indicators are nowhere near the euro requirements, 84 percent of the deputies interviewed claimed that Turkey could indeed meet the requirements for participating in the adoption of the euro. The results from this question and the one discussed above indicate that, unfortunately, those who are making decisions about Turkey's adoption of the EU *acquis* seem to have very little knowledge about the EU itself. Turkish ability to meet the economic aspects of the Copenhagen criteria and the euro requirements are two different things. If the deputies responded "yes" based on the assumption that once Turkey meets the economic aspects of accession criteria this would also suffice for entering the euro-zone, this demonstrates a lack of knowledge about the EU's monetary standards for the euro.

CONCLUSION

With the EU's enlargement process going ahead at full speed, there is much discussion in Turkey among politicians and media personalities about orchestrating reforms—such as economic restructuring and changing the legal and penal codes—solely for the sake of finally being accepted into the "club." However, despite its importance, we find surprisingly little information regarding mass or elite opinions on the issue until very recently. This analysis was an attempt to fill this gap by gauging the thoughts and concerns of one part of the Turkish public—its nationally elected officials.

What insights do these elites provide into the nature of Turkish-EU relations? First, the consensus regarding full EU membership is encouraging. There does not appear to be any opposition whatsoever to Turkey entering the EU as a full member someday. Such overwhelming support will, of course, be necessary during a time of extensive reform in preparation for accession. Additionally, the level of hope is quite high. Even before the Helsinki summit, at which Turkey was granted candidacy, such hope among non-political elites was also surprisingly high.[42] In other words, political and non-political elites alike do not express too much concern that the EU will never allow Turkey into the "club." This hopefulness is important because if elites believe that the effort of preparation—especially the adoption of EU legislation—is in vain, then their support is likely to wane quickly. This is also an important consideration as, in July 2002, the Turkish parliament adopted a major constitutional package dealing with such issues as the abolition of death penalty and the right of education and broadcasting in languages other than Turkish. This was quite an important step towards EU membership, but, as noted, far more is likely to be required, and the political will of Turkish elites will be necessary to carry out these reforms. One should note that MHP parliamentarians voted "no" on the reform package despite the repeated reassurances from the MHP that they support EU membership.

Second, based on the emphasis on the political aspects of EU membership, it appears that Turkish MPs believe that significant improvements in the political system—primarily in the functioning of the democratic institutions and the improvement of human rights—will be necessary before obtaining full EU membership *and* that these improvements will be a result of finally achieving full membership. In other words, in the eyes of the political elite the prospect of EU membership is working to help consolidate democracy in Turkey and will ultimately guarantee that Turkey will be a consolidated democracy, *a la* Spain and Portugal.

The next most emphasized problem facing Turkish membership—as well as an advantage if Turkey is indeed accepted into the EU—is related to socio-economic development. This is not surprising given the current problems of inflation, income disparities and regional development disparities. It is apparent that many deputies realize that the level of development in Turkey lags significantly behind that of even the poorest EU country, and that—as in the case of political development—the process of preparing for full membership, as well as the membership itself, should dramatically improve the economy of Turkey. The financial problems facing Turkey since the November 2000 and February 2001 crises clearly illustrate the need for macroeconomic stability.

We encountered two potential problems in elite perceptions of Turkish-EU relations. The first of these was discussed extensively above, and relates to the Cyprus issue. The problem, as we see it, is that elites in Turkey do not perceive this issue to be a major obstacle to Turkish membership of the EU, implying that the other factors are more important and, if those are resolved, Turkey should still be able to enter the EU even if the dispute with Greece over Cyprus continues. Unless Greek leaders suddenly change their position on this issue, it seems highly unlikely that Greece will allow Turkey to join the EU if Turkey continues with the position outlined by Ecevit (that there are two separate countries on Cyprus). The failure of our sample of deputies to acknowledge the importance of this problem indicates a lack of understanding of how the voting on the accession of new member states occurs within the EU (by unanimous vote in the EU Council of Ministers, with the assent of the European Parliament and each member state parliament). Thus, even though Cyprus is not part of the EU's accession criteria, the EU's decisionmaking structures will make it an equally important factor influencing Turkey's accession.

This research has focused on political elite views of Turkish-EU relations. We should stress that—other than a few opinion polls—very little is known about mass opinion regarding the EU within Turkey, particularly regional and social sector variation in support of Turkish membership of the EU. However, the TESEV-sponsored mass opinion survey on Turkish people's attitudes towards the EU conducted in spring 2002 (the results of which are discussed in this volume) is an important step in that regard. Thus, while our research can be seen as a "first attempt" at understanding the nature of opinion towards internationalized governance in Turkey, much more work in this area is necessary, particularly on *mass* opinion, which is likely to be quite different from the opinions of Turkish political elites. The national elections in Turkey that took place in November 2002 altered the configuration of the parliament. The newly founded Justice and Development Party (*Adalet ve Kalkınma Partisi*—AKP), representing the religious and center-right conservative vote, and the Republican People's Party, representing the social democratic vote, were elected to parliament. Although these two parties also repeatedly voice their support for EU membership, the November 2002 elections changed the Turkish political elite's opinion, making it somewhat different from that pictured in this essay.

APPENDIX: THE SURVEY INSTRUMENT
(ONLY THE PORTION RELATED TO EUROPEAN UNION ISSUES)

1. Are you in favor or opposed to Turkey eventually joining the EU as a full member? Would you say you are:

    ☐ Strongly in favor 1
    ☐ In favor 2
    ☐ Opposed 3
    ☐ Strongly opposed 4
    ☐ Don't know 5
    ☐ Other 6

2. What about the citizens living in your district: Do you believe they are in favor, opposed, or do they not care very much whether Turkey joins the EU as a full member?

   ☐ They are definitely in favor   1
   ☐ They are mostly in favor   2
   ☐ They are mostly opposed   3
   ☐ They are definitely opposed   4
   ☐ They do not care one way or the other   5
   ☐ Don't know   6

3. In your opinion, what is the most important obstacle that must be overcome before Turkey will be admitted to the EU as a full member?

4. What do you believe would be the best thing about Turkey becoming a full EU member?

5. What do you believe would be the worst thing about Turkey becoming a full EU member?

6. Do you believe that Turkey will eventually join the EU as a full member, and if so, in what time frame? Would you say that:

   ☐ Turkey will never join (Please explain below)   1
   ☐ Turkey will join within the next 5 years   2
   ☐ Turkey will join within the next 10 years   3
   ☐ Turkey will join within the next 15 years   4
   ☐ Turkey will join within the next 20 years   5
   ☐ Turkey will join, but it will take more than 20 years 6
   ☐ Other   7

   a) [If response is "Turkey will never join"] Please explain.

7. The following is a list of potential obstacles for Turkey with regards to full membership in the EU. Please state which of these potential obstacles you consider to be important and then indicate on the list which is most important, second most important, etc.?

   —The position of the military in politics   1
   —The level of human rights violations in Turkey   2
   —The level of democratization in Turkey   3
   —The lack of economic development in Turkey   4
   —The large size of the population in Turkey   5
   —The problem in the southeastern part of the country   6
   —Political Islam   7
   —Turkey being a Muslim country   8
   —The conflict with Greece over Cyprus   9
   —Other_____   10

8. In your opinion, which group in Turkey will benefit most from full membership in the EU? (Please explain.)

9. Which group will suffer most? (Please explain.)

10. Does the recent change in the Austrian government affect Turkey's prospects for joining the EU?
    ☐ Yes 1
    ☐ No 2

    a) [If YES] Please explain.

11. Would any government change in any other country affect Turkey's prospects for joining the EU?

   ☐ Yes 1
   ☐ No 2

   a) [If YES] Please explain.

12. Which of the following statements best describes your belief about how the conflict with Greece over the Cyprus issue will eventually be resolved, or do you have another view on this?

   ☐ The only viable solution is for Northern Cyprus to be recognized as an independent sovereign state. 1
   ☐ The only viable solution is for Northern and Southern Cyprus to be reunited in a federal state, as equal parties. 2
   ☐ The issue will probably never be resolved. 3
   ☐ Other 4

   a) [If "The issue will probably never be resolved"] Please explain.

For the following statements, can you please say whether you strongly agree, agree, disagree, strongly disagree, or are undecided?

	Strongly Agree	Agree	Disagree	Strongly Disagree	Undecided	Other
13. In Turkish-Greek relations, the European Union tends to favor the Greek side.	1	2	3	4	5	6
14. Turkey's sovereignty will be decreased considerably as a result of full membership in the EU.	1	2	3	4	5	6
15. Turkish institutions are currently capable of managing the process of adopting the EU criteria for full membership.	1	2	3	4	5	6
16. A referendum should be conducted before Turkey enters the EU as a full member.	1	2	3	4	5	6

17. If Turkey joins the EU, will it be able to comply with the requirements of the euro?

   ☐ Yes
   ☐ No

   a) Please explain.

NOTES

Special thanks to Burcu Gezgör, Yusuf Gözükücük, Fatih Gülgönül, Ayşe Sargın and Ahu Tatlı for their invaluable assistance in conducting the interviews for this project. Any errors in interpretation are the sole responsibility of the authors.

1. The Council of the European Union, Luxembourg *Presidency Conclusions*, Dec. 12–13, 1997, <http://www.europa.eu.int/council/off/conclu/dec97.htm>.
2. The Copenhagen criteria consist of political aspects (the functioning of democratic institutions), economic aspects (the stability of macroeconomic factors and functioning market economy) and the adoption of the EU's *acquis communautaire*.
3. Vast reforms have already been adopted in the Turkish Grand National Assembly (TBMM) since October 2001. However, the adoption of these particular laws is likely to be only the first—albeit important—step in the process of actually having the type of political system that the EU envisions. In addition, there is some doubt as to whether the reforms that have been passed thus far are enough to meet EU political standards. Thus, the political will to continue with reforms must be present.
4. Another important factor in Turkey's application for associate membership was, of course, Greece's application for associate member status. The Turkish application was lodged just 16 days after the Greek application. Traditionally, Turkish policy has been to balance Greece in international organizations and platforms.
5. A military coup and disarray in the government after the military returned power to the civilian government delayed the signing.
6. These association agreements gave Turkey and Greece a privileged status in their relationship with the EC and acted as a testament to both their eligibility for membership and Europeanness. In all the other association agreements, specifically the Europe Agreements signed with the Central and Eastern European countries, such references to full membership were cleverly evaded, perhaps in the light of the Turkish experience.
7. In the 1970s there were several disagreements over key issues. For a summary, see Meltem Müftüler-Baç, *Turkey's Relations with a Changing Europe* (Manchester: Manchester University Press, 1997), pp.53–74.
8. Atilla Eralp, "Değişen Savaş-Sonrası Uluslararası Sistemde Türkiyeve AT" [Turkey and EC in the Changing Post-War International System], in Canan Balkır and Alan Williams (eds.), *Türkiye ve Avrupa ilişkileri* [Turkey and Europe Relations] (Istanbul: Sarmal Yayınevi, 1996), p.112.
9. The current proposal by the European Commission suggests that in 2004 there will be a "big bang" enlargement that includes all of the Central and Eastern European (CEE) applicants, as well as Cyprus and Malta. The only CEE candidates not slated for full membership at that date are Romania and Bulgaria. It is not definite that the big bang will occur, but clearly countries like Slovenia, Poland, Hungary, the Czech Republic and Estonia will be admitted in the very near future.
10. This change in the configuration of preferences was seemingly due to two factors. One was the September 1998 general election in Germany, which produced a Social Democratic-Green governing coalition. From the start of this new government's term the leadership was quite clear about its support for Turkish membership of the EU. The other important change in the configuration was that Greece became considerably less hostile toward Turkey, presumably prompted by the major earthquakes that hit the Istanbul and Athens areas in August and September 1999. These natural disasters produced a significant warming of Turkish-Greek relations as the two sides moved to assist one another with rescue and relief efforts. See Ayten Gündoğdu, "Identities in Question: Greek-Turkish Relations in a Period of Transformation," *Middle East Review of International Affairs* (MERIA), Vol.5, No.1 (March 2001), <http://meria.idc.ac.il>.

11. The EU claims that until Turkey fulfils the Copenhagen criteria accession negotiations with Turkey cannot begin.
12. Fuad Aleskerov, Gamze Avcı, Ian Iakouba and Ziya Ümit Türem, "European Union Enlargement: Power Distribution Implications of the New Institutional Arrangements," *European Journal of Political Research*, Vol.41, No.3 (2002), pp.379–94.
13. Lauren M. McLaren, "Turkey's Eventual Membership of the EU," *Journal of Common Market Studies*, Vol.38, No.1 (2000), pp.117–29.
14. Piret Ehin, "Determinants of Public Support for EU Membership: Data from the Baltic Countries," *European Journal of Political Research*, Vol.40, No.1 (2001), pp.31–46.
15. Quoted in Peter Norman, "Bold Approach Carries Risk," *Financial Times*, Dec. 3, 1999.
16. See <http://www.europa.eu.int/comm/dg1a/enlarge/report_11_98_en/turkey/b10.htm>.
17. For example, in 1997 Luxembourg's Prime Minister Jean Claude Junckers stated with regard to Turkey that "the EU cannot sit at a negotiating table with a country where torture is widespread." See Nurdan Bernard, "Turkey Pains in the Summit," *Yeni Yüzyıl* (Turkish Daily Newspaper), Dec. 13, 1997.

    Similarly, Anna Lindh, Sweden's Minister of Foreign Affairs, initially opposed Turkey's candidacy status until it made improvements on its human rights record. See Leyla Boulton, "EU Protests to Turkey at Kurd Mayors' Arrest," *Financial Times*, Feb. 25, 2000.
18. See Freedom House website country ratings, <http://www.freedomhouse.org/ratings/index.htm>.
19. See Eurostat, *Statistical Yearbook on Candidate and South-East European Countries* (Brussels: The European Commission, 2000), Vol.3, pp.51–5.
20. Meltem Müftüler-Baç, "Through the Looking Glass: Turkey in Europe," *Turkish Studies*, Vol.1, No.1 (Spring 2000), pp.21–35.
21. John Redmond, *The Next Mediterranean Enlargement of the European Community: Turkey, Cyprus, and Malta?* (Aldershot: Dartmouth, 1993), p.17.
22. See Nurdan Bernard, "Turkey Pains in the Summit," *Yeni Yüzyıl*, Dec. 13, 1997.
23. Chris Nuttall and Ian Traynor, "Kohl Tries to Cool Row with Ankara," *Guardian*, March 7, 1997.
24. For further information on the Turkish population figures, see <http://www.die.gov.tr/konularr/nufusSayimi.htm>.
25. As the Nice summit occurred several months after these interviews, we do not contend that the deputies are reacting to the Nice summit results in this survey. However, even before Nice, it was common knowledge that Turkey had a very large and very poor population and, for this reason, we expected that deputies might think this is one of the causes for problematic relations with the EU.
26. Members of parliament have rather busy schedules, and we realized that they might give hasty responses to our questions. For this reason, we posed this particular question in two different ways so that the MP would have another chance to think carefully about it. In addition, in previous research conducted by McLaren (2000) certain issues—such as Cyprus and the role of the military—were severely de-emphasized. Thus, the current survey attempted to understand if the respondent would "remember" that these issues were important once they were presented together in a list.
27. Ziya Öniş, "Greek-Turkish Relations and the European Union: A Critical Perspective," *Mediterranean Politics*, Vol.6, No.3 (2001), pp.31–45.
28. Douglas Frantz, "Some in Turkey see Minefield Along road to European Union," *New York Times*, Dec. 1, 2000.
29. "A Survey of European Union Enlargement," *Economist*, 19 May 2001; Neil Nugent, "EU Enlargement and the Cyprus Problem," *Journal of Common Market Studies*, Vol.38, No.1 (2000), pp.131–50.
30. For the positions of Turkey and the EU on Cyprus, see pp.55–78 of this volume.

31. The Accession Partnership is also relatively clear about this, but since it was released long after this survey was conducted, the deputies could not possibly be taking cues from it.
32. McLaren (2000), pp.117–29.
33. Ecevit's declaration, *Milliyet*, July 23, 2000.
34. Another five percent gave an answer that did not fit into any of these categories.
35. However, because of the small sample size, some caution in interpreting these results is advised.
36. Note that since we are trying to make inferences here about the views of party members in the parliament we have weighted the responses according to the actual size of the party in the TBMM.
37. Joseph Fitchett, "Turkey's Warning on Cyprus Vexes Western Allies," *International Herald Tribune* (Europe), Sept. 11, 2001.
38. Erol Manisalı, "Post Helsinki EU-Turkey Relations," *Turkish Daily News*, July 11, 2000.
39. McLaren (2000), pp.117–29.
40. Ibid.
41. The question posed to the MPs was as follows: Would any government change in any other country affect Turkey's prospects for joining the EU?
42. See McLaren (2000), pp.117–29.

Implementing the Economic Criteria of EU Membership: How Difficult is it for Turkey?

MİNE EDER

This essay analyzes Turkey's situation regarding the European Union's (EU) economic criteria established in the Copenhagen agreement as a condition for membership. It assesses the prospects and constraints that Turkey faces in meeting these criteria. Broadly defined as a "fully functioning market and a capacity to compete with the EU,"[1] the economic conditionality is largely seen as the least problematic side of Turkey's membership. Yet, the economic crises in the country in 2000 and 2001 and the consequent slow-down in the economy coupled with difficulties encountered in the Customs Union increasingly suggest that meeting the economic criteria will be more difficult than expected. The fact that most of the economic adjustment and technical assistance funds, which are largely available for the prospective and negotiating new members, will not be available for Turkey, exacerbates the country's economic prospects further.

However, some of the economic reforms being implemented under the current International Monetary Fund (IMF) program coincide with some of those expected for membership. Banking and agricultural reforms along with transparency requirements are some examples of this overlap. To what extent will these reforms be enough? Can Turkey overcome its persistent problem in its political economy and meet the Copenhagen criteria? How realistic and consistent are EU's economic expectations? This study offers some answers to these questions with emphasis on the economically contingent factors that can make and unmake Turkey's membership of the EU.

Despite the fact that Turkey has considerable experience with a market economy, particularly when compared to the other candidate countries in Eastern Europe, and has some capacity to compete with its European counterparts, the country faces serious dilemmas and challenges in meeting these economic criteria. The first part of this contribution provides a brief overview of Turkey's economic indicators and discusses the fundamental problems embedded in Turkey's political economy as main barriers to meeting the Copenhagen criteria. Economic liberalization since the 1980s, which has not gone far enough to push for public sector reform, and the persistent legacy of populism and/or patronage politics are cited as fundamental barriers to Turkey's accession. The second part of this paper argues that the changes within the European project itself and problems embedded in the Copenhagen criteria have further complicated Turkey's accession. The European project has shifted from a largely Keynesian strategy with emphasis on integration and cohesion to the neo-liberal one. The "neo-liberalization" of European integration was largely intertwined with the EU's enlargement and Turkey's accession.[2] This neo-liberal agenda was most evident in the annual progress reports the EU Commission prepared on Turkey and other candidate countries. The shortage of EU funds and the timing of these grants and credits available for Turkey as it undertook significant liberalization reforms with the hope of accession also troubled the Turkey-EU economic relationship.

What makes Turkey's accession most problematic is that the country's economy is strikingly different from that of the EU countries—as well as the candidate countries—in many ways. For instance, the 13 candidate countries' populations range from 388,000 people (Malta) to 67.8 million (Turkey).[3] Upon membership, Turkey would become the most populous country after Germany. The total population of the other candidate countries is only about 105 million. The entry of all 13 countries into the EU will bring EU's total population from 376 million to 550 million, which would mean that approximately one in ten Europeans would be Turkish.[4] Geographically, Turkey would become the biggest country within the EU.[5] In terms of Gross Domestic Product (GDP), Turkey has the largest economy among the candidate countries by far, even in the aftermath of the 2000 and 2001 financial crises. On the other hand, in terms of GDP per capita, Turkey ranked twenty-forth among the total 28 countries (EU and candidate countries) in 1998, which indicates the disadvantages of a rapidly increasing population.[6] In the 1995–2000 period, GDP per capita in terms of purchasing power parities has remained at around 28 percent of the EU average.[7]

Human development indicators in Turkey also show striking divergence from EU as well as other candidate countries. For example, while 42 of every 1,000 children die in Turkey before the age of five every year, the EU average is six deaths per 1,000.[8] (Turkey is followed by Romania with 25 and Lithuania with 19 deaths per 1,000.) The ratio of public expenditure on education to GDP is lowest in Turkey with 2.2 percent (1998 figures), while the other candidate countries range between 3.3 percent (Bulgaria) and 7.3

percent (Estonia); the EU average is 5.3 percent.[9] The number of doctors per each 100,000 people is 119, while the average of the 12 other candidate countries is 289.[10] Turkey is also at the bottom of the list in terms of internet connections, use of computers in schools and the ratio of university graduates to the overall population.[11] With an average life expectancy of 69 years, Turkey also shares the lowest ranking among the 28 EU and candidate countries with Lithuania and Romania.[12]

Finally, Turkey's macroeconomic indicators also alert the observer to the country's divergence from EU members and candidate countries. Though the average annual Gross National Product (GNP) growth rate in the 1990s is not far from the EU average, the volatility in GNP growth rates is visible, with a minus 6.1 percent growth in 1994 and 1999, 6.3 percent growth in 2000 and a galloping minus 9.4 percent—the worst in the republic's history—in 2001.[13] The crisis has essentially brought Turkey's 200 billion dollars GDP down to 148 billion. Inflation rates are yet another example of Turkey's exceptionality. While the 12 months' average of the Consumer Price Index (CPI) increased with an annual 1.3 percent in the EU in 1998, this number was 84.6 percent in Turkey in the same year. As of 2000, only Turkey, Romania and Slovakia had inflation rates higher than ten percent.[14] While the IMF program, which began to be implemented in 1999, aimed to bring down the inflation, as of 2002 the rates did not fall below an annual 50 percent. The same is true for fluctuations in the rates of foreign exchange. In the 1996–98 period for instance, the Turkish lira (TL) has literally evaporated *vis-à-vis* the ECU (European Currency Unit). With the February 2001 crisis, the TL lost an additional 50 percent of its value *vis-à-vis* the dollar and euro by the summer of the same year. Not surprisingly, the public budget deficits and current account deficit numbers also indicate similar instability. In the year 2000, for instance, the eurozone countries had budget surpluses, while Turkey's budget deficit to GDP ratio reached almost 20 percent in 2001.[15] None of the other candidate countries have such a high level of budget deficits (see Table 1).

How can we account for this rather bleak picture? Can Turkey overcome these barriers and meet the Copenhagen economic criteria? Clearly, Turkey's prospects for converging with the EU will depend on the economic and social reforms that the country is able to undertake on the domestic front. However, there are tremendous problems embedded in Turkey's own domestic political economy. These entrenched problems have made it very difficult for the country to engage in radical reforms and consolidate these reforms in the long run, creating and perpetuating instead what Uğur calls an "anchor/credibility dilemma." He defines this dilemma as:

TABLE 1
TURKEY AND OTHER CANDIDATE COUNTRIES

Country	GDP per capita at purchasing power parity (ECU/euro) European Union (15) average = 1000	Budget deficits (percentage of GDP)	Where Turkey stands in global competitiveness (Current competitiveness index)
Year	2000	2000	2001
Czech Rep.	59	-4.3	35
Hungary	53	-3.1	26
Poland	41	-3.6	41
Slovak Rep.	41	-4.8	32
Slovenia	73	-1.6	39
Bulgaria	25	-0.7	68
Romania	27	-4.0	61
Estonia	41	-0.5	27
Latvia	30	-2.8	42
Lithuania	30	-3.3	49
Austria	112	-1.0	13
Turkey	28	-11.0	33
EU 15 average	100	0.3*	NA
Candidate countries' (13) average		-5.9	NA

Note: NA = not applicable.

Sources: GDP per capita figures: Bernard Funck and Lodovico Pizzati (eds.), *Labor, Employment and Social Policies in the EU Enlargement Process* (Washington, DC: World Bank, 2002), p.31. Budget deficits: Eurostat. Competitiveness figures: World Economic Forum, *Global Competitiveness Report, 2001–2002*.

two tendencies working at cross purposes. On the one hand, state-society interaction in EU member states limits the EU's capacity to undertake commitments and/or impose sanctions with a view to anchor Turkey's convergence towards European standards. On the other hand, the type of state-society interaction in Turkey induces Turkish policy makers to engage in frequent deviations from the policy reform required for convergence. The combination of both tendencies leads to a typical prisoners' dilemma where the EU's failure to act as an effective anchor increases the probability of policy reversals in Turkey, which, in turn, induced the EU to be even more reluctant about anchoring Turkey's convergence towards European standards.[16]

The frequent policy reversals and the difficulty in undertaking these reforms stem from Turkey's troubled economic liberalization experience, as well as the patronage-based politics that has typified Turkey's political economy since the 1980s.

PROBLEMS EMBEDDED IN TURKEY'S LIBERALIZATION AND LINGERING PATRONAGE POLITICS

Reviewing the fundamental problems embedded in Turkey's political economy is beyond the scope of this contribution. The difficulties that Turkey faces in meeting the Copenhagen economic criteria, however, can be linked to two fundamental problems rooted in Turkey's political economy. One is that Turkey has suffered from a perverse and rather premature neo-liberal development. The country was unable to balance its liberalization with efforts to mediate the impact that such liberalization might have on various sectors of the economy. More importantly, Turkey has failed to complement its economic liberalization with sufficient regulatory institutions and broader investment and development strategy.

Second, Turkey's liberalization has only recently begun to push for public sector reforms. The persisting legacy of populism and patronage politics has made it very difficult for governments to engage in policy reforms with short-term costs and long-term benefits, which are, after all, what the EU-related economic reforms are all about. Increasing political fragmentation within the parliament, the need for coalition governments throughout the 1990s and frequent elections also induced populist policies as each party tried to use state resources for their own constituencies. The severity of the recent economic crises has also lowered the degree of patience for policies with long-term results. Undertaking public sector reform that will result in ending patronage, establishing transparency in public accounts and eliminating the politicization of economic decisionmaking—which are all necessary conditions for a "functioning market economy" and "capacity to compete"—have thus proven too difficult.

Indeed, one of the fundamental problems in Turkey's political economy has been the unorthodox economic liberalization that the country underwent since the 1980s.[17] While there was considerable liberalization in trade and capital flows, undertaking long-term structural reforms such as privatization and achieving the so-called retreat of the state at the domestic front were much more difficult. As Waterbury, Buğra, Öniş and Waldner have all argued,[18] for instance, Turgut Özal, the prime minister and later the president of the country, left his imprints on Turkey's liberalization agenda in the 1980s. In describing the decade, Waterbury argued, "Özal government favors turning the economy over to the private sector *and* reinforcing the state. It has promoted deregulation and liberalization in the name of efficiency *and* increased the scope of discretionary allocations in the economy. It has promoted the survival of the fittest in the export sector *and* entitlements elsewhere" (original emphasis).[19] As such, Turkey's neo-liberalism was also accompanied by the expansion and concentration of the state's economic power. The public sector still remained dominant in the economy and the problem of endemic fiscal deficits with inadequate tax revenues and rising external/internal debt remained unresolved. The creation of the extra-budget funds, such as Mass Housing and Public Transportation Funds, which were under the direct control of the prime minister, was only one small example of such an expansion. The total number of such funds ranged from 96 to 134 and total assets in 1987–88 at 3.5 to 5.7 billion dollars. The 1988 estimated Mass Housing and Public Transportation Funds reached a value of 2.2 billion dollars.[20]

More importantly, economic liberalization and export-led growth in 1980s has largely failed to restructure state-society relations in Turkey. In essence, Turkey's liberalization did not result in transforming the behavior of the economic groups that have long relied on import substitution policies. Some of the industrial conglomerates of the 1960s and 1970s have begun to shift towards exports largely thanks to the extraordinary conditions of the post-coup era, such as frozen wages, as well as the generous export incentives. Özal's economic program ended up creating an alternative, but equally rent-seeking, export elite. This new rent-seeking elite of exporters created yet another cleavage in the business community between big industrialists and exporters.[21] Just like its predecessors they relied on state patronage such as export incentives, tax breaks and credits leading to "fictitious" exports.[22]

Side payments across various interest groups, such as subsidies for the agricultural elite, industrial incentives for various industrial groups and lowering import tariffs on certain goods, were all crucial for building various large electoral coalitions for successive governments in the 1980s and 1990s. Democratic pressures and electoral concerns increased the need for more side payments and extending state patronage.[23] Thus, even though the economic policies have changed, both the institutional setting and the nature of bureaucracy remained largely statist. Despite Özal's attempt to create an alternative technocratic elite, a personalized, highly politicized distribution of state patronage remained intact. It was, therefore, not surprising that the fate of economic reforms were very much linked to who was in power and what kind of side payments were being made. The stagnant exports in the 1990s and lack of export-related investment growth showed how much the export coalition during the Özal years relied on patronage and how fragile such coalitions are when they lose their leader.

Another net result of the state patronage, which has encouraged rent-seeking activities, was, as Öniş and Webb point out, the complete negligence of the distributional issues and institutional reforms.²⁴ The continuous populist discourse has masked such fundamental problems as regional discrepancies, wages and skewed taxation. Both of the center-right coalitions of the Özal governments since 1983, as well as Süleyman Demirel's and later Tansu Çiller's coalition with the Social Democrats, have largely ignored such structural issues, continuing instead with the side payments to their constituencies.²⁵ These constituencies included the farmers in the case of Çiller's True Path Party (*Doğru Yol Partisi*—DYP) and this explains the base prices for the farmers that were above the world market prices. In the case of the Republican People's Party (*Cumhuriyet Halk Partisi*—CHP), it included urban workers, which explains increasing wage rises in the 1990s. Increasing support for the new Anatolian business community and small-to-medium enterprises during the True Path and Welfare Party (*Refah Partisi*—RP) coalition (July 1996–June 1997) and the rising base prices for tea during the Motherland Party-led coalition (*Anavatan Partisi*—ANAP) government between 1997 and 1999 constitute the best-known examples of side payments by existing governments.²⁶

Two major factors explain the failure of public sector reform, the persisting problem of rent distribution and the reasons behind the populist strategies of successive governments.²⁷ One is that this problem is clearly associated with the nature of state-society relations in Turkey and the absence of what Evans has called "embedded autonomy of the state."²⁸ The absence of institutionalized channels of information and negotiation between state and society ("embeddedness") along with a certain degree of insulation of state bureaucracy (autonomy) to provide for policy coherence have led to continuous policy oscillations and inconsistencies throughout the 1990s. At times, the Turkish state suffered from too much rent-seeking and falling prey to interest groups and incumbents' electoral desires. At other times it was too much autonomy of the Turkish state or the lack of embeddedness that proved problematic.²⁹

Secondly, and perhaps more importantly, populist pressures emerge from the nature of distributional conflicts. Turkish liberalization, for instance, created a number of losers. The agricultural sector, urban workers and industrialists accustomed to the import substitution policies, were among those who opposed the liberalization agenda. As described above, various governments since the late 1980s have tried to mediate these conflicts by distributing the state rents to their respective constituencies. The income distribution in the country has systematically worsened, for instance, since the beginning of liberalization in the 1980s. While the share in income in the lowest 20 percent of households has dropped from 5.23

percent in 1987 to 4.86 percent in 1994, the share of the highest 20 percent increased from 49.93 to 54.88 percent. The share of children, moreover, living in poor population remains staggeringly high at 47 percent.[30] The more inequality in income distribution increases, and the more there is regional discrepancy, the stronger the tendency for rent distribution, which typifies Turkey's experience in the 1990s.

These populist pressures and the tendency to engage in patronage politics have eliminated all the incentives for public sector reform, limiting, in effect, Turkey's prospects for meeting the Copenhagen criteria. Regardless of what may have caused these populist strategies and distribution of state rent by the political elite, increased state spending and growing public deficits had fully returned in the second half of the 1980s after a small break in the 1980 post-military-intervention period. Pay-offs to constituents, particularly to the rural sector, and financing the deficits of State Economic Enterprises (SEEs) resulted in the relaxation of the austerity measures and spiraling inflation. Even though commitment to liberal reforms did not change with successive governments in the 1990s, the return of macroeconomic instability coupled with increasing political fragmentation and uncertainty began to make Turkey less and less attractive for potential foreign direct investors. All the expected benefits of liberalization, particularly of the customs union agreement, such as increased capital flows, foreign direct investments and exports, failed to materialize. Declining investor confidence launched a well-known vicious cycle of rising interest rates and spiraling public debt, leading to further loss of confidence, higher deficits and higher interest rates.[31]

This vicious cycle also precipitated the November 2000 and February 2001 financial crises in the country. A 14-month anti-inflation program, beginning in April 1999, had initial success and had brought the inflation levels from an average of 80 percent for much of the 1990s to an annual 36 percent. Yet, the weak banking system in the country, which was used to live off the high coupon government bonds, delayed privatization, and increasing current account deficits coupled with the widening gap between the pegged currency rates and inflation gradually undermined the foreign investors' confidence in Turkey's economy. An estimated 7.5 billion dollars was withdrawn from the country in November 2000 when the fragility of banking system first became evident. The already fragile banking system could not accommodate the February 2001 crisis, which initiated a renewed outflow of 3 billion dollars. The government was then forced to allow the TL to float, which resulted not only in a 36 percent devaluation of the TL in just one week but also brought the country to the brink of total financial collapse. In effect, the February 2001 crisis highlighted the fundamental problems of the premature liberalization of capital flows.

But the crisis also precipitated many structural reforms and aimed at limiting, if not ending, rent distribution in the public sector and patronage based dispersion of public funds. The IMF funds, which Turkey desperately needed to revolve its massive debt, were linked to a series of conditionalities written into the stand-by agreements.[32] These included both further liberalization of the economy, which involved significant restructuring of the agricultural and banking sector, as well as a series of institutional reforms such as the independence of the central bank and the creation of apolitical regulatory boards in banking, telecommunication, energy and tobacco and sugar. Agricultural liberalization included the elimination of product subsidies and its replacement with direct income subsidies to farmers. These subsidies, seen as the major reason behind huge public deficits, were cut dramatically. Restructuring the public sector banking system was also aimed at limiting the so called "duty losses" of the banks, which referred to the non-performing credits mostly paid on a patronage or populist basis. These gaping losses of the public banks had largely financed the political ambitions of the incumbent governments. Yet, because of the crisis, cheap credit and loans to farmers and shopkeepers all became unsustainable. The growing independence of the central bank in May 2001 and the establishment of autonomous regulatory boards, such as the Banking Regulatory and Supervisory Board in June 1999, along with other regulatory boards mentioned above (established throughout 2000 and 2001), also meant that political use of fiscal policy and state bureaucracy would now be even more difficult.

To what extent can the IMF reforms really end patronage politics? Can the short-term policies be replaced by long-term structural reforms? Will these reforms succeed and take Turkey out of its financial and economic crisis? The answers to these questions still remain to be seen. One thing, however, is clear. These IMF-induced reforms have brought Turkey closer to meeting the Copenhagen criteria. As will be discussed below, the economic agenda set out in the Commission's progress report significantly overlaps with that of the IMF.

THE CUSTOMS UNION AGREEMENT AS A MIRROR OF TURKEY'S ENDEMIC PROBLEMS

Though it is difficult to discern the exact effect of EU-Turkey economic ties on Turkey's economy, it is clear that these ties, in and of themselves, reflect the fundamental problems embedded in Turkey's political economy. This is particularly true for Turkey's customs union agreement with the EU. Turkey has become the first country to sign a customs union agreement with the EU without full membership benefits. The agreement, which came into effect in January 1996, reduced the 10.22 percent nominal rate of protection Turkey had with EU countries to 1.4 percent and brought down the overall rate against third parties to 6.92 percent. As more than half of Turkey's trade is with EU and about half of this volume is with Germany, this level of liberalization was significant for Turkey.[33]

Though it is difficult to measure the exact benefits of the Customs Union, some of the main expected benefits of it—such as the increased Foreign Direct Investment (FDI) flows, easier access to the EU and third-country markets, and further deepening of integration with the EU—has not really occurred. Given its limited impact, Mehmet Uğur rightly raises the question of whether the customs union agreement is significant enough to act as an incentive inducing Turkey to view the Customs Union as an anchor.[34]

There are also clear short-term costs associated with the Customs Union. For instance, most extra-budgetary funds, which had allowed the government to circumvent its revenue-raising problems and increase its non-tax resources, were eliminated. The remaining incentives were to be removed gradually within five years (Articles 32–38 of the customs union agreement).[35] Harrison *et al.* estimate the tariff revenue loss from the Customs Union at 1.4 percent of GDP.[36] The welfare gain does increase, however, if Turkey completes the bilateral trade agreements as a part of adopting the Common Customs Tariffs (CCT). Given the significant reduction in effective rate of protection, and the fact that Turkey has not really been able to negotiate effective bilateral trade deals (except with Israel), and hence open third-country markets for its own goods, also raised the short-term costs of the agreement.

Increasing short-term costs also explains the slow pace at which customs union-related reforms are being implemented in Turkey. The 2001 Progress Report observes, for instance:

> According to the Decision 1/95 of the EC-Turkey Association Council on implementing the final phase of the Customs Union, Turkey undertook to adopt Community legislation relating to the removal of technical barriers to trade by the end of 2000 ... However, Turkey has not been able to meet its obligation under Decision 1/95. The transitional arrangements have expired by the end of 2000 while a substantial part of the *acquis* remains to be transposed and implemented in Turkey. Although industrial goods

largely circulate freely within the Customs Union territory, the number of non-tariff barriers has in practice increased during 2001. This distorts trade and prevents the Customs Union from being used to its full potential.[37]

Issues such as standardization, preparation and implementation of technical legislation on products, and the independent and effective functioning of the Competition Authority still remain problematic. Even though talks have begun to extend the Customs Union into agriculture and services, no significant progress has been made.

Moreover, the stop-and-go nature of the Customs Union's implementation also reflects the patronage-based politics. From the very start, the Customs Union has been a victim of political posturing and calculations. A governing coalition of the DYP and CHP (June 1993 to March 1996) undertook the bargaining and completion of the customs union agreement with the EU. Moderate opposition came from the major opposition party on the right, ANAP, even though it was Turgut Özal, the party founder, who initiated Turkey's application to the EU in 1987. (The same party's leader, Mesut Yılmaz, later became the deputy prime minister responsible for EU affairs in another coalition government, which has been in power since April 1999.) The most visible and consistent source of opposition was the Islamist Welfare Party (RP), which saw membership as incompatible with the country's national interest, as well as its religious and cultural heritage.[38] Necmettin Erbakan, then the leader of the RP, who became the prime minister two months after the Customs Union went into effect, suggested during his election campaign that, once in office, his party would seek renegotiation of the agreement. Erbakan later retracted this statement, but these events showed the political fragility and reversibility of the Customs Union.[39]

Immediate politicization of the agreement is another problem, as was the case when the French parliament passed a resolution accepting the claims of Armenian genocide in January 2001. The Ministry of Agriculture, controlled by the nationalistic Nationalist Action Party (*Milliyetçi Hareket Partisi*—MHP) went on to propose a tariff increase on many of the processed agricultural imports from France with absolutely no regard for the provisions of the Customs Union.[40] The result has been a sub-optimal policy and incomplete customs union, which causes frequent friction and has not enabled Turkey to reap the benefits of the agreement. Rather, Ankara suffers from the Customs Union's short-term costs, and the EU, suspicious of Turkey's commitment, is reluctant to carry out its end of the bargain.[41]

Hence, Turkey-EU economic ties within the context of the Customs Union, reflect the typical problematic elements of Turkish political economy. Trade liberalization occurred as an end in itself, not as a part of a development strategy. While there has been a reduction of tariffs, the regulatory aspects of this liberalization have lagged behind. Indeed, one of the striking aspects of Turkey's political economy since the 1980s has been the inability or incapacity of the state to couple its liberalization strategies not only with investment and productivity growth but also with sufficient regulatory framework.

Problems in Turkey's relations with the EU in general and the customs union agreement in particular, however, cannot be limited to Turkey's structural problems embedded in the country's domestic political economy. Has the EU done enough to "anchor" Turkey into Europe?[42] To what extent are the Copenhagen criteria realistic?

HAS THE EU DONE ENOUGH: ADJUSTMENT AID—TOO LITTLE, TOO LATE?

In contrast to IMF conditionality, where financial aid is primarily linked to the implementation of specific economic policies and is given immediately once the policy changes take place, the EU conditionality has suffered from a timing problem offering benefits not *during* the implementation but long *after* it. IMF and World Bank conditionality is a "means of ensuring the execution of a contract, a promise by one party to do something now in exchange for a promise of the other party to do something else in the future."[43] Indeed, Turkey has received a significant amount of IMF funds, reaching an approximate 30 billion dollars, which makes Turkey the second highest borrower from the IMF after Brazil.[44] The World Bank has also provided considerable grants and loans on a project basis, particularly in the implementation of agricultural and trade reforms. On the other hand, as Grappe argues in the context of Central and Eastern Europe (CEE) countries:

> In sharp contrast, EU demands on CEE are not just sets of conditions to receive defined benefits, but an evolving process that is highly politicized, especially on the EU side. The linkage between fulfilling certain tasks and receiving particular benefits is much less clear than in IFI [International Financial Institutions] conditionality because the tasks are complex, and many of them are not amenable to quantitative targets that show explicitly that they have been reached.[45]

The amount of aid that Turkey received in its membership ordeal clearly reflects this problem as well. According to the Turkish Ministry of Foreign Affairs, Turkey received a total of ECU1.05 billion from the EU during

1964–95, prior to the Customs Union: within the framework of the four Financial Protocols, the Supplementary Protocol and the Special Aid Package, 78 million of this was as grants and 927 million as low-interest credits.[46] More importantly, the absence of full membership to the EU meant Turkey would not be able to benefit from much of the social and regional funds designed to ease the costs of adjustments required to enter the Customs Union. The ECU375 million promised to Turkey as fiscal aid to be spread over five years in the Joint Council meeting on March 1995 as a part of adjustment to the Customs Union was suspended by the European Parliament on political grounds, particularly the human rights issue. Similarly, the aid that Turkey was supposed to receive as a part of the European Mediterranean Development program was also suspended for similar reasons. An ECU750 EIB (European Investment Bank) credit could not be used due to a Greek veto.[47]

Apart from the Customs Union, Turkey's access to the pre-accession funds has also proved problematic. For instance, the Commission has taken a stand, largely due to budgetary constraints, against the extension (in order to include Turkey) of the "Instrument for Structural Policies for Pre-accession" (ISPA) and the "Special Accession Programme for Agriculture and Rural Development" (SAPARD). Despite emphasis in progress reports that Turkey desperately needs a regional integration and social policy, Turkey is also not part of the European Regional Development and Cohesion Fund.[48] Thus, the overall aid that Turkey has received in the context of both the Customs Union and pre-accession has been too little and too late to have any significant impact on Turkey's economy. CEE countries, however, have received considerably more aid. While Turkey has received only four euros per capita, this number ranged between ten and 45 euros for CEE countries.[49]

The fact that most of this aid is made available *after* meeting the Copenhagen economic criteria also creates a "chicken and egg" problem.[50] As noted above, the implementation of the customs union agreement and EU-related reforms have been painstakingly slow largely due to the long-term nature of the expected benefits and patronage-based politics in the country. In sum, the absence of access to EU funds *during* the implementation of these reforms has reduced Turkey's prospects of meeting the Copenhagen criteria.

Furthermore, the definition of the Copenhagen criteria has also proved problematic. In "Agenda 2000," in which the Commission discussed the challenge of enlargement, the EU defined the "functioning market economy" as liberalization of prices and trade, an enforceable legal system that includes property rights, macroeconomic stability consensus on economic policy to enhance the performance of a market economy, a well-developed financial sector and the absence of significant barriers to market entry and exit so as to improve efficiency of the economy.[51] The second economic Copenhagen criteria—"capacity to compete in the EU markets"—is seen as a function of a functioning market economy and a stable macroeconomic framework which allows for predictability, a sufficient amount of human and physical capital including infrastructure, and the restructuring of state enterprises and investments to increase efficiency.

At first glance, these criteria look deceptively straightforward. But since no specific definition of a market economy has been provided and there is no one single model of capitalism at work in Europe, how and when the applicant countries will meet these criteria remains extremely vague. Furthermore, with the exception of the country progress reports, there is no published rationale of how these EU demands will bring the applicants closer to west European political and economic norms. As Grappe puts it when discussing all three Copenhagen criteria, they:

> are very broad and open to considerable interpretation; elaboration of what constitutes meeting them has progressively widened the detailed criteria for membership, making the Union a moving target for applicants. The conditions are not fixed and definite, new conditions have been added and the old ones redefined at the biannual summits of the EU leaders. Moreover, the benefits do not come in stages, but only at the end. As the arbiter of what constitutes meeting the conditions and when the benefits will be granted, the Union changes the rule of the game. This moving target problem also has implications for relative strength in negotiating the terms of accession, because the Union is a referee as well as a player in the accession process.[52]

The moving target problem and the ambiguity embedded in the Copenhagen criteria has clearly blurred the link between expected benefits of membership and ongoing structural reforms.

THE CHANGING EUROPEAN PROJECT AND THE PROBLEM OF COHERENCE IN THE COPENHAGEN CRITERIA

The problems with the Copenhagen criteria and the enlargement process are inevitably linked to the transformation of the EU project itself. On the whole, the EU project itself has been largely Keynesian, emphasizing regional and social integration, accepting the state's role in the economy as an integral part of market correction and using fiscal tools to address employment problems as well as social and regional discrepancies. Yet, the focus has visibly shifted in the 1990s towards increasing the EU's competitiveness in an increasingly globalized economy in comparison to the rest of the world. In fact the project of a single internal market emerged against a background of a perceived loss of competitiveness in comparison to Japan and the United States in the mid-1980s. These global market pressures pushed European governments to endorse the neo-liberal agenda. This new concern for competitiveness and the consequent neo-liberal restructuring ignored the social harmonization with common and high health standards, labor conditions (such as the Social Protocol, Charter of Basic Social Rights for workers, etc.) that, to a large extent, had long been a part of the European project. The neo-liberal agenda was also easier to carry out for the states than the social policies.

Spreading neo-liberal policies became an effective "legitimizing" agent as the nation states unload their responsibility to the world markets. Eliminating fragmentation within the European market through predominantly "negative integration," such as removing trade barriers and distortion of competition, was the initial step to compete in the global economy.[53] The neo-liberal shift was most evident in the Maastricht Treaty (1993), which was a qualitatively new step in European integration, as the European Monetary Union (EMU) and the euro became the centerpiece of supranationalism in the EU system. While, externally, the EMU was designed to give the euro a chance in global currency competition, internally it aimed at cementing the political actors to orthodox monetarist/fiscal policies.[54]

The changing nature of European integration has inevitably influenced the dynamics of enlargement and the associated Copenhagen economic criteria. The core of the EU's economic agenda for enlargement became increasingly neo-liberal, emphasizing privatization, overall retreat of the state's involvement in the economy and further liberalization of trade. Despite the immense variety of economic systems within the EU, ranging from the "Anglo-Saxon" model to "Rhenish" social market economies to Latin style economies of southern Europe, the progress reports have presented a uniform set of expectations based on the Anglo-Saxon recipe.[55]

TURKEY'S PROGRESS REPORTS: 1998-2001

The Neo-liberal Dimension

The progress reports on Turkey provide a good example of the neo-liberal shift in the economic dimension of EU enlargement. Under the rubric of a functioning market and capacity to compete, several themes dominated the progress reports when evaluating the economic criteria. First, the issue of macroeconomic stability. Excessive public borrowing requirements, political instability and dysfunctional financial system are singled out as main sources of macroeconomic instability. Second, the overall retreat of the state a la privatization, restructuring of state-economic enterprises and agricultural liberalization. Third, the issue of price liberalization and elimination of barriers to market entry. Here, too, the institutional framework of market dynamics and the competition and intellectual property rights law are emphasized. Finally, commercial liberalization and external integration to the European and world markets are assessed in the progress reports and are seen as hallmarks of meeting the Copenhagen economic criteria.

All of these themes also form the core issues of the IMF structural adjustment agenda for Turkey and Turkey's letters of intent to the IMF.[56] It is important to note that even though some economic reforms orchestrated by Ankara had to do with harmonization in accordance with the customs union agreements (such as intellectual property rights and competition laws), almost *all* the economic reforms discussed and praised in the progress reports have been undertaken following IMF supervision. The financial crises of November 2000 and February 2001 have accelerated these reforms under the immense pressures of resolving the existing domestic and public debt.

The Commission's 1998 progress report on Turkey—the first of its kind—points out that "Turkey has not attained a degree of macroeconomic stability required to participate in the internal market and not interfere with its smooth working."[57] Given the political instability, and more importantly the "lack of an enduring consensus on economic strategy among main political, social and economic forces," the report shows skepticism towards the government's new stabilization program.[58] In the 1999 progress report it is suggested that while the response to external crises (particularly the ruble crisis of August 1998) has shown the flexibility and adaptability of the Turkish economy, it has also revealed its vulnerability, particularly in terms of access to liquid capital.[59] The most comprehensive review of Turkey's economy is provided in the progress report of 2000. In this report, there is a congratulatory tone for the reforms Turkey is undertaking within the IMF framework. The coalition government, which was in place from April 1999, is praised for maintaining an unprecedented level of consensus on the essentials of economic policy.[60] Remarkable decline in interest rates and reduction in inflation, fiscal discipline and consequent improvements in public sector accounts are noted as important successes towards macroeconomic stability. Not surprisingly, the 2001 progress report loses this optimistic tone due to the November 2000 and February 2001 financial crises in Turkey. The report concludes that, "the two financial crises brought to a halt economic recovery and put an end to the prior economic stabilization program. Macroeconomic stability has been shaken, and many macroeconomic imbalances have reappeared." But the report adds that "Turkey has adopted and has been implementing an ambitious economic reform programme that addresses better than its predecessor the risks and vulnerabilities of the domestic financial sector and seeks to reduce government intervention in many areas of the economy. These problems were at the heart of the crises."[61]

Indeed, the need for reducing the state's role in the economy by restructuring the public sector is another common theme of the progress reports. While the 1998 progress report cites the disappointing degree of privatization and very high level of external protection of agricultural goods as problems of too much involvement of the Turkish state in the economy, the 1999 progress report adds the financial sector to the list of problems and explains that in Turkey:

> the process of achieving a smoothly functioning market economy is not completed as there are still considerable areas of state dominance and market distortions—especially in agriculture and the financial sector. Structural imbalances, such as the close link between the banking sectors' profitability and the existence of high and short-term financing need of the public sector, lead to a distorted capital market and high real interest rates.[62]

The commission recommends that, "in order to cure such chronic imbalances and to unveil Turkey's slumbering growth potential, the authorities should continue to focus on bringing down inflationary pressures and public deficits and on developing further structural reforms."[63] The 2000 report, on the other hand, praises the successful privatization of state economic enterprises, such as POAŞ (a petroleum distributor), and public offerings for Turkish Petroleum Refineries (TÜPRAŞ), and goes on, in typical liberal fashion, to criticize the inefficiencies embedded in state economic enterprises.[64]

There is also a cautionary emphasis on the need for deepening the agricultural liberalization reforms, which have been the centerpiece of the country's structural reform under the IMF and World Bank program:

> The financial support system (on agriculture) represents a heavy burden on public finances, distorts prices and the allocation of resources and aggravates social disparities, since the artificially high prices for agricultural commodities are disproportionably affecting low-income households. The government's new approach so far has been to reduce support prices in line with the inflation target and to end subsidized credits to the agricultural sector. The reform of the agricultural sector aims at switching to direct income support for farmers. Given Turkey's resource endowment, this sector has great potential. However, in order to improve the sector's competitiveness and sustainability, the initiated reform has to be sustained and deepened.[65]

But the most explicit call for the reduction of state interference is expressed in the 2001 report, where the Commission finds that:

> state interference has been declining further in the agricultural and financial sector. The most important measures in this respect have been initiatives to liberalize the tobacco and sugar markets, the establishment of the autonomy of the agricultural sales cooperatives and the elimination of political influence in the state banks. The role of the Telecommunication Regulatory Authority has been strengthened and the latest amendments to the regulation of the electricity and gas sector call for the establishment of independent regulatory institutions.[66]

As noted above, these reforms have again been central to IMF reforms in Turkey.

Price liberalization, eliminating barriers to market entry and providing the institutional framework for a functioning market economy are other themes in the progress reports. Here, there seems to be less of an adjustment problem, but intervention into the agricultural prices—the role the state still plays in setting prices in stated-owned enterprises—is still underlined as market distorting. Nevertheless, the 1998 report states that "Turkey has the institutional framework for a market economy" and underscores the important role the Customs Union played with regards to the economic legislation, particularly in competition and intellectual property rights laws.[67] The establishment of the independent Competition Authority in 1998 and the constitutional change passing through the parliament to allow for international arbitration are both noted as important steps in the 1999 report.[68] But the 2001 report still suggests that "Despite fairly liberal regulations concerning market entry and exit, remaining barriers impede economic activity." Prohibitively high interest rates and reluctance on the part of private banks to provide credits to the private sector are cited as fundamental problems.[69] Problems in the implementations of laws and regulations are yet another challenge.

Finally, Turkey's commercial integration with the EU and the degree of trade liberalization are discussed extensively in the progress reports. Here, the centerpiece of discussion is the Customs Union with the EU. The fact that Turkish enterprises have been able to survive the customs union agreement is hailed as a building block for creating a functioning market and increasing the competitiveness of Turkish industries. Turkey's harmonization of customs legislation with the EU and the adoption of CCT have also lowered Turkey's tariffs *vis-à-vis* the third countries. The 2000 progress report provides a very positive account:

> The major economic effect of the Customs Union was the redirection of Turkish third country imports towards the EC. Turkish enterprises had no major problems in adjusting to the new competitive situation ... The trade integration between Turkey and the EU rose continuously, reaching a trade share of more than 50 percent of Turkey's total trade. Simultaneously, the commodity structure of Turkey's trade improved, with the share of manufactured commodities rising from 66 percent in 1990 to 70 percent in 1999. In particular, the value-added in key automotive and textile industries increased markedly. The share of intra-industry trade with the EU is relatively high.[70]

The fact that Turkey's overall exports to the EU have not particularly risen after the Customs Union was implemented is explained by the overvalued lira (due to the currency peg system implemented under IMF supervision between April 1999 and February 2001) and the rising importance of the Russian and Central Asian market. Overall, the customs union agreement, according to the progress reports, is a very important sign for the EU regarding Turkish ability to meet the Copenhagen economic criteria.

Social Dimension

Nevertheless, it would be a mistake to suggest that the economic assessment of the Commission was based *only* on this neo-liberal agenda. Repeatedly, the progress reports underscore the importance of addressing the regional inequalities that have persistently worsened in the country and call for the need to invest in physical and human capital. In the 2001 report, for instance, the Commission observes that, in Turkey:

> the composition of human and physical capital is very heterogeneous in terms of quality and regional distribution and needs urgent improvement. The demographic structure of Turkey, with a relatively young population, represents a considerable potential but also generates the need to provide adequate resources for schooling and training. Turkey's human capital reflects years of insufficient funding ... The health system does not provide sufficient support to the labor force. Besides insufficient resources, provision of health services differs significantly between regions. The quality of physical capital is also heterogeneous, leading to considerable productivity differentials. Export-oriented companies work with state-of-the-art technology while many small to medium enterprises still deal with worn-out capital and outdated management techniques.[71]

Despite these observations, however, the commission simply concludes that the authorities "should redefine their budgetary priorities, in a medium-term perspective, in order to provide a sufficient level of investment in education, health, social services and public infrastructure across the country."[72] Given the two financial crises that Turkey experienced and the very serious budgetary constraints due to the burden of debt, carrying out these investments is bound to be difficult. The progress reports are silent regarding how exactly such developmental projects can be financed in the midst of macroeconomic instability and consequent limits on public expenditures.

In effect, despite the lip service being paid to the social policies and concerns on regional disparities, the commission does not provide any guidelines on how, particularly in the absence of EU aid, these problems can be tackled. This problem, as Grappe explains, is not limited to Turkey and reflects a degree of inconsistency embedded in the Copenhagen criteria:

> At a general level, applicants are encouraged to maintain fiscal and monetary discipline and the Union stresses the need to control budget deficits while undertaking systemic reforms (such as pensions, health care and industrial restructuring). But at the same time, the Union also demands major investments in infrastructure, environmental protection, agricultural reform, and a whole range of other sectors. The room for additional public spending on

implementing the *acquis* is reduced if it is to be accompanied by tight fiscal and monetary policies aimed at macroeconomic stability. This creates an inconsistency in the EU's recommendations that would only be resolved by massive external funding (foreign or private), of which the Union is willing to provide only a very small proportion.[73]

Indeed, as noted above, the absence of adjustment aid has been particularly acute in the case of Turkey.

CONCLUSION

Turkey faces serious dilemmas and challenges in meeting the Copenhagen economic criteria. Part of the difficulty is that the EU's own project and strategies are also changing from a Keynesian strategy—emphasizing integration and cohesion—to a neo-liberal one, emphasizing deregulating markets in the face of growing global competition. This shift has inevitably influenced the EU's enlargement process and the associated conditionality for accession, known as the Copenhagen criteria. The progress reports prepared on Turkey by the EU Commission very much reflect this trend. These reports predominantly focus on neoliberal recipes such as privatization and price and trade liberalization, which have been on Turkey's economic agenda due to the IMF stand-by agreements. In contrast to IMF conditionality, however, EU conditionality has not come with definite, immediate and quantifiable benefits. IMF conditionality meant money flow to get out of crises whereas Customs Union benefits remained small and EU adjustment money was never delivered. Indeed, most of the EU-related reforms, as is most evident in the customs union agreement, bring short-term costs and long-term benefits. The fact that EU adjustment aid has largely been absent in the case of Turkey has further complicated the country's prospects. Hence, Turkey-EU ties, particularly the Customs Union, resulted in reflecting, rather than solving, the two fundamental problems of Turkey's political economy: a sub-optimal liberalization experience that did not go far enough to push for public reforms, the side effects of which were not mediated through an investment and growth strategy, and patronage-based politics, which makes long term planning impossible—if not irrational—for politicians.

Can the EU-related economic reforms eventually end patronage politics and policy reversals? Clearly, neither the Customs Union nor Turkey-EU economic ties will be sufficient in order to address the deeply rooted problems in Turkey's political economy. Nevertheless, the EU offers a priceless opportunity for governments to "lock-in" their reforms and to increase their credibility. The extent to which Turkey can resolve these dilemmas and challenges will depend on the ability of successive governments to balance the neo-liberal and socio-economic strategies. Those governments coupling the liberalization agenda with a growth/investment strategy and able to make use of the EU within that context, will be the most likely to succeed. Only then, perhaps, can Turkey put an end to the so many stop-and-go cycles, systematic policy reversals and short-term dynamics of its economic policymaking.

POSTSCRIPT

The December 12, 2002 Copenhagen summit of the European Council has irreversibly linked Turkey's future with that of the EU. Once again, however, Turkey's candidacy was blocked due to insufficient implementation of political reforms and, once again, economic reforms were seen as unproblematic. Early months of the new Justice and Development Party (*Adalet ve Kalkınma Partisi*—AKP) government, which came to power with a considerable electoral victory in the November 2002 elections, indicate, however, that implementation of the economic reforms the earlier coalition government had launched under the tutelage of the IMF may prove just as problematic. The AKP government, for instance, is attempting to delay and/or change the public procurement law designed to bring more transparency and openness in public procurements. The government's concerns regarding the independent status of regulatory boards and its reluctance to undertake the fiscal reforms also indicate that some of the institutional reforms embedded in the IMF program that are crucial for meeting the Copenhagen economic criteria may not be implemented. These early signs suggest that the old-style patronage-based politics, which lie at the heart of the problems embedded in Turkey's political economy, may indeed be here to stay.

NOTES

1. Europa, European Commission, Enlargement, <http://www.europa.eu.int/comm/enlargement/intro/criteria.htm>.
2. Dorothee Bohle, "The Ties that Bind the New Europe: Neo-Liberal Restructuring and Transnational Actors in the Deepening and Widening of the European Union," Paper presented at Workshop 4, "Enlargement and European Governance," ECPR Joint Session workshops, Turin, March 22–27, 2002; Bastiaan van Apeldoorn, "Transnational Class

Agency and European Governance: The Case of the European Roundtable Industrialists," *New Political Economy*, Vol.4, No.2 (2000), pp.157–81.
3. 2000 population statistics, Institute of State Statistics, <http://www.die.gov.tr>.
4. TİSK (*Türkiye İşveren Sendikaları Konfederasyonu*—Confederation of Turkish Employers Union), *Avrupa Birliği'ne Aday Ülkeler Kıyaslama Raporu* [Comparative report on candidate countries to the EU] (Ankara: Yayın No.220, 2002), p.35.
5. Another striking factor is that, with 30.5 percent of its population under the age of 15, Turkey has a very young population, which is in sharp contrast to the rapidly aging EU population. It is estimated that by 2015, approximately one-fifth of the EU population will be 65 or older. World Bank, *World Development Indicators* (Washington DC: World Bank, 2000).
6. Ibid.
7. EU Commission, *Regular Report from the Commission on Turkey's Progress Towards Accession* (Brussels, 2001), p.37.
8. Ibid.
9. The World Bank, *World Development Indicators* (Washington DC: World Bank, 1999).
10. TİSK (2002), p.53.
11. TİSK, *Avrupa Birliği'ne üyelik sü recinde AB ülkeleri ve diğer aday ülkeler arasında Türkiye'nin durumu: TİSK kıyaslama raporu* [The condition of Turkey during the membership process in comparison to EU and other candidate countries: TİSK benchmarking report] (Ankara: Ajanstürk Press, 2000), pp.97–127.
12. Ibid., p.63.
13. All figures given in relation to 1987 prices. See Institute of State Statistics, Economic Panorama, <http://www.die.gov.tr/seed/nation/page27.html>.
14. TİSK (2002), p.24.
15. Ibid., p.26.
16. Mehmet Uğur has extensively discussed this issue in his book *The European Union and Turkey: An Anchor/Credibility Dilemma* (London: Ashgate, 1999), pp.x–xi.
17. The term is borrowed from Ziya Öniş, "Political Economy of Turkey in the 1980s: Anatomy of Unorthodox Liberalism," in Metin Heper (ed.), *The State and Economic Interest Groups: The post-1980 Turkish Experience* (Berlin and New York: Walter de Gruyter, 1991), pp.27–40.
18. See John Waterbury, "Export-led Growth and Center-Right Coalition in Turkey," *Comparative Politics*, Vol.24, No.2 (1992a), pp.127–45; Ayşe Buğra, *State and Business in Modern Turkey: A Comparative Study* (New York: State University of New York Press, 1994); David Waldner, *State Building and Late Development* (Ithaca, NY: Cornell University Press, 1999); Öniş (1991).
19. John Waterbury, "Export-led Growth and the Center-Right Coalition in Turkey," in Tevfik Nas and Mehmet Odekon (eds.), *Economics and Politics of Turkish Liberalization* (Bethlehem, PA: Lehigh University Press, 1992b), p.46.
20. Ibid., p.52.
21. Yeşim Arat, "Politics and Big Business: Janus-faced Link to the State," in Heper (1991), pp.135–49.
22. For an extensive discussion of why Turkey's export-led growth did not result in successful industrialization, see Waldner (1999).
23. For the discussion of state patronage during Özal years, see Waterbury (1992a).
24. Ziya Öniş and Steven B. Webb, "Turkey: Democratization and Adjustment from Above," in Steven B. Webb and Stephan Haggard (eds.), *Voting for Reform* (New York: Oxford University Press and World Bank, 1994), pp.128–85.
25. See Heper (1991).
26. There is extensive literature on the basis of patronage politics in Turkey. For good examples, see Ali Çarkoğlu, "The Interdependence of Politics and Economics in Turkey: Some Findings at the Aggregate Level of Analysis," *Boğaziçi Journal: Review of Social, Economic and Administrative Studies*, Vol.9, No.2 (1995), pp.85–108 and Metin Heper,

"Double-Faced State: Political Patronage and Consolidation of Democracy in Turkey," *Middle Eastern Studies*, Vol.34, No.4 (1998), 259–78.
27. Populism has always been endemic to Turkey's political economy. For an excellent analysis of the origins and development of populism, see İlkay Sunar, "Populism and Patronage: The Demokrat Party and its Legacy in Turkey," *Il Politico*, anno.V (1990), pp.745–57 and "The Politics of State Interventionism in Populist Egypt and Turkey," in Ayşe Öncü, Çağlar Keyder and Saad Eddin İbrahim (eds.), *Developmentalism and Beyond: Society and Politics in Egypt and Turkey* (Cairo: American University in Cairo Press, 1994).
28. For extensive discussion of this concept, see Peter Evans, *Embedded Autonomy: States and Industrial Transformation* (Princeton, NJ: Princeton University Press, 1995).
29. For the problem of too much autonomy of the state, see Mine Eder, "Becoming Western: Turkey and the European Union," in Jean Grugel and Will Hout (eds.), *Regionalism Across the North-South Divide: State Strategies and Globalization* (London: Routledge, 1999), pp.79–95. For a more in-depth look at Turkey's political economy, see Mine Eder, "Globalization and Turkey's Changing Political Economy," in Barry Rubin and Kemal Kirişci (eds.), *Turkey in World Politics: An Emerging Multi-Regional Power* (Istanbul: Boğaziçi University Press, 2002), pp.249–84.
30. Ümit Cizre-Sakallıoğlu and Erinç Yeldan, "Politics, Society and Financial Liberalization: Turkey in the 1990s," *Development and Change*, Vol.31, No.2 (2000), p.488. Also see OECD, *Economic Survey of Turkey* (Paris: OECD, 2001), pp.101–2.
31. For an analysis of Turkey's public deficits, see İzak Atıyaş and Şerif Sayın, "A Political Economy Perspective on Turkish Budget Deficits," *Boğaziçi Journal: Review of Social, Economic and Administrative Sciences*, Vol.12, No.1 (1998), pp.55–79.
32. For the complete content of letters of intent and structural reforms, see the Turkish Treasury home page: <http://www.treasury.gov.tr>.
33. See Undersecretariat of Trade, <http://www.foreigntrade.gov.tr>.
34. Uğur (1999), p.78.
35. So much so that, in 1988, 11.2 percent of public investment was financed through these extra-budgetary funds. Ziya Öniş, *State and Market: The Political Economy of Turkey in Comparative Perspective* (Istanbul: Boğaziçi University Press, 1998), p.188.
36. Glenn W. Harrison, Thomas Rutherford and David Tarr, "Economic Implications for Turkey of a Customs Union with the European Union" (1996), available at <http://econpapers.hhs.se/paper/wopwobaie/1599.htm>. Harrison adds that if VAT was to be used to compensate for this loss, VAT rates would have to increase by 16.2 percent in each sector.
37. EU Commission (2001), p.49.
38. Welfare Party, *Election Manifesto*, p.29.
39. Uğur (1999), p.79.
40. Interview with the Ministerial Undersecretary, Hamit Ayanoğlu, Ministry of Agriculture and Rural Affairs, Ankara, July 8, 2001.
41. For example, the Commission has consistently complained about the post-verification of the origins of the product. In the case of the canned tuna fish and Turkish televisions, the European Commission issued a warning to EU importers in 1999.
42. For an extensive discussion of this issue, see Uğur (1999), pp.75–85.
43. Paul Mosley, Jane Harrigan and John Toye, *Aid and Power: The World Bank and the Policy-Based Lending* (London: Routledge, 1991), p.65, cited in Heather Grappe, "European Union Conditionality and the *Acquis Communautaire*," *International Political Science Review*, Vol.23, No.3 (2002), p.252.
44. Turkish Treasury, <http://www.treasury.gov.tr>.
45. Grappe (2002), p.252.
46. Within the context of the Customs Union, the EU committed credits of a total of ECU557 million, 340 million of which were given in the framework of the New Mediterranean Policy, 205 million in the framework of MEDA-I and 12 million as risk capital. During the same period, the EU's grant commitment totaled ECU393 million, 376 million of which came from

MEDA-I, 3 million from Administrative Cooperation, and 14 million from various individual projects on the environment, the fight against drugs, AIDS, etc. These grants are still being distributed on a project-by-project basis. See Turkey-EU Financial Cooperation, Ministry of Foreign Affairs, Feb. 19, 2002, <http://www.mfa.gov.tr>.

47. "In the post-Helsinki period, the EU took the initiative to make available a portion, if not all, of the above-mentioned 750 million. In this context, on 4 December 2000, the EU General Affairs Council adopted the Regulation on the allocation to Turkey of EUR 450 million EIB credits. The programming of those credits covering the period 2000–4 is pending. Actual disbursements are planned to start in 2002. As for the 375 million worth of grants, the EU Commission prepared two regulations of 15 and 135 million respectively, the process for the adoption of which have been completed. The regulations have also been promulgated in the Official Journal of the European Communities. A part of those grants is committed in 2001 for projects that will start to be implemented as of 2002. The remaining resources will be allocated to projects in the framework of the 2002-4 Financing Agreement." See Ministry of Foreign Affairs, Turkey-EU Financial Cooperation, <http://www.mfa.gov.tr>.
48. Gamze Avcı, "Putting the Turkish Candidacy into Context," *European Foreign Affairs Review*, Vol.7, No.1 (2002), p.106.
49. A. Gugenbuehl and M. Theelen, "The Financial Assistance of the European Union to its Eastern and Southern Neighbours: A Comparative Analysis," in Marc Marsceau and Erwan Lannon (eds.), *The EU's Enlargement and Mediterranean Strategies: A Comparative Analysis* (Basingstoke: Palgrave, 2000), p.251, cited in Avcı (2002), p.109.
50. The best example is the European Investment bank credits. On May 15, 2001, Turkey completed the legal ground to open the country to the Pre-Accession Facility, which offers a total of EUR8.5 billion EIB credits during 2000–3 to the public and private sectors from all the candidates. However, for this money to be used in public projects, the EIB works as a rigorous commercial bank and requires a minimum of "BBB" international credit rating from the beneficiary country. Similarly, for private sector projects, the beneficiary is required to bear a credit rating of "A+." Due to the recent economic crisis, Turkey is currently unable to meet those prerequisite criteria. See Avcı (2002), p.106.
51. The Commission presented the Agenda 2000 report in July 1997 and, based on the Commission's recommendation, the Luxembourg European Council decided to launch the enlargement process in December 1997.
52. Grappe (2002), p.251. See also Laszlo Bruszt, "Making Markets and Eastern Enlargement: Diverging Convergence?," *West European Politics*, Vol.25, No.2 (April 2002), pp.12–34.
53. Fritz W. Scharpf, "Negative and Positive Integration in the Political Economy of European Welfare States," in Gary Marks, Fritz W. Scharpf, Phillipe C. Schmitter and Wolfgang Streeck (eds.), *Governance in the European Union* (London: Sage, 1996), p.15.
54. Bohle (2002), p.7.
55. Michele Albert, *Capitalisme Contre Capitalisme* (Paris: Le Seuil, 1991); Martin Rhodes and Bastiaan van Apeldoorn, "Capitalism Unbound? The Transformation of European Corporate Governance," *Journal of European Public Policy*, Vol.5, No.3 (1998), pp.406–27.
56. T.C. Başbakanlık Hazine Müsteşarlığı, *Eflasy onla Mücadele Programı Politika Metinleri: Niyet Mektupları, Ekonomik kararlara ilişkin mevzuat* [Political Documents regarding the anti-inflation program: Letters of intent and legal texts of economic decisions] (Ankara: Undersecretariat of Treasury, July 2000). Also see Turkish Treasury, <http://www.treasury.gov.tr>.
57. EU Commission, *Regular Report from the Commission on Turkey's Progress Towards Accession* (Brussels, 1998), p.22.
58. Ibid.
59. EU Commission, *Regular Report from the Commission on Turkey's Progress Towards Accession* (Brussels, 1999), p.22.
60. EU Commission, *Regular Report from the Commission on Turkey's Progress Towards Accession* (Brussels, 2000), p.22.

61. EU Commission (2001), p.45.
62. EU Commission (1999), p.23.
63. Ibid., pp.23–4.
64. EU Commission (2000), p.25.
65. Ibid., p.26.
66. EU Commission (2001), p.44.
67. EU Commission (1998), p.22.
68. EU Commission (1999), p.23.
69. EU Commission (2001), p.41.
70. EU Commission (2000), p.26.
71. EU Commission (2001), pp.42–3.
72. Ibid., p.45.
73. Grappe (2002), p.263.

13
Conclusion

ALİ ÇARKOĞLU

After a long period of silence and stagnation that resulted in a deep economic crisis and an equally formidable lack of trust in government, the seeds of change in Turkish politics were showing signs of growth towards the end of the spring of 2002. On the surface, the painful process of transformation took the form of party infighting around Prime Minister Bülent Ecevit's health condition. However, scratching deeper, one sees the inability of the Turkish party system to effectively respond to mass demand and expectations in times of crisis.

The coalition of the DSP, MHP and ANAP in the aftermath of April 1999 elections was full of crises. While some of these crises came with natural disasters, such as the two massive earthquakes in August and November of 1999, the coalition partners themselves sowed the seeds of the others. The ineffective organization of public relief efforts in the aftermath of the August 1999 earthquake not only enervated the grieving public but also proved once again the inaptitude of public authorities to respond to the needs and demands of the Turkish public. However, the arithmetic of parliamentary seat distribution, together with the inability of the civic anger to pressure the coalition to take responsibility, helped the coalition survive the political aftershocks of the earthquake.

The impact of the financial crisis that hit the country first in November 2000 and next in February 2001 has been much more severe on the political front. Political manipulations of fiscal policies leading to an unsustainable public debt are commonly diagnosed as the underlying reason for the crisis. The new post-crisis economic policy initiative, under the guardianship of Kemal Derviş, aims to do away with political manipulations in the economy. As Mine Eder's discussion (pp.219–44) shows, these economic policy initiatives largely overlap with the adjustment of the Turkish economic policy framework for EU membership. As such, the struggle to implement these new policy initiatives reflects the attempt to adjust to the EU and the consequent resistance among the domestic interest groups.

The dilemma of the new program rests on this very objective. The capacity to politically manipulate economic policies has been the only tool in the hands of the politicians to build and maintain political support in Turkey. Other, more subtle ideological tools, have either been oppressed—as in the case of the once quite potent left-wing groups of the late 1970s, and the once rising pro-Islamists of the early 1990s—or they are quite risky, as is the ethnic nationalism of the Turkish or Kurdish variants, domestically as well as internationally. If the economic patronage distribution mechanisms were to be taken away from the politicians, the Turkish party system risked being reduced to an impotent player. Parties had so far failed to respond to the demands of their constituencies in any other way than simple patronage distribution, which led to huge public deficits and inefficient production structures. Intricate and obscure budgeting practices helped disguise the responsibility of the politicians while ruining the public budget. Politicians could not design foreign policy, which remained an almost exclusively bureaucratic or military arena. They also could not design much of domestic policy. Many, for example, in the political circles of the center-right would want to concede on the issue of the headscarf ban in universities, but that option was perceived to lead to an effective veto by the military. Many in the pro-European political circles would also want concessions on minority issues, regarding for instance education rights in Kurdish, but that, too, was very hard to push against complex bureaucratic coalitions in Ankara with potent political power.

Within the framework of the new economic policy initiative that was primarily imposed by the international financial institutions, politicians cannot deliver patronage-based economic policy because they do not have the necessary resources any more. They no longer have the means to postpone dealing with structural issues in the economy for future generations. The new dilemma for Turkish politicians then becomes one of whether or not they have the power to be potent players with the political responsibility to deliver policies. In contrast to being in "power without responsibility" for decades of patronage-based policymaking, for the first time in multi-party politics in Turkey the present political parties seem unable to escape from "responsibility without power."[1] The issue of EU membership gains potency within this larger framework of running politics in the Turkish party system.

The ruling coalition of the DSP, MHP and ANAP has survived immense economic difficulties, which seem to have exhausted public trust in the future of the country. It was time for the ultimate political punishment associated with this failure. The discussions of early elections

Conclusion 247

began within this general atmosphere of failure in the executive office. As the idea of early elections took root, a surprising pro-EU initiative also started to assert itself on the public agenda. Parliament first decided on an early election and then, again to the surprise of many, started the debate over the so-called EU adjustment package. One by one, a series of changes was adopted on many sensitive issues ranging from the abolishing of the death penalty to making the education of mother tongues other than Turkish possible under Turkish law. As William Hale explains (pp.107–26), the issues involved were very deeply rooted in the Turkish Republican psyche that remained deeply suspicious of foreign infringement in issues of sovereignty. However, domestic constituencies mobilized around EU membership and courageous political leadership tilted the balance in favor of change towards Europe for Turkey.

The courage of the leaders seems to have been rooted in desperation for facing the downfall of electoral support in approaching elections rather than in sincere principles of the so-called EU coalition of ANAP, DSP, the newly founded YTP, and DYP that pushed the legislation in parliament. As Ziya Öniş (pp.9–34) potently puts it, the EU's role as a catalyst for change and reform in candidate countries became evident once more in the case of Turkey, where a long tradition of multi-party politics created and maintained a network of entrenched patronage groups standing for opposing interests that nourished various forms of Euro-skepticism in the country. The leaders of the EU coalition seem to have jumped into the EU lifeboat just prior to a decisive election in which they saw themselves at risk for being perhaps eliminated by the newly rising pro-Islamist AKP (Justice and Development Party—*Adalet ve Kalkınma Partisi*).

The characteristics of resistance of the EU and Euro-skepticism were most evident in the opposition of MHP against and the hesitation of AKP towards the EU package. As Canefe and Bora effectively argue (pp.127–48), the skeptical and resistant attitude towards anything that is Western and European has deep roots in the Turkish intellectual tradition. Although it is hard to argue that during the founding years of multi-party democracy in Turkey this long-standing resistance among the elites has had widespread support among the masses, their support bases seem to have been spreading over the last few years. As Gamze Avcı (pp.149–70) and Ali Çarkoğlu (pp.171–94) show in detail, the modern Turkish political scene also contains a sizeable political constituency resistant or hesitant towards integration with the EU. In some respects, these elite movements resemble their European counterparts. However, despite sizeable pockets of resistance, the overall mass support seems to run against them.

Suddenly, in early August 2002, the Turkish political scene seemed cleared in terms of the political aspects of the Copenhagen criteria. Given Lauren McLaren and Meltem Müftüler-Baç's account of the parliamentary elites (pp.195–218), the parliamentarians' ability to take the initiative for EU adjustments despite the pressures of early elections might not be surprising. Ali Çarkoğlu's discussion (pp.171–94) shows the missing link between the elite initiative and the popular bases of EU support available among the electorate. At least on paper, Turkey seemed willing and ready to start the long and arduous process of membership negotiations. While the realization of legal changes in practice remains to be seen, there was no question as to the decisiveness of the representatives of the Turkish electorate. What was questionable was the real basis of mass support behind these changes.

The early general election on November 3, 2002 became a test of potency for the pro-EU coalition. Among the political parties, the nationalist MHP and, to a lesser extent, the pro-Islamist AKP resisted these EU adjustment laws. However, as the election approached, the populist GP's rhetoric took an anti-European shape and, as the electoral support for AKP surfaced in predictive polls, the fate of the Euro-skeptics in the elections became a critical issue. The leaders of the pro-EU coalition, Mesut Yılmaz (ANAP) and İsmail Cem (New Turkey Party— *Yeni Türkiye Partisi*), used the EU card to appeal to the electorate, but they seemed to lack any credibility in the eyes of the voters. The only two real winners of the election, Deniz Baykal (Republican People's Party— *Cumhuriyet Halk Partisi*) and Recep Tayyip Erdoğan (AKP), chose not to appeal to their electorate using the EU debate in its full capacity to build their argument for a new set of promises. However, their main campaign issues, addressing the economic crisis and the transformation necessary to lift the country out of the deep economic crisis, were all linked to EU debates and membership criteria. Thus the two leading parties, AKP and Republican People's Party (CHP), successfully kept the EU debate at low salience. They therefore freed themselves from taking sides on sensitive issues concerning minority rights or binding themselves to strict positions concerning the specificities of the Copenhagen criteria yet at the same time preserved their commitment to the EU membership cause. In the aftermath of the November 2002 election no party that opposed the EU membership remained in the parliament. As a result, following the first round of the debate in early August, the second round was also won by the pro-EU coalition in the general elections.

Having been brought to power on the promise of economic relief, the AKP is under pressure to deliver. The AKP's open and welcoming stance towards the EU in the immediate aftermath of the general elections should thus not be surprising. Since the AKP leadership left the EU and related reform largely untouched during their campaign beyond mere linkages to modernization and democratization rhetoric, they felt largely uninhibited and uncommitted facing their electorate on these issues. Despite the fact that their constituency contained a sizeable minority of Euro-skeptics, they chose to push the EU membership issue in both Europe and Turkey just before the Copenhagen summit. The AKP was riding on the wave of electoral victory—they were the single party in power and there was no opposition that could legitimately claim a sizeable Euro-skeptic constituency backing in the parliament. AKP leader Recep Tayyip Erdoğan was not an MP and thus was conveniently available for deliberations with the European and American leadership on the start of negotiations for Turkey's membership. Most importantly, a date for the start of membership negotiations in Copenhagen 2002 would have lifted most of the economic and political uncertainty from the agenda, which would have helped relieve the economic pressures on the government. Considering all these factors, the AKP leadership perhaps saw this as a potential windfall gain, but their gamble did not fully pay off. For a host of reasons, strategic and otherwise, a clear and close-by date was not given in Copenhagen although, pending a number of interim evaluations, it has now been set for December 2004. This date did not lift the uncertainties that faced Turkish polity and economy and thus could not be viewed with optimism in domestic or international markets. Nevertheless, the AKP leadership had its first international experience in Europe and Washington DC when they lobbied enthusiastically for a start date for Turkish membership negotiations in the EU rather than a crisis on the eastern front.

Turkish public opinion in the aftermath of the Copenhagen 2002 summit is not easy to gauge. There was certainly a sense of disillusionment with Europe although an influential circle of public opinion leaders also portrayed the December 2004 decision as an irreversible process of Turkish accession to full membership, unless of course the country did not play the game according to its written and unwritten rules. As argued on many occasions throughout this collection, the gamble of the AKP government rests on the resolution of the Cyprus conflict. If the negotiations reach no agreement and the debate lingers beyond the honeymoon months of the new government, the AKP is more likely to face a growing resistance coalition. This resistance will take root among not only the security establishment, but also the opposition within and without the parliament who might be tempted to use this as an opportunity to revitalize their electoral support. The credibility of the pro-European drive in the AKP government is also being tested with the implementation of the EU adjustment package passed in early August, as well as in their decisiveness in legislating a number of other relatively less controversial bills. The longer it takes the AKP to pass these new pieces of legislation and the more reluctant they act in implementing the already passed laws, the more ammunition they will place in the hands of the anti-European camp. The growth of the opposition to the EU rather than the pro-EU coalition will in turn undermine the AKP's hopes for optimism on the economic front. Solidification, if not growth, of their support base among the alienated centrist masses and expansion of their legitimacy in the eyes of the secularist circles in the country will also become problematic.

Taken together, these considerations explain the determined push of EU membership by the AKP government immediately after they came to power. They seem still to be standing behind Turkey's EU membership commitment, but whether they will still be as enthusiastic and capable of pushing the reform packages in the face of a crisis in Iraq or the larger Middle East remains to seen.

Turkey's membership in the EU is not only a central theme in the domestic political scene, it also occupies a central position in the security circles of Europe, the United States, the countries of the Caucuses and the larger Middle East that lies at the borders of an enlarged EU. Being a key member of NATO, especially in the expanded security environment of the post-September 11 world, Turkey's security concerns have been a central concern in the founding discussions of a new European security system. As Esra Çayhan's discussion (pp.35–54) indicates, while the difficulties in meeting the Copenhagen criteria perhaps provided a push factor for Turkey's bid for full membership in the EU, the security assets and Turkey's decisive role in NATO provided a pull factor. A key element in shaping Turkey's reactions to EU membership requirements revolves around the problematic case of Cyprus' accession to full membership. Semin Suvarierol's discussion (pp.55–78) provides the intricate details of the issues involved, but also highlights the potentially problematic nature of EU enlargement and the link between Turkey's long-standing issue over the rights of the Turkish population on the island as it relates to its own membership bid in the EU. Of equal importance is the impact of the EU on the recent move towards resolution of the conflict on the island, a fact which is also apparent in these discussions. As such, the EU's impact on not only the domestic political scene but also on Turkish security and foreign policy principles is also highlighted. Kemal Kirişci's discussion of justice and home affairs issues (pp.79–106) is yet another example of a significant number of impacts by the EU on one of Turkey's key policy roles in the eastern Mediterranean and the Middle East, lying on the path of a very active migration route. Kirişci's discussion of the interplay between the domestic policy concerns in Turkey and the necessities of EU membership and how that leads to a new path of policymaking, provides an interesting case study of the impact of EU enlargement on candidate countries' policymaking.

The essays in this volume were completed by early September 2002 when Turkey was heading somewhat hesitantly toward general elections in November. The authors were asked to re-evaluate their essays and write short postscripts in light of the developments during the fall of 2002. In stark contrast to the campaign period, the aftermath of the elections witnessed intense debate of a range of issues concerning the European identity in Turkey, strategic mutual dependence of Turkey and Europe and the potential fragility of the foreign policy futures in the wake of a crisis in the Middle East. The MHP's application to the Constitutional Court for the annulment of some key parts of the EU package was rejected and the legal bases of the Copenhagen criteria were once again consolidated. A firm date for the start of membership negotiations finally appeared on the horizon, but it depended on the drafting and implementation of essential legislation, particularly in the sphere of human rights. Both sides of the EU debate seem to have come to the understanding that the informal rules of democratic deliberation, policymaking and conflict resolution are perhaps as important as the formal economic and legal conditionality requirements, the functioning of the judiciary and the supremacy of law. These aspects concern first and foremost the role of the security establishment—military and civilian—in Turkish politics.

Concerns that Turkey might be a cultural misfit in the Europe of the future were voiced preceding the Copenhagen summit. The question of where the geographic boundaries of EU should end was asked once again. What was the ultimate aim of the EU? Was it just another trading area? Should geography or religion dictate who might join?[2] The *Economist* argued that "if the European idea is to inspire, it ought to be about values, not maps or tribes. Countries that can subscribe to the core values of democracy and freedom should be eligible as candidates, be they Slavs or Muslims, and no matter how far they are in miles from Paris or Berlin."[3] As portrayed in the Turkish media, these arguments seem to have remained either as mere reflection of Orientalism and stereotyping for domestic political concerns or friendship gestures. However, they also reflected a major difficulty for the European elites who find it difficult to convince their domestic constituencies about the worthiness of Turkey's bid for EU membership. Any negotiation between international players always has its reflections in the respective domestic politics. The obsessive focus on the formalities of the Copenhagen criteria seem to have pushed the lower level of negotiations at the domestic players' level behind, especially in the minds of the Turkish side. As the discussion above clearly showed, the domestic resistance to EU membership in Turkey is a powerful coalition, but it is nevertheless the minority. The picture from the European perspective is obviously dissimilar and unless Turkey convinces the domestic players of the enlarging Europe about the merits of its bid for membership, the disappointment of the Turkish public opinion might continue summit after summit. The continually disgruntled public opinion only undermines support for EU membership in the country.

So far, the EU initiatives and membership requirements have had a deep impact on the Turkish domestic and foreign policy priorities; all in the direction of further integration with the western hemisphere. The Turkish domestic scene has witnessed the most widespread discussion of EU issues only during the second half of 2002. However, the divide between the EU supporters and resisters in the party system touches upon the very heart of the Turkish republican concerns with national unity, modernization, security and democracy. So far it seems that the anti-European camp has lost the major battles. Given the infertile ground that exists in Turkey for creating and developing issues of relevance for the electorate, the EU debate remains a prominent candidate for occupying the focal point of a new cleavage in Turkish politics that rests on the idea of reform in the system. However, it remains to be seen whether the new leadership can effectively maintain the long-term drive for policy creativeness and determination necessary to fulfil the opening and closing of negotiations with the EU; the crowning jewel of Turkish modernization and integration with the West.

NOTES

1. See Thomas L. Friedman's account in the *New York Times*, June 6, 2001.
2. "Turkey belongs in Europe," *Economist*, Dec. 7, 2002, p.13.
3. Ibid.

Abstracts

Domestic Politics, International Norms and Challenges to the State: Turkey-EU Relations in the post-Helsinki Era *by Ziya Öniş*

Developments in Turkish politics following the endorsement of Turkey's candidacy for full membership at the EU's Helsinki summit of December 1999 underline the significant role that the EU can play as a catalyst for change and reform in candidate countries. The essay draws attention to the emergence of a "pro-EU coalition" in Turkey during the post-Helsinki era and highlights the formidable barriers on the path to Turkey's full membership given the presence of a powerful and vocal "anti-EU coalition." A central argument of this piece is that the EU can help in overcoming the existing stalemate and shift the balance in favor of the pro-EU coalition through an improved mix of conditions and incentives as it has done so effectively in other national contexts.

Towards a European Security and Defense Policy: With or Without Turkey? *by Esra Çayhan*

The European Union, a unique example of successful economic integration, aspires to become a major international relations actor. Recently, the Union has been trying to develop its own military capabilities in order to play a greater role on the international scene. This essay serves as an introduction to the process of framing a security and defense policy in Europe. It explains the evolution of the European Security and Defense Policy (ESDP), describes how it plans to tackle the challenges ahead and emphasizes Turkey's position in terms of this new dimension in European security.

The Cyprus Obstacle on Turkey's Road to Membership in the European Union *by Semin Suvarierol*

The compromise reached as of March 6, 1995, and the 1999 Helsinki European Council within the European Union (EU) framework concerning Turkey and Cyprus confirms the linkage between the Turkish and Cypriot candidatures for membership to the EU. Turkey cannot block the accession of Cyprus to the EU by not contributing to the resolution of the Cyprus conflict. This strategy would jeopardize the accession of Turkey, as well as the accession of Turkish Cypriots. Therefore, the *status quo* is to the benefit of the Greek Cypriots, who will be able to join the EU even if the Cyprus problem is not settled.

The Question of Asylum and Illegal Migration in European Union-Turkish Relations *by Kemal Kirişci*

In the aftermath of the September 11, 2001 terrorist attacks in the United States, the question of illegal migration and asylum has re-emerged at the top of the agenda of many European Union member countries. Hearing of the capture of a boat or a container full of illegal immigrants in Europe is almost a daily incident. There are also frequent stories in the international media referring to Turkey as a country at the center of illegal movements of people. Turkey finds itself located between regions of emigration and immigration. During the last few years, Turkey has become a country of transit for illegal migration as well as a country of destination, as some of these migrants choose to stay on in Turkey or become stranded. This article surveys Turkish government practice in the area of illegal migration and asylum and examines how the European Union policies impact and shape change in Turkish policy.

Human Rights, the European Union and the Turkish Accession Process *by William Hale*

In the political crisis that gripped Turkey during the summer of 2002 the question of completing reforms in civil rights and the protection of minorities was a crucial issue which divided the Ecevit government. This contribution explores the question of human rights in Turkey and its relation to the EU accession process with regard to four leading issues: freedom of expression and association, and of political parties; treatment of ethnic minorities; abolition of capital punishment; and the political role of the military. At appropriate points, it also discusses some important questions about the definition and extent of human rights in general.

The Intellectual Roots of Anti-European Sentiments in Turkish Politics: The Case of Radical Turkish Nationalism *by Nergis Canefe and Tanıl Bora*

This contribution examines the intellectual roots of current anti-European sentiments actively embraced by the radical Turkish nationalists and their parliamentary representative, the Nationalist Action Party (MHP). Particularly in the aftermath of the acceptance of the new legislation in accordance with European Union membership criteria, radical Turkish nationalists appear to be the main group vehemently opposing Turkish efforts to join Europe. The authors argue that the concerns raised by this movement have a long history in Turkish political thought. The most appropriate context for such an analysis is identified as the Republican tradition of nationalism/conservatism. Consequently, this study reveals that the MHP in particular, and the radical nationalist movement in general, do not constitute a singular example of anti-European sentiments and criticism in Turkish politics. Instead, this engagement with the intellectual history of the current political stand of radical Turkish nationalists confirms that ideological approaches and normative values pronounced among these circles are a reflection of the intertwined traditions of Turkism, Islamism, cultural purism, defensive nationalism and reverse Orientalism in Turkish political culture. Finally, the authors make the claim that anti-European attitudes of radical nationalist pedigree are an integral part of grander political transformations rather than being an end in themselves.

Turkey's Slow EU Candidacy: Insurmountable Hurdles to Membership or Simple Euro-skepticism? *by Gamze Avcı*

This contribution focuses on how the issue of EU membership has affected the domestic political debates in Turkey in the context of the Copenhagen political criteria. It concentrates on the period since the Helsinki summit, where Turkey was granted official candidacy status. This analysis seeks to unveil the bottlenecks within the government concerning the political Copenhagen conditions and discusses the positions of the coalition partners. After presenting a background and history to recent EU-Turkish relations, it evaluates the progress reports of the EU and subsequently the political discourse in Turkey since 1999. Finally, the contribution concludes by linking the Turkish domestic discourse to discussions in the EU and other candidate countries.

Who Wants Full Membership? Characteristics of Turkish Public Support for EU Membership *by Ali Çarkoğlu*

This essay examines the popular bases of support and resistance to EU membership among Turkish voters. Data from a nationwide representative survey collected just prior to the passage of the EU adjustment package in summer 2002 is used to analyze the determinants of support and opposition to EU membership. It is diagnosed that religiosity, Euro-skepticism and democratic values are all significant attitudinal bases for preferences about EU membership. On the basis of survey findings an evaluation of the likely resistance to EU is provided.

Turkish Parliamentarians' Perspectives on Turkey's Relations with the European Union *by Lauren M. McLaren and Meltem Müftüler-Baç*

This contribution addresses the lack of information on Turkish opinion regarding the European Union (EU) by interviewing a sample of deputies in the Turkish Grand National Assembly (TBMM). The results indicate overwhelmingly favorable attitudes towards Turkey joining the EU as a full member and great hope that this will happen within 10–15 years. Furthermore, the deputies tend to emphasize the political problems that must be overcome before joining the EU as well as the political benefits to be gained by obtaining full membership, but they also point to economic problems that must be overcome and economic benefits that will result from full membership. On the other hand, findings indicate a lack of emphasis on a few key problems facing Turkish membership in the EU, particularly the Cyprus issue and the role of the military in the political system. Overall, despite a sometimes lukewarm attitude towards Turkey from EU leaders, Turkish political elites remain quite favorable and hopeful regarding Turkish membership of the EU.

Implementing the Economic Criteria of EU Membership: How Difficult is it for Turkey? *by Mine Eder*

This contribution examines the serious dilemmas and challenges Turkey faces in meeting the Copenhagen economic criteria. The author begins by describing briefly Turkey's economic indicators and the fundamental problems in its political economy which have complicated Turkey's accession to the EU. Next, the paper argues that the changes within the European project itself (the move from a Keynesian strategy, emphasizing integration and cohesion, to a neo-liberal one with emphasis on deregulating markets in the face of growing global competition) and problems of coherence in the Copenhagen criteria, have further confounded Turkey's prospects for membership.

Notes on Contributors

Gamze Avcı is an assistant professor at the Department of Political Science and International Relations at Boğaziçi University, Istanbul. She received her BA from Bogazici University, MS from the London School of Economics, and MA and Ph.D. from the University of Georgia.

Tanıl Bora graduated from the Ankara Faculty of Political Sciences. Upon graduation he worked for several influential Turkish magazines, including *Yeni Gündem* [New Agenda] and *Birikim* [Accumulation]. Since 1989 he has worked as an editor in İletişim Publications in Istanbul. He is on the editorial board of *Birikim* and is the editor-in-chief of *Toplum ve Bilim* [Society and Science]. He is the author of many books on nationalism in Turkey, including *Devlet, Ocak, Dergah* [State, Hearth, Convent] (co-authored with Kemal Can), *Milliyetciligin Kara Baharı* [Dark Spring of Nationalism] and *Türk Sağının Hali* [The State of Turkish Nationalism].

Nergis Canefe studied history and sociology in Turkey, the United States and Canada. She worked for several years at the Center for Refugee Studies at York University, Canada, from where she received her doctorate at the Graduate Programme of Social and Political Thought. She acted as the first Past and Present Society post-doctoral fellow at the Institute of Historical Research, University of London, between 1998 and 2000. She then worked as a research associate and lecturer at the European Institute, London School of Economics, until 2002. She is currently a lecturer at the Department of Sociology, Bilgi University, Turkey.

Ali Çarkoğlu is currently an associate professor at the Faculty of Arts and Social Sciences in Sabancı University, Istanbul. He regularly teaches courses on Turkish politics, comparative political parties and interest groups, formal modeling, research methods and statistics. He received his Ph.D. from the State University of New York—Binghamton in 1993. He co-authored *The Political Economy of Cooperation in the Middle East* with Mine Eder and Kemal Kirişci (1998).

Esra Çayhan is the associate dean of the Faculty of Economics and Administrative Sciences and the director of the Center for Strategic Research at Akdeniz University, Antalya. She graduated from Boğaziçi

University, Istanbul (BA Hons, Political Science), Carleton University NPSIA, Ottawa (MA, International Affairs), and Istanbul University, Faculty of Economics (Ph.D., International Relations). She was a Jean Monnet Scholar at the University of Amsterdam in 1992–93. She is the author of two books, *Turkey-EU Relations and Political Parties in Turkey* (1997) and *The New Search for Security in Europe NATO-EU-Turkey* (with Nurşin Güney—1996).

Mine Eder is an associate professor in the Department of Political Science and International Relations at Boğaziçi University, Istanbul. She received her Ph.D. from the University of Virginia, where she specialized in the political economy of newly industrializing countries. She is the co-author of *Political Economy of Regional Cooperation in the Middle East* (1998) and has written extensively on regionalism and the comparative political economy of Turkey.

Özgül Erdemli is assistant director of the Turkish Studies Institute and assistant editor of *Turkish Studies*.

William Hale is professor of Turkish Politics at the School of Oriental and African Studies, University of London. He is the author of *The Political and Economic Development of Modern Turkey* (1981), *Turkish Politics and the Military* (1994) and *Turkish Foreign Policy, 1774–2000* (2001), besides numerous essays on Turkey's modern politics and international relations.

Kemal Kirişci is a professor at the Department of Political Science and International Relations at Boğaziçi University, Istanbul, and holds the Jean Monnet Chair in European Integration. He received his Ph.D. from City University, London in 1986. He is the author of *The Kurdish Question and Turkey* (with Gareth Winrow—1997) and *Turkey in World Politics: An Emerging Multiregional Power* (with Barry Rubin—2001).

Lauren M. McLaren received her Ph.D. from the University of Houston in 1996. She is currently lecturer in the Department of Politics and International Relations, University of Oxford, and on leave from Bilkent University, Department of Political Science and Public Administration.

Meltem Müftüler-Baç is an associate professor of International Relations at Sabancı University, Istanbul. She received her Ph.D. in Political Science from Temple University, Philadelphia in 1992. She served as faculty member and as the associate dean of the Faculty of Economics, Administrative and Social Sciences at Bilkent University. She was a Fulbright Fellow at the University of Chicago in 1999–2000. She is the author of *Turkey's Relations with a Changing Europe* (1997).

Ziya Öniş is a professor of international relations at Koç University, Istanbul. His current research interests include the role of civil society organizations in the democratization process, Turkey-EU relations as well as the political economy of financial globalization and emerging market crises. He is the author of *State and Market: The Political Economy of Turkey in Comparative Perspective* (1998) and co-editor of the forthcoming *Turkish Studies* special issue *Turkey's Economy in Crisis*.

Barry Rubin is director of the Global Research in International Affairs Center and of its Institute for Turkish Studies. He is editor of *Turkish Studies* journal and of the *Middle East Review of International Affairs* (MERIA). His publications include *The Transformation of Palestinian Politics: From Revolution to State-Building* (1999) and *Assimilation and its Discontents* (1995).

Semin Suvarierol is a graduate of the Department of Political Science and International Relations of Boğaziçi University. She obtained her MA in International Relations at the Institut d'Études Politiques de Paris; her thesis was on Cyprus' accession to the EU. She has worked as a project manager at TESEV (Turkish Economic and Social Studies Foundation) and is currently a Ph.D. student in the Department of Public Administration at the University of Leiden on a Jean Monnet Scholarship.

Index

abolition of the death penalty 118–19, 122, 163, 187, 247
Accession Partnership (AP—March 2000) 12–13, 150–51, 159
Accession Partnership Document (EU December 2000) *see* APD
Ad Hoc Committee of Contributors 47
Aegean 48, 50, 180–81
Agenda 2000 (July 1997) 60, 195, 231
agriculture elite, subsidies and 224–5
Akif, Mehmet (poet with Islamic beliefs) 138
AKP,
   Cyprus and 74
   death penalty and 161
   electoral victory (November 2002) 30, 240
   human rights reforms and 109
   religious and center-right conservative vote 213
   stance towards EU 163, 166, 178, 190–92, 247–50
Albanian refugees, Humanitarian Evacuation Program (1999) 85
Amnesty International, Turkish refugees and 86
ANAP 135
   Cyprus problem and 25, 30, 206
   economic problems with EU 209
   EU reforms and 107, 157–8, 161–3
   issues related to EU conditionality 17–18
   language courses in mother tongue 15
   opposition to Customs Union 229
   rift with MHP 161
   side payments and 225
   survey 200
Ankara Agreement (1963) 70, 197–8
Annan, Kofi (UN Secretary General) 30, 74
"Annan Plan," Cyprus dispute and 30–31, 74–5
anti-EU coalition 29, 252
Anzar, Jose 79
APD (November 2001) 80, 108–9, 112, 198
   de facto moratorium on capital punishment 118
   European Union Adaptation Law (*Avrupa Birliği Uyum Yasasi*) 122
   Greece and 205
   justice and home affairs issues 87
   National Security Council and 120
   NP and 100
   political parties and 115
   readmission treaty and 97–8
   resolution of Cyprus issue 195
   word "Kurdish" and 117
appendix: the survey instrument 213–15
armed forces, Turkish politics and 119
Armenian genocide 95, 137, 229
Asia 80
"associate membership" of WEU 39, 45
Association Council (AC),
   issues between EU and Turkey 97
   Turkey and TRNC 59–60
asylum 79–80, 81–92, 96, 98–100, 102
   illegal migration and 80
Atatürk 119
Austria 39, 222

Bahçeli, Devlet (leader of MHP) 107, 130, 164
   amendments to Article 312 and 162
   attitude to EU 135–7, 144, 159–60
   death penalty and 160
   EU's attitude to terrorism and 161
   MHP would appeal to Constitutional Court 163–4
   reforms and 162–3
Baku-Ceyhan pipeline construction project 67
Balkans 46, 49–50, 89, 145
   interviews regarding adopting the *acquis* 199
   political violence 143
   prostitution in Turkey by women from 93
Balladur Stability Pact 65
Banarlı, Nihad Sami 139
Bangladesh 98
Banking Regulatory and Supervisory Board (June 1999) 227
Basis for Agreement on a Comprehensive Settlement of the Cyprus Problem (November 11, 2002) 74
Baykal, Deniz (CHP) 248
Blair, Tony 79
Bosnia 46, 52
Brazil 230
Britain 42, 79, 98–9, 162
British House of Commons (Foreign Affairs Committee April 2002) 121–2

Budapest process, forum for cooperation on irregular migration 97
Buğra, Ayse 223
Bülent-Ecevit-Yılmaz-Bahçeli coalition government 154–5, 161, 235, 245
Bulgaria 39, 98, 220, 222
Bush administration 49

Can, Ahmet Selçuk 137
Capabilities Commitment Conference (November 2000) 38
capital punishment, democratic government and 118, 122
Cardiff Council (1998), Turkey could work towards EU membership 201
Caucuses 143, 250
CEE countries,
  agreements on returning nations 97
  Balladur Stability pact and 65
  EU demands on 230
  EU membership and 149, 195
  interviews regarding adopting *acquis* 199
  received more aid than Turkey 231
Cem, İsmail 62, 122, 163, 189, 248
Central and Eastern European countries *see* CEE countries
CFSP 35–6, 50
Charter of Basic Social Rights for workers 233
Chechen refugees 84
China 98
CHP 163, 166, 213
  election (November 2, 2002) 248
  EU issues and 191–2
  Kemalism and 134
  side payments to urban workers 225
Çiller, Tansu (Turkish PM) 58, 109, 158, 225
Clinton administration, famous three Ds 43, 49
Clinton, Bill 95
cold war,
  anti-communism in Turkey 132
  Turkey's role in 46, 63, 83, 98, 101
Cologne European Council Presidency Conclusions 37–9
Common Customs Tariffs (CCT), Customs Union and 228, 237
Common Foreign and Security Policy *see* CFSP
communism,
  associated with Europe and cosmopolitanism 142–3
  asylum seekers from Eastern Europe and 83–4
Community regional funds, basic economic infrastructure and 10

Competition Authority (1998) 229, 236
competitiveness 233–4
Confederation of Turkish Labor Unions (*Türkiye İşçi Sendikalari Konfederasyonu*—TÜRK-İŞ) 20
Convention (1951), status of refugees and 83–4, 89
Copenhagen Council Conclusions (December 2002) *see* Copenhagen (December 2002) summit
Copenhagen criteria (1993) 203, 216n.2
  accession negotiations and 195
  Accession Partnership and 12, 108
  aid to be received after meeting 231
  AKP and CHP attitude to EU debate (2002) 248
  can Turkey meet 219, 221, 226
  conditionality and 151–2, 219
  Customs Union and 237
  Cyprus dispute and 26, 205
  democratic environment in Turkey and 182
  difficulties Turkey faces in meeting 223–4, 250
  economic and euro requirements 211
  evaluation of progress by European Commission 201
  IMF reforms and Turkey 227, 240
  inconsistency embedded in 238
  mixed support for 22
  NPAA and 13
  obsessive focus on formalities 252
  policy approval to conform to EU standards 181
  problematic definition 231–2
  problem of coherence and changing European project 232–3
  "protection of minorities" 117
  reforms to meet extensive and painful 196
  religious differences and 202
  security considerations and 27
  stability of institutions 108, 153
  Turkey,
    dilemmas and challenges 239
    economic reform process and 16
    membership process and 68, 74, 149, 183, 187
    parliament and 190
    political parties and 188
    progress on human rights insufficient 155
    reforms it must meet 80
Copenhagen (December 2002) summit, accession negotiations and 8, 30–31, 123, 149, 151, 166, 249
Cyprus and 74–5

Index

resolution of conflicts between Turkey and Greece 51–2, 136
Corfu summit 1994 (Greek Presidency), next enlargement would include Cyprus 64
corruption 96, 155, 189
Council of Europe (1949) 197
crises after (1999) election, coalition of DSP, MHP and ANAP 245
Cumhuriyet, articles on Turkey 137
Customs Union,
  ANAP opposition to 18
  benefits failed to materialize 226, 239
  difficulties meeting economic criteria 219
  favorable attitude and support for EU membership 181
  Greek veto and financial assistance 23, 57
  mirror of Turkey's endemic problems 227–30
  role in economic legislation 236
  short-term costs 228–9
  Turkey's membership (1996) 9, 29, 45–6, 197–8, 237
  negotiations with Cyprus for EU membership 58
Cyprus,
  1998 Report on Turkey and 154
  2000 Report on Turkey 155
  2001 expected to be amongst first wave of EU members 62
Cyprus 205–7
  accession criteria and 60–61
  acquis to north suspended 74
  chronology of events 70–74
  compromise (March 6, 1995) 57
  developments in negotiations 190
  dialogue between EU and Turkey 68
  discussions on by AKP 191
  dispute 143, 180–81
  EU membership 2004 52, 198
  lack understanding by TBMM 196
  sine qua non for Turkey's EU membership 55
  "stationary aircraft carrier" (*sabit uçak gemisi*) 57
  strategic interests of Turkey as EU member 66
  Turkish policy on 56–61, 80
  whether it will join EU as unified island 69
Cyprus problem 12
  AKP gamble on resolution 249–50
  ANAP and 18
  EU and indirect resolution of 25–6
  limitation of NPAA 14
  MHP and 131
  no resolution despite successful RoC negotiations 64

political parties and 17
pro-EU coalition in Turkey and 23–6
resolution proof that Turkey would be asset to EU 27
Turkey and EU membership 50, 63, 205, 250
Turkey's domestic politics and 23
TÜSİAD and solution 19
Czech Republic 11, 39–40, 45, 222

D'Alema, Massimo (Italian PM) 95
Danish Presidency 48, 152
Danişmend, İsmail Hami 139–40
Dayton Peace Treaty (1995) 84
decentralization 11
"de-coupling" United States from Europe 43
Demirel, Süleyman 225
democratization 10, 28, 182, 249, 251–2
  EU and mutual provides peace 26
  human rights improvement and 203–4, 208–9, 212
  TÜSİAD and 19
Democrat Left Party (*Demokratik Sol Parti*) *see* DSP
Denktaş, Rauf (TRNC president) 59–60, 74–5
  supported by MHP 159
Denmark 39, 79
Derviş, Kemal 163, 245
"discrimination" against non-EU member allies 43, 46
Doğan, D. Mehmet 141
Drevet, Jean-François 67
drug trafficking 95
DSP 122, 158
  Cyprus reunification and 206
  economic problems and 209
  human rights improvements and 107
  life time imprisonment 161, 163
  resignations from 19, 122, 165, 189
  survey of 200
"duplication" of NATO structures and capabilities 43
DYP 18, 109, 135, 157
  Coalition with CHP and Customs Union 229
  mixed attitude to EU reforms 163
  side payments and 225
  survey of 200
  trying to lure support from MHP 161

East Sea (freighter) 95
Ecevit, Bülent (Turkish PM) 122–3
  coalition government and Turkey's EU candidacy 157, 164
  coalition wiped out (November 2002) 166
  constitutional amendments and 114, 119

contrast with Bahçeli's position 160
Customs Union and 197
Cyprus and 57, 62
desire to work with Yılmaz 158
illness 107, 149, 162–3, 165, 245
reform of Human rights 109
sensitivity on Cyprus issue 206–7, 213
thinks of EU in economic terms 199
ECHR 58, 87, 108, 160
economic benefits and costs of integration 11
Economic Development Foundation (*İktisadi ve Kalkinma Vakfi*—IKV) 19–20
Economist, The 251
education rights in mother tongues 12, 118, 161, 163, 246–7
election in Turkey (November 2002) 143, 149, 191, 213, 248
 AKP on Cyprus 74
 human rights reforms 163
enlargement of EU,
 Anglo-Saxon recipe 233
 candidate countries' policymaking 251
 common grounds in security and defense issues 41
 more difficulties for ESDP 50
 problematic nature of issues involved 250
 protecting geographically and 101, 251
 respect for human rights *sine qua non* 108
enosis 58, 64, 71
Erbakan, Necmettin (Islamist leader) 109, 112, 143, 229
Erder, Necat 173
Erdoğan, Recep Tayip (AKP leader) 74, 109, 248–9
Eriş, Meral Gezgin 20
ESDI,
 became ESDP 38
 discussions and American role 43
 EU military capabilities 40
 Euro-Atlantic crisis management 36
 NATO and European security 37
 problem for Turkey 162
ESDP,
 agreement between US, Britain and Turkey (December 2001) 162
 Atlanticists and 43
 Copenhagen summit (2002) and Greece and Turkey 51–2, 80
 European willingness to take initiative in its "backyard" 43
 from ESDI to 36–40
 goal to deploy people on range of Petersberg tasks 44–5
 NATO's ability to manage crises and 41
 peacekeeping in Bosnia (2003) 52
 strategic concept missing from 50
 strengthening or weakening European security 40–45
 Turkey and 45–8, 155
Esmer, Yılmaz 172–3
Estonia 221–2
ethnic minorities, treatment of 116–18
EU,
 accession negotiations of RoC with 24
 anchor in new democracies 10–12
 Christian "club" 150, 164, 182
 Cyprus' accession based on Helsinki decisions 65
 Cyprus policy and Greek factor 62–6, 136
 democratic deficit becoming greater 41
 effect of merger of WEU into 39, 45
 elite in favor of European integration 166
 focus shifted to competitiveness (1990s) 233
 framing common security and defense policy 41
 Greek-Turkish conflicts and 60, 63
 issue of protecting geographically 101, 251
 let Greece Europeanize the Cyprus question 64
 military forces and conflicts between NATO and EU members 48
 military operation in fYROM 52
 NATO and 50, 162
 negotiations for Turkey (2004) 166, 249
 "post-modern" character of 29
 prime issue for MHP is Cyprus 159
 role of in Turkey and 15
 "security community" 26
 security and defense policy to become a major world power 49
 solution to Greek-Turkish problems and Cyprus issue 60
 Southern Cyprus and membership 31
 successful economic integration and 51
 Turkey
  difficult to accommodate 156
  important partner to 66
  mix of conditions and incentives for 28
  policy is impediment to "European army" 51
  question of domestic situation 2
  trade and 228
 Turks including Kurds who live in 82
EU *acquis*,
 asylum and Turkey's accession process 87, 89, 100, 102
 implementing and funding 239
 National Program (March 2001) for implementation 109, 198–9

Index

suspended in northern Cyprus 74
Turkish laws and Constitutional Amendments 13
EU Association Agreement,
  Greece and 63, 197
  with Turkey 63
EU membership,
  AKP and 30
  completion of long-term Atatürk revolution 1
  conditionality 28, 230, 239
  creates conditions and incentives 9
  foreign direct investment and 11
  impact on Turkish domestic and foreign policy 252
  perceived costs and benefits in support for 207–10
  Turkey,
    candidacy and 171–2
    foreign policy since (1960s) 155–6
    public and 149
    slow pace of advance towards 2
    worthiness of bid for 251–2
EU project, Keynesian, regional and social integration 232–3, 239
EU rapid reaction force (RRF), opposition from Ankara 162
EU-related issues, military-security establishment and 18
Europe 2002 (*Avrupta*) 20
Europe,
  demographic trends 101
  Europeanness and Turkish national identity 134–7
  failure to learn from September 11 attacks 161
  nationalist-conservative tradition and 138–42
  neo-liberal agenda 233
  Twentieth-century wars and American involvement 43
European Commission,
  Accession Partnership (March 2000) 12–13
  economic assessment of 237–8
European Convention on Human Rights 108
  Article (10) 112–13, 115
  Article (11) 113, 115
  death penalty and 118, 153
  minority rights and 116
  Sixth Protocol 118–19, 160
European Council, EU's military operation in Bosnia 52
European Council Luxembourg summit,
  accession negotiations with Cyprus 59–60
  Greece and first-wave candidates including Cyprus 64
European Court of Human Rights *see* ECHR
European Economic Community (EEC— established 1957) 35, 172
European Human Rights Convention, Turkey a party to 86
European integration process, "pooling of sovereignty" 11
European Mediterranean Development program, aid suspended 231
European Monetary Union (EMU) 50, 233
European Parliament,
  "against Turkey" 137
  solution of Cyprus problem, relations between EU and Turkey 63, 205
European People's Party, EU has no place for Turkey 201
"European Political Cooperation" (EPC) 35
European projects,
  neo-liberal strategy 220
  Turkish reactions 108–10
European Regional Development and Cohesion Fund 231
Europeans,
  choose "butter" instead of "guns" 45
  critical of American dominance of NATO 42
  troops deployed in the Balkans 42
European Security and Defense architecture, European security and 26
European Security and Defense Identity *see* ESDI
European strategic concept, difficult to develop 41
Europe and Europeanness, Turkish intellectuals and 127
Europhobia, Europe and West as forces of evil 145
euro requirements, TBMM and 210–11
Euro-skepticism 40–41, 192
  AKP and 249
  cost of 165
  decline of support for EU membership 182
  patronage groups and 247
  Turkish 67, 164
EU standards, legal and human rights and 90
Evans, Peter 225
"Exceptional Situation," Hakkâri and Tunceli 121

family reunification arrangements, Turkish citizens and 80–81
February 2001 crisis, problems of premature liberalization 227

Feira European Council Presidency
   Conclusions, EU military crisis
   management 39–40, 46–7
Felicity Party (*Saadet Partisi*) see SP
Finland 39
Finland (Tampere 1999), EU on common
   asylum and immigration policy 80
foreign direct investment 11, 226, 228
former communist countries, EU membership
   and 198
former Soviet Union 28, 84, 93, 98
Former Yugoslav Republic of Macedonia see
   fYROM
"Fortress Europe" 79
FP 109, 112, 135, 155, 190, 200, 209
Framework Convention for Protection of
   National Minorities (1994) 116
France 42, 80, 92, 95, 229
Franco-British initiative, EU's own military
   capabilities 37–8
Fraternity of Turkish Culture (*Türk Kültür
   Ocağı* 1946) 132
freedom of expression, association and of
   political parties 110–15

Geneva Convention, rights of asylum seekers
   and 83
geographical limitation on refugees,
   APD and 87
   expected to be lifted (2004) 100, 102
   status determination of refugees and 91
   Turkey's willingness to lift 88
   "Turkish descent and culture" 89
   Turkish national security and 92
   two-tiered asylum policy 83
geographic location, support for EU
   membership and 186
Georgia, refugees and 84
Germany 42, 99, 210
globalization 11, 145
globalized nature of "domestic politics" 22
Gökalp, Ziya 140
Gothenburg European Council (June 2001)
   150
GP 191–2
Grappe (2000) 230, 232, 238
Gray Wolves 129
Greece,
   accession has rendered *enosis* obsolete 64
   EU and conflict over Aegean or Cyprus 48
   illegal immigrants 80, 92
   influence on EU policy vis-à-vis Cyprus 62
   membership of EU (1981) 23, 55, 58, 63,
      197
   readmission agreement signed by Turkey
      with 98
   reunification of Cyprus and 31
   solutions of Cyprus and "Aegean
      problem" 137
   veto if Cyprus excluded from first wave
      of enlargement 65, 212
Greece and RoC, "Joint Defense Dogma" 59
Greek Cypriots,
   EU could force Turkey to solution of
      Cyprus 69
   indirect *enosis* through membership of EU
      59
   willing to sign agreement 75
Greek *Megali Idea* 129

HADEP 112, 175, 178
Haider (Austrian right-wing politician) 145
hard Euro-skepticism 164
"Harmonization Laws" 13, 18
   financial and technical assistance to
      Turkey 100
headscarf ban in universities 246
Heinze, Christian 57
Helsinki summit 12–16, 37–9, 155
   Cyprus and Turkey candidates for EU
      membership 55, 108
   dialogue between EU and Turkey over
      Cyprus 68
   granted "candidacy status" to Turkey 61,
      108, 150, 156, 195, 202
   Greek agreement to Turkey's candidacy
      64–5
   its aftermath and 61–2
   opportunities after 27, 29, 207
   Turkish-EU relations and 80, 198
   TÜSİAD and 19
"historical compromise" (1995), give-and-
   take process on Cyprus 64
human rights,
   access process and EU standards 90
   DSP and ANAP and 107
   European Convention of 116, 118
   sine qua non for EU candidates 108, 153,
      208–9, 251
   Turkey and 203–4, 212
Hungary 11, 39, 45, 222
Huntingtonian thesis on clash of civilizations
   145

Iceland 39, 45
Idealist Associations (*Ülkü Ocakları*) 133,
   142
illegal arms trade 95
illegal immigrants, difficulties of deportation
   96
illegal migrants 80, 86, 90, 92, 94, 96
   allegations about Turkish vessels 95

Index

illegal migration 92–100
illegal transit migrants 93–4
  dialogue between Italy and Turkey 97
IMF 9, 12, 21
  agricultural liberalization reforms 236
  economic reforms and EU 219
  funds for Turkey linked to conditionality 227, 230, 239
  reforms and patronage politics 227
  structural adjustment agenda 234
  supervision of Turkey (April 1999 and February 2001) 237
import substitution policies, Turkish economic groups and 20, 224–5
inflation in Turkey 221
"Instrument for Structural Policies for Pre-accession" (ISPA) 231
intellectual property rights 234, 236
Intergovernmental Conference (IGC 1996), Cyprus and 57
International Catholic Migration Commission 83
International Financial Institutions (IFI) 230
International Monetary Fund *see* IMF
Iran 85, 98, 164
Iraq, American forces and 52, 190, 250
Ireland 39
irregular transit migration, Turkish use as political weapon 95
Islamic world, Turkey and Europe 27–8
Islamists, pro-EU 17
Italy 42, 80, 92

Japan, competitiveness and EU 233
JHA 80, 87, 250
  asylum and illegal migration 80
  Expert Mission report, Turkey's refugee status and 81, 87
  joint military exercises (*Nikiphoros*), Joint Defense Dogma and 59
Justice and Development Party (*Adalet ve Kalkınma Partisi*) *see* AKP
Justice and Home Affair *see* JHA
Justice Party (*Adalet Partisi*—AP) 133

Kabakı, Ahmet 140, 143
Karacakurt, Osman 137
Karakoç, Sezai 140
Karayalçın, Murat 58
Kemalist principles,
  authoritarian tendencies 134
  military and 119
  radical nationalist politics and 131, 133, 140
  secular reactionaries 142
  Turkish intelligentsia 141
  Turkish minorities and 116
  Western-oriented 138
Kılınç, General Tuncer 164
Kıvrıkoğlu, General Hüseyin 121
Kosovo,
  Albanians and Turks entered Turkey 84
  turning point for EU 42
Kosovo air campaign 42
Kosovo crisis, Europe dependent on United States 37
Kurdish language,
  broadcasting and education 163
  lessons 154
  option in state schools 117–18
  support for joining EU and 175, 184
Kurdistan Workers Party (*Partiya Karkaren Kurdistan*) *see* PKK
Kurds,
  amendments to Constitution and 96–7
  asylum in EU 79–80
  asylum seekers entering Europe from Turkey 96
  asylum seekers in Turkey 82
  influx from Iraq (1988 and 1991) 83, 92
  problems of in southeast 143
  Turkey blamed when they landed on Adriatic coast of Italy 95
Kuzu, Selim 137
Kutan, Recai 109

Laeken (December 2001) 40–41, 151
Latvia 39, 222
Lausanne Treaty (1923), definition of "minority rights" 14–15, 116, 154
Law on Settlement (1934) 88–9
left-of-center social democratic parties, pro-EU versus anti-EU axis 18
Le Pen, Jean-Marie 79, 145
liberal internationalism 18
liberalization 222
  agriculture,
    deepening reforms 236
    elimination of subsidies 227, 234
    benefits failed to materialize 226
  deregularization and 223
  economic 220, 227
    groups in Turkey and 224
    and regulatory institutions 223, 230
    income distribution and (1980s) 225–6
  price 234, 236, 239
  reforms 220
  sub-optimal that did not give public reforms 239
  trade 230, 237, 239
    and capital flows 223
Lithuania 39, 220–22

Luxembourg summit (1997) 60, 108, 150, 195, 198, 202, 205

Maastricht Treaty 35–6, 39, 233
Malta 52
market economy, no specific model defined 232
Mass Housing Funds 224
Mediterranean enlargement process, Spain, Greece and Portugal 10
Mendelson, Maurice H. 57–8
Meriç, Cemil 141
MHP 14–15, 107, 158–9, 190
   1974 invasion of Cyprus and 129
   accused EU of inconsistency 159
   anti-EU attitude 18, 20, 25, 127, 145, 157, 165, 191, 247
   application to Constitutional Court over EU package 251
   Article 312 of Constitution and 162
   beginnings of 129
   Caucasus, the Middle East and Balkans 135–6
   cultural degeneration 209
   Cyprus problem and 25, 206
   death penalty and 119, 135, 160
   EU membership and 17
   Europeanness and 145
   no overlap with GP 192
   opposed EU reform package 163, 212
   opposition to human rights 109
   pamphlet 142
   pivotal role in EU reforms 158
   protection of the state and 130, 134
   question worth of EU membership 189
   racism and fascism 131
   radical Turkish nationalists and 132
   resisted EU adjustment laws 248
   rift with ANP 161
   survey of 200
   tariff increase on French processed agricultural imports 229
   Turkey's relations with Europe and 128, 137
   Turkish society and political culture 144
   voters and support for EU membership 178, 180
Middle East 28, 46, 80, 250–51
migration 80–83, 91
   illegal 92–100, 123
military,
   anti–EU label and 157
   attitude to EU and Öcalan issue 164
   Cyprus problem and 25
   political role of 119–22
   regime (1980–83) 110

minorities, broadcasting and education in mother tongues 12, 14
Mithad, Ahmet (Felatun Bey) 141
modernization 10, 17, 249, 252
Mongolia 98
Motherland Party (*Anavatan Partisi*) see ANAP
Movement for Europe 2002 (*Avrupa Hareketi 2002*) see Europe 2002
multiculturalism 18, 28

Nadi, Yunus (journalist) 138
National Action Party (*Milliyetçi Hareket Partisi*) see MHP
national conservatism (*milliyetçi muhafazakarlık*) 127
national identity, Turkish definition 100
nationalism, definition of 179
nationalist/patriotic attitudes, impact on EU membership support 184
National program for the Adoption of the Acquis see NPAA
National Security Council see NSC
national sovereignty, definition 101
NATO,
   Article 5 commitment 44, 47, 54n.24
   cornerstone of European security 41, 44
   ESDI and 36
   founded (1952) 197
   importance of underlined 37
   role of should not be undermined 43
   Turkey's decisive role in 250
NATO-ESDP, Turkey and 69
"New Europe," human rights and quality of democratization 10
New Turkey Party (*Yeni Türkiye Partisi*) see YTP
NGOs 20, 122, 157
Nice meeting of European Council (2000) 108, 198
"non-Convention" refugees 85
non-EU member European allies, NATO and ESDP 45
non-EU member NATO allies, position of Turkey and 50
non-EU NATO members, ESDP mechanisms and 41
non-governmental organizations see NGOs
non-military crisis management mechanism 38
non-Muslim religious foundations, allowed to buy and sell real estate 163
North American Free Trade Agreement (NAFTA) 10
North Atlantic Council/North Atlantic Cooperation Council (January 1994) 36

North Atlantic Treaty Organization (1952)
see NATO
Norway 39–40, 45
NPAA 13, 80, 98, 150–51, 158
NSC 15, 120–21, 153–5, 164, 199

Öcalan, Abdullah (leader of PKK) 94–6, 119, 129, 160, 187
official EU documents, significance of NATO and ESDP 43–4
Operation Provide Comfort 85–6
optimistic federalist, united Europe becoming a reality 40
Organization for Economic Cooperation and Development (OECD 1948) 197
Özal, Turgut (Turkish PM) 197, 199, 223–5, 229

Pakistan 98
Papandreou, George 52
"Partnership for Peace" 52
patronage politics,
    Customs Union's implementation and 229, 239–40
    public sector reform and 226, 246
People's Democracy Party (*Halkin Demokrasi Partisi*) see HADEP
People's Labour Party (*Halkýn Emek Partisi*—HEP) 112
pessimistic Euro-skeptic, "Brussel-ize" security and defense 40–41
"Petersberg tasks" 37–9, 44–5
PKK 86, 94, 136–7
    campaign of violence (1984–99) 120, 160
    smuggling people into Europe 95
    struggle between and Turkish army 92, 96, 109, 161
POAS (petroleum distributor), privatization of 235
Poland 11, 39–40, 45, 145, 222
political elite,
    benefits of EU membership and 208–9, 248
    Cyprus problem and 212
    Helsinki summit and 207–8
    resistance to political change 187
Political Parties Law 154
political problems 22, 203–4
populism in Turkey's political economy 223, 225–6, 242n.27
Portugal 197, 212
post-cold war environment, Turkey becoming a regional power 129
post-cold war period, transatlantic Alliance and mutual criticisms 41
post-Communist Central and Eastern Europe, EU membership and 11

post-Helsinki era,
    realignments in domestic politics and 16–23
    Turkey-EU relations 9
post-Helsinki period, political discourse in 155–64
post-modern state, minority rights and 11–12
post-September 11 world, security environment and Turkey 28, 30, 250
presidency of Britain (1998), readmission agreements 98
primary schools, resentment of Kurdish or Arabic language in 15
principle of *non-refoulement*,
    "non-Convention" refugees 86, 104n.31
    Turkey and 87, 90
privatization 223, 226, 233–5, 239
"problem of Turkey" 47–8
Prodi, Romano (President of European Commission) 61
pro-EU coalition, after Helsinki summit 29–30
pro-EU versus Anti-EU axis,
    EU and incentives 23–4
    left-of-center social democratic parties 18
pro-Islamic Virtue Party (*Fazilet Partisi*) see FP
Protocol (1967), status of refugees 83
public opinion and the EU,
    general observations 172–3
    support for membership
        attitudes toward democracy and 182–3, 247
        basic demographic characteristics 173–5
        geography of 175–8
        multivariate analysis of 183–6
        nationalist/patriotic values and 179–82
        party preferences and 178–9
        religiosity and 182
        socio-economic status and 179
public sector banking system, restructuring to limit "duty losses" 227
public sector in Turkey, endemic fiscal deficits 224, 226, 246
Public Transportation Funds 224

qualified majority voting 80

radical nationalist politics 131–4
    Official Turkish History Thesis 135
radical Turkish nationalism,
    Europeanness an "alien" concept 145
    how to approach it 129–31
    likely to remain 143
    Turkey-based Turanism 132

radical Turkish nationalist movement 128, 130–31
Rasmussen, Anders Fogh (Danish PM) 152
readmission agreements 97–8
readmission treaties 81
"refugee," definition 83
refugees 81–92, 100, 102, 104n.31
religious problems 163, 202, 204
rent-seeking elite of exporters, state patronage and 224
Republican People's Party (*Cumhuriyet Halk Partisi*) *see* CHP
Republic of Cyprus *see* RoC
Revolutionary People's Liberation Party-Front (*Devrimci Halk Kurtulus Partisi-Cephesi*—DHKP-C) 161
RoC,
  accession negotiations and 64
  "Annan Plan," RoC votes against 75
  application for EU membership and Turkish reaction 57–61
  Association Agreement with EU (1973) 71
  dispute with TRNC 24
  resolution of Cyprus problem and EU membership 55
  Russian S-300 missiles (January 1997) 59
Romania 39, 98, 202, 220–22
RP 112, 115, 135, 153, 225, 229
Russia 145

Safa, Peyami 141
St Malo summit (December 1998) 37, 43
Schengen visa regime, need to harmonize Turkish policy 80–81, 98, 100
Schröder, Gerhard 150, 210
security considerations, democratic reforms and 27
September 11, basic pre-conditions since 28
Seville summit (June 2002) 65, 69, 79, 151
Sezer, Ahmet Necdet 121
SHAPE 48
side payments 225
Single European Act, legalized (EPC) 1986 35
Slovakia 39, 221–2
Slovenia 39, 222
smugglers, illegal immigration and 91, 95, 123
social harmonization 233–4
Social Protocol 233
socio-economic problems 132, 179, 203, 208–9, 212, 240
soft Euro-skepticism 164
"soft security" 79
Somalia to Bosnia, Turkish experience of peacekeeping 46

sovereignty 11, 70, 101, 209–10, 247
SP 109, 161, 163, 178, 183–4, 186
  Cyprus problem and 206
Spain 197, 212
Spanish Presidency (2002) 48, 152
"Special Accession Programme for Agriculture and Rural Development" (SAPARD) 231
"Special Situation Region" (*Olaganüstü Hal Bölgesi*) 120
stable democracies, economic stability and progress 11
State Economic Enterprises (SEEs) 226, 234–5
state patronage, rent-seeking activities 224
State Security Courts (*Devlet Güvenlik Mahkemeleri*), reformation of 129–30, 154
status quo, benefits Greek Cypriots 66
subsidies, public deficits and 227
Sun-Language Theory, Republican years of Turkey 138
Supreme Headquarters Allied Powers Europe *see* SHAPE
Syria 98
Szczerbiak, Aleks 164–5

Taggart, Paul 164–5
TBMM 127, 152, 196, 199–200
  knowledge about EU 210–11
  population factor and 203, 220
temporary refuge in Turkey 84, 87, 98
TESEV 3, 20, 22, 213
third way politics 18
Topçu, Nurettin 141
trafficking of human beings 93, 96
"transnational businesss elites," EU anchor and 20–22
transnational civil society groups, domestic politics of individual states and 11
transnational issues, international action required 49
transparency 219, 223, 240
Treachery of Westernization, The (*Batılılaşma İhaneti*) 141
Treaty of Amsterdam 35–6, 80
Treaty of Nice (2001) 35
TRNC 24–5
  broke off contacts with EU 59
  effect of Turkey's compromise over Cyprus 59
  must be recognized as sovereign state 206
  support for Annan Plan 75
  Turkish authorities and 67–8, 207
True Path Party (*Doğru Yol Partisi*) *see* DYP
Türkeş, Alpaslan (1917–97) 129–30

Index

Turkey 222
  accession partnership (2001), political requirements and 2, 70
  accused EU of submission to Greek blackmail 64
  aid received 230–31
  anti-EU bloc 23–4
  association with EU since 1963 195
  asylum recognition rates 90–91, 100
  Asylum Regulation (November 1994) 86–7
  attitudes towards EU and membership process 3, 248
  basic pre-conditions since September 11 28
  concerns about Greek intentions 51
  constraints and complaints against 2
  contribution to multicultural Europe 27
  Convention (1951) on status of refugees 83
  cooperation with EU *sin qua non* of accession process 81, 100
  could become country of first asylum 81
  Cyprus
    intervention by (1974) 57
    a national cause (*milli dava*) 56
  democratization and 10
  difficulty over work permits 89
  dilemmas facing 101
  earthquakes August and November (1999) 245
  economic adjustment and technical assistance funds 219, 237
  education spending 220–21
  emigration 79–80
  ESPD and 45–6, 51
  EU access to SHAPE and 48
  EU adjustment package (August 2002) 247–8, 250
  European Council and EU-led operations 40
  European organizations after Second World War 197
  Feira arrangements and 46–7
  human development indicators diverge from EU 220
  human rights and 107
  illegal immigrant flow towards Europe 96
  immigration 82–3
    pressure to prevent irregular 94, 100
  import-substitution era and 20
  integration process in Europe and 51
  interest associations 19
  international law about RoC EU membership 57–8
  irregular migrants from EU 98
  labor migration from to Europe 81–2
  Left parties nationalistic stand 18
  mass refugee crisis (April 1991) 85
  military coup (1980) 197
  modernization and westernization 17
  NATO member 26, 39, 46, 157, 250
  non-credibility of European orientation of 64
  non-EU member ally 45
  performance of economy and EU membership 16
  political crises (2002) 107
  pro-EU coalition could challenge security-conscious mindset 27
  proximity to potential crisis areas 46
  question of
    EU membership 1
    including in security and defense 36
  reform package (August 3, 2002) 149
  removal of death penalty (2002) 14
  resolution of Cyprus problem and EU membership 55
  restless relations with EEC/EC/EU 45
  second largest army in Atlantic alliance 162
  TRNC annexed if EU admitted Cyprus before settlement 62
  twin economic crises 21, 155, 219–20, 226, 234, 245
  warnings to EU 47
  withdrawal of troops from Cyprus required of 66
Turkey-EU debate, broad terms and 156
Turkey-EU relations 197–9
  chronology of 4–8
  developments in aftermath of September (2002) 30
  domestic-political constraints 21
  EU hoped Greece's accession would not affect 63
  fostering closer 26–8
  Greece's membership of EU and 23
  obstacles to Turkey's accession 195–6
  post-Helsinki era 9
  Turkey and Politics journal (*Türkiye ve Siyaset*) 136
Turkey's Accession Partnership 55
Turkey's candidacy for EU membership and 171–2
Turkey's military-security establishment, argument by 26
Turkey and the TRNC,
  common declaration on Cyprus (December 28, 1995) 59
  (January 20, 1997) 59

Turkish authorities,
   Article (159) 111
   burden-sharing expectations about
     refugees 88
   illegal immigrants and 92–3, 99
   relations with UNHCR over refugees
     86–7
Turkish Constitution,
   Article (3) 117
   Article (8) 111–12
     changes to 114–15
   Article (13) 110–11
   Article (14) 111
     changes to 113–15
   Article (26) 116–17
   Article (28) 110, 117
   Article (34) 110
   Article (38) 119
   Article (42) 117–18
   Article (68) 111, 114
   Article (69) 114–15
   Article (87) 118
   Article (101), changes to 114–15
   Article (117) 120
   Article (118) 120–21
   Article (125) 118–19
   Article (159), changes to 112, 114–15, 122
     EU and 199
   Article (312) 111–12, 162
     changes to 114–15
   Articles (13 and 14) 110
     changes to 113, 115
   Articles (22–6) 110
   Articles (146–7) 118
   Articles (159 and 312) 111–12
     repeal of Law No.2932 117
Turkish and Cypriot accessions, links
   between 66–7
Turkish Economic and Social Studies
   Institute (*Türkiye Ekonomik ve Sosyal
   Etüdler Vakfi*) *see* TESEV
Turkish-EU relations,
   asylum issues and 89–90, 99
   date back to (1950s) 198
   elites and lack of knowledge of EU 211
   Helsinki summit (December 1999) 80
   interviewing people regarding *acquis* 199
   major breakthrough December (1999) 198
   obstacles to Turkey's accession 196
   role of Cyprus question 67
   via Athens and Nicosia 55
Turkish Foreign Ministry, December 18,
   longstanding Turkish position and 75
Turkish Grand National Assembly (*Türkiye
   Büyük Millet Meclisi*) *see* TBMM
Turkish-Greek relations 55, 97, 191, 195

Turkish Industrialists' and Businessmen's
   Association (*Türkiye Sanayici ve
   İsadamlari Derneği*) *see* TÜSİAD
Turkish intellectuals, attitude to Western and
   European 127, 141, 247–8
Turkish lira 226
   ECU and 221
Turkish nationalism,
   totalitarian fanaticism and 144
   xenophobic branch of 128
Turkish nationalists, communist threat of cold
   war era and 180
Turkish National Program 87–8, 109, 198–9
"Turkish National Program for the Adoption
   of the Acquis" *see* NPAA
Turkish parliament, 34 Constitutional
   Amendments since NPAA 13, 96–7, 109,
   155, 190, 212
Turkish parliamentarians 3
   approval to EU-related proposals 196
   cultural degeneration and 209
   "power without responsibility" 246
   survey of 199–200
     perceived obstacles 201–4
   what EU membership entails and 198–9
Turkish Petroleum Refineries (TÜRPAŞ) 235
Turkish politicians, separate Cyprus problem
   from EU membership 61
Turkish progress reports,
   (1998–2001) 234
     neo-liberal dimension 234–7, 239–40
     social dimension 237–9
   1998 Report 153–4, 234–6
     political and economic problems 201–2
   1999 Report 154, 201–2, 234–5, 237
   2000 Report 155, 201, 234–5, 237
   2001 Report 155, 201, 228–9, 235–6, 238
   2002 Report 201
   commercial integration with EU and trade
     liberalization 237
   perceptions of 153–5
Turkish representation system 187–8
Turkish Republic of Northern Cyprus *see*
   TRNC
Turkish society, socio-economic changes
   (1950 and 1970) 132
Turkism and Sunni Islam (*Türk-İslam
   sentezi*—TIS) 133
Turkish Cypriots, EU and 25
TÜSİAD 19, 25

Uğur, Mehmet 221, 228
Ukraine 98
UNHCR 82–3, 85–6, 89–91
United Nations High Commission for
   Refugees *see* UNHCR

Index

United Nations Security Council Resolution 688 85
United States 28, 31, 41–2, 44, 162, 233
United States and Canada, security of Europe and 36
UN Plan for Cyprus 30–31

Verheugen, Günter 68–9, 201
Vietnam syndrome, US troops on the ground and 42
Vitorino, Antonio (EU Commissioner for JHA matters) 99

Waldner, David 223
Waterbury, John 223
Webb, Steven B. 224–5
Welfare Party (*Refah Partisi*) *see* RP
westerners, lack ethical principles 142
Western European Union (WEU) 36, 39, 46
western governments, refugee advocate organizations and 86
Western ills, imperialism, crusades communism and other 142–3
westernization 2, 16–17, 45, 140
women, in Turkey 154

Yılmaz, Mesut (ANAP leader) 17–18, 59, 107, 159, 229
　ANAP and reforms 163
　EU card to appeal to electorate 248
　on Luxembourg decision 202
　objection to working with Çiller 158
　terrorism and 161
　Turkey needs to be active about Cyprus 160
Young Party (*Genç Parti*—GP) 191–2
young women, forced across frontiers 93
YTP 122, 163, 189, 248

Printed in the United States
102514LV00003B/140/A